REAL ESTATE
FUNDAMENTALS NINTH EDITION

Wade E. Gaddy Jr.

Robert E. Hart

Marie S. Spodek, DREI, *Consulting Editor*

Dearborn™
Real Estate Education

This publication is designed to provide accurate and authoritative information in regard to the subject matter covered. It is sold with the understanding that the publisher is not engaged in rendering legal, accounting, or other professional advice. If legal advice or other expert assistance is required, the services of a competent professional should be sought.

President: Dr. Andrew Temte
Chief Learning Officer: Dr. Tim Smaby
Executive Director, Real Estate Education: Melissa Kleeman-Moy
Development Editor: Christopher Kugler

REAL ESTATE FUNDAMENTALS NINTH EDITION
©2015 Kaplan, Inc.
Published by DF Institute, Inc., d/b/a Dearborn Real Estate Education
332 Front St. S., Suite 501
La Crosse, WI 54601

Printed in the United States of America

ISBN: 978-1-4754-2838-4

PPN: 1513-0109

Contents

Introduction

The real estate industry has experienced significant change since the first edition of this textbook was released in 1981. From the manner in which real estate professionals establish business relationships to the means through which real estate is advertised and purchased, aspects of the real estate transaction continue to grow and evolve.

Also changing is the role of the real estate professional. Now, more than ever, brokers and their affiliated licensees are responsible for grasping the broadest principles and specific practices of the real estate industry. This ninth edition of *Real Estate Fundamentals* celebrates 34 years of excellence by giving students the foundation they need to prepare for their licensing exams and providing the fundamentals they need to know as they begin their careers as real estate professionals.

Real Estate Fundamentals begins with an introduction to the real estate business by studying different types of real estate, underlying economic principles, and the variety of professions that help drive the sale and purchase of real estate. From there, the text delves into real estate's essential components: land descriptions, rights and interests, agency and brokerage, finance, contracts, and closings.

What distinguishes *Real Estate Fundamentals* as a textbook is the clear and concise manner in which these essential components are described. Even real estate's most sophisticated concepts become easy to comprehend. All chapters begin with a list of learning objectives and key terms designed to help reinforce students' learning, while numerous charts, figures, and illustrations help visualize key concepts along the way. Each chapter concludes with review questions that allow students to gauge their understanding of the material.

Real Estate Fundamentals is also an excellent source for exam preparation. Chapter 18: Real Estate Mathematics and the 100-question practice examination are designed to familiarize students with real estate's basic computations and the test-item style of today's license exams. Students will also find an answer key with rationales that explain why an answer is correct, along with a page reference to where that material can be found in the text.

A FINAL NOTE

Please take a few moments to let us know what you thought of this edition. Did it help you? Has your understanding of real estate increased? How did you do on your course or licensing exam? Please be sure to indicate that you used the ninth edition of *Real Estate Fundamentals* and send your comments to contentinquiries@dearborn.com.

Acknowledgments

CONSULTING EDITOR

The authors would like to express special appreciation to the consulting editor, Marie S. Spodek, DREI, for her invaluable assistance in revising and preparing this text's ninth edition as well as her contributions to previous editions. Spodek has been in the real estate business for more than 30 years, working first for a city real estate office, and then in a suburban office. She owned and operated a real estate school in Charleston, South Carolina. For the past 15 years, she has combined classroom instruction with the development of course materials. She is an active member of the Real Estate Educators Association (REEA) and was awarded the first Jack Wiedemer Distinguished Career Award in 2001.

Spodek is co-author of *Environmental Issues in Your Real Estate Practice*, *Manufactured and Modular Housing*, *Insurance for Consumer Protection*, *Mortgage Fraud and Predatory Lending*, and *Sustainable Housing and Building Green: What Agents Should Know*, all published by Dearborn Real Estate Education. She was also the consulting editor for *The Language of Real Estate Sixth Edition* suite, also published by Dearborn.

CONTRIBUTORS

This ninth edition of *Real Estate Fundamentals* would not have been possible without the input of Alton E. Duncanson, CBR.

The following individuals have contributed to the success of this text's previous editions:

- Patricia Anderson

- John Ballou, Moraine Valley Community College, Illinois

- Doris Barrell, NeighborWorks®

- Joseph M. Brice, JMB Real Estate Academy, Massachusetts

- Fred Brodsky, DREI, Brodsky School of Real Estate, Arizona

- James C. Clinkscales, American Institute of Real Estate, Inc., Georgia

- Rose Mary Chambers, Dean, First Institute of Real Estate, Alabama
- Mary Coveny, CareerMatch Consultants, Inc., Illinois
- John R. Dickinson, Moseley-Dickinson Academy of Real Estate, Virginia
- Gregory J. Dunn
- David A. Floyd, Tennessee Real Estate Education Systems, Inc.
- Judith Geesell, Mykut Real Estate School, Washington
- Kenneth R. Greenwood, Southern Oaks School of Real Estate, Alabama
- William Harrington
- Paul Harris, National Real Estate School, Arkansas
- Lorna Horton
- Terri Keyes, Real Estate School of Nevada in Las Vegas
- Robert Marshall
- Ed Mathews, Tennessee Real Estate Systems, Inc.
- Ronnie H. Minnick, The Real Estate Institute for Career Advancement, Inc., Arkansas
- D.D. Nordstrom, PRO/ED, South Dakota
- Ron Oslin, Tennessee Real Estate Educational Systems, Inc., Tennessee
- Katherine A. Pancak, University of Connecticut
- Roy L. Ponthier, Jr., Ph.D., First Professional Real Estate School, Inc., Louisiana
- Dr. Jack N. Porter, The Spencer Group: School of Real Estate, Massachusetts
- John F. Rodgers III, Catonsville Community College, Maryland
- Ben C. Scheible, Truckee Meadows Community College, Nevada
- Fraser Sparkman, Alabama School of Real Estate
- Bill Whisnant, Tennessee Real Estate Educational Systems, Inc., Tennessee
- Nancy Daggett White, Mississippi County Community College, Arkansas
- Don W. Williams, Alabama Courses in Real Estate
- George Williams
- Kathleen M. Witalisz, Richard S. Thomas REALTOR®, Massachusetts
- Terrence M. Zajac, DREI, Terry Zajac Seminars, Arizona

An Introduction to the Real Estate Business

LEARNING OBJECTIVES

When you finish reading this chapter, you will be able to

- identify different careers that are real estate-related and the organizations that support them,
- list five types of real estate properties,
- describe the economic principles that affect real estate markets, and
- differentiate between factors that affect supply and those that affect demand.

agricultural	financing	rental market
appraisal	industrial	residential
broker	market	sales market
brokerage	property manager	salesperson
commercial	real estate counseling	seller's market
demographics	REALTOR®	special purpose

Real estate transactions take place all around you, all the time. When a commercial leasing company rents space in a mall or the owner of a building rents an apartment, it's a real estate transaction. If an appraiser gives an expert opinion on the value of a marina or the bank lends money to a business to expand its office and manufacturing facilities, it's a real estate transaction. Most common of all, when a family sells its home and buys a new one, it takes part in the real estate industry. Consumers of real estate services include buyers and sellers of homes, tenants, landlords, investors, and developers. Nearly everyone, at some time, is involved in a real estate transaction. All this adds up to big business, involving billions of dollars every year in the United States alone.

REAL ESTATE SPECIALTIES

Many real estate professionals are involved in the real estate business. Real estate brokerage, appraisal, property management, financing, subdivision and development, counseling, and education are all separate businesses within the real estate field. To succeed in this complex industry, real estate professionals should have a basic knowledge of the work carried out by other specialists within the industry. What follows is a brief description of these specialties; most of them are discussed in more detail in later chapters.

Brokerage

Brokerage is the business of bringing people together in a real estate transaction. A brokerage firm acts as a point of contact between two or more people negotiating the sale, purchase, or rental of property. State law dictates that persons conducting brokerage activities must be licensed. Although some states have implemented single licensing, most still have two license categories—**brokers** and **salespersons**—that require different experience, education, and testing requirements. Brokers can perform the same functions as an affiliate licensee or can be the firm's designated broker. A designated broker, typically in charge of the brokerage office, is the person who enters into contractual arrangements with buyers and sellers, and is ultimately responsible for licensees affiliated with the office. Affiliate licensees act on behalf of the firm and the firm's clients as either employees or independent contractors. Each state has specific rules and regulations with regard to the operation and activities of a brokerage firm (see Chapter 7).

Appraisal

Appraisal is the process of estimating a property's value. An **appraisal** is an appraiser's opinion of value, based on established methods of valuation and the appraiser's professional judgment. Although training gives brokers some understanding of the valuation process, lenders generally require a professional appraisal conducted by a state-licensed or certified appraiser (see Chapter 11).

Property Management

A **property manager** is a person hired to maintain and manage property on behalf of its owner. A manager's basic responsibility is to protect the owner's investment and maximize the owner's return. A manager is considered an agent of the property owner and, therefore, owes the owner either fiduciary duties of care, obedience, accounting, loyalty, and disclosure or statutory duties as established by law for that state.

The scope of the manager's work depends on the terms of the individual employment contract, called a *management agreement*. The management agreement defines the manager's authority and responsibilities and establishes the manager's rate of compensation. Many states require a property manager to hold a real estate or property manager's license (see Chapter 9).

Financing

Financing is the business of providing funds for the purchase and development of real estate. Real estate financing differs from other forms of financing in that real property is pledged as collateral for the repayment of the loan through a mortgage or deed of trust. Different entities involved in the process of loaning money to real estate owners include commercial banks, savings associations, real estate investment trusts, mortgage banks, and mortgage brokerage companies (see Chapters 12 and 13).

Insurance

Property owners purchase insurance to minimize risks associated with ownership. Insurance brokerage requires a specific state insurance license. Buying insurance transfers the financial risks to the insurance company. However, hazard insurance was never meant to cover maintenance and replacement, only to cover the costs of a major catastrophe. Real estate licensees should encourage their buyers to start the insurance process early because the buyer's credit score may affect the availability and cost of insurance. Because the insurance industry has found that those with low credit scores are more likely to file frivolous or maintenance types of claims, some borrowers with lower scores may find it difficult to obtain insurance, and those who do will have to pay more.

All lenders require that the mortgaged property be insured, not only for fire and lightning, but also for flooding if located in a special flood hazard area (SFHA). The best policy for owner-occupants is the homeowners' policy, which provides insurance coverage for the building, its contents, liability, and more.

Real estate licensees should avoid giving insurance advice. Instead, they should strongly encourage buyers and sellers to ask their insurance agents about any special real estate situations, such as vacant homes, rentals while the home is on the market, and dual-use dwellings (second homes sometimes rented out). Licensees should encourage their clients to be totally honest about the use of the property when talking with their insurance agents.

The following policies are available to owner-occupants:

- *HO-1 basic form homeowner policy.* This policy covers damage caused by fire, lightning, hail, and a number of other perils. It is the default when the property has been empty for a certain length of time, which varies from company to company.

- *HO-2 broad form homeowner policy.* This includes more comprehensive coverage than HO-1 and is often available for second homes (not to be confused with rental properties).

- *HO-3 special form homeowner policy.* The HO-3 traditionally offers the most coverage for the most reasonable price. Replacement costs vary and might include caps on the amount covered. Personal liability may be expanded. Sellers who move before the property is sold should consult with their own insurance agents to determine at what time the policy will convert to a basic HO-1 policy.

- *HO-6 condominium policy.* The HO-6 covers the portions of the property that the condo owner owns; many policies must be customized to comply with the association bylaws. Town homes may be covered by HO-6 or HO-3 policies, depending on what is owned by whom.

Rental properties present other issues. Owners can only insure that which they own. Thus, a landlord cannot insure the tenant's personal property and vice versa. Different policies are available for rental properties:

- *HO-4 renter's insurance.* This is very similar to the HO-3, but it does not cover the real property owned by someone else.

- *Rental home or landlord's policy.* The landlord's policy is the reverse of the HO-4 policy and covers very little personal property (only the real property).

Flood insurance. Flooding can occur anywhere—inland and along coastal areas. Licensees should encourage buyers to obtain flood insurance even if not required by a lender because a homeowner's policy does not cover rising water (i.e., flooding that may be caused by a broken water main, inadequate or overloaded drainage areas, melting snow, rising river water, and dam bursts).

Flood insurance is always a separate policy. Before making a price quote, the insurance agent must receive an elevation certificate, prepared by a licensed surveyor. The cost of flood insurance can affect the buyer's financial ratios and thus affect the price that buyers can pay for the property.

The National Flood Insurance Program (NFIP) sets the rates nationally, and its policies cover buildings and/or contents. The Biggert-Waters Act of 2012 requires that flood insurance premiums reflect real actuarial risk, especially those for "repetitive loss properties" (those that repeatedly flood). However, many of the act's provisions have been delayed with 2014 legislation. Professionals should refer all questions about the insurance program and current FEMA guidelines to insurance agents who can write flood policies. To determine the level of risk, the Federal Emergency Management Agency (FEMA) has graded nearly every county in the United States into two types of zones: A (inland) and V (coastal). The most flood-prone areas are designated SFHAs. If a property is located in an SFHA, federal law requires flood insurance before closing any property purchased with federally related monies.

To enforce compliance, the Federal Deposit Insurance Corporation (FDIC) can fine and withdraw FDIC insurance from lenders who hold mortgages that do not carry required flood insurance. Flood insurance becomes effective 30 days after purchase, unless the lender requires flood insurance, in which case, it is immediately effective.

Subdivision and Development

Subdivision is the process of splitting a single property into smaller parcels. *Development* involves the construction of improvements on the land. These processes, which are normally related but can occur separately, are integral to the growth of geographic areas and expansion of real estate uses (see Chapter 14).

Real Estate Counseling

Real estate counseling involves providing clients with competent independent real estate advice based on sound professional judgment and expertise. A real estate counselor helps clients make informed decisions when purchasing, using, or investing in real property, without actually representing them as an agent.

Education

Real estate education is available to both real estate professionals and consumers. Colleges, universities, private schools, and trade organizations all conduct real estate courses and seminars on subjects ranging from prelicensing principles to the technical aspects of tax law. State licensing laws establish the minimum educational requirements for both obtaining and maintaining a real estate license. Continuing education helps ensure that real estate professionals keep their skills and knowledge current.

Other Areas

Many other real estate career options are available. Specialists are needed in a variety of areas, including law, tax, corporate real estate, and land use.

PROFESSIONAL ORGANIZATIONS

Many real estate professions have associated trade industries that serve that specialty. The largest brokerage trade organization is the National Association of REALTORS® (NAR). NAR is composed of state, regional, and local associations. NAR members subscribe to a code of ethics and are called **REALTORS®** or REALTOR-ASSOCIATES®. Note the difference between a *REALTOR®*, who is a person who holds membership in NAR, and a *licensee*, who is a person who holds either a state broker or salesperson license. All REALTORS® are licensees, but some licensees are not REALTORS®.

A sampling of other professional organizations includes the National Association of Real Estate Brokers (NAREB), whose members are called Realtists, the Appraisal Institute, the Real Estate Educators Association (REEA), the Real Estate Buyers' Agent Council (REBAC), the Building Owners and Managers Association (BOMA), the Institute of Real Estate Management (IREM), the Commercial Investment Real Estate Institute (CIREI), and the American Society of Real Estate Counselors (ASREC). Each organization has a website that provides additional information about that association.

TYPES OF REAL ESTATE

Just as there are different real estate industry specializations, there are different types of property. Real estate can be classified as follows:

- **Residential**—all property used for single-family or multifamily housing, whether in urban, suburban, or rural areas

- **Commercial**—business property, including office space, shopping centers, stores, theaters, hotels, and parking facilities

- **Industrial**—warehouses, factories, industrial districts, and power plants

- **Agricultural**—farms, timberland, ranches, and orchards

- **Special purpose**—churches, schools, cemeteries, and government-held lands

REAL ESTATE MARKETS

A **market** is a place where goods can be bought and sold and a price established. The real estate market is not a set location, but rather the setting in which supply and demand establish market value for real estate interests. The real estate market is really a group of *submarkets*, which can be defined in a number of ways.

A submarket may be defined by property type, such as whether the real estate is residential, commercial, industrial, agricultural, or special purpose. A submarket can also be defined by geographic level, such as whether properties at a specific national, regional, community, or neighborhood level are being analyzed. Also, the market can be divided into the **sales market**, which involves the transfer of title and ownership rights, and the **rental market**, which involves the temporary leasing of space.

Economic Principles

Real estate markets are local markets—each geographic area has different types of real estate and different conditions that drive prices. This relates to the old adage of location being important; a parcel of real estate cannot be moved, is never exactly like another parcel, and its value is impacted by surrounding land uses. These characteristics of real estate are discussed more thoroughly in Chapter 2. Therefore, it is the *specific* supply of real estate and *specific* demand for real estate in an area that determine the price of a parcel of real estate in that area.

Seller's market.   Basically, when the demand for a product exceeds the supply, the result will be an increase in price. Because development and construction are lengthy processes and needed supply cannot be built immediately, a shortage creates a seller's market. When demand exceeds supply, prices rise and the shortage creates an incentive for developers to build new buildings.

Buyer's market.   When the supply exceeds the demand, prices fall, creating a buyer's market. The real estate market experienced a period of overbuilding in the 1980s, which led to lower real estate prices in the early 1990s. However, by the late 1990s and into the early first years of the new millennium, not only did demand for housing increase, but liberal mortgage lending practices allowed more buyers to enter the market, thus driving up prices.

Unfortunately, the financial crisis that began in 2007 accelerated the number of foreclosures, which increased supply; prices plummeted in many areas of the country. This would indicate a strong buyer's market, but unfortunately, financing is more difficult to obtain because of tighter qualifying standards and fewer affordable loan products.

Factors Affecting Supply

Factors that affect the supply of real estate include labor force and construction costs, government controls, and financial policies.

Labor force and construction costs.   A shortage of skilled labor or building materials or an increase in the cost of the materials can decrease the amount of new construction.

Government controls and financial policies.   Virtually any government action can affect the real estate market. The negative influences of taxes, zoning, high interest rates, and the like may deter investors and new construction. On the other hand, government incentives in these areas can attract developers.

Factors Affecting Demand

Many factors affect the demand for real estate, including population, demographics, and employment and wage levels.

Population.   Demand or lack of demand for housing and amenities varies as the population in that area grows or declines. Populations may grow or decline due to economic reasons (increase or decrease in jobs in the area), social concerns (such as quality of schools and recreational amenities), or geographic preferences (such as population shifts from warmer to colder climates).

Demographics.   The population, or **demographics**, of a community is a major factor in determining the quantity and type of housing in that community. Family size, the ratio uuuggof adults to children, the number of retirees, family income, lifestyle, and the growing number of single-parent and empty-nester households are all demographic factors that contribute to the amount and type of housing needed.

Employment and wage levels.   Income levels deeply affect decisions about renting or buying and how much to spend. When job opportunities are scarce or wage levels low, demand for real estate usually drops, but that can change with rumors that new jobs are coming to the community.

SUMMARY

Many real estate industry professions provide a variety of specialized services. These professions include real estate brokerage, appraisal, property management, subdivision and development, counseling, financing, insurance, and education. Trade associations offer education and training for those involved in various real estate markets.

A market is a place where goods and services can be bought and sold and price established. Real estate markets can be classified by submarkets such as general use (residential, commercial, industrial, agricultural, or special purpose), geographic (national, regional, community, or neighborhood), sales, and rental.

The best insurance policy for owner-occupied properties is the HO-3 special form homeowners' policy, which includes liability as well as basic fire and lightning coverages. Owners can only insure what they own, so landlords can insure the building, but renters must buy their own insurance to cover their personal property. Flood insurance is available only as a separate policy and may be purchased through private insurance companies that work with the National Flood Insurance Program (NFIP).

The supply and demand for real estate are affected by many factors, including changes in population and demographics, wage and employment levels, construction costs, availability of labor, governmental controls, and interest rates.

REVIEW QUESTIONS

Please complete all the questions before turning to the Answer Key on page 334.

1. All of the following are commercial real estate transactions *EXCEPT*
   a. a midtown office building for sale.
   b. a fifth-floor residential condominium unit for rent.
   c. 2,000 square feet of retail space for lease in a mall.
   d. a fast-food restaurant for sale.

2. With three times as many homes for sale in one section of town as there were this time last year, house prices can be expected to
   a. continue to increase but at a slower rate than seen previously.
   b. begin to show a reduction in price.
   c. immediately drop by 20%–30%.
   d. stay approximately the same.

3. Of the following, which is *MOST* likely to increase the demand for real estate?
   a. The opening of a very large new real estate brokerage firm
   b. The closing of two small equipment factories
   c. An increase in employment levels and wage schedules
   d. The number of new homes being built

4. The supply of real estate is *MOST* directly affected by
   a. population.
   b. construction costs.
   c. wage controls.
   d. demographics.

5. A large company announces that it will relocate one of its corporate offices, along with 2,000 employees, to a different city. What effect will this announcement *MOST* likely have on the housing market in the new location?
   a. Houses will likely become less expensive.
   b. Houses will likely become more expensive.
   c. Housing prices will stay the same, although the price of office space will likely increase.
   d. Housing prices will stay the same, as will prices of all other property types.

6. Property management, appraisal, financing, and development are all examples of
   a. factors affecting demand.
   b factors affecting supply.
   c. government regulation of the real estate industry.
   d. specializations within the real estate industry.

7. Which of the following is a REALTOR®?
   a. A specially licensed real estate professional who helps clients negotiate real estate transactions
   b. Any licensed real estate broker or salesperson
   c. A member of the National Association of Real Estate Brokers who specializes in residential property
   d. A real estate licensee who is a member of the National Association of REALTORS®

8. A real estate licensee with many years' experience decided to retire from actively marketing properties. Now she helps clients choose among the various alternatives in purchasing, using, or investing in real estate. Her new profession is that of a real estate
   a. counselor.
   b. appraiser.
   c. educator.
   d. salesperson.

9. A farmer is nearing retirement. He intends to divide his 50-acre farm, selling 20 acres to a residential home developer and giving the remainder to his son. This process of dividing the land is called
   a. development.
   b. agricultural property management.
   c. subdivision.
   d. retirement planning.

10. A small community near a major city has experienced a period of significant overbuilding of office buildings. This will likely lead to
    a. an increase in the number of offices rented.
    b. an increase in the cost of renting an office.
    c. a decrease in the cost of renting an office.
    d. an increase in the number of office buildings planned.

11. Flood insurance is required when the
    a. property is located near an ocean.
    b. buyer pays cash.
    c. property is located in a special flood hazard area (SFHA).
    d. property is located outside a SFHA.

12. What must be provided before an insurance agent can provide a quote for the cost of flood insurance?
    a. Elevation certificate
    b. Federal Deposit Insurance Corporation (FDIC) approval
    c. Estimate of replacement costs
    d. Federal Emergency Management Agency (FEMA) approval

13. The owner of three warehouses uses them to stockpile truck and tractor parts. This property falls into the real estate category of
    a. commercial.
    b. industrial.
    c. agricultural.
    d. special purpose.

14. The owner of a 50-acre tract of land decides to sell it. The appropriate asking price will be determined primarily by the
    a. specific supply and demand for real estate in the area.
    b. property's current use.
    c. property's potential use.
    d. price paid for it.

15. Demographics is the study and description of the
    a. current sales market in an area.
    b. master planning by a city or county.
    c. characteristics of the population within a given area.
    d. factors affecting supply and demand.

16. The sellers have moved out of their home while it is still for sale. The listing agent should suggest that they
    a. talk with the lender about reducing the principal owed.
    b. ask their neighbors to keep an eye on the property.
    c. consider renting out the home until it is sold.
    d. notify their insurance agent.

17. A home is located in a SFHA. Will this designation have any effect on its market value?
    a. Enhances the value of the property because it is close to water
    b. Might reduce the market value of the property because of increased insurance costs
    c. No effect at all
    d. Not if it is a cash sale

18. A buyer has purchased a home located in an SFHA. The lender requires that the buyers purchase flood insurance. When does this flood insurance policy become effective?
    a. Immediately upon transfer of title
    b. 7 days after purchase
    c. 15 days after purchase
    d. 30 days after purchase

19. The buyers paid cash for their home. At closing, they also purchased flood insurance and homeowners insurance. When do the insurance policies become effective?
    a. The homeowners' policy becomes effective within 24 hours of recording the title.
    b. The homeowners' policy is effective after 30 days.
    c. The flood insurance is effective after 30 days.
    d. The flood insurance is effective when the title is transferred.

20. Who is responsible for insuring the personal property of the renter?
    a. Tenant
    b. Property manager
    c. Landlord
    d. Both landlord and tenant

The Nature and Description of Real Estate

LEARNING OBJECTIVES

When you finish reading this chapter, you will be able to

- identify the ownership rights that convey with the transfer of property;
- explain the rights included in land, real estate, and real property;
- differentiate between the physical and economic characteristics of real estate;
- describe three methods to identify real property; and
- summarize the differences between real and personal property.

air rights	land	real estate
appurtenance	legal description	real property
benchmarks	littoral rights	rectangular survey system
bundle of legal rights	metes-and-bounds description	riparian rights
chattel	monuments	severance
emblements	nonhomogeneity	situs
fixture	permanence of investment	subdivision lot and block
immobile	plat map	subsurface (mineral) rights
improvements	prior appropriation	trade fixture
indestructible		

The real estate business centers around the ownership, possession, and transfer of real estate. However, as you will learn in this chapter and in following chapters, real estate is more than just the earth we walk on. The ownership and possession of real estate brings into play a body of highly complex laws that define the various rights and interests of property owners, third parties, and the general public. Real estate is further affected by local, state, and federal laws and court decisions that regulate the orderly transfer.

PROPERTY RIGHTS

The word *property* refers to both the physical article owned and, more importantly, to the rights or interests involved in its use and ownership. These rights are called the **bundle of legal rights** (see Figure 2.1). At the time of transfer, a person receives the ownership rights previously held by the seller.

FIGURE 2.1   **The Bundle of Legal Rights**

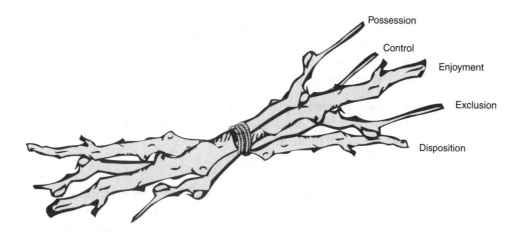

Possession
Control
Enjoyment
Exclusion
Disposition

These rights of ownership include the rights of

- possession,

- control within the framework of the law,

- enjoyment in any legal manner,

- exclusion (to keep others from entering or occupying the property), and

- disposition (to be able to sell or otherwise convey the property).

The bundle of rights is not absolute; owners may sell, will, devise, mortgage, encumber, cultivate, explore, lease, license, dedicate, give away, share, trade, or exchange their rights. In some cases, the owners may lose a right through use by someone else, not paying taxes, delinquency in debt repayment, or other such circumstances. Furthermore, one's ownership is subject to any rights that others may have in the property. The various rights and interests in property ownership will be discussed in detail in Chapter 3.

Property may be classified as *real property* (that which is immovable) and *personal property* (that which is movable). The early English courts distinguished between a lawsuit in which a wrongfully ousted landowner could recover the land itself and those lawsuits in which the owner could recover monetary damages only. Over time, the ownership interest in the land became called *real property* or *realty*. Because the suit for monetary damages was called a personal action, over time, property other than real property became called *personal property*, *personalty*, or a *chattel*.

LAND, REAL ESTATE, AND REAL PROPERTY

The terms *land*, *real estate*, and *real property* are often used interchangeably. Though they may seem to be describing the same thing, there are important differences in their meanings.

Land

Land is defined as the earth's surface extending downward to the center of the earth and upward to infinity, including those things permanently attached by nature, such as trees and water and those things **appurtenant** to the land. An *appurtenance* is defined as anything that, by right, is used by the land for its benefit, often referenced as runs with the land. Such rights include subsurface (mineral) rights, air rights, and water rights. An *easement appurtenant* is discussed in Chapter 3.

Subsurface (mineral) rights.   Subsurface rights include minerals and other substances located below the surface of the land; each may be transferred separately. For example, a landowner may sell the rights to any oil and gas found in the land to an oil company and later sell the property to a purchaser and, as a condition of the sale, reserve the rights to all coal that may be found in the land. After these transactions, three parties have ownership interests in this real property: (1) the oil company owns all oil and gas, (2) the seller owns all coal, and (3) the purchaser owns the rights to all the rest of the real property. In the absence of an agreement to the contrary, any individual acquiring the rights to minerals in the subsurface also acquires what is called an implied easement, which allows the holder of the subsurface (mineral) rights to come back onto the surface of the land for the purpose of removing the minerals. Easements are discussed in Chapter 3.

Air rights.   Likewise, the rights to use the air above the land may be sold independently of the land itself. **Air rights** are an increasingly important part of real property, particularly in large cities. Huge office buildings such as the Met Life building in New York City and the Prudential building in Chicago have been built over railroad tracks. The developer must acquire not only the air rights above the tracks but also numerous small portions of the surface of the land in order to construct the building's foundation supports. The finished foundation must not interfere with the operation of trains on the railroad's remaining land.

Until the development of airplanes, a property owner's air rights were considered unlimited. Today, however, the courts permit reasonable interference with these rights as long as the owner's right to use and occupy the property is not lessened. For example, an airplane flying through unused airspace would not interfere with the property owner's ability to occupy the property. Governments and airport authorities often purchase air rights adjacent to an airport to provide glide patterns for air traffic.

Water rights.   In the United States, the ownership of water and the right to use the water is determined by the doctrines of riparian rights, littoral rights, or prior appropriation. Navigable waters are considered public highways on which the public has an easement or right to travel. Thus, the land is generally owned to the water's edge, with the state holding title to the submerged land.

Riparian rights are granted to owners of land located along the course of flowing water, such as a river or stream, and to owners who have water located within the subsurface of their land. Such subsurface water is called *percolating water*. The level at which such water is located beneath the surface of the earth is called the *water table*.

While there are state laws governing riparian rights, generally, riparian owners have the right to make use of the water for irrigation, swimming, boating, fishing, or any legal way that does not interfere with the same rights of owners downstream. In addition, an owner of land that borders a non-navigable waterway owns the land to its exact center.

Closely related to riparian rights are the **littoral rights** of owners whose land borders on large, navigable but nonflowing lakes and oceans. These owners may make reasonable use of the available waters but generally only own the land adjacent to the water down to the mean high-water mark.

In states where water is scarce, the ownership and use of water is often determined by the doctrine of **prior appropriation**. Under prior appropriation, the right to use water for any purpose other than limited domestic use is controlled by the state rather than by the adjacent landowner. However, ownership of the land bordering bodies of water is generally determined by the rules for riparian and littoral ownership.

Property purchasers are also interested in potable water—available water that is safe and agreeable for drinking (see Figure 2.2).

FIGURE 2.2   **Land, Real Estate, and Real Property**

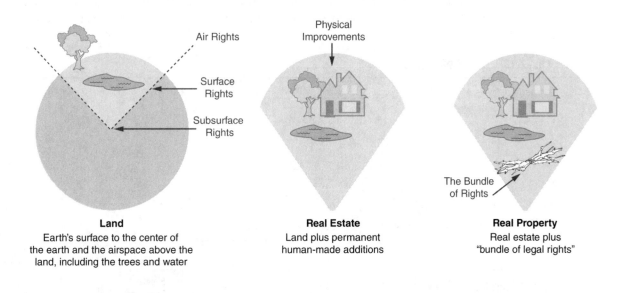

Land
Earth's surface to the center of the earth and the airspace above the land, including the trees and water

Real Estate
Land plus permanent human-made additions

Real Property
Real estate plus "bundle of legal rights"

Real Estate

Real estate is defined as the earth's surface extending downward to the center of the earth and upward into space, including all things permanently attached to it by nature or by people (see Figure 2.2). In practice, the term *real estate* is most often used to describe that commodity with which real estate as a business and the real estate broker and salesperson are concerned. It is sometimes called *realty*.

Products of the earth that are naturally grown and require no annual labor or cultivation, such as trees and bushes, are considered real property (called "fruits of nature" or by the Latin term *fructus naturales*). Products of the earth that require annual planting or cultivation, such as unharvested wheat or vegetables, are considered personal property (called "fruits of industry" or *fructus industriales*).

Artificial attachments, called **improvements**, are normally those things that have been placed on the land by people. Improvements may be embedded in the land, such as walls, footings, in-ground swimming pools, and water or gas lines. They may be placed or resting upon the land (such as building slabs, driveways, streets, and patios) or erected on the land (such as buildings, towers, or any other human-made additions to property). Land that has been improved has not necessarily been made better—it has only been changed in some way by human activity.

Real Property

The term **real property** further broadens the definition of real estate to include the bundle of legal rights involved in real estate ownership. Thus, real property is defined as the earth's surface extending downward to the center of the earth and upward into space, including all things permanently attached to it by nature or by people, as well as the interests, benefits, and rights inherent in its ownership (see Figure 2.2).

CHARACTERISTICS OF REAL ESTATE

Unlike many commodities sold on the open market, real estate possesses certain unique characteristics that affect its use both directly and indirectly. These characteristics fall into two broad categories—physical characteristics and economic characteristics (see Figure 2.3).

FIGURE 2.3   **Characteristics of Real Estate**

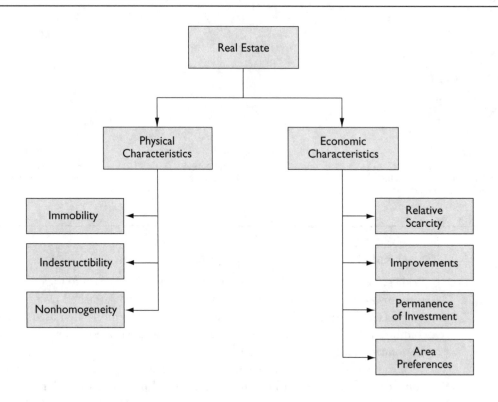

Physical Characteristics

The basic physical characteristics of land are (1) immobility, (2) indestructibility, and (3) nonhomogeneity.

Immobility.   Land, which is the earth's surface, is **immobile**. Although some of the substances of land are removable and topography can be changed, that portion of the earth's surface always remains. The geographic location of any given parcel of land can never be changed. It is rigid and fixed.

Because land is immobile, the rights to use land are more easily regulated than other forms of property and are controlled by the laws of the state in which it is located. Records concerning land are located and maintained in the city or county where the land is located. For example, local governments are supported largely by property taxes on real estate. The fixed amount of land in a given area enables the local government to rely on a certain amount of annual property tax revenue, which, in turn, allows the government to make long-range plans based on the projected income. For these reasons, real estate markets tend to be local in character.

Indestructibility.   Just as land is immobile, it is durable and **indestructible**. This permanence, which also holds for the improvements placed on it, has tended to stabilize investments in land. The fact that land is indestructible does not, of course, change the fact that improvements do depreciate and can become obsolete, thereby reducing, or possibly destroying, values. This gradual depreciation should not be confused with the fact that the economic desirability, or situs, of a given location can change and thus create a ghost town.

Nonhomogeneity.   No two parcels of land are ever exactly the same. Although there may be substantial similarity, all parcels differ geographically, as each parcel has its own location. Because of land's nonhomogeneity, the courts have long held that a person cannot be required to accept a substitute for a specific parcel of land. The law grants the right to either a buyer or a seller to sue for specific performance. This means that the seller must convey, or the buyer must buy, the specific parcel for which the parties contracted. The subject of specific performance will be discussed later in the text.

Economic Characteristics

The basic economic characteristics of land are: relative scarcity, improvements, permanence of investment, and area preferences.

Relative scarcity.   Although the total supply of land is fixed, land is not scarce in this country. Despite the considerable amount of land not in use, available land in a given location or of a particular quality may be limited.

Improvements.   The improvement of one parcel of land has an effect on the value and use of other neighboring tracts and often has a direct bearing on whole communities. For example, constructing a steel plant or a reactor can directly influence a large area. Such land improvements can influence other parcels and communities favorably or unfavorably and may affect not only the land use itself but also the value and price of land.

Permanence of investment.   Once land has been improved, capital and labor expenditures represent a fixed investment. Although older buildings can be razed to make way for new buildings or other land uses, improvements such as drainage, electricity, water, and sewerage remain fixed investments because they generally cannot be dismantled or removed economically. The income return on such investments is long term and relatively stable, and it usually extends over what is called the economic life of the improvement. However, this permanence may make improved real estate unsuitable for short, rapid-turnover investing.

Area preferences.   The economic characteristic, often called **situs**, does not refer to a geographic location per se, but rather to people's choices and preferences for a given area. It is the unique quality of people's preferences that results in different valuations being attributed to similar units. This nonhomogeneity, as previously discussed, means that no two parcels are exactly the same, partly because of the variable likes and dislikes people possess.

Preferences are not static; they are constantly changing. For example, social influences caused the rapid movement of people to suburban areas. However, some are now returning to urban areas, preferring the environments and amenities of a city to those of a suburb.

The effect of situs on land value can be seen in the approach of salespeople selling homes in a new development who try to influence prospects into preferring the location of the new development over other locations. The same model home may be available in several different areas, but the personal preference of the buyer for a certain location illustrates the saying "people make value."

Real Estate Characteristics Define Land Use

The various characteristics of a real estate parcel affect its desirability for a specific use. Physical and economic factors that affect land use include (1) contour and elevation of the parcel, (2) prevailing winds, (3) transportation, (4) public improvements, and (5) availability of natural resources, such as water. For example, hilly, heavily wooded land would need considerable work before it could be used for industrial purposes, but it might be ideally suited for residential use. Likewise, flat land located along a major highway network is undesirable for residential use but might be well located for industry.

LAND UNIT MEASUREMENTS

Before we discuss legal descriptions, it is important to understand land unit measurements because they are commonly used to describe real estate. Some commonly used measurements are listed in Figure 2.4.

FIGURE 2.4   **Units of Land Measurement**

Unit	*Measurement*
Mile	5,280 feet; 1,760 yards
Square mile	640 acres (5,280 feet × 5,280 feet = 27,878,400 square feet ÷ 43,560 square feet per acre)
Acre	43,560 square feet
Cubic yard	27 cubic feet
Square yard	9 square feet
Square foot	144 square inches

LEGAL DESCRIPTIONS

In conveying title to real property or preparing an instrument for recording, a legally sufficient description of the real property is required. A **legal description** is one that describes no other property but the one in question. It characterizes the property in such a manner that a competent surveyor could locate it, as it appears on the surface of the earth, using nothing more than the description. Descriptions of real property are classified as being informal or formal.

Informal descriptions, while considered adequate to locate and identify a parcel of real estate, are not accepted as legal descriptions by the courts. Title companies will not insure the title to real property described in this manner. Informal descriptions may be in the form of street number (6065 Roswell Road, Atlanta, Georgia), name (the Met Life building in New York City), or blanket ("all the real property of John Adams").

Formal descriptions, or legal descriptions, constitute three basic types used throughout the United States: metes and bounds, rectangular survey, and subdivision lot and block (plat).

The oldest form of describing land is the **metes-** (distance and direction) **and-bounds** (landmarks, monuments) **description** that makes use of the boundaries and measurements of the land in question. These descriptions start at a designated point called the *point of beginning (POB)* and proceed around the boundaries of the tract by reference to linear measurements and directions returning to the point of beginning (see Figure 2.5). The boundary must always return to the point of beginning so that the tract being described is fully enclosed (this is called *closure*). Often, a metes-and-bounds description will use compass directions and measurements to the one one-hundredth of a foot.

FIGURE 2.5   **Metes-and-Bounds Description Map**

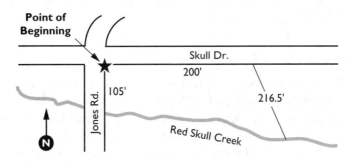

The metes-and-bounds description of the parcel of land shown in Figure 2.5 is as follows:

A tract of land located in Red Skull, Boone County, Virginia, described as follows: beginning at the intersection of the east line of Jones Road and the south line of Skull Drive; then east along the south line of Skull Drive 200 feet; then south 150 degrees east 216.5 feet, more or less, to the center thread of Red Skull Creek; then northwesterly along the center line of said creek to its intersection with the east line of Jones Road; then north 105 feet, more or less, along the east line of Jones Road to the point of beginning.

Metes-and-bounds descriptions are complicated and should be handled with extreme care. When they include compass directions of the various lines (always called from a true north-south heading) and concave and convex curved lines, metes and bounds can be difficult to understand. Metes-and-bounds descriptions also tend to be lengthy, especially when naming the owners of adjoining parcels. Descriptions that vary from those used in previous conveyances tend to cause gaps and overlaps. Because of the possibility of discrepancies and disputes concerning property by metes and bounds, it is particularly important to have the land surveyed by an authorized surveyor in order to clearly establish the tract's boundaries. Another obvious problem arises when the monuments (points of reference) change or disappear—a fence may be moved, the big oak tree may die, or a stream may change its course.

Monuments. *Monuments* are fixed objects used to establish real estate boundaries. Monuments may be either natural or artificial. Artificial monuments include roads, fences, canals, and iron pins or posts placed by surveyors as markers. Natural monuments include rocks, trees, lakes, and streams. The actual distance between monuments takes precedence over linear measurements set forth in the description, if the two measurements differ.

Benchmarks. A *benchmark* is a permanent reference point used in land descriptions. In a metes-and-bounds description, the point of beginning is usually tied to being located a certain distance from a benchmark. Although the U.S. Geological Survey has identified standard benchmarks throughout the country, local surveyors normally use street intersections as benchmarks.

For example, in preparing a metes-and-bounds description of a particular parcel, a surveyor might reference a benchmark as follows:

> Beginning at a point on the south side of Hammond Drive 325 feet east of the corner formed by the intersection of the south side of Hammond with the east side of Roswell Road.

Rectangular Survey

The rectangular survey system, sometimes called the government survey method, was established by Congress in 1785, soon after the federal government was organized. The system was developed as a standard method of describing all lands conveyed to or acquired by the federal government, including the extensive area of the Northwest Territory.

The **rectangular survey system** is based on two sets of intersecting lines: *principal meridians* and *base lines*. Principal meridians are north and south lines, and base lines run east and west. Both can be located exactly by reference to degrees of longitude and latitude. Each principal meridian has a name or a number and is crossed by its own base line. Each principal meridian and base line is used to survey a specific area of land.

Ranges. The land on either side of a principal meridian is divided into six-mile-wide strips by lines that run north and south, parallel to the meridian. These north-south strips of land are called *ranges* (see Figure 2.6). They are designated by consecutive numbers east or west of the principal meridian. For example, Range 3 East is a strip of land between 12 miles and 18 miles east of its principal meridian.

FIGURE 2.6 **Townships in the Rectangular Survey System**

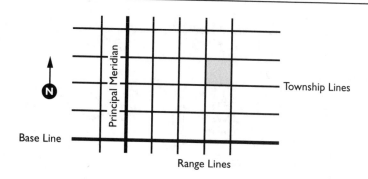

Townships. Lines running east and west and parallel to the base line six miles apart are called township lines and form strips of land (or *tiers*) called *townships* (see Figure 2.6). These tiers of townships are designated by consecutive numbers north or south of the base line. For example, the strip of land between 6 miles and 12 miles north of a base line is Township 2 North.

The shaded square in Figure 2.6 is described as Township 3 North, Range 4 East.

The township squares formed by the intersecting township and range lines are the basic units of the rectangular survey system. Theoretically, townships are 6 miles square and contain 36 square miles (see Figure 2.6).

Sections. Each township contains 36 *sections*. Sections are numbered consecutively, 1 through 36, as illustrated in Figure 2.7, with section 1 being in the upper right-hand corner of the township. By law, each section numbered 16 has been set aside for school purposes and is called a school section. The sale of or rental proceeds from this land were originally available for township school use.

FIGURE 2.7 **Sections**

			N		
6	5	4	3	2	1
7	8	9	10	11	12
18	17	16	15	14	13
19	20	21	22	23	24
30	29	28	27	26	25
31	32	33	34	35	36

W / E at sides, S at bottom

Each section contains 1 square mile, or 640 acres of land, and is commonly divided into half-sections (containing 320 acres), quarter-sections (160 acres), and further divisions of halves and quarters for reference purposes (see Figure 2.8).

FIGURE 2.8   **A Section**

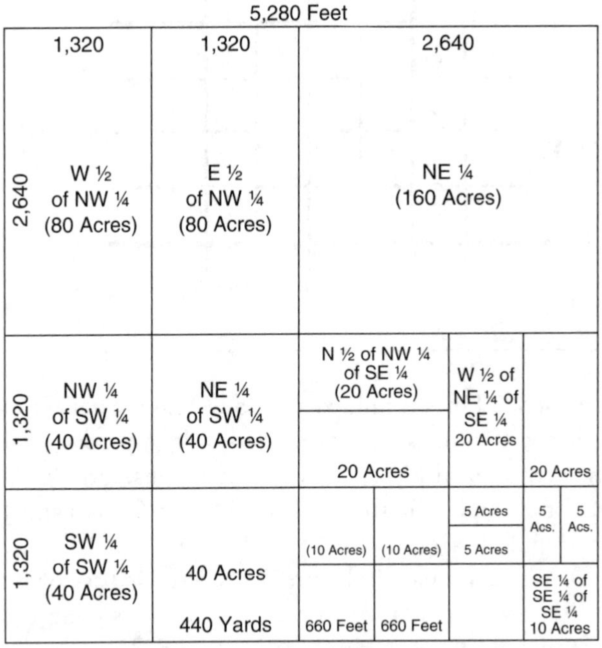

5,280 Feet		
1,320	1,320	2,640

W ½ of NW ¼ (80 Acres)	E ½ of NW ¼ (80 Acres)	NE ¼ (160 Acres)
NW ¼ of SW ¼ (40 Acres)	NE ¼ of SW ¼ (40 Acres)	N ½ of NW ¼ of SE ¼ (20 Acres) / 20 Acres	W ½ of NE ¼ of SE ¼ 20 Acres	20 Acres
SW ¼ of SW ¼ (40 Acres)	40 Acres / 440 Yards	(10 Acres) / 660 Feet	(10 Acres) / 660 Feet	5 Acres / 5 Acres	5 Acres / SE ¼ of SE ¼ of SE ¼ 10 Acres	5 Acs. / 5 Acs.

Land descriptions are made by referring to a particular portion of a section in a township that is either north or south of a specified base line and either east or west of a certain meridian. The following is a sample of a rectangular survey description:

The E½ of the NW¼ of Section 17, Township 14 North, Range 4 West of the 6th Principal Meridian.

In this sample, the land described would have an area of 80 acres (the NW¼ equals 160 acres; ½ of this ¼ equals 80 acres). Generally, the smaller a parcel of land is, the longer its legal description will be.

Subdivision Lot and Block

The newest method of land description is by **subdivision lot and block** in a subdivision plat. When subdividing land, the licensed surveyor or engineer first prepares a **plat map**. After referencing the official legal description of the larger property described either by the metes-and-bounds method or the rectangular survey method, the land is divided into blocks that are further subdivided into lots. Each block and each lot is assigned a number or letter. Lot sizes and street details must be completely indicated and must comply with all local ordinances and requirements. Some states have passed *plat acts*, which regulate the minimum size tract that may be conveyed without a subdivision plat being prepared, approved, and recorded.

When approved, the subdivision plat is recorded in the county in which the land is located, thereby becoming part of the legal description. When describing a lot from a recorded subdivision plat, the lot and block number, name or number of the subdivision plat, plat book number and page number, and name of the county and state are listed.

Measuring Elevations

Air lots. The owner of a parcel of land may subdivide the air above that land into air lots. *Air lots* consist of airspace within specific boundaries located over a parcel of land. This type of description is found in titles to tall buildings that are located on air rights, generally over railroad tracks. Similarly, a surveyor, in preparing a subdivision plat for condominium use, describes each condominium unit in reference to the elevation of the floors and ceilings on a vertical plane above the city datum.

Datum. A *datum* is a point, line, or surface from which elevations are measured or indicated. For the purpose of the U.S. Geological Survey, datum is defined as the mean sea level at New York Harbor. While most cities throughout the country have established a local datum in relation to the U.S. Geological Survey, the most common datum used for a particular property is simply the surface of the land. Therefore the location of a particular unit in a high-rise condominium could be referenced as being "Air Lot _____, located _____ feet above the surface of the land." A datum is also used to describe the area of the subsurface subject to an oil lease, to establish the grade of streets, and other situations requiring a vertical elevation.

PERSONAL PROPERTY

Personal property, also called **chattels**, is different from real property in that it is movable. Personal property includes such items as furniture, clothing, money, stocks and bonds, notes, mortgages, leases, trade fixtures, annual flowers and plants, and growing crops (emblements).

Fixtures

A **fixture** is an item that was once personal property but is now affixed to the real estate in such a way as to become part of the real property. The process is called accession. For example, wall-to-wall carpeting is personal property when it sits uninstalled at the warehouse, but once installed it becomes immovable. Courts apply five tests to determine whether an article has become a fixture or is still personal property: (1) method of attachment, (2) agreement between the parties, (3) relationship of the parties, (4) intention of the parties, and (5) adaptation of the article to the real property. The acronym *MARIA* is useful for remembering these five tests.

1. *Method.* The permanence of the manner of annexation or attachment often provides a basis for court decisions relating to fixtures. For example, a furnace, although it is removable, is usually attached in such a way that it cannot be taken out without causing extensive damage to the property. Moreover, the furnace is considered an essential part of the complete property and, as such, a fixture.

2. *Agreement.* Normally, the first test to be applied by the court is the existence of an agreement between the parties involved as to the nature of the property affixed to the land. If the existence of an agreement can be established, all other tests are generally disregarded. For example, if an agreement clearly stated that the tenant could remove any articles attached by the tenant during the lease term, the court would infer that this agreement should be followed because the parties had displayed sufficient foresight to anticipate the problem.

3. *Relationship.* Another test applied by the court is the relationship between the person who adds the article and the person with whom a dispute arises. The relationship is typically between a landlord and a tenant or between a seller and a purchaser.

4. *Intention.* The intention of the parties at the time an article was attached is a very important factor in deciding whether or not an article is a fixture. For example, a tenant who opens a jewelry store may bolt the display cases to the floor and later remove them. Because these items are an integral part of business property and it was never the intent to make them a permanent part of the structure, they are considered personal property essential to conducting a business, or trade fixtures (see more about trade fixtures later in this chapter).

5. *Adaptation.* How an article is adapted for use in a particular building is another test. For example, air conditioners installed by a tenant into wall slots specifically constructed for that purpose are considered fixtures even though they could be removed. Likewise, storm windows custom-made for a particular house are considered fixtures even though they could be readily removed. In addition, all the integral parts necessary for the operation of a fixture are considered real estate. Examples are house keys, garage door openers, and the remote control of a built-in television.

Not only is it possible to convert an item of personal property into real property, it is also possible to convert real property into personal property by **severance**. A growing tree is real property, but if the owner cuts down the tree, severing it from the land, the tree becomes personal property. Likewise, clay existing in the subsurface of the land is real property; but if the owner mines the clay and mills it into bricks, the bricks are considered personal property.

The final question to be asked is this: once the tree has been severed and milled into lumber and the clay has been milled into bricks, becoming personal property, can either once again become real property? The answer is yes. If the lumber and bricks are used in the construction of a house, they become real property again.

Trade Fixtures

A **trade fixture** is an article attached to a rented space or building by a tenant for use in conducting a business. While fixtures are legally construed to be real estate, trade fixtures are considered personal property. Examples of trade fixtures are bowling alleys, store shelves, restaurant equipment, and agricultural fixtures such as chicken coops and tool sheds. Trade fixtures must be removed on or before the last day the business property is rented, or they become the real property of the landlord by accession. After the expiration of the lease, the tenant has no right to come back onto the landlord's property to remove trade fixtures.

Emblements

Growing crops that are produced annually as a result of someone's labor are called **emblements** (*fructus industriales*, as discussed earlier). Emblements are regarded as personal property even before harvest. Thus, a tenant farmer has the right to take the annual crop resulting from that farmer's labor, even if the harvest occurs after the lease has expired. A landlord cannot terminate a tenant farmer's lease and not give the tenant the right to reenter the land to harvest the crops.

Manufactured Housing

Manufactured housing is constructed in a factory and identified by the red label—the manufacturer's certification that the home has been built in compliance with HUD construction and safety standards. At the time of manufacture, a manufactured home is movable and personal property.

By definition, a manufactured home is constructed on a permanent chassis and must be at least 8 feet wide, at least 40 feet long, and when erected on-site, at least 320 square feet. Manufactured homes can consist of one or multiple sections assembled on-site. More than 95% of the homes are never moved again. The homes are usually sited on privately owned property or in manufactured home communities (parks).

Most homes are financed by installment contracts and treated as personal property, but the interest rate is higher than mortgage interest rates. Both Fannie Mae and Freddie Mac will buy loans secured by a manufactured home, but the home must be classified as real property, a process that varies from county to county.

Briefly, the wheels must be removed and the purchase, conveyance, and financing must be a single real estate transaction evidenced by a first lien mortgage or deed of trust properly recorded. The home must be permanently connected to a septic or sewage system meeting local and state requirements. Most importantly, the home must be placed on a foundation in accordance with the manufacturer's requirements for anchoring, support, stability, and maintenance and appropriate to soil conditions meeting local and state codes.

Real estate licensees are not usually involved in the initial purchase, but are consulted for resales. Licensees should help the owner locate the necessary paperwork to show that the home has been converted from personal to real property. Without the paperwork, buyers will find it very difficult to obtain financing.

SUMMARY

The definition of land not only applies to the earth's surface, but also includes everything below the surface to the center of the earth and the air above the surface. Real estate, on the other hand, refers to the earth's surface, everything below and above it, plus all things permanently attached to it. The term *real property* further expands this definition to include those rights associated with ownership of the land and improvements.

The unique nature of land is apparent in both its economic and physical characteristics. The economic characteristics are relative scarcity, improvements, permanence of investment, and area preferences. The physical characteristics are immobility, nonhomogeneity, and indestructibility. All of these characteristics affect the investment potential of and competition for a specific parcel of land.

Documents affecting or conveying interests in real estate must contain a legal description that accurately identifies the property involved. Three methods of description are used in the United States: (1) metes and bounds, (2) rectangular survey, and (3) subdivision lot and block. A legal description is a precise method of identifying a parcel of land as it exists on the surface of the earth. Air lots, condominium descriptions, and other measurements of vertical elevations may be computed from the U.S. Geographical Survey datum, which is the mean sea level at New York Harbor. Most large cities have established local survey datums for surveying within the area. The elevations from these datums are further supplemented by reference points, called benchmarks, placed at fixed intervals from the datum.

All property that does not fit the definition of real property is classified as personal property, or chattels. When articles of personal property are permanently affixed to the land, they become fixtures and, as such, are considered a part of the real property. Five tests are used to determine whether an article has become a fixture or is still personal property: (1) method of attachment, (2) agreement between the parties, (3) relationship of the parties, (4) intention of the parties, and (5) adaptation of the article to the real property. However, personal property attached to real property by a tenant for business purposes is classified as a trade (or chattel) fixture. Trade fixtures must be removed by the tenant before the end of the lease period.

Manufactured housing, built in a factory, is personal property at the time of manufacture. It can be converted to real property by removing the wheels, attaching it to a septic system, and meeting other local requirements.

REVIEW QUESTIONS

Please complete all the questions before turning to the Answer Key on page 335.

1. Which of the following is personal property?
   a. Land
   b. Fixtures
   c. The bundle of rights
   d. Trade fixtures

2. A metes-and-bounds legal description must include
   a. a datum.
   b. an acreage for the parcel.
   c. a point of beginning (POB).
   d. a meridian.

3. Personal property is distinguished from real property by its
   a. cost.
   b. mobility.
   c. scarcity.
   d. size.

4. The legal description on the purchaser's contract is Lot 4 in Block C at Happy Acres, Washington County. This method of legal description is based on
   a. a rectangular survey.
   b. a subdivision plat.
   c. metes and bounds.
   d. a government survey.

5. Items that are attached to the land are considered
   a. trade fixtures.
   b. emblements.
   c. real estate.
   d. chattels.

6. A builder constructs the same model home in many different locations. The fact that a young couple only wants to buy that particular model in the center city is an example of the economic characteristic called
   a. scarcity.
   b. permanence of investment.
   c. situs.
   d. improvements.

7. A farmer and rancher is worried that owners of property upstream are diverting all the available water, leaving nothing for watering crops and stock. He may be protected by the concept of water rights called
   a. riparian rights.
   b. subsurface rights.
   c. littoral rights.
   d. prior appropriation.

8. A farmer sold his cornfield. The farmer has the right to harvest the corn because the corn is an example of
   a. an emblement.
   b. personal property.
   c. a chattel.
   d. a trade fixture.

9. A county supports its local government through property taxes. This ability to make long-range plans based on projected income is based on the physical characteristic of land called
   a. immobility.
   b. scarcity.
   c. indestructibility.
   d. nonhomogeneity.

10. The bundle of rights of ownership allow a new homeowner to do all of the following *EXCEPT*
    a. take possession of the property.
    b. exercise complete control of the property with no restrictions.
    c. exclude others from entering the property.
    d. sell, rent, or give away the property.

11. A new homeowner installed ceiling fans in all the rooms in the house. The factors that will determine whether these fans are now considered part of the real property include all of the following *EXCEPT*
    a. the method by which they are attached.
    b. their cost.
    c. the homeowner's intention when installing them.
    d. the adaptation of the fans to the house.

12. The definition of *land* includes
    a. man-made additions.
    b. the right to possession.
    c. subsurface rights.
    d. emblements.

13. All metes-and-bounds descriptions must
    a. include natural monuments.
    b. return to the point of beginning.
    c. use U.S. Geological Survey benchmarks.
    d. include lot and block numbers.

14. A parcel of land containing 640 acres is called a
    a. township.
    b. section.
    c. range.
    d. plat.

15. A truckload of lumber has been left on the drive-way for use in building a new deck. At this point, the lumber is considered
    a. a fixture because it will be permanently affixed to real property.
    b. personal property because it is movable.
    c. real property because it will be a man-made addition.
    d. a trade fixture because it is part of a business contract.

16. An owner sells several large trees for use as lumber. The growing trees become personal property through the process called
    a. accession.
    b. rescission.
    c. severance.
    d. acceptance.

17. A lease for a commercial tenant ended before the tenant removed several large counters and a large refrigerator. The landlord may acquire this property by a process called
    a. accession.
    b. severance.
    c. common law.
    d. custom.

18. A seller recently installed a heat pump used to heat the house. The heat pump is installed outside the house. Because the heat pump is new and cost a lot of money, the seller wants to take it with him. Can he do this?
    a. Yes, because the seller paid for it.
    b. Yes, because the owner can take anything that is not indoors.
    c. No, because any item that heats any part of the home is considered real property.
    d. No, the item is an essential part of the property.

19. In which property will the surveyor *MOST* likely use an air lot to describe the property?
    a. High-rise commercial building
    b. High-rise condominium unit
    c. Shopping mall
    d. A duplex consisting of two rental units

20. A metes-and-bounds legal description appears to be very complicated. Whom should the buyer consult for accurate boundary lines?
    a. An attorney
    b. An appraiser
    c. A surveyor
    d. Current owner

3

Rights and Interests in Real Estate

LEARNING OBJECTIVES

When you finish reading this chapter, you will be able to

- identify the four government powers,
- recognize the different types of freehold estates,
- list and describe the effect of encumbrances on the transfer of property, and
- recognize how deed restrictions can impact the use of property.

ad valorem	easement by prescription	inverse condemnation
allodial system	easement in gross	judgment
covenants, conditions, and restrictions (CC&Rs)	eminent domain	leasehold estate
community property	encumbrance	license
condemnation	encroachment	lien
curtesy	escheat	life estate
deed restriction	fee simple absolute	lis pendens
dower	fee simple defeasible	mechanic's lien
easement	fee simple subject to a condition subsequent	pur autre vie
easement appurtenant		spot survey
easement by necessity	freehold estates	remainder interest
	homestead	reversionary interest

As discussed in Chapter 2, a person who holds title to a parcel of real estate owns not only the land itself, but also certain rights to the property—possession, control, enjoyment, exclusion, and disposition. These rights, however, are not absolute; certain rights are always retained by the government. In addition, ownership rights may be restricted, depending on the type of interest held, or may be subject to the rights of third parties who might have some legal interest in the real estate.

HISTORICAL BACKGROUND OF REAL ESTATE OWNERSHIP

According to English common law, the government or king held title to all lands under the **feudal system** of ownership, a system in which the individual was merely a tenant whose rights to use and occupy real property were held by an overlord. Through a series of social reforms in the 17th century, the feudal system evolved into the **allodial system** of ownership, under which the individual was entitled to property rights without being subject to control.

Land in the United States is held under the allodial system. The Bill of Rights of the U.S. Constitution firmly establishes the private ownership of land free from any of the overtones, obligations, or burdens of the feudal system.

GOVERNMENTAL POWERS

An individual has maximum rights in the land that individual owns, but these rights are subject to certain powers, or rights, held by federal, state, and local governments. Government limitations on ownership of real property are for the general welfare of the community and include police power, eminent domain, taxation, and escheat. The acronym *PETE* makes it easier to remember.

- *Police power.* Under police power, every state may establish legislation to preserve order, protect public health and safety, and promote general welfare. The use and enjoyment of property is affected by this legislation, which includes zoning and building ordinances that regulate the use, occupancy, size, location, construction, and rents of real property, as well as environmental protection laws.

- *Eminent domain.* The right of government to acquire private land for public use is **eminent domain**; the action to acquire this land is **condemnation**. Two conditions must be met: (1) the proposed use must be declared by the court to be a public use, and (2) fair compensation must be paid to the owner. The right of eminent domain is generally granted by state laws to agencies such as land clearance commissions and public housing or redevelopment authorities, as well as to railroads and public utility companies.

  Inverse condemnation is the legal action for compensation taken by a property owner because the action of a government entity has negatively impacted the value of the property. The action can be a physical taking or because of other actions—sewage leaks onto the property, flooding occurs after a road was built, changing flight patterns at an airport creates an unbearable noise level, and so on. Several lawsuits have upheld this right. *Lucas v. South Carolina Coastal Council* successfully argued that restrictions placed by the South Carolina Coastal Council on his two lots valued at $975,000 prevented him from erecting any home on his property. The justices ruled that a government body may not regulate away all the economic beneficial use of a property.

  In 2000, the case of *Kelo v. New London* created a storm of controversy in Connecticut. The City of New London turned over the power of eminent domain to the New London Development Corporation (NLDC) to take the entire neighborhood of Fort Trumbull for an extensive redevelopment project. The city argued that economic rejuvenation justified the taking. Although fought all the way to the Supreme Court, in June 2005, the Court ruled against the homeowners. The significance of this case prompted more than 40 states to consider legislation limiting a government's use of eminent domain powers to promote private use. For more information on this historic case, visit www.ij.org/kelo.

- *Taxation.* Taxation is a charge on real property to raise funds to meet the operating costs of a government. Taxation is discussed later in this chapter and in greater detail in Chapter 10.

- *Escheat.* Property becomes ownerless when the owner dies intestate (without a will) and no known heirs. **Escheat** is the process by which the ownership of such property transfers to the state or the county in which the property is located. Governmental powers are discussed in more detail in Chapter 14.

ESTATES IN LAND

An *estate in land* is the character and extent of ownership interest that a person has in real property. As illustrated in Figure 3.1, estates in land are divided into two major classifications: (1) freehold estates and (2) leasehold estates (also called *nonfreehold estates*).

FIGURE 3.1   **Freehold and Leasehold Estates**

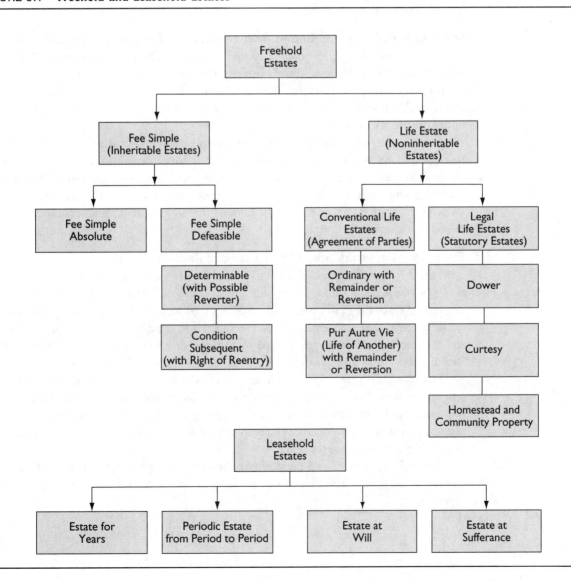

Freehold Estates

Estates that may be for an indefinite time, existing for a lifetime, or longer are called **freehold estates** and include (1) fee simple absolute, (2) fee simple defeasible, and (3) life estates (see Figure 3.1). Fee simple absolute and defeasible fee estates continue for an indefinite period and can be inherited; life estates terminate upon the death of the person on whose life the estate is based.

Fee simple absolute.   The most complete type of interest in real estate recognized by law is a fee simple absolute. A **fee simple absolute** estate is one in which the holder is entitled to all rights of property ownership. Because this estate is of unlimited duration, upon the death of its owner, it passes to the heirs or as provided in the owner's will. The terms *fee*, *fee simple*, and *fee simple absolute* are basically the same. The holder of a fee simple estate is, of course, subject to governmental powers.

Fee simple defeasible.   A fee estate that can be inherited is called a **fee simple defeasible**, sometimes called a *qualified fee* or *conditional fee*. However, this estate is subject to the occurrence or nonoccurrence of a certain event. There are two types of fee simple defeasible: (1) an estate subject to a condition subsequent and (2) an estate qualified by a special limitation.

Fee simple defeasible qualified by a condition subsequent.   This means that the new owner must not perform some action or activity. The former owner retains a *right of reentry* so that if the condition is broken, the former owner can retake possession of the property through legal action. Conditions in a deed are different from restrictions or covenants because of the grantor's right to reclaim ownership, a right that does not exist under private restrictions.

For example, when the deed of conveyance for a parcel of real estate specifically states that the transfer is made on the condition that there be no consumption of alcohol on the premises, the estate conveyed is a **fee simple subject to a condition subsequent**. If alcohol is consumed on the property, the former owner has the right to reacquire full ownership. It will be necessary for the grantor (or the grantor's heirs or successors) to go to court to assert that right, however.

Fee simple defeasible qualified by special limitation.   The estate ends automatically on the current owner's failure to comply with the limitation. The former owner retains a *possibility of reverter*. If the limitation is violated, the former owner (or heirs or successors) reacquires full ownership, with no need to reenter the land or go to court. A fee simple with a special limitation is also called a *fee simple determinable* because it may end automatically. The language used to distinguish a special limitation—the words *so long as*, *while*, or *during*—is the key to creating this estate.

For example, a grant of land from an owner to a church "so long as the land is used for religious purposes" is a fee simple determinable. The church has the full bundle of rights possessed by the property owner, with one string attached. If the church ever uses the property for nonreligious purposes, the property will automatically revert to the original grantor (or to heirs or successors).

The right of reentry and possibility of reverter may never take effect. If they do, it will be in the future. Therefore, both of these rights are considered future interests (see Figure 3.1).

Conventional life estates. A conventional **life estate** is an estate that is limited to the life of the owner or to the life of some other designated person or persons. It is not an estate of inheritance—that is, the rights cannot be passed on to the owner's heirs—because the estate terminates at the death of the owner or designated person.

There are two types of conventional life estates—ordinary and pur autre vie (see Figure 3.2). When the owner of a fee simple estate grants an ordinary life estate to someone, it is limited to the lifetime of the owner of the life estate, the life tenant. However, a life estate can also be created based on the life of a third party. For example, a man conveyed a home to his father's caretakers for as long as his father lives. When his father dies, ownership of the home reverts to the original owner. This is called an estate **pur autre vie**, meaning "for the life of another." In this type of life estate, the caretakers are the life tenants.

FIGURE 3.2 Ordinary Life Estates

Ordinary Life Estate, Based on Life Tenant's Life

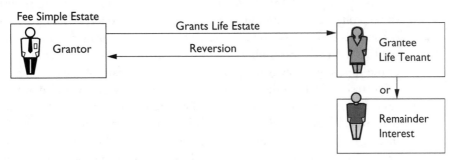

Pur Autre Vie Life Estate, Based on Another's Life

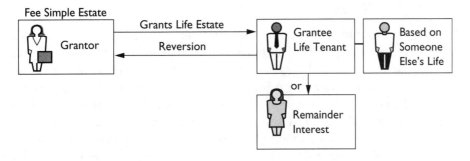

When creating a life estate, the original fee simple owner must also consider the future ownership of the property after the life tenant's death. The future interest may take one of two forms:

1. **Remainder interest.** If the deed or will creating the life estate names a third party or parties to whom title will pass upon the death of the life estate owner, then this third party is said to own the remainder interest, or estate.

2. **Reversionary interest.** If the creator of a life estate (the original fee simple owner) does not convey the remainder interest to a third party or parties, then upon the death of the life estate owner, full ownership reverts to the original fee simple owner. If the original owner is deceased, it reverts to the heirs or devisees set forth in the deceased's will. This interest or estate is called a *reversion*.

Upon the death of the life estate owner or other designated person, the holder of the future interest, whether remainder or reversion, will be the owner of a fee simple estate.

A life tenant's interest in real property is a true ownership interest. In general, the life tenant is not answerable to the holder of the future interest, called the *remainderman*, to whom the right of possession will pass upon termination of the life estate. However, the life tenant cannot perform any acts that would permanently injure the land or property. Such injury to real estate is known in legal terms as *waste*.

A life tenant is entitled to all income and profits arising from the property during the term of ownership and is also responsible for paying the real estate taxes. A life interest may be sold, leased, or mortgaged, but finding an interested party can be difficult. Life tenants may only lease, mortgage, or sell the interests they have. The interest of any buyer, tenant, or lender will terminate at the end of the life interest.

Legal life estates (statutory estates).   Legal life estates are created by state law. **Curtesy** is a husband's life estate in the real estate of his deceased wife. **Dower** is the life estate that a wife has in the real estate of her deceased husband. A dower or curtesy interest means that upon the death of the owning spouse, the surviving spouse has a right to either a one-half or a one-third interest in the real property. The right of dower or curtesy becomes effective only upon the death of a spouse. During the lifetime of the parties, the right is merely the possibility of an interest. It is *inchoate*, or incomplete, until the death of the spouse who owns the property. Upon the death of the owning spouse, the dower or curtesy right becomes *consummate* (complete). Curtesy and dower rights have been abolished in many states and replaced by the Uniform Probate Code elective share rules that provide the surviving spouse with a share of the property regardless of provisions made in the deceased spouse's will. Due to any possible future interests (dower, curtsey, or elective shares), it is always advisable to obtain both spouses' signatures on listing and contract agreements even though only one of the parties may be the owner of record of the property.

Homestead.   Other interests in real estate created by state law include homestead and community property. A **homestead** is a tract of land that is owned and occupied as the family home. In those states that have homestead exemption laws, a portion of the value is protected from judgment debts. In some states, it is necessary to file a declaration of homestead. This is not to say that the homestead cannot be sold—it can. Should judgment be awarded against the property, the homestead exemption simply sets aside a portion of court-ordered sale proceeds to go to the property owner before any disbursement is made to the creditor. In most cases, the homestead exemption is only operative against unsecured judgment creditors and has no effect on the claim of a mortgage lender whose loan is secured by the property, a governmental claim for unpaid property taxes, or a mechanic's lien against the property for labor and materials supplied in improving the real estate. In some states, the homestead exemption relieves the property owner from paying property taxes on a portion of the value of the home.

Community property.   **Community property** consists of all property, real and personal, acquired by either spouse during the marriage. Any conveyance of, or encumbrance on, community property requires the signature of both spouses. Upon the death of one spouse, the survivor automatically owns one-half of the community property. The other half is distributed according to the deceased's will. If the deceased died without a will, the other half is inherited by the survivor or by the deceased's other heirs, depending upon state law. The concept of community property originated in Spanish law, not English common law, and has been adopted by many U.S. western and southwestern states. The only property not subject to the community property statutes in these states is *separate property*, which is acquired and owned by either spouse prior to marriage or acquired by either spouse during marriage through gift, devise, or descent.

Leasehold Estates

A **leasehold estate** is one of predetermined duration. Through a *lease*, an owner of real estate transfers to a tenant the right to exclusive possession and use of the owner's property for a specific period of time. Because the leasehold estate is not an estate of ownership, the ownership interest in the property remains with the landlord as an *estate in reversion*. The landlord has the right to retake possession of the property after the lease term has expired. All leasehold estates are classified as being either *definite* or *indefinite*. The four most important are (1) *estate for years*, (2) *estate from period to period*, (3) *estate at will*, and (4) *estate at sufferance*. The legal specifics of the relationship between landlord and tenant will be discussed in detail in Chapter 9.

ENCUMBRANCES

An **encumbrance** is defined as a charge or burden on a property that may diminish its value or obstruct the use of the property but that does not necessarily prevent a transfer of title. Encumbrances may be divided into two general classifications: (1) *money encumbrances* or *liens*, which affect the title, and (2) *nonmoney encumbrances*, which affect the physical condition and use of the property (see Figure 3.3).

FIGURE 3.3 **Encumbrances**

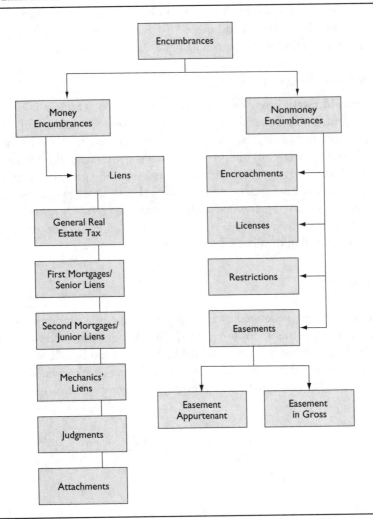

Liens

A **lien** is a monetary claim or charge on a property by which the property is made security for the performance of some act, usually the payment of a debt. A lien allows a creditor to force the sale of property given as security by a debtor to settle debt in case of default. Liens may be *voluntary* or *involuntary*. They are further classified into two categories: *specific* and *general*.

Voluntary liens. A lien is *voluntary* when the owner of the property agrees to use the title to real estate as security for a debt. The best example of a voluntary lien is the mortgage lien.

Involuntary liens. A lien is considered *involuntary* when the lien is placed on the title to real estate by statute or by court order, against the express will of the property owner. Examples of involuntary liens are real estate tax liens and court-ordered judgment liens.

Specific liens. Specific liens are those secured by one or more specific parcels of real estate, and they include mortgages, taxes, special assessments, liens for public utilities, mechanics' liens, vendees' liens, vendors' liens, surety bail bond liens, attachment liens, and execution liens.

General liens. General liens usually affect all of the debtor's nonexempt property, both real and personal. Included are real and personal property, judgment liens, debts of a deceased person, state inheritance taxes, federal estate taxes on a decedent's estate, and franchise taxes levied against corporations.

A typical real estate owner's fee simple estate may be reduced in value by the lien and encumbrance rights of others. The fee simple title to encumbered property can be conveyed to another party by the owner, but the existence of one or more liens against the property threatens the buyer with possible loss of the real estate if creditors take court action to enforce payment.

Real estate tax liens. State and local governments have the right to levy taxes on real property. Because the location of real estate is permanently fixed, the government can levy taxes with a high degree of certainty that the taxes will be collected. Because annual taxes levied on real estate usually have priority over previously recorded liens, if the property is subjected to a court-ordered sale to satisfy unpaid debts, outstanding real estate taxes will be paid from the proceeds first.

Real estate taxes can be divided into two types: (1) *general real estate tax* or *ad valorem tax* and (2) *special assessments* or *improvements tax*. Both of these taxes are levied against specific parcels of property and automatically become liens on those properties. Real estate tax liens are specific, involuntary liens.

General real estate taxes are levied for the general support or operation of the governmental agency authorized to impose the levy, such as the state, county, municipality, and/or local school district. These taxes are called **ad valorem** taxes (from the Latin phrase meaning "to the value") because the amount of the tax varies in accordance with the value of the property being taxed. To be enforceable, real estate taxes must be valid, meaning that they must be (1) properly levied, (2) for a legal purpose, and (3) applied equitably to all affected property. Real estate taxes that have remained delinquent for the period specified by state law can be collected through either tax foreclosure or tax sale. While there are substantial differences in the methods and details of the various states' tax sale procedures, the results are the same.

Special assessments are special taxes levied on real estate that require property owners to pay for municipal improvements that benefit the real estate they own. Such taxes often are levied to pay for streets, street lighting, curbs, public sewers, and similar items and may be involuntary or voluntary, if requested by the property owners. They are enforced in the same manner as general real estate taxes. Both general and special assessment real estate taxes will be covered in more detail in Chapter 10.

Mechanics' liens. A **mechanic's lien** is a right granted by statute to give security to those who perform labor or furnish materials for the improvement of real property. The mechanic's lien right is based on the *enhancement of value theory*. Because of the labor performed and material furnished, the real estate has been enhanced in value. Therefore, the parties who performed the work or supplied the materials are given the right of lien on the real estate on which they worked as security for the payment of their proper charges. A mechanic's lien is a specific, involuntary lien.

In order for a person to be entitled to file for a mechanic's lien, the work completed must have been done by contract with the owner or the owner's representative. Such a lien is relied on to cover situations in which the owner has not fully paid for work or when the general contractor has been paid but has not paid the subcontractors or suppliers. Generally, a person claiming a mechanic's lien must record a notice of lien within a limited time after the work is completed.

The point at which a mechanic's lien attaches to the real estate varies according to state law. For example, priority may be established as of the date

- the construction began or materials were first furnished (the beginning of what is called the *scheme of improvements*),

- the work was completed,

- the individual subcontractor's work was either commenced or completed,

- the contract was signed or work ordered, or

- a notice of lien was recorded.

Mechanics' liens may be filed according to the laws of the state in which the real estate is located. These laws usually provide that a claimant must take steps to enforce a lien within a certain time, usually one or two years after the filing of the lien claim, or the lien will expire. Enforcement usually requires a court action to foreclose the lien through the sale of the subject real estate in order to obtain the money to satisfy the lien.

Judgment liens.   A **judgment** is a final order or decree of the court. When the decree awards money and sets forth the amount owed to the creditor, the judgment is called a *money judgment*. The details of the judge or jury's final determination are put in writing in an *abstract of judgment*. Until the abstract of judgment is recorded, it has no direct effect upon the debtor's property. However, the judgment constitutes a potential *cloud on the title*. Once recorded, it becomes an involuntary, general lien on all nonexempt real and personal property in that county that is either possessed by the debtor or subsequently acquired, as long as the judgment is effective.

Writ of execution.   If a money judgment is awarded by the court and the debtor fails to pay, the creditor may force payment through sale of the property. The court issues a writ of execution, which authorizes an officer of the court to seize and sell the debtor's property in order to satisfy the judgment. From the time the writ of execution is issued by the court until the debtor's property is actually sold to satisfy the debt, the writ constitutes another type of involuntary lien awarded by the court, an *execution lien*.

Lis pendens.   Because a judgment or other decree affecting real estate is rendered at the conclusion of a lawsuit, there may be a considerable time lag between the filing of a lawsuit and the rendering of a judgment. When any suit is filed that affects title to a specific parcel of real estate, a notice called **lis pendens** is recorded. A lis pendens filed in the public records gives constructive notice to all interested parties of the creditor's possible claim against the real estate and constitutes a cloud on the title. For more information about constructive notice, see Chapter 6.

Attachments.   To prevent a debtor from conveying title to unsecured real estate (realty that is not mortgaged or encumbered) while a court suit is being decided, a creditor may seek a *writ of attachment*, or an attachment lien. By this writ, the court retains custody of the property until the suit is concluded. To obtain an attachment, a creditor must first post with the court a surety bond or deposit sufficient to cover any possible loss or damage the debtor may sustain during the period the court has custody of the property, in case the judgment is not awarded to the creditor. The writ of attachment and subsequent attachment lien are placed against the debtor's property before the court suit is decided.

Although a judgment lien is said to affect all property of a debtor, the courts hold that certain property is exempt from attachment or execution. When a written *declaration of homestead* is filed for record prior to the recording of an abstract of judgment, it protects the debtor's equity up to the amount of the exemption. A *joint tenant's interest* is another example of exempt property. A lien or a joint tenant's interest is extinguished if the joint tenant dies before the court-ordered sale of the property.

Failure to pay federal income, estate, or payroll taxes would result in a general lien against all property owned by the delinquent taxpayer.

Nonmoney Encumbrances

Although all liens are encumbrances, not all encumbrances are liens. Nonmoney encumbrances are those that affect the physical condition or limit the use of real estate. Nonmoney encumbrances are normally classified as *easements, deed restrictions, licenses,* or *encroachments.*

Easements. An **easement** is a right acquired by one party to use the land of another party for a special purpose. It is also possible to have an easement right in the air above a parcel of real estate. Because an easement is a right to use land, it is classified as an interest in real estate, but it is not an estate in land. The holder of an easement merely has a right, but does not have an estate or ownership interest in the land over which the easement exists. An easement is sometimes called an *incorporeal right* in land (a nonpossessory interest). An easement may be either appurtenant or in gross (see Figures 3.4 and 3.5).

FIGURE 3.4 **Easement Appurtenant**

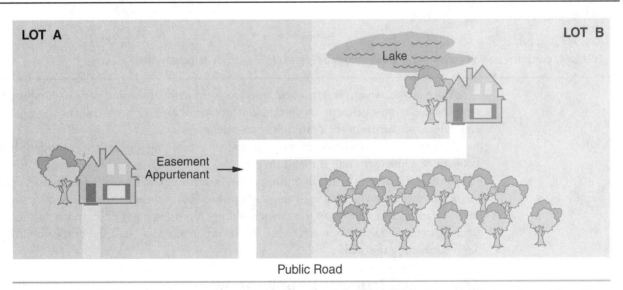

The owner of Lot B has an easement appurtenant across Lot A to gain access to his property from the public road. Lot B is dominant, and Lot A is servient.

An **easement appurtenant** is an easement that is annexed to the ownership and used for the benefit of another party's land; for example, access to a property may only exist on a neighbor's property. For an easement appurtenant to exist, there must be two tracts of land owned by different parties. The tract over which the easement runs is called the *servient estate (tenement)*; the tract that is to benefit from the easement is the *dominant* *estate (tenement)*. An easement appurtenant is considered part of the dominant estate. If the dominant tenement is conveyed to another party, the easement will pass with the title. In legal terms, it is said that the easement runs with the land. However, title to the actual land over which an easement runs is retained by the owner of the servient estate.

An **easement in gross** is a mere personal interest in or right to use the land of another and is not appurtenant to any ownership estate in the land. Commercial easements in gross include the easement right a railroad or utility company has for its tracks, pipeline, or high tension power lines (see Figure 3.5). It may be assigned, conveyed, or inherited.

FIGURE 3.5   **Easement in Gross**

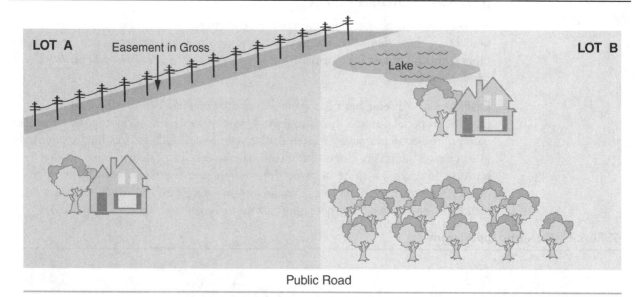

The utility company has an easement in gross across both parcels of land for its power lines.

A personal easement in gross is granted to an individual for that person's lifetime. It permits access to the property for some use. This type of easement is usually not assignable and will terminate upon the death of the easement holder.

A *party wall easement* exists when a wall of a building sits on the boundary line between two lots, with half the wall on each lot. For example, neighboring office buildings built right up to the lot line might share a common wall on the lot line between them. Lot owners own the side of the wall on their lot, and they have an easement right in the other side for support of their own building. A written party wall agreement should be used to create these easement rights. Each owner must pay half the cost of building and maintaining the wall.

Creation and Termination of Easements

Creation of an easement requires two separate parties, one of whom owns the land over which the easement runs. It is impossible for the owner of a parcel of property to hold an easement running over that property. Thus, where a valid easement exists and the dominant tenement is acquired by the owner of the servient tenement, the easement becomes dormant. The user's express or implied intention is required to terminate the easement.

Easements may be created by the following:

- *Mutual agreement expressed by the parties*—generally in writing, through a grant or by reservation in a deed of conveyance.

- *Necessity*—for ingress to and egress from an otherwise landlocked property, often by a court order. An **easement by necessity** is an appurtenant easement that arises when an owner of land sells a part that has *no access* to a street or public way except over the seller's remaining land. An easement by necessity arises because all owners have rights of ingress to and egress from their land—they cannot be landlocked.

- *Prescription*—through visible, open, and notorious use of another person's property. An **easement by prescription** is acquired when the claimant has used another's land for a certain period of time as defined by state law. This *prescriptive period* varies by state but is usually from 5–20 years. The claimant's use must have been continuous, exclusive, and without the owner's approval. Additionally, the use must be visible, open, and notorious so that the owner has or could have had knowledge of it.

- *Condemnation*—such as when a public utility installs new towers or pipelines across a property.

- *Implication*—when the situation or the parties' actions imply the intention to create an easement.

Easements may be terminated when the

- purpose for which the easement was created no longer exists,

- owner of either the dominant or servient tenement becomes the owner of both in a process called merger,

- owner of the dominant tenement releases the right of easement,

- easement is abandoned (again, the intention of the parties' controls),

- easement is taken by eminent domain or is lost through adverse possession, and

- person acquiring the easement uses it for an improper or illegal purpose.

Private restrictions.   Private agreements that affect the use of particular property are called **deed restrictions,** while those affecting an entire subdivision are covenants, conditions, and restrictions (CC&Rs). A real estate owner can create a deed restriction by including it in the deed when the property is conveyed; the restrictions are binding on future owners. Deed restrictions are privately enforced, not by government entities. Deed restrictions are legal so long as they do not violate the law.

There is a distinction between restrictions on the owner's right to *sell* and restrictions on the right to *use*. In general, provisions in a deed conveying a fee simple estate that bar the grantee from selling, mortgaging, or conveying it are considered void. Such restrictions attempt to limit the basic principle of the *free alienation (transfer) of property*, and the courts usually consider them against public policy and therefore are unenforceable.

Covenants, conditions, and restrictions (CC&Rs).   A subdivider may establish restrictions on the right to use land through a covenant in a deed or by a separate recorded declaration. These restrictions are commonly called **covenants, conditions, and restrictions (CC&Rs)** and are binding on all grantees. CC&Rs are considered valid if they are legal, reasonable restraints and are for the benefit of all property owners in the subdivision. CC&Rs usually relate to the (1) type of building; (2) use to which the land may be put; and (3) type of construction, height, setbacks, and square footage. For example, a subdivision may have a restriction dictating the style of home built or banning the use of clotheslines. If such restrictions are too broad in their terms, however, they may prevent the free transfer of property and may not be enforceable. Any restrictive covenant or condition considered void by a court does not affect the validity of the deed and does not prevent divestiture by the grantee.

Time limitations. Most CC&Rs have a *time limitation*, for example, "effective for a period of 25 years from this date." After that time, the restrictions become inoperative, unless they are extended by majority agreement of the owners of subdivision property at that time. Frequently, the effective term of the restrictions may be extended with the consent of a majority (or two-thirds) of owners in a subdivision. Generally, a deed restriction may only be removed by unanimous consent of all lot owners.

Generally, if there is conflict between a zoning ordinance (public restriction) and a deed restriction (private restriction), the more stringent will prevail.

Injunctions against violators of restrictions. Subdividers usually place restrictions on the use of all lots in a subdivision as a general plan for the benefit of all lot owners. Such restrictions give each lot owner the right to apply to the court for an *injunction* to stop a neighboring lot owner from violating the recorded restrictions. If granted, the court injunction will direct the violator to stop the violation upon penalty of being in contempt of court. The court retains the power to punish the violator for failure to obey the court order. Adjoining lot owners who stand idly by while a violation is being committed can lose the right to the court's injunction by their inaction; the court might claim *laches*, that is, loss of a right through undue delay or failure to assert it.

Licenses. A license is a privilege to enter the land of another party for a specific purpose. It is not an estate in land; it is a personal right of the person to whom it is given. A license differs from an easement in gross in that it can be terminated or canceled by the licensor (the person who granted the license) and is usually not transferable. An example of license is permission to park in a neighbor's driveway.

Encroachments. An *encroachment* arises when a portion of a building, a fence, or driveway illegally *extends beyond its owner's land* and covers some land of an adjoining owner or a street or alley. Encroachments are usually disclosed by either a physical inspection of the property or a spot survey. A **spot survey** shows the location of all improvements located on a property and reveals whether any improvements extend over the lot lines. Encroachments are not disclosed by the usual title evidence provided in a real estate sale, unless a survey is submitted at the time the examination is made. If the building on a lot encroaches on neighboring land, the neighbor may be able to either recover damages or secure removal of the portion of the building that encroaches. Encroachments of long standing may give rise to easements by prescription.

Public restrictions. Public restrictions are those that are imposed on private property by governmental authorities because they are considered necessary to protect the public health, safety, and general welfare. These are discussed in more detail in Chapter 14.

SUMMARY

Under the allodial system, an individual in the United States may acquire the ownership rights of possession, use and enjoyment, control, and disposition in real property, but an individual may not acquire absolute ownership of real property because certain rights—such as police power, eminent domain, taxation, and escheat—are always retained by the government. The government is obligated to reimburse property owners when it acquires private land for public use through eminent domain. The taking may be by agreement, by condemnation, or inverse condemnation.

An estate in real property is the degree, quantity, nature, and extent of interest that a person has in that property. If the estate is of indeterminable length, it is called a freehold estate and may be a fee simple, defeasible fee, or life estate, with either an estate in reversion or a remainder estate. If the estate exists less than a lifetime, it is called a leasehold estate and may be an estate for years, estate from period to period, estate at will, or estate at sufferance.

Although an owner of real estate generally controls the various rights to that real estate, an owner's rights in real estate may be subject to the rights of others. These rights are called encumbrances and include money encumbrances, where the right is acquired due to some monetary debt or obligation, and nonmoney encumbrances, where the right affects the physical condition and use of the property.

Liens (money encumbrances) may be voluntary or involuntary and are classified as general or specific. They include mortgage liens, attachment liens, judgment liens, execution liens, and tax liens.

Easements and restrictions are nonmoney encumbrances. Easements may be either appurtenant or in gross, while restrictions are largely of two kinds—private or public. Easements may be created by deed or by use, condemnation, or implication. They may be terminated when the use for which they were created no longer exists, the properties merge under one owner, the dominant releases the servient tenement, the easement is used for an illegal purpose, or by abandonment or eminent domain.

Deed restrictions are binding on subsequent owners and affect only one property. Covenants, conditions, and restrictions (CC&Rs) are for the benefit of all owners in the subdivision. They may not be illegal. If there is a conflict between a zoning ordinance (public restriction) and a deed restriction or CC&Rs, the more restrictive prevails.

A license is a personal privilege to enter another's property for a specific purpose, and it can be revoked at any time. An encroachment is the illegal extension of one owner's property onto another's and may be discovered by physical inspection or by a spot survey that shows the location of all improvements located on the property and, if any, extend over the lot lines.

REVIEW QUESTIONS

Please complete all of the questions before turning to the Answer Key on page 335.

1. A town condemns all property in four downtown blocks to build a new courthouse and social services building. It is able to do this under the governmental power of
   a. taxation.
   b. police power.
   c. eminent domain.
   d. escheat.

2. A man owns 20 acres of farmland with a farm-house, two barns, and numerous outbuildings that he will leave to his son when he dies. The man has a
   a. freehold estate.
   b. leasehold estate.
   c. life estate.
   d. tenancy at will.

3. A widow is willed property from her deceased husband for the rest of her life. Upon her death, the title passes to her children. This type of ownership is *BEST* described as a
   a. fee simple absolute.
   b. fee simple defeasible.
   c. life estate with a reversionary interest.
   d. life estate with a remainder interest.

4. A construction company placed a new roof on a house four months ago. Because the owner of the property has not paid for the work done, the company may need to place a
   a. general lien on the owner's other properties.
   b. mechanic's lien on the owner's other properties.
   c. mechanic's lien on the property with the new roof.
   d. judgment lien on the property with the new roof.

5. An electric company is planning to bury electric lines across the backyards of 40 homes in a new subdivision. They will need to apply for
   a. an easement appurtenant.
   b. a commercial easement in gross.
   c. a license.
   d. a dominant tenement.

6. A money encumbrance that affects the title to property is called
   a. a restriction.
   b. an easement.
   c. an encroachment.
   d. a lien.

7. A man has an easement appurtenant to cross over another's property in order to reach the public road. This man is considered to have
   a. a dominant tenement.
   b. a servient tenement.
   c. an encroachment.
   d. a license.

8. A family is struggling financially. Unfortunately, they find that their homestead exemption will only protect them against
   a. the remaining balance due on their mortgage.
   b. debt on a credit card issued by a local bank.
   c. the mechanic's lien filed by the company that built their garage.
   d. property taxes they still owe from last year.

9. A grandmother left her home and 100 acres to her church to be used as a camp. In the event the church attempts to sell or make some other use of the property, the estate would then go to the grandmother's heirs. This is an example of a
   a. fee simple absolute estate.
   b. fee simple determinable estate.
   c. leasehold estate.
   d. life estate.

10. A town is levying charges to all homeowners along a street where the town is putting in curb and gutters plus streetlights. The charges for these improvements, which will add to the value of the real estate, are called
   a. ad valorem taxes.
   b. general real estate taxes.
   c. special assessments.
   d. judgment liens.

11. A brother gave property to his sister for her lifetime, and at her death the property is to be transferred to their cousin. In this situation, the cousin's interest in the property is
   a. reversionary.
   b. remainder.
   c. fee simple with possible reverter.
   d. fee simple subject to a condition subsequent.

12. An example of a specific voluntary lien is a
    a. unpaid property tax lien.
    b. court-ordered judgment lien.
    c. heating and air-conditioning company mechanic's lien.
    d. bank mortgage lien.

13. The interest of a husband in the real estate of his deceased wife is the
    a. dower right.
    b. curtesy right.
    c. elective share.
    d. community property share.

14. A landscaping company has not been paid for its work on a property. In order to give public notice of intent to file a mechanic's lien, the company must file
    a. an attachment.
    b. a judgment.
    c. a lis pendens.
    d. a writ of execution.

15. A man has an easement appurtenant as a dominant tenement across a woman's property, which allows him to have an extra-wide driveway big enough for him to store his boat. This easement may be terminated if the
    a. man sells his property.
    b. woman gets tired of looking out her window at the boat.
    c. woman sells her property.
    d. man sells his boat and wants to terminate the easement.

16. Which encumbrance is typically removed before the transfer of title?
    a. Restrictive covenant
    b. Life estate
    c. Lien
    d. Encroachment

17. Who enforces covenants, conditions, and restrictions (CC&Rs)?
    a. Local zoning board
    b. Tax assessor
    c. Previous owner
    d. Other owners in the subdivision

18. Which of the following is a public limitation on private ownership?
    a. Eminent domain
    b. Deed restriction
    c. Covenants, conditions, and restrictions (CC&Rs)
    d. Encroachment

19. An elderly woman passed away. She had no other living family members but did have a will. In this case, her estate will
    a. escheat to the state because she outlived her relatives.
    b. pass to whoever is named in the will.
    c. become the subject of a lawsuit to determine ownership.
    d. revert to the heirs of the previous owners, if any.

20. A person has full rights to use and occupy the property for a certain period, after which the person must return the property to its owner. This person holds a
    a. freehold estate.
    b. leasehold estate.
    c. legal life estate.
    d. homestead estate.

4

The Acquisition and Transfer of Title

LEARNING OBJECTIVES

When you finish reading this chapter, you will be able to

- define voluntary alienation,
- list the requirements for a valid conveyance,
- differentiate between different types of deeds,
- identify methods of involuntary alienation, and
- explain the transfer of a deceased person's property.

accession	deed in trust	intestate
accretion	descent	partition suit
acknowledgment	devise	power of attorney
administrator	eminent domain	probate
adverse possession	erosion	quitclaim deed
alienation	escheat	testate
attorney-in-fact	executor	testator
avulsion	grant deed	title
bargain and sale deed	grantee	warranty deeds
cloud on title	granting clause	wills
consideration	grantor	
dedication	habendum clause	

Title is defined as the right to or the ownership of land and as the evidence of ownership. Each state has adopted legislative acts that affect the methods of transferring title or other interests in real estate. Property may be transferred from one owner to another in three ways:

1. Through voluntary alienation (by sale or gift)
2. Through involuntary alienation (by operation of law)
3. By will or descent (after an owner's death)

VOLUNTARY ALIENATION

Voluntary **alienation** (transfer) of title may be made by gift, will, or sale. An owner who wants to transfer title by voluntary alienation during the owner's lifetime must normally use some form of deed of conveyance.

A *deed* is a written instrument by which an owner of real property intentionally conveys to another the right, title, or interest in a parcel of real property. All deeds must be in writing in accordance with the requirements of each state. The person conveying the property is called the **grantor**, and the person acquiring the property is called the **grantee**. A deed is executed (signed) by the grantor. A grantor who is incapable of signing the deed can make a *mark* (see Figure 4.1).

FIGURE 4.1   **Transfer by Deed**

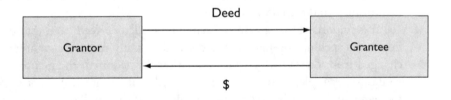

Examples of voluntary alienation involving a gift include a patent, a public grant in which the state or federal government conveys title to public land to an individual, and **dedication**, which generally results from the intention of the owner to turn over private property to the government for public use. For example, many developers and subdividers build streets to certain specifications so that later they can dedicate these streets to the municipality, which then is responsible for their maintenance and upkeep. Dedication is normally accomplished by use of a deed.

The best example of voluntary alienation involving a sale is a typical real estate sales transaction, in which a property owner negotiates price and terms with a purchaser, with the understanding that, at the closing, the property owner will convey title to the purchaser through use of a deed.

Requirements for a Valid Conveyance

Although the formal requirements for a valid deed are not uniform in all states, certain requirements are basic. These are

- a *grantor* having legal capacity to execute (sign) the deed;

- a *grantee* named with reasonable certainty so that the grantee can be identified;

- a *recital of consideration*;

- a *granting clause* (words of conveyance);

- an *habendum clause* (specifies type of estate to be conveyed and any recorded encumbrances);

- a designation of any *limitations* on the conveyance of a full fee simple estate;

- a *legal description* of the property conveyed;

- *exceptions* and *reservations* affecting the title ("subject to" clause);

- the *grantor's signature*, sometimes with a seal; and

- the *delivery* of the deed and acceptance to pass title during the lifetime of both the grantor and grantee.

Grantor.   The laws of the state in which the real estate is located control the precise legal requirements to convey title. A grantor must be of sound mind and lawful age, usually at least 18 years old. If capable of understanding the action, a grantor is generally held to have sufficient mental capacity to execute a deed. If these conditions are not met, the grantor may void the contract at a later time.

It is important that a grantor's name be spelled correctly and that there be no variation in its spelling throughout the deed. If, for any reason, a grantor's name has been changed from that by which title was originally acquired, the grantor must show both names(for example, "John Smith, now called John White"). A grantor should first state the name under which the title was acquired and then indicate the current name. When title to property is originally acquired under a woman's maiden name and she subsequently marries, if she takes her husband's name, the conveyance must show both her maiden name and her married name. In addition, in many states, her spouse, if living, must join in the deed to release marital rights, or when the husband is the grantor, the wife must also join in the deed.

Grantee.   To be valid, a deed must name a grantee in such a manner that the grantee is readily identifiable. A deed naming as the grantee a wholly fictitious person, a company that does not legally exist, or a society or club that is not properly incorporated is considered void and, as such, has no legal effect.

Consideration.   In order to be valid, all deeds must contain a clause acknowledging the grantor's receipt of a **consideration**—something given by the grantee in exchange for the property. The amount of consideration is usually stated in dollars although when a deed conveys real estate as a gift to a relative, love and affection may be sufficient consideration. In deeds conveying property as a gift to a nonrelative, it is customary in most states to specify a nominal consideration, such as "ten dollars and other good and valuable consideration." The full dollar amount of such other consideration is seldom set forth in the deed except when the instrument is executed by a corporation or trustee or is carrying out a court order.

Granting clause. A deed of conveyance transfers a current interest in real estate. Therefore, it must contain words of grant, or conveyance, that state the grantor's intention to convey the property at this time; an expression of intent to convey at some future time is inadequate. Such words of grant are contained in the **granting clause**. Depending on the type of deed and the obligations agreed to by the grantor, the wording is generally either "convey and warrant," "grant," "grant, bargain, and sell," or "remise, release, and quitclaim." (These terms will be explained under the discussions of the individual types of deeds that follow.)

If more than one grantee is involved, the granting clause should cover the creation of their specific rights in the property and state(for example, that the grantees will take title as joint tenants or tenants in common). The wording is especially important in states where specific wording is necessary to create a joint tenancy. Joint tenancy and tenancy in common will be discussed in Chapter 5.

Habendum clause. The **habendum clause** follows the granting clause and begins with the words "to have and to hold" when it is necessary to define or explain the extent of ownership to be enjoyed by the grantee, such as a fee simple, life estate, or easement. The provisions of the habendum clause must agree with those set forth in the granting clause. If there is a discrepancy between the two, the provisions of the granting clause are usually followed.

Limitations. The granting clause should also specify what interest in the property is being conveyed by the grantor. Deeds that convey the entire fee simple interest of the grantor usually contain a phrase such as "to Jacqueline Walton and to her heirs and assigns forever." If the grantor is conveying less than a complete interest—for example, a life estate to property—the wording must indicate this limitation on the grantee's interest. For example, a deed creating a life estate would convey property "to Jacqueline Walton for the duration of her natural life."

Legal description. For a deed to be valid, it must contain an adequate description of the real estate conveyed. Land is considered adequately described if a competent surveyor can locate the property from the description. A street address alone is not an adequate legal description of real estate, as discussed in Chapter 2.

Exceptions and reservations ("subject to" clause). A deed should specifically note any encumbrances, reservations, or limitations that affect the title being conveyed. Exceptions to a clear title include mortgage liens, taxes, restrictions, and easements that run with the land. For example, a deed may convey title to a grantee "subject to an existing first mortgage loan, which the grantee assumes and agrees to pay."

In addition to existing encumbrances, a grantor may reserve some right in the land for personal use (an easement, for example). A grantor may also place certain restrictions on the grantee's use of the property. For example, a developer may restrict the number of houses that may be built on a one-acre lot. Restrictions must be clearly stated in the deed or contained in a previously recorded document that is expressly cited in the deed.

Grantor's signature. To be valid, a deed must be signed by all grantors named in the document. Most states permit a grantor who is unable to write to sign by using a *mark*. Generally, with this type of signature, two persons must witness the grantor's execution of the deed and sign as witnesses.

Most states permit a grantor's signature to be signed by an attorney-in-fact acting under a **power of attorney**. An **attorney-in-fact** is any person who has been given power of attorney (specific written authority) to execute and sign legal instruments for a grantor. Note that a person does not have to be an actual licensed attorney to act as an attorney-in-fact. It is usually necessary for a power of attorney to be recorded in the county where the property is located. Because the power of attorney terminates upon the death of the person granting such authority, adequate evidence must be submitted that the grantor was alive when the attorney-in-fact signed the deed.

An **acknowledgment** is a form of declaration voluntarily made by a person who is signing a formal, written document before a notary public or authorized public officer. This acknowledgment (notarized document) usually states that the person signing the deed or other document is known to the officer or has produced sufficient identification and is signing freely and voluntarily. The acknowledgment provides evidence that the signature is genuine.

Although it is customary to acknowledge the execution of a deed to real property, it is not essential to the validity of the deed. In some states, however, an unacknowledged instrument is not admissible as evidence in court without proof that the signature is genuine, and an unacknowledged deed cannot be recorded. Although an unrecorded deed is valid between grantor and grantee, it often is not a valid conveyance against subsequent innocent purchasers. To help ensure that good title is received, a grantee should always require acknowledgment of the grantor's signature on a deed.

Delivery and acceptance.   Before a transfer of title by conveyance can take effect, there must be an actual *delivery* of the deed by the grantor and either actual or implied *acceptance* by the grantee. Delivery may be made personally or to the grantee's attorney. The transfer is done inter vivos; title passes from a living grantor to a living grantee and must happen during the lifetime of each to be valid. Arrangements may also be made for delivery and for acceptance requirements to be fulfilled by a third party, commonly called an *escrow agent* or *escrowee*, for ultimate delivery to the grantee upon the completion of certain requirements. Title is said to pass when a deed is delivered. The effective date of the transfer of title is the date the deed itself is delivered. When a deed is delivered in escrow, the date of delivery of the conveyance is generally the date that it was deposited with the escrow agent. However, when property is registered under the Torrens system, title does not pass until the deed has been examined and accepted for registration. For more information about the Torrens system, see Chapter 6.

Execution of Corporate Deeds

Under the law, a corporation is considered to be a legal entity. The laws affecting a corporation's rights to convey real property vary widely from state to state, but the following are some basic rules that must be followed:

- A corporation can convey real property only upon the proper resolution passed by its board of directors. If all or a substantial portion of the corporation's real property is being conveyed, a resolution authorizing the conveyance usually must be secured from the stockholders as well.

- Deeds to real property can be signed only by authorized officers. The authority of the officer who signs must be granted by a resolution properly passed by the board of directors.

- The corporate seal must be affixed to the conveyance.

Types of Deeds

The forms of deeds used in any given state are regulated and authorized by the laws of the state in which the land is located. The most common forms are (1) *warranty deed*, (2) *grant deed*, (3) *bargain and sale deed*, (4) *quitclaim deed*, (5) *deed in trust*, (6) *trustee's deed*, and (7) *deed executed to carry out to a court order*.

Warranty deeds. **Warranty deeds** are normally divided into two types: general warranty deeds and special (or limited) warranty deeds.

For a purchaser of real estate, a general warranty deed provides the greatest protection of any deed (see Figure 4.2). In a *general warranty deed*, the grantor is legally bound by certain *covenants* or *warranties*. In many states, these warranties are simply implied by the use of certain words, such as "convey and warrant," "warrant generally," and, in some states, "grant, bargain, sell, and convey." Other states require that such warranties be expressly written into the deed itself. Following are the basic warranties:

- *Covenant of seisin.* The grantor warrants that the grantor is the owner of the property and has the right to convey title to it. The grantee may recover damages up to the full purchase price if this covenant is broken.

- *Covenant against encumbrances.* The grantor warrants that the property is free from any liens and encumbrances except those specifically stated in the deed. Encumbrances generally include such items as mortgages, mechanics' liens, and easements. If this covenant is breached, the grantee may sue for expenses to remove the encumbrance.

- *Covenant of quiet enjoyment.* The grantor guarantees that the grantee's title is good against third parties who might bring court actions to establish superior title to the property. In such cases, if the grantee's title is found to be inferior, the grantor is liable for damages.

- *Covenant of further assurance.* The grantor also promises to obtain and deliver any instrument needed in order to make the title good. For example, if the grantor's spouse has failed to sign away dower rights, the grantor must deliver a quitclaim deed executed by the spouse to clear the title.

- *Covenant of warranty forever.* The grantor guarantees that if at any time in the future the title fails, the grantor will compensate the grantee for the loss.

Note that these covenants in a general warranty deed are not limited to matters that occurred during the time the grantor owned the property, but they extend back through the chain of title to its origins.

A *special warranty deed* is a conveyance that carries only one covenant by the grantor. That is, the grantor warrants only that the property was not encumbered during the time the title was held, except as noted in the deed. Special warranty deeds carry additional warranties only when they are specifically stated in the deed. Some states may refer to this as a *statutory warranty deed*.

A special warranty deed is usually used by fiduciaries—those entrusted to handle the monies of others. Fiduciaries include trustees, executors, and corporations. In addition, special warranty deeds are sometimes used by grantors who have acquired title at tax sales. Such deeds are based on the theory that a fiduciary or corporation has no authority to warrant against acts of its predecessors in title.

FIGURE 4.2   **Sample Deeds**

This Warranty Deed *Made this   day of   , A.D. 19*

by hereinafter called the grantor, to

whose post office address is

hereinafter called the grantee:

> *(Wherever used herein the terms "grantor" and "grantee" include all the parties to this instrument and the heirs,*
> *legal representatives and assigns of individuals, and the successors and assigns of corporations.)*

Witnesseth: *That the grantor, for and in consideration of the sum of $ and other valuable considerations, receipt whereof is hereby acknowledged, hereby grants, bargains, sells, aliens, remises, releases, conveys and confirms unto the grantee, all that certain land situate in   County,   Florida, viz:*

Together, *with all the tenements, hereditaments and appurtenances thereto belonging or in anywise appertaining.*

To Have and to Hold, *the same in fee simple forever.*

And *the grantor hereby covenants with said grantee that the grantor is lawfully seized of said land in fee simple; that the grantor has good right and lawful authority to sell and convey said land; that the grantor hereby fully warrants the title to said land and will defend the same against the lawful claims of all persons whomsoever; and that said land is free of all encumbrances, except taxes accruing subsequent to December 31, 19   .*

This Special Warranty Deed *Made this   day of   , A.D. 19*

by hereinafter called the grantor, to

whose post office address is

hereinafter called the grantee:

> *(Wherever used herein the terms "grantor" and "grantee" include all the parties to this instrument and the heirs, legal*
> *representatives and assigns of individuals, and the successors and assigns of corporations.)*

Witnesseth: *That the grantor, for and in consideration of the sum of $ and other valuable considerations, receipt whereof is hereby acknowledged, hereby grants, bargains, sells, aliens, remises, releases, conveys and confirms unto the grantee, all that certain land situate in   County,   Florida, viz:*

Together, *with all the tenements, hereditaments and appurtenances thereto belonging or in anywise appertaining.*

To Have and to Hold, *the same in fee simple forever.*

And *the grantor hereby covenants with said grantee that the grantor is lawfully seized of said land in fee simple; that the grantor has good right and lawful authority to sell and convey said land, and hereby warrants the title to said land and will defend the same against the lawful claims of all persons claiming by, through or under the said grantor.*

This Quit-Claim Deed, *Executed this   day of   , A.D. 19*

by first party, to

whose post office address is

second party:

> *(Wherever used herein the terms "first party" and "second party" shall include singular and plural, heirs, legal*
> *representatives and assigns of individuals, and the successors and assigns of corporations, wherever the context*
> *so admits or requires.)*

Witnesseth, *That the said first party, for and in consideration of the sum of $ is hand paid by the said second party, the receipt whereof is hereby acknowledged, does hereby remise, release and quit-claim unto the said second party forever, all the right, title, interest, claim and demand which the said first party has in and to the following described lot, piece or parcel of land, situate, lying and being in the County of   State of   , to wit:*

To Have and to Hold *the same together with all and singular the appurtenances thereunto belonging or in anywise appertaining, and all the estate, right, title, interest, lien, equity and claim whatsoever of the said first party, either in law or equity, to the only proper use, benefit and behoof of the said second party forever.*

Grant deeds.   In certain areas of the country, the **grant deed** has replaced the warranty deed as the most popular form of conveyance. A grant deed carries two implied warranties: (1) that the owner has the right to convey the property as stated in the deed and (2) that the owner has not encumbered the property except as noted in the deed. In addition, the grant deed conveys to the grantee any future title to the property. For example, if at the time of conveyance, the grantor had an interest in the property that was less than the grantor thought or the title was defective and the grantor subsequently acquired or perfected the title, this new title would automatically pass on to the grantee. These warranties are not stated in the deed, but are implied by the use of the word *grant* in the deed's words of conveyance. Clearly, a grant deed contains fewer warranties than a general warranty deed; specifically, it does not warrant against the acts of any previous owners. The grant deed is commonly used in many western states only in conjunction with a title insurance policy that protects the new owner against prior liens and claims against the property.

Bargain and sale deeds. A **bargain and sale deed** contains no real warranties against encumbrances; it only implies that the grantor holds title and possession of the property (see Figure 4.2). Because the warranty is not specifically stated, the grantee has little legal recourse if defects later appear in the title. In some areas, the grantor may add a covenant against encumbrances to create a bargain and sale deed with covenant against the grantor's acts, which is roughly equivalent to a special warranty deed.

Quitclaim deeds. A **quitclaim deed** provides the grantee with the least protection of any deed. It carries no covenant or warranties whatsoever; and, in most states, it conveys only whatever interest the grantor may have when the deed is delivered (see Figure 4.2). The grantor "remises, releases, and quitclaims" interest in the property to the grantee. In some states, a quitclaim deed does not actually convey property; rather, it conveys only the grantor's right, title, and interest, whatever that may be. If the grantor has no actual interest in the property, the grantee will acquire nothing by virtue of the quitclaim deed nor acquire any right of warranty claim against the grantor. A quitclaim deed can convey title as effectively as a warranty deed if the grantor has good title when delivering the deed, but it provides none of the guarantees of a warranty deed.

A quitclaim deed is frequently used to cure a technical defect in the chain of title (a *cloud on the title*). A **cloud on title** is any encumbrance that may impair the title to real property or that makes the title doubtful. It is usually discovered during a title search (see Chapter 6) and is removed by either a quitclaim deed or suit to quiet title. For example, if the warranty deed misspells the name of the grantee, a quitclaim deed with the correct spelling may be executed to the grantee in order to perfect the title. When a quitclaim deed is used for the special purpose of clearing a cloud on the title or releasing an interest in property of which the grantor never had possession, the wording should read "releases and quitclaims all interest, if any."

Deeds in trust. A **deed in trust** is used to convey real estate to a trustee, usually in order to establish a land trust or living trust. Under the terms of such an instrument, full powers to sell, contract to sell, mortgage, subdivide, and the like are granted to the trustee. The trustee's use of these powers, however, is controlled by the beneficiary under the provisions of the trust agreement. The *deed in trust* should not be confused with the *deed of trust* that establishes a property as collateral for a loan in some states.

Trustee's deeds. A trustee's deed is executed by a trustee acting in accordance with the powers and authority granted by trust instrument. It is typically used when a trustee named in a will, agreement, or deed in trust sells or conveys title to real estate out of the trust.

Deeds executed to carry out a court order. This classification includes such deed forms as *executors' deeds, masters' deeds, administrators' deeds, sheriffs' deeds*, and many others. These statutory deed forms are used to convey title to property that is transferred by court order or by will. The forms of such deeds must conform to the laws of the state where the property is located.

As mentioned earlier in this chapter, one characteristic of such instruments is that the deed states the full amount of consideration. Because the deed is executed to carry out a court order that has authorized the sale of the property for a given amount, verification of this amount must be included in the document.

INVOLUNTARY ALIENATION

Title to property can be transferred involuntarily—without the owner's consent. This is called *involuntary alienation.* Such transfers are usually carried out by (1) *operations of law,* (2) *court order,* and (3) *natural forces.* These methods are illustrated in Figure 4.3.

FIGURE 4.3   **Involuntary Alienation**

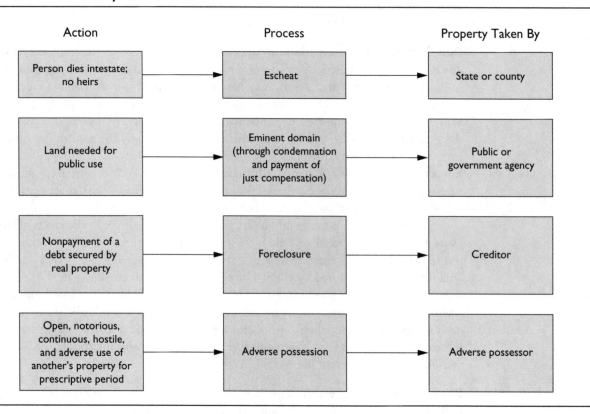

Operations of Law

When a person dies leaving no will and no heirs, the title to the deceased's property passes to the state (or county, in some states) by operation of law based on the principle of **escheat.** Likewise, federal, state, and local governments, school boards, some governmental agencies, and certain public and semipublic corporations and utility companies have the power of **eminent domain** to acquire private property through a *condemnation action* if two conditions are fulfilled: (1) the use for which the property is being taken must benefit the public and (2) an equitable amount of compensation must be paid to the property owner for the taking. Recall the discussion of *Kelo v. New London* in Chapter 3.

Adverse possession is another means of involuntary transfer by operation of law. A property owner who does not use the land or does not inspect it for a number of years may lose title to another person who has taken possession of the land and, most importantly, used it. The person claiming title by adverse possession substantiates that claim through an action to *quiet title*. Usually the claimant's possession must be *open, exclusive, notorious, hostile,* and *uninterrupted* for the number of years set by state law. State laws generally require that possession be uninterrupted, although several states recognize the concept of *tacking on*; if several claimants possess the property at different but continuous times, they can add to, or *tack on*, each successive time of occupation in order to reach the statutory number of years needed for the adverse possession claim of title.

Court Order

Title to real property may also be transferred without the owner's consent by court order. Under a suit for *specific performance*, the court can order the title transferred as promised by the seller in the purchase agreement. The court may order a sale in order to satisfy debts such as real estate taxes, mortgage loans, mechanics' liens, and judgment liens against the property owner. A **partition suit** results in the division of cotenants' interests in real property when the parties do not all voluntarily agree to terminate the co-ownership. Property may also be sold to satisfy creditors of an estate or in a bankruptcy.

Natural Forces

Owners of land bordering on rivers, lakes, oceans, and other bodies of water may acquire or lose additional land through natural forces. When land is acquired through natural causes, the owner acquires title to the new land by **accession**. The property may be expanded by **accretion**, the slow increase in land mass caused by *alluvion*, the accumulation of soil, rock, and other matter deposited by the movement of water or by *reliction*, the gradual withdrawal of water from along a shore, which uncovers more land. An owner may lose land through natural forces, such as **erosion**, the gradual wearing away of land by the action of water and wind, or **avulsion**, the sudden tearing away of land generally caused by a change in the course of a river or other body of water.

TRANSFER OF A DECEASED PERSON'S PROPERTY

When a person dies **intestate**, that is, without leaving a will, the decedent's real estate and personal property pass to the heirs, according to the state's *statute of descent and distribution*. In effect, the state makes a will for such decedents. In contrast, people who die **testate** are those who have prepared their own will indicating the way their property should be disposed of after death.

Legally, when a person dies, title to the deceased's real estate immediately passes either to heirs by descent, to persons named in the will, or to the state under the laws concerning *escheat*. Before the heirs can take possession of the property, however, the will must be probated, and all claims against the estate must be satisfied.

Transfer of Title by Will

A *last will and testament* is an instrument made by an owner to voluntarily convey title to property after death. A will takes effect only after the death of the decedent. Until that time, any property covered by the will can be conveyed by the owner, the executor named in the will can be changed, and any other provisions of the will itself can be changed. Until the death of the decedent, the will is *ambulatory* (changeable). Amendments to the will are called *codicils*.

A person who has died and left a will is said to have died testate. A party who makes a will is called a **testator**. A gift of real property by will is called a **devise**. A person who receives a gift of real property by will is called a *devisee*, and the decedent who has willed the property is a *devisor*. A gift of personal property by will is called a *bequest*, and a person who receives a gift of personal property by will is called the *legatee*.

The privilege of disposing of property by will is statutory. To be effective, a will must conform to all the statutory requirements of the state in which the real estate is located. To execute a valid will, a person generally must be of legal age and sound mind and the drawing of the will must also be a voluntary act, free of any undue influence by other people. In addition, a will cannot supersede state laws of dower and curtesy (or elective share) that were enacted to protect the inheritance rights of the surviving spouse. If a will does not provide the minimum inheritance allowed by law, the surviving spouse can, upon notice to the court, take the minimum statutory share rather than the lesser share provided in the will. This practice, called *renouncing the will*, is a right reserved only to a surviving spouse. In states with community property laws, a surviving spouse automatically owns one-half of the couple's community property acquired during the marriage. No statutory inheritance rights are necessary to protect the surviving spouse's interest in the community property.

Three types of **wills** are recognized: (1) *formal* or *witnessed will*, (2) *holographic will*, and (3) *nuncupative will*.

Formal or witnessed will. An attorney typically prepares a formal or witnessed will. The testator signs the document before two or more witnesses, who also must sign the will. Usually the witnesses cannot be people named in the will as devisees or legatees.

Holographic will. This is a handwritten will. Normally it is prepared, dated, and signed in the testator's own handwriting with no witnesses.

Nuncupative will. This is an oral will, usually a declaration made by someone in immediate fear of dying. The oral declaration must be committed to writing within 30 days, and it can generally only bequeath personal property.

Many states do not permit the use of holographic or nuncupative wills.

Transfer of Title by Descent (Succession)

By law, the title to real estate and personal property of a person who dies intestate passes to the heirs. Under the **descent** statutes, the primary heirs of the deceased are the spouse and blood relatives, such as children, parents, brothers, sisters, aunts, uncles, and first and second cousins. The closeness of the relationship to the decedent determines the specific rights of the heirs.

The right to inherit under descent laws (also called *laws of intestate succession*) varies from state to state (Figure 4.4 shows sample statutory distributions). When a husband dies leaving a wife and one child, the wife and child usually take the entire estate between them, some states dividing it equally and some allowing one-third to the surviving spouse. If, however, a wife and two or more children survive, it is customary for the wife to take one-third and the children to divide the remaining two-thirds equally among them. If a wife survives, but no children or descendants of children survive, some state laws give the wife one-half of the estate and divide the other half equally among collateral heirs, such as parents and siblings of the decedent. In other states, the wife receives the entire estate.

FIGURE 4.4 **Sample Statutory Distributions**

Decedent Status	Family Status	How Property Passes
Married, surviving spouse[1]	No children No other relatives	100% to surviving spouse
	Children	50% to surviving spouse 50% shared by children or descendants of deceased child
Married, no surviving spouse	Children	Children share equally, with descendants of a deceased child taking their parent's share
Unmarried, no children	Relatives	100% to father or mother, brothers or sisters, or other relatives (such as grandparents or great grandparents, uncles or aunts, nieces or nephews, first or second cousins) in order of priority
	No relatives or heirs as defined by state law	100% to state by escheat

[1] Some states allow the decedent's spouse the right to elect a life estate of dower or curtesy (as discussed in Chapter 7) in place of the share provided for in the law of descent.

As discussed earlier, if no heirs are found, the deceased person's real estate will escheat to the state (or county) in which the land is located.

Probate

Probate is a legal process by which a court determines the assets of the estate and who inherits the property of the deceased. Probate proceedings vary from state to state. If the person died testate, the court rules on the validity of the will, and if the will is upheld, the property is distributed according to its provisions. If, for any reason, the court declares a will invalid, any property owned by the decedent will pass by the state's laws of descent.

If a person dies intestate, the court must determine the rightful heirs. The court decides which parties will receive what portion of the estate based on personal information, usually prepared by an attorney, regarding the decedent's spouse, children, and relatives.

When the heirs are established, the court approves someone to oversee the administration and distribution of the estate. If named in the will, this party is called an **executor** or an **administrator** if appointed by the court.

The administrator must see that federal estate taxes and, if appropriate, state inheritance taxes are paid. The administrator or executor has the authority to satisfy all debts that were owed by the decedent; this may involve selling some or all of the assets. Once all liens against the estate have been satisfied, the executor or administrator distributes the remaining assets of the estate according to the provisions of the will or the state law of descent.

SUMMARY

Title to real estate may be transferred voluntarily or involuntarily. The voluntary transfer of an owner's title (voluntary alienation) is made by a deed, executed (signed) by the owner as grantor to the purchaser, as grantee. The form and execution of a deed must comply with the statutory requirements of the state in which the land is located. The obligation of a grantor is determined by the form of the deed; that is, whether it is a general warranty deed, grant deed, special warranty deed, bargain and sale deed, or quitclaim deed. The words of conveyance in the granting clause are important in determining the form of the deed.

In order to create a valid conveyance, a deed must meet the appropriate state requirements. Among the most common of these are a grantor with legal capacity to contract; a readily identifiable grantee; a granting clause; a legal description of the property; a recital of consideration, exceptions, and reservations on the title ("subject to" clause); and the signature of the grantor, properly witnessed if necessary. In addition, the deed should be acknowledged before a notary public or other officer in order to provide evidence that the signature is genuine and to allow recording. Title to the property passes when the grantor delivers a deed to the grantee and it is accepted, during the lifetime of the parties. The deed may also be accepted on the buyer's behalf by an agent, such as the buyer's attorney.

A title may be transferred without the title owner's permission (involuntary alienation) by a court action, such as a foreclosure or judgment sale, a tax sale, condemnation under the right of eminent domain, adverse possession, or escheat. Land may also be transferred by the natural forces of water and wind; the owner receives title to the new land by accession.

The real estate of an owner who makes a valid will (who dies testate) passes to the devisees through the probating of the will. Generally, an heir or a devisee will not receive a deed, as title passes by the law or the will. The title of an owner who dies without a will (intestate) passes according to the provisions of the law of descent of the state in which the real estate is located.

REVIEW QUESTIONS

Please complete all of the questions before turning to the Answer Key on page 336.

1. A will that is drawn in its maker's own handwriting and then signed by that person without witnesses is called a
   a. formal will.
   b. witnessed will.
   c. nuncupative will.
   d. holographic will.

2. In the early days of development of the United States, the government often conveyed public land to individuals. This type of conveyance is called a
   a. patent.
   b. dedication.
   c. devise.
   d. bequest.

3. If the grantee wants to be sure to have the greatest measure of protection from the grantor who is conveying title of the property, the grantee should request that the grantor provide a
   a. general warranty deed.
   b. special warranty deed.
   c. bargain and sale deed.
   d. quitclaim deed.

4. In order for a deed conveying property to be valid, the deed must contain
   a. the grantee's signature.
   b. the grantor's signature.
   c. a court order.
   d. the sales price.

5. The seller has already moved and won't be present at settlement when title to a property is conveyed to the purchasers. The person designated to sign the deed on the seller's behalf under a power of attorney is called an
   a. agent.
   b. executor.
   c. attorney at law.
   d. attorney-in-fact.

6. A hurricane will often shift large quantities of sandy soil from one end of a barrier island to the other. Title to this additional land created by the natural forces of accretion is acquired by the owner through a process called
   a. alluvion.
   b. reliction.
   c. accession.
   d. avulsion.

7. A man died, leaving no will and no heirs. His property will be transferred to the state (or county) where the property is located based on the operation of law called
   a. escheat.
   b. condemnation.
   c. dedication.
   d. patent.

8. The covenant in a deed in which the grantor guarantees the title against third parties who might bring a court action to establish superior title is the covenant
   a. of further assurance.
   b. of quiet enjoyment.
   c. of seisin.
   d. against encumbrances.

9. Three men are not able to agree on the management of their investment property. They may find it necessary to terminate their joint tenancy through the court-ordered action of
   a. foreclosure.
   b. partition.
   c. dedication.
   d. probate.

10. The type of deed that provides no covenants or warranties of any kind and may only convey whatever interest the grantor has at the time of conveyance is a
    a. general warranty deed.
    b. special warranty deed.
    c. bargain and sale deed.
    d. quitclaim deed.

11. A man has planted strawberries in an empty field near his home for the past 15 years. In order for him to make a legitimate claim of adverse possession, he will have to prove that his possession of the property was
    a. subtle.
    b. involuntary.
    c. hostile.
    d. profitable.

12. A young couple has just purchased their first home. Title to the property transfers to the purchasers when
    a. the sellers sign the deed.
    b. all parties appear at the settlement table.
    c. the deed is delivered and accepted.
    d. the purchasers sign the deed.

13. The executor for a person's estate must convey a deed to the buyers. The buyers will *MOST* likely receive a
    a. general warranty deed.
    b. special warranty deed.
    c. bargain and sale deed.
    d. quitclaim deed.

14. A woman bought property in another state and never visited the land. A man moved his mobile home onto the land, had a water well drilled, and lived there for 22 years. This man may become the owner of the land if he has complied with the state law regarding
    a. requirements for valid conveyance.
    b. adverse possession.
    c. avulsion.
    d. voluntary alienation.

15. The granting clause of a deed includes the words "do hereby grant, bargain, sell, and convey." The grantee has received a
    a. special warranty deed.
    b. quitclaim deed.
    c. general warranty deed.
    d. bargain and sale deed.

16. All of the following are required for a valid deed *EXCEPT*
    a. the grantor's signature.
    b. the grantee's signature.
    c. be in writing.
    d. a granting clause.

17. The owner of an old plantation plans to deed the property to the state for use as a state park. This gift is an example of
    a. dedication.
    b. a patent.
    c. involuntary alienation.
    d. accession.

18. What is the effect of signing a document in front of a notary public?
    a. Adds to the cost of settlement
    b. Ensures that all parties have been properly identified
    c. Validates that the information in the document is true
    d. Verifies that the signature is genuine and voluntary

19. Which is an example of involuntary alienation?
    a. Title passed at settlement
    b. Dedication
    c. Father wills farm to his son
    d. Court order for specific performance

20. The beach has been gradually washing away so that the house that was 50 feet from the beach is now only 10 feet away. This is a result of
    a. erosion.
    b. accretion.
    c. accession.
    d. avulsion.

How Ownership Is Held

LEARNING OBJECTIVES

When you finish reading this chapter, you will be able to

- describe the implications inherent in form of ownership;
- explain the differences between ownership in severalty, tenancy in common, joint tenancy, and tenancy by the entirety;
- discuss the use of trusts;
- summarize the advantages and disadvantages of different types of business entity ownership of real estate; and
- differentiate between cooperative and condominium ownership.

beneficiary	general partnership	syndicate
community property	joint tenancy	tenancy by the entirety
condominium	limited liability company (LLC)	tenancy in common
cooperative	limited partnership	time-share
co-ownership	right of survivorship	trust
corporation	separate property	trustee
fiduciary	severalty	trustor
four unities of ownership		

A fee simple estate in land may be owned by one individual or by two or more co-owners. The type of ownership determines such matters as an owner's legal right to sell the real estate without the consent of others, the right to choose who will own the property after the owner's death, and the future rights of creditors. In many cases, the type of ownership also has tax implications, in terms of a possible gift tax resulting from a present transfer or future income and death taxes.

THE IMPORTANCE OF FORM OF OWNERSHIP

The form by which property is owned is important to the real estate broker and salesperson for two reasons: (1) the form of ownership existing at the time a property is sold determines who must sign the various documents involved (listing contract, acceptance of offer to purchase, or sales contract and deed), and (2) the purchaser must determine in what form title is taken. Parties in a marriage have alternatives affected by state law. Additionally, property may be owned by artificial entities, such as corporations, or a combination, as in condominium and cooperative ownership.

The available forms of ownership are controlled by the laws of the state in which the land is located. When questions regarding holding ownership are raised, a real estate licensee should recommend that the parties seek legal advice.

In most states, real estate may be owned in three basic forms: (1) in *severalty*, where title is held by one owner; (2) in *co-ownership*, where title is held by two or more persons; or (3) in *trust*, where title is held by a third person for the benefit of another.

OWNERSHIP IN SEVERALTY

Property is owned in **severalty** when title is *vested in* (currently owned by) one person or one organization. All states have special laws that affect title held in severalty by either a husband or a wife. In most states, when either the husband or wife owns property in severalty, the spouse must join in signing documents for the following three reasons:

1. To release *dower* or *curtesy* in states that have such rights

2. To release *homestead rights* in states that provide a homestead exemption

3. When the other spouse is a minor (in a few states, only the owner's signature is needed)

CO-OWNERSHIP

When title to a parcel of real estate is vested in two or more parties, such persons or organizations are said to be *co-owners*, or *concurrent owners*, of the property. Each concurrent owner shares in the rights of ownership, possession, and so forth. Several forms of **co-ownership** exist, each with unique legal characteristics. The forms of co-ownership most commonly recognized by the various states are

- *tenancy in common,*

- *joint tenancy,*

- *tenancy by the entirety,*

- *community property*, and

- *partnership property.*

Each form will be discussed separately.

Tenancy in Common

When a parcel of real estate is owned by two or more people as *tenants in common*, each owner holds an undivided interest in severalty; that is, *each owner's portion of interest is held just as though that owner were a sole owner.* There are two important characteristics of a **tenancy in common**.

First, the ownership interest of a tenant in common is an *undivided interest.* Although a tenant in common may hold a one-half or one-third interest in a property, it is impossible to physically distinguish which specific half or third of the property. The deed creating a tenancy in common can state the portion of interest held by each co-owner, but if no fractions are stated and two people hold title to the property as co-owners, each has an undivided one-half interest. Likewise, if five people hold title, each would own an undivided one-fifth interest.

Second, each owner holds an undivided interest in severalty and can sell, convey, mortgage, or transfer that interest without consent of the other co-owners. Upon the death of a co-owner, that undivided interest passes to heirs or devisees according to the deceased's will (see Figure 5.1). The interest of a deceased tenant in common does not pass to another tenant in common unless the surviving co-owner is an heir, devisee, or purchaser. In many states, the spouse of a married tenant in common is generally required to sign a deed to a purchaser in order to release the spouse's dower or homestead rights.

FIGURE 5.1 **Tenancy in Common**

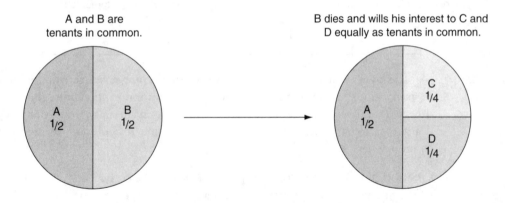

A and B are tenants in common.

B dies and wills his interest to C and D equally as tenants in common.

A 1/2   B 1/2

A 1/2   C 1/4   D 1/4

When two or more people acquire title to a parcel of real estate and the deed of conveyance does not identify the form of tenancy created, then by operation of law, the grantees usually acquire title as tenants in common. However, if the conveyance is made to a husband and wife with no further explanation, this presumption may not apply. In some states, a conveyance made to a husband and wife creates tenancy by the entireties; in others, community property; and in at least one state, a joint tenancy. Therefore, it is important to know the legal interpretation of such a situation under your particular state's law.

Joint Tenancy

A **joint tenancy** is an estate, or unit of interest, in land owned by two or more persons and is based on unity of ownership. Only one title exists, and it is vested in a unit made up of two or more persons. The death of one of the joint tenants does not destroy the unit. It only reduces by one the number of persons who make up the owning unit. The remaining joint tenants receive the interest of the deceased tenant by **right of survivorship** (see Figure 5.2).

FIGURE 5.2   **Joint Tenancy with Right of Survivorship**

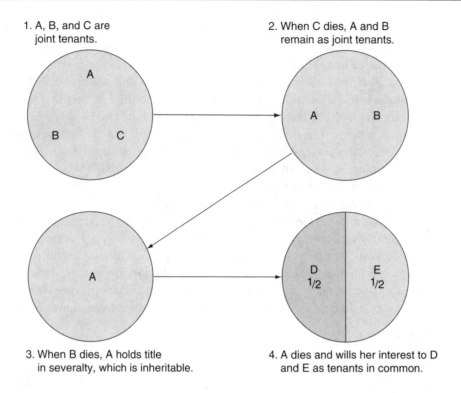

1. A, B, and C are joint tenants.

2. When C dies, A and B remain as joint tenants.

3. When B dies, A holds title in severalty, which is inheritable.

4. A dies and wills her interest to D and E as tenants in common.

This right of survivorship is one of the distinguishing characteristics of joint tenancy. As each successive joint tenant dies, the surviving joint tenants acquire the interest of the deceased joint tenant. The last survivor takes title in severalty, and upon such person's death, the property goes to the heirs or devisees. Some form of joint tenancy is recognized by most states.

Creation of joint tenancies.   A joint tenancy can be created only by grant or purchase (through a deed of conveyance) or by devise (giving the property by will). It cannot be implied or created by operation of law. The conveyance must specifically state the intention to create a joint tenancy, and the grantees or devisees must be explicitly identified as joint tenants. For example, typical wording in a conveyance creating a joint tenancy is "to A and B as joint tenants and not as tenants in common." A number of states have abolished automatic right of survivorship as a distinguishing characteristic of joint tenancy. In these states, the conveyance to two or more parties as joint tenants must explicitly indicate the intention to create the right of survivorship in order for that right to exist. In such cases, appropriate wording might be "to A and B and to the survivor(s) of their heirs and assigns, as joint tenants."

The following **four unities of ownership** are required to create a valid joint tenancy:

1. Unity of *time*—all joint tenants acquire their interest at the same time.

2. Unity of *title*—all joint tenants acquire their interest by the same instrument of conveyance.

3. Unity of *interest*—all joint tenants hold equal ownership interests.

4. Unity of *possession*—all joint tenants hold an undivided interest in the property.

These four unities are present when title is acquired by one deed, executed and delivered at one time, and conveys equal interests to all the grantees who hold undivided possession of the property as joint tenants. A, B, and C are joint tenants. When C dies, A and B remain as joint tenants. When B dies, A holds title in severalty, which is inheritable. When A dies, she wills her interest to D and E who now hold title as tenants in common (see Figure 5.2).

In many states, if real estate is owned in severalty by a person who wishes to create a joint tenancy between herself and others, the owner will have to convey the property to an intermediary (usually called a *nominee*), and the nominee must convey it back to all parties, naming them as joint tenants in the conveyance.

Some states have eliminated this legal fiction by allowing an owner in severalty to execute a deed to himself and others "as joint tenants and not as tenants in common," thereby creating a valid joint tenancy without the actual presence of the four unities. However, in a few states that have tried to accomplish this, the courts have held that such a conveyance creates a wholly new estate, usually called an *estate of survivorship*.

Termination of joint tenancies.   A joint tenancy is destroyed when any of the previously mentioned essential unities has been destroyed. Although joint tenants have the legal right to convey their own interest in the jointly owned property, such a conveyance destroys the unity of interest and, consequently, voids the joint tenancy. For example, if A, B, and C hold title as joint tenants and A conveys her interest to D, D will then own an undivided one-third interest as a sole owner, while B and C will continue to own the undivided two-thirds interest as joint tenants. D will be a tenant in common with joint tenants B and C (see Figure 5.3).

FIGURE 5.3   **Termination of Joint Tenancy**

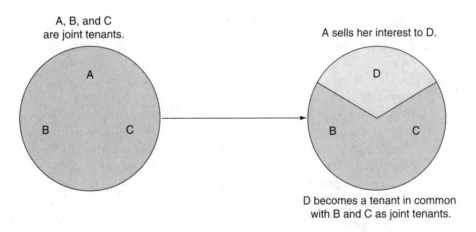

A, B, and C are joint tenants.

A sells her interest to D.

D becomes a tenant in common with B and C as joint tenants.

Joint tenancies may also be terminated by operation of law, such as in bankruptcy or foreclosure sale proceedings. Joint tenants who mortgage their own interest without the other joint tenants joining in the mortgage will destroy the existing joint tenancy.

Most state laws do not provide dower or curtesy rights in joint tenancy. For example, business associates can hold title to a parcel of real estate as joint tenants, and their spouses will not be required to join in a conveyance in order to waive dower or curtesy rights.

Termination of co-ownership by partition suit.   Tenants in common or joint tenants who wish to terminate their co-ownership of real estate may file in court a suit to partition the land. The right of *partition* is a legal way to dissolve a co-ownership when the parties do not voluntarily agree to its termination. If the court determines that the land cannot actually be divided into parts, it will order the real estate to be sold and divide the proceeds of the sale among the co-owners in accordance with their interests.

Tenancy by the Entirety

A **tenancy by the entirety** is a special joint tenancy between husband and wife. The distinguishing characteristics of this tenancy are

- the owners must be husband and wife;

- the owners have rights of survivorship;

- during the owners' lives, title can be conveyed only by a deed *signed by both parties* (one party cannot convey a one-half interest); and

- there is generally no right to partition. Under early common law, a husband and wife were held to be one legal person—the wife's legal personality was merged with that of her husband. As a result, real estate owned by a husband and wife as tenants by the entireties is considered as being held by one indivisible legal unit.

Like a joint tenancy, a tenancy by the entirety cannot be created by operation of law; it must be created by grant, purchase, or devise. Most states now require that the intention to create a tenancy by the entirety be specifically stated in the original document, or a tenancy in common usually results.

A number of states recognize tenancy by the entirety in some form. Real estate licensees who practice in a state that recognizes this form of tenancy should become familiar with the legal aspects of this form of ownership.

Community Property Rights

The concept of community property originated in Spanish law, rather than English common law, and has been adopted by eight western and southern states: Arizona, California, Idaho, Louisiana, Nevada, New Mexico, Texas, and Washington. Wisconsin recognizes *marital property* that is similar to community property. There are many variations among the community property laws of these states. Community property laws are based on the concept that a husband and wife, rather than merging into one entity, are equal partners. Thus, any property acquired during a marriage is considered to be obtained by mutual effort. Community property states recognize two kinds of property.

Separate property is that which is owned solely by either spouse before the marriage or is acquired by a gift or inheritance during the marriage. Such separate, or exempted, property also includes any property purchased with separate funds during the marriage. Any income earned from a person's separate property generally remains part of that separate property. Property classified as sole and separate can be mortgaged or conveyed by the owning spouse without the signature of the nonowning spouse.

Community property consists of all other property, real and personal, acquired by either spouse during the marriage. Any conveyance or encumbrance of community property requires the signature of both spouses. Upon the death of one spouse, the survivor automatically owns one-half of the community property. The other half is distributed according to the deceased's will. If the deceased died without a will, the other half is inherited by the survivor or by the deceased's other heirs, depending on state law.

Examples of Types of Co-ownership

To further clarify the concepts of co-ownership, note the following three examples of co-ownership arrangements:

1. A deed conveys title to A and B. The intention of the parties is not stated, so ownership as tenants in common is created. If A dies, her one-half interest will pass to her heirs or according to her will.

2. A deed conveying title one-third to C and two-thirds to D creates a tenancy in common, with each owner having the fractional interest specified.

3. A deed to R and M as husband and wife may create a tenancy by the entirety, community property, or other interests between the husband and wife as provided by state law.

A conveyance of real estate to two persons (not husband and wife) by such wording as "to J and H, as joint tenants and not as tenants in common" may create a joint tenancy ownership. Upon the death of J, the title to the property will usually pass to H by right of survivorship. However, in states that do not recognize the right of survivorship, additional provisions are required, such as "and to the survivor and his or her heirs and assigns."

A combination of interests can exist in one parcel of real estate. For example, while P and his spouse may hold title to an undivided one-half as joint tenants, the relation between the owners of the two half interests is that of tenants in common.

TRUSTS

In most states, title to real estate can be held in a trust. To create a trust, the **trustor**, or person originating the trust, must convey title to a **trustee**, who will own the property for one or more persons or legal entities, called **beneficiaries**. The trustee is a **fiduciary**, or one who acts in confidence or trust, and has a special legal relationship with the beneficiary or beneficiaries. The trustee can be either an individual or a corporation, such as a trust company. The trustee has only as much power and authority as is given by the instrument that creates the trust. Such an instrument may be a trust document, will, trust deed, or deed in trust (see Figure 5.4). Trusts may be classified as (1) *living and testamentary trusts*, (2) *land trusts*, or (3) *business trusts*.

FIGURE 5.4   **Trust Ownership**

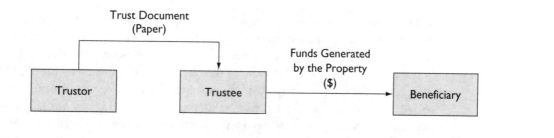

Living and Testamentary Trusts

Property owners may provide for their own financial care and/or that of their families by establishing a **trust**. Trusts may be created by agreement during a property owner's lifetime (living) or established by will after that person's death (testamentary). The individual makes an agreement with a trustee by which the trustor conveys the deceased's assets (real and/or personal), or a certain portion of them, to the trustee with the understanding that the trustee will assume certain duties. These duties include the care and investment of the trust assets to produce an income. After payment of operating expenses and trustee's fees, this income is paid to or used for the benefit of the beneficiaries. Trusts may continue for the lifetime of the beneficiaries, or the assets can be distributed when children reach certain predetermined ages.

Land Trusts

A few states permit the establishment of *land trusts* in which real estate is the only asset. As in all trusts, legal title to the property is conveyed to a trustee, and the beneficial interest is in the beneficiary, who in the case of land trusts is usually the trustor.

One of the distinguishing characteristics of a land trust is that the public records do not indicate the beneficiary's identity. A land trust agreement is executed by the trustor and trustee. Under this agreement, the trustee deals with the property only upon the beneficiary's written direction. While the beneficial interest in the trust real estate is considered to be personal property, the beneficiary retains management and control of the property and has the right of possession as well as the right to any income from it or proceeds from its sale.

Usually only individuals create land trusts, but corporations can also be beneficiaries. A land trust generally continues for a definite term, such as 20 years. At the expiration of the term, if the beneficiaries do not extend the trust term, the trustee is obligated to sell the real estate and distribute the net proceeds to the beneficiaries.

Business Trusts

This form of trust, when used in a real estate syndicate operation, is usually designated a *real estate investment trust (REIT)*. Much like mutual fund operations, real estate investment trusts pool an assortment of large-scale income-producing properties (apartment buildings, shopping centers, and so forth) and sell shares to investors. The distinguishing benefit of a REIT is that the trust is exempt from corporate taxation of profits as long as it distributes at least 95% of its income to the investors. In order to meet the requirements to form a REIT, a group of 100 or more members must hold shares in the trust.

BUSINESS ENTITY OWNERSHIP OF REAL ESTATE

A business entity is an organization that exists independently of its members. Ownership by a business organization makes it possible for many people to hold an interest in one parcel of real estate. There are various ways in which investors may be organized to finance a real estate project. Some provide for the real estate to be owned by the entity itself; others provide for direct ownership of the real estate by the investors. Business organizations may be categorized as (1) *partnerships*, (2) *corporations*, or (3) *syndicates*. The purchase or sale of real estate by any business organization involves complex legal questions, and legal counsel is usually required.

Partnerships

A partnership is an association of two or more persons who carry on a business as co-owners and share the profits and losses of the business. There are two kinds of partnerships, general and limited. In a **general partnership**, all partners participate to some extent in the operation and management of the business and may be held personally liable for business loses and obligations. A **limited partnership** includes general partners as well as limited, or silent, partners. The business is run by the general partner or partners. The limited partners do not participate and can be held liable for the business's losses only to the extent of their investment. The limited partnership is a popular method of organizing investors in a real estate project.

Generally, a partnership is not a legal entity, and technically, under common law, a partnership cannot own real estate. Title must be vested in the names of the partners as individuals in a tenancy in common or joint tenancy and not in the name of the firm. Most states, however, have adopted the Uniform Partnership Act, under which realty may be held in the partnership name, and the Uniform Limited Partnership Act, which establishes the legality of the limited partnership form and also provides that realty may be held in the partnership name.

General partnerships are dissolved and must be reorganized if one partner dies, withdraws, or goes bankrupt. In a limited partnership, the agreement creating the partnership may provide for the continuation of the organization upon the death or withdrawal of one of the partners.

Corporations

A **corporation** is an artificial person, or legal entity, created under the authority of the laws of the state from which it receives its charter. Because the corporation is a legal entity, real estate ownership by a corporation is an ownership in severalty or as a tenant in common. A corporation is managed and operated by its board of directors. A corporation's charter sets forth the powers of the corporation, including its right to buy and sell real estate after passage of a resolution to that effect by its board of directors. Some charters permit a corporation to purchase real estate for any purpose; others limit such purchases to land that is needed to fulfill its corporate purpose.

As a legal entity, a corporation may exist in perpetuity, meaning that the death of one of the officers or directors does not affect title to property that is owned by the corporation.

Individuals participate, or invest, in a corporation by purchasing stock certificates. Because stock is personal property, stockholders do not have a direct ownership interest in real estate owned by a corporation. Each stockholder's liability for the corporation's losses is usually limited to the amount of the stockholder's investment.

One of the main disadvantages to corporate ownership of income property is that the profits are subject to double taxation. As a legal entity, a corporation must file an income tax return and pay tax on its profits. In addition, portions of the remaining profits distributed to stockholders as dividends are taxed again as part of the stockholders' individual incomes.

A *subchapter S corporation*, also called a *tax-option corporation*, combines the features of corporate and partnership ownership. Under this arrangement, the Internal Revenue Service permits stockholders to enjoy the limited liability of a corporation while avoiding double taxation of profits.

Participation in a subchapter S corporation is limited to a maximum of 100 stockholders. The corporation's profits are not taxed at the corporation level, but they are taxed at the shareholder's level. On their individual income tax returns, stockholders declare their share of the profits as personal income and can also deduct a proportional share of corporate losses.

Limited Liability Companies (LLCs)

The **limited liability company (LLC)** is a form of business entity that combines features of limited partnerships and corporations. The members of an LLC enjoy the limited liability offered by a corporation, the tax advantages of partnership, and flexible management without the complicated requirements of S corporations or limited partnerships. The structure and establishment of an LLC varies from state to state. LLCs may be attractive for small groups of owners who hold real property.

Syndicates

Generally speaking, a **syndicate** is a joining together of two or more persons or firms in order to make and operate a single real estate investment. A syndicate, also called a *joint venture*, is not in itself a legal entity; however, it may be organized into a number of ownership forms, including co-ownership (tenancy in common, joint tenancy), partnership, trust, or corporation. A syndicate differs from a real estate investment trust in that a syndicate is formed to purchase one particular property; a REIT is formed to pool a number of different properties. Furthermore, joint ventures differ from partnerships in that syndicates are characterized by a time limitation; the investors do not intend to establish a permanent relationship.

Real estate licensees are required by state law to possess a separate securities license to be able to sell ownership shares in an investment syndicate.

COOPERATIVE AND CONDOMINIUM OWNERSHIP

During the first half of the 20th century, the country's population grew rapidly and was concentrated in large urban areas. This population concentration led to multiple-unit housing—high-rise apartment buildings in the city and low-rise apartment complexes in adjoining suburbs. Initially, these buildings were occupied by tenants under the traditional rental system. However, the traditional urge to own a part of the land, together with certain tax advantages that come with ownership, gave rise at first to **cooperative** ownership and, more recently, to the **condominium** form of ownership of multiple-unit buildings.

Cooperative Ownership

Under the usual cooperative arrangement, title to the land and the building is held by a corporation (or land trust). Each purchaser of an apartment in the building receives stock in the corporation when paying the agreed-upon price for the apartment. The purchaser then becomes a stockholder of the corporation and, by virtue of that stock ownership, receives a *proprietary lease* to the apartment for the life of the corporation. Real estate taxes are assessed against the corporation as owner. The mortgage is signed by the corporation, creating one lien on the entire parcel of real estate. Taxes, mortgage interest and principal, and operating and maintenance expenses on the property are shared by the tenant-shareholders in the form of monthly assessments similar to rent. Thus, while the tenant-owners do not actually own an interest in real estate (they own stock, which is personal property), for all practical purposes they control the property through their stock ownership and their voice in the management of the corporation.

Under the cooperative form of ownership, tenants are not subject to annual rent increases or to the possibility of losing possession if the landlord refuses to renew the annual lease. In an effort to maintain a congenial group of occupants in the building, the bylaws of the corporation generally provide that each prospective buyer must be approved by an administrative board. There must be no discrimination based on any of the federally protected classes of race, color, religion, national origin, sex, familial status, or mental or physical disability.

One disadvantage of cooperative ownership became particularly evident during the depression years and must still be considered. This is the possibility that if enough owner-shareholders become financially unable to make prompt payment of their monthly assessments, the corporation may be forced to allow mortgage and tax payments to go unpaid. Through such defaults, the entire property could be ordered sold by court order in a foreclosure suit. Such a sale would usually destroy all occupant-shareholders' interests. Another disadvantage is that some cooperatives provide that tenant-owners can only sell their interest back to the cooperative at the original purchase price, so that the cooperative gains any profits made on the resale. These limitations have diminished the attraction of this form of ownership and resulted in greater popularity for the condominium form of ownership.

Condominium Ownership

The condominium form of ownership has gained increasing popularity. Condominium laws, often called *horizontal property acts*, have been enacted in every state. Under these laws, the occupant-owner holds a *fee simple title* to a unit, as well as a specified share of the indivisible parts of the building and land, called the *common elements*. The individual unit owners in a condominium own these common elements together as tenants in common (Figure 5.5 provides a drawing depicting the elements of condominium ownership). State law usually limits this relationship among unit owners in that there is no right to partition.

FIGURE 5.5   **Condominium Ownership**

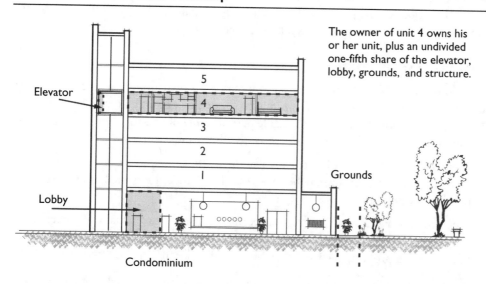

The owner of unit 4 owns his or her unit, plus an undivided one-fifth share of the elevator, lobby, grounds, and structure.

Condominium ownership may also be used for many types of properties, such as office buildings, retail stores, or large buildings that contain offices and shops in addition to residential units, but it is most frequently used for residential communities ranging from freestanding high-rise buildings to town house communities. Common elements include the land, walls, hallways, elevators, stairways, and roof. Landscaping and recreational facilities, such as swimming pools, clubhouses, tennis courts, and golf courses, may also be considered common elements.

To create a condominium, a condominium declaration and a plat of subdivision are recorded in the county in which the real estate is located. The condominium declaration sets out the rights and obligations of each unit owner. The plat subdivides the land and building into apartment units, describes each apartment by unit number, and assigns a fractional share of the common elements to each unit. The apartments are described by the airspace that each actually occupies (the boundary planes extending through the floor, walls, and ceiling). The total of all units and their respective shares of common elements represent the entire parcel of real estate.

Covenants, conditions, and restrictions (CC&Rs). A developer of a condominium project draws up a list of restrictions that affect all purchasers. These are called *covenants, conditions*, and *restrictions (CC&Rs)* and address such issues as what vehicles are permitted in the common parking areas and what alterations homeowners may make to the exterior of their units. The CC&Rs should be recorded with the deed and should include provisions for how the existing CC&Rs may be changed in the future.

Once the property is established as a condominium, each unit becomes a separate parcel of real estate and can be conveyed by deed. A condominium unit is owned in fee simple and can be held by one or more persons in any type of ownership or tenancy recognized by state law.

Real estate taxes are collected on each unit as an individual property. Default in the payment of taxes or a mortgage loan by a unit owner may result in a foreclosure sale of that owner's unit, but it will not affect the interests of the other unit owners.

The condominium property is generally administered by an association of unit owners, established by the condominium declaration. The association is responsible for the maintenance, repair, cleaning, sanitation, and insurance of the common elements and structural portions of the property. These expenses are paid for by the unit owners in the form of monthly assessments collected by the owners' association.

Time-Share Ownership

Time-share ownership permits multiple purchasers to own undivided interests in real estate (usually a building or condominium unit located in a resort or vacation area) with a right to use the facility for a fixed or variable period, generally one or two weeks each year. This time-shared ownership may take one of the following two forms:

1. *Fee simple ownership*—unlimited ownership in the property for a specified period each year. This ownership may be sold, leased, or otherwise treated as any other real property owned in fee.

2. *Right-to-use*—ownership limited to a specific length of time, usually anywhere from 15 years to 50 years. This ownership may likewise be sold, leased, or otherwise treated like other real property owned in fee, but only for the specified right-to-use period.

The purchaser's initial cost depends upon the time of year desired, the location and popularity of the resort, and the form of ownership, with right-to-use generally being somewhat less expensive. Annual maintenance fees are also charged and include the general management and staffing of the project, hazard and liability insurance premiums, record keeping, maid service, structural maintenance, and pool and golf club services—plus fees for the replacement of furniture, linens, and glassware.

Developers of multiple properties may provide an exchange service for a fee. Resort exchange companies have also become popular in order to permit owners to trade their time and location for alternative spots at other resorts around the world, depending on the value of what they own.

Both the development and selling of time-shares are complicated and usually dictated by state law. Generally, but not always, those selling time-shares must hold a real estate license. In some situations, one must hold a securities license.

SUMMARY

Sole ownership, or ownership in severalty, indicates that title is held by one person or entity. Title to real estate can be held concurrently by more than one person, a situation called co-ownership.

Under a tenancy in common, each party holds an undivided interest in severalty and may sell that interest. Upon death, an owner's interest passes to the heirs or according to the will. There are no special requirements for creating this interest. When two or more parties acquire title to real estate, they will hold title as tenants in common, unless there is an expressed intention otherwise.

Joint tenancy indicates two or more owners with the right of survivorship. The intention of the parties to establish a joint tenancy with right of survivorship must be clearly stated. In some states, the four unities of time, title, interest, and possession must be present; other states have eliminated this legal requirement.

Tenancy by the entirety, in those states where it is recognized, is actually a joint tenancy between husband and wife giving the husband and wife the right of survivorship in all property acquired by them jointly during marriage. Both must sign the deed for any title to pass to a purchaser.

Community property rights exist only in certain states and pertains to all property owned by husband and wife. The property acquired by joint efforts during the marriage is community property, and one-half is owned by each spouse. Properties acquired by a spouse before the marriage and through bequests, death, or gifts during the marriage are termed separate property. Community property is a statutory right and each state defines those specific rights.

Real estate ownership may also be held in trust. In creating a trust, title to the property involved is conveyed to a trustee under a living trust, testamentary trust, land trust, or a business trust.

Various types of business organizations may own real estate. A corporation is a legal entity and can hold title to real estate in severalty or as a tenant in common. While a partnership is technically not a legal entity, the Uniform Partnership Act and the Uniform Limited Partnership Act, adopted by most states, enable a partnership to own property in the partnership's name. A syndicate is an association of two or more persons or firms to make a single investment in real estate. Many syndicates are joint ventures and are organized for only a single project. A syndicate may be organized as a co-ownership, trust, corporation, or partnership.

Cooperative ownership of property indicates title in one entity (corporation or trust) that must pay taxes, mortgage interest and principal, and all operating expenses. Shareholders have long-term proprietary leases entitling them to occupy their units and obligating them to pay their portion of operating expenses, usually through monthly assessments. Under condominium ownership, each occupant-owner holds fee simple title to the unit plus a share of the common elements. Each owner receives an individual tax bill and may mortgage the unit as desired. Expenses to operate the building are collected by an association of unit owners through monthly assessments. Time-share ownership may be as a fee simple ownership of a specific property or as a right-to-use for a specific period of time.

REVIEW QUESTIONS

Please complete all of the questions before turning to the Answer Key on page 337.

1. A woman lives in an apartment in a high-rise building. She owns a certain number of shares of stock in a development corporation and has a proprietary lease to her unit. Her form of ownership is
   a. a condominium.
   b. a cooperative.
   c. a time-share.
   d. an investment trust.

2. A couple lives in a two-story town house and holds a fee simple interest in their town house plus an undivided interest in the common elements of the community: swimming pool, tennis courts, landscaping, and exterior maintenance. Their form of ownership is a
   a. condominium.
   b. cooperative.
   c. time-share.
   d. right-to-use.

3. All of the following are unities of joint tenancy *EXCEPT*
   a. time.
   b. title.
   c. interest.
   d. survivorship.

4. A man has four pieces of land that he would like to have held in trust for his grandson. An attorney friend has offered to assume the duties of care and maintenance of the trust. The grandson will be called the
   a. trustor.
   b. trustee.
   c. beneficiary.
   d. fiduciary.

5. Two doctors purchased a condominium unit where they practice medicine. Later, one of the doctors died. The other doctor, who was not named in the deceased doctor's will, now owns the entire interest in the property. They apparently held the property as
   a. tenants in common.
   b. community property.
   c. joint tenants with right of survivorship.
   d. tenants by the entirety.

6. Two businessmen regularly travel back and forth between two cities. They decide to purchase a small condominium in one city instead of staying in a hotel every time they work there. They will *MOST* likely take title as tenants in common due to the provision that
   a. if either one of them dies, the other will receive the entire interest in the property.
   b. if either one of them dies, that person's interest will convey to the heirs.
   c. they will each have a divided one-half interest in the property.
   d. the other party's consent is required in order to sell their own interest.

7. A young couple plans to be married next month in a part of the United States that is most influenced by Spanish common law. Any property they acquire during marriage will be considered
   a. separate property.
   b. joint property.
   c. community property.
   d. divisible property.

8. One of the principal disadvantages of corporate ownership of income property is
   a. personal liability for its profits and losses.
   b. inability to transfer its stock.
   c. double taxation of all of its profits.
   d. control by the general partner.

9. A group of investors wishing to invest in real estate, while limiting their losses to the amount of their investment, would probably be *BEST* satisfied with a
   a. general partnership.
   b. limited partnership.
   c. corporation.
   d. joint venture.

10. A financial advisor with over a hundred clients is planning to have all the clients join together to purchase shares in a trust. The trust will then purchase a combination of income-producing properties, including two apartment buildings, a small shopping mall, and an office building. The advisor is originating a
    a. syndicate.
    b. REIT.
    c. joint venture.
    d. subchapter S corporation.

11. If tenants in common cannot agree on a voluntary method of terminating their co-ownership, an action may be filed in court to legally dissolve the co-ownership. This action is called a
    a. foreclosure suit.
    b. quiet title action.
    c. partition suit.
    d. separation action.

12. A time-share in which the owner has unlimited ownership for a specified time period each year takes the form of
    a. fee simple ownership.
    b. right-to-use.
    c. cooperative.
    d. participation.

13. A parcel of real estate was purchased by two brothers. The deed they received from the seller at the closing conveyed the property "to A and B" without further explanation. A and B probably took title as
    a. joint tenants.
    b. tenants in common.
    c. tenants by the entirety.
    d. community property owners.

14. Three sisters are joint tenants with rights of survivorship in a tract of land. One sister conveys her interest to her cousin. The two remaining sisters are now
    a. joint tenants along with the cousin.
    b. tenants-in-common along with the cousin.
    c. joint tenants with the cousin as a tenant-in-common.
    d. joint tenants with the cousin as severalty owner.

15. Four brothers have decided to purchase the family homestead, with the intent that the property will remain in the family. They will each have an undivided interest in the property, with right of survivorship. There will be one title issued at settlement. They are apparently holding title as
    a. tenants in common.
    b. joint tenants.
    c. tenants by the entirety.
    d. community property.

16. A corporation can take title
    a. in severalty.
    b. as a joint tenant.
    c. as tenancy by the entirety.
    d. with survivorship.

17. Depending on the state, a married couple can take title as any of the following *EXCEPT*
    a. joint tenancy.
    b. tenancy by the entirety.
    c. in severalty.
    d. tenants in common.

18. Who inherits under the right of survivorship when a joint tenant dies?
    a. Depends on the will
    b. Spouse and children of the deceased
    c. Depends on the state's statute of descent and distribution
    d. The surviving owners

19. Generally, co-owners may petition the court to dissolve the co-ownership. Which parties may *NOT* do so?
    a. Tenants by the entirety
    b. Joint tenants
    c. Tenants in common
    d. Tenants with the right of survivorship

20. A real estate licensee has approached several investors. In return for the investment money, the licensee promises to run the business for the benefit of himself and the investors, who will not have to be involved in the day-to-day business. The licensee is proposing a
    a. general partnership.
    b. limited partnership.
    c. sub-S corporation.
    d. limited liability company.

Chapter 6

Title Records

LEARNING OBJECTIVES

When you finish reading this chapter, you will be able to

- explain the importance of recording documents in the public record;
- discuss different forms of evidence of title; and
- explain how title insurance protects buyers and their lenders.

abstract of title	evidence of title	subrogation
actual notice	marketable title	suit to quiet title
certificate of title	priority	title insurance
chain of title	recording	Torrens system
constructive notice	security agreement	Uniform Commercial Code

A seller of real estate can only convey what the seller owns; in other words, a seller can never transfer an interest in real estate that the seller does not have. Therefore, when purchasing a parcel of real estate, a buyer must ascertain what interest the seller has in the real estate and whether the seller is able to convey ownership to the property. A purchaser also wants to know about any encumbrances that might limit the use of the property and any liens that should be paid prior to settlement. Recording documents in the county where the property is located provides information necessary to determine the condition of the title as well as public notice for anyone with an interest in the property. Although anyone may review recorded information about the property, in the typical real estate transaction, a professional—an attorney, abstractor, or title company—performs the research. Real estate licensees should recognize what is available in the public records, how this information can impact transferability, and what are the generally accepted practices in their marketplace.

State law requires that designated officials maintain public records for the protection of real estate purchasers, owners, taxing bodies, and creditors. Such records help establish real estate ownership, give notice of encumbrances, and establish the priority of liens. Records involving taxes, special assessments, ordinances, and zoning and building codes also fall into this category. Local officials, such as the recorder of deeds, county clerk, county treasurer, city clerk, and clerks of various courts of record administer these records.

All states have enacted a statute of frauds, which requires that instruments affecting interests in real estate be in writing in order to be enforceable. In addition, state laws require owners or parties with interests in real estate to file as a public record all documents affecting their interest, in order to give the world legal, public, and constructive notice of their interest. The public records should reveal the condition of a title, and a purchaser should be able to rely on a search of such public records.

PUBLIC RECORDS AND RECORDING

Recording is the process of placing documents in the public record. Under each state's recording acts, all written instruments affecting any estate, right, title, or interest in real estate must be recorded in the county where the property is located. Recording gives public notice of the various interests of all parties in title to a parcel of real estate. From a practical point of view, the recording acts give legal priority to the interests that are recorded first.

To be eligible for recording, an instrument must be drawn and executed in accordance with local recording statutes. The prerequisites for recording are not uniform. For example, many states require that the names be typed below the signatures on a document and that the instrument be acknowledged before a notary public or other authorized officer. In a few states, the instrument must also be witnessed. Many states require that the name and address of the attorney or other authorized person who prepared the document appear on it as well.

Notice

Through the common law doctrine of *caveat emptor* ("let the buyer beware"), the courts charge a prospective real estate buyer or mortgagee (lender) with the responsibility of inspecting the property and searching the public records to learn of the possible interests of other parties. **Constructive notice** is a presumption of law that makes the buyer responsible for acquiring this information (see Figure 6.1). Failure to do so is no defense for not knowing of a right or interest because the recording of that interest in the public records or possession of the real estate gives constructive notice of various rights in the property.

FIGURE 6.1 **Notice**

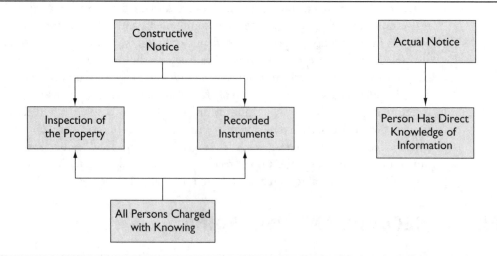

Constructive notice, what the buyer should know, is distinguished from **actual notice**, what the person actually knows (see Figure 6.1). Once an individual has searched the public records and inspected the property, that person has *actual notice*, or direct knowledge, of the information. If an individual has actual knowledge of information concerning a parcel of real estate and this knowledge can be proven, that person cannot rely on a lack of constructive notice, such as an unrecorded deed or an owner who is not in possession.

Real estate taxes and special assessments are direct liens on specific parcels of real estate and need not be recorded in the recorder's office because they are already considered matters of public record. Real estate taxes are collected by and filed at the county tax collector's office. Special assessments may be found at the municipal clerk's or city clerk's office.

Other liens, such as inheritance taxes and franchise taxes, are placed by statutory authority against all real estate owned either by a decedent at the time of death or by a corporation at the time the franchise tax became a lien; these are not recorded.

Foreign language documents. Deeds or mortgages written in a foreign language, although valid between the parties to a transaction, do not impart constructive notice when recorded. Recorded documents must be in English. An official translation by a consulate of the country representative of the language being used, when attached to a foreign language document, may meet state recording requirements.

Priorities. The order of rights or position in time is called **priority**. Many complicated situations can arise that affect the priority of rights in a parcel of real estate. For example, a purchaser may receive a deed and take possession, but not record the deed. By taking possession of the property, the purchaser gives constructive notice of an interest in the land. Such purchaser's rights are considered superior to those of a subsequent purchaser who acquired a deed from the original owner at a later date and recorded the deed, but did not inspect the property to determine who was in possession. How the courts will rule in any situation depends, of course, on the specific facts of the case. A real estate licensee must recognize that these are strictly legal questions that the parties should refer to their lawyers.

Chain of Title

A **chain of title** is a record of ownership of the property over a period of time, depending on the length of the title search. Chain of title in the original colonial states frequently dates back to a grant from the King of England. Later, the deeds of conveyance in the chain of title generally stem from the patent issued by the federal government. In a few states, such as Louisiana and Texas, chain of title dates back to a point prior to the acquisition and annexation of the states by the federal government.

By examining the chain of title, usually in the grantor/grantee indexes, the ownership of the property from its origin to its present owner can be traced. Any gap in ownership names becomes a cloud on the title. A gap might be caused by the purchase under transfers by the same person with two different names (maiden name and married name) or a fraudulent deed was recorded. In such cases, a court action, a **suit to quiet title**, is necessary to establish ownership.

EVIDENCE OF TITLE

Purchasers want to know that they are receiving a **marketable title**, one that is free from significant defects, such as undisclosed liens and encumbrances. An unmarketable title does not mean that the property cannot be transferred; rather, it means that certain defects in the title may limit or restrict future transfers. A marketable title assures the buyer against having to defend the title after purchasing the property and that it can be mortgaged or sold later.

Evidence of title is the documentary proof that the seller is the owner and has good title to the property. A recorded warranty deed or other conveyance is not evidence of title because it does not provide any proof of the kind or condition of the grantor's title. The only effective proof is one of the evidences of title based upon an adequate search of the public records. There are four forms of title evidence: (1) *abstract of title and lawyer's opinion*, (2) *title insurance policy*, (3) *Torrens certificate*, and (4) *certificate of title*.

Abstract of Title and Lawyer's Opinion

An **abstract of title** is a brief history of the instruments appearing in the county record that affect the title to the parcel in question. An abstract usually begins with the government's ownership of the land followed by several sections, or continuations, each covering a specific period. Each succeeding section must begin with a search of the public record from a date immediately following the date of the previous section, to eliminate the possibility of a gap in the abstract. The abstractor lists and summarizes each instrument in chronological order, along with information about taxes, judgments, special assessments, and the like. The abstractor concludes with a certificate indicating which records were examined and when and then signs the abstract. An abstractor must exercise due care or risk being held liable for negligence for any failure to include or accurately record all pertinent data. However, an abstractor does not pass judgment on or guarantee the condition of the title.

In a real estate transaction, the seller's attorney orders the abstract continued through the current date. When the abstract has been completed, it is submitted to the purchaser's attorney, who examines the entire abstract from the origin of that title. Following a detailed examination, the purchaser's attorney evaluates all the facts and material in order to prepare a written report, called an attorney's opinion of title, on the condition of the ownership.

The title evidence system of abstract examination and opinion and of the certification of title by attorneys is imperfect and open to objection. For example, it is difficult to detect forged documents or false statements, including incorrect marital information and transfers involving incompetent parties or minors. As previously noted, not all encumbrances are directly recorded against the property. Title insurance provides a purchaser with protection against these types of errors while providing insurance along with defense of the title.

Title Insurance

A **title insurance** policy is a contract by which a title insurance company agrees, according to the terms of its policy, to indemnify (compensate or reimburse) the insured (the owner, mortgagee, or other interest holder) against loss sustained as a result of defects in the title other than those exceptions listed in the policy. The title company agrees to defend, at its own expense, any lawsuit attacking the title if the lawsuit is based on a defect in title. The maximum loss for which the company may be liable cannot exceed the face amount of the policy. The premium is paid once for the life of the policy.

Under the contract, the title insurance company provides for the defense of the title at its own expense, as well as for the payment of any claims against the property if the title proves to be defective, subject to the conditions and stipulations of the policy. When a title company makes a payment to settle a claim, the company acquires, by right of **subrogation**, all of the legal remedies and rights that the insured party might have against anyone responsible for the settled claim. The title insurance company does not agree to insure against defects in or liens against the title that are found by the title examination, only certain undiscovered defects (coverage varies) (see Figure 6.2). A *standard coverage* policy usually insures against defects found in the public records plus such matters as forged documents, documents of incompetent grantors, incorrect marital statements, and improperly delivered deeds. An *extended coverage* policy generally includes all the protection of a standard policy plus additional protection to cover risks that may be discovered only through inspection of the property, inquiries of persons in actual possession of the land, or examination of a correct survey. The company does not agree to insure against defects in or liens against the title that are found by the title examination. An owner's policy usually excludes coverage against the following exceptions: unrecorded documents, unrecorded defects of which the policyholder has knowledge, rights of parties in possession, and questions of survey.

FIGURE 6.2   **Owner's Title Insurance Policy**

Standard coverage	Extended coverage	Not covered by either policy
Defects found in public records	Standard coverage plus defects discoverable through the following:	Defects and liens listed in policy
Forged documents		Defects known to buyer
Incompetent grantors	• Property inspection, including unrecorded rights of persons in possession	Changes in land use brought about by zoning ordinances
Incorrect marital statements		
Improperly delivered deeds	• Examination of survey	
	• Unrecorded liens not known of by policyholder	

Owner's and lender's title insurance.   The most common forms of title insurance are the *owner's* and *lender's* (or *mortgagee's*) policies. The *lender's title insurance policy* insures a mortgage lender that it has a valid first lien against the property. This policy only insures the lender's interest, not an owner's. The property owner must purchase an *owner's policy* for the benefit of the owner and the owner's heirs.

There are several differences between these policies: the owner's policy is valid for the full amount of the policy as long as the insured or the insured's heirs have an interest in the property, whereas the lender's policy amount decreases as the amount owed on the mortgage loan decreases. Also, the lender's policy can be transferred if the loan is sold, but the owner's policy terminates upon the sale to another party.

A tenant's interest can be insured with a *leasehold policy. Certificate of sale policies* are available to insure the title to property purchased in a court sale.

American Land Title Association.   The *American Land Title Association (ALTA)* is an association of approximately 2,000 land title companies throughout the nation, organized to maintain professional standards and ethics within the industry. Some ALTA members provide abstracts only, others issue title insurance, and still others act as agents for title insurance underwriting companies. Many members are both abstractors and title insurance agents. ALTA members use uniform ALTA title insurance forms, designed by the association to achieve standardization within the industry. For more information, visit the ALTA website at www.alta.org.

The Torrens System

Under the **Torrens system** of land registration, all records regarding a parcel of real estate are filed with a public official, generally called the *registrar of titles*. Today, few states recognize this land registration system.

Transferring title under the Torrens system.   Once real estate is registered under the Torrens system, a **certificate of title** is prepared by the registrar, who keeps the original and issues a duplicate to the owner of the property. At the same time, the owner signs a signature card for protection against forgery.

Under the Torrens system, it may be necessary to verify the payment of taxes and special assessments because the county treasurer and county collector are not usually required to register their tax liens on the Torrens records.

A certificate of title is issued for Torrens registered properties instead of a title insurance policy. The certificate does not set forth a dollar amount. In the event that a claim or suit regarding title arises, the holder of a Torrens certificate must defend the suit at personal expense and be able to prove loss in order to gain a right to any compensation from the registrar.

Certificate of Title

In some localities, a certificate of title prepared by an attorney is used in place of an abstract. The attorney examines the public records and issues a certificate of title that expresses the attorney's opinion of the validity of the title. The certificate identifies the title owner and gives the details of all liens and encumbrances against the title. It is not a title insurance policy and does not carry the full protection of such a policy.

Title and escrow agents.   Many states do not require that an attorney prepare the title search and conduct real estate settlements. A title and escrow agent obtains the abstract of title, arranges for title insurance, and conducts the closing. In Western states settlement occurs in escrow, where an escrow agent performs all required actions leading to settlement, resulting in delivery of the deed to the purchaser and the funds of the sale to the seller.

UNIFORM COMMERCIAL CODE

The **Uniform Commercial Code** is a codification of commercial law that has been adopted in practically all states. While this code generally does not apply directly to real estate, it has replaced state laws relating to chattel mortgages, conditional sales agreements, and liens on chattels, crops, or items that are to become fixtures. Some states have made variations in the details of the code's provisions.

To create a security interest in a chattel, including chattels that will become fixtures, the code requires the use of a **security agreement**. A short notice of this agreement is called a *financing statement*. It includes the legal description of the real estate involved, and it must be filed in the recorder's office. The recording of the financing statement constitutes notice to subsequent purchasers and mortgagees of the security interest in chattels and fixtures on the real estate. Many mortgagees require the signing and recording of a financing statement when the mortgaged premises include chattels or readily removable fixtures (such as major appliances) as part of the security for the mortgage debt.

Article 6 of the code covers *bulk transfers*, which are defined as the sale of the major part of the materials, supplies, merchandise, or other inventory of an enterprise not made in the ordinary course of the transferor's business. The purpose of this article is to outlaw the fraud perpetrated when a businessperson who is in debt sells the business and all stock in trade (personal property) and disappears without having paid creditors. Under Article 6, a bulk sale does not give the purchaser of such goods a clear title, unless the purchaser complies with the article's requirements, which include giving notice of the sale to the seller's creditors.

SUMMARY

The recording acts give the world legal, public, and constructive notice of interests in real estate. The interests and rights of the various parties in a particular parcel of land must be recorded so that those rights will be legally effective against third parties who do not have knowledge, or notice, of them. In addition, such records show whether or not a seller is conveying marketable title. Marketable title is generally one that is so free from significant defects that the purchaser can be assured that the title will not have to be defended.

Possession of real estate is generally interpreted as notice of the rights of the person in possession. Actual notice is firsthand knowledge acquired directly by a person.

The four forms of title evidence commonly in use throughout the United States are (1) abstract of title and lawyer's opinion, (2) owners' title insurance policy, (3) Torrens certificate, and (4) certificate of title.

A deed of conveyance is evidence that a grantor has conveyed interest in real estate to the grantee, but it does not prove that the grantor had good and marketable title—even though the interest is conveyed via a warranty deed containing implied promises or warranties. The grantee should seek evidence of good title prior to accepting any conveyance.

Each form of title evidence bears a date and is evidence up to and including that date. All forms of title evidence show the previous actions that affect the title. A Torrens certificate, title insurance policy, certificate of title, and abstract of title relate to a title based on its history. Each must be later dated, or continued or reissued, to cover a more recent date.

Under the Uniform Commercial Code, security interests in chattels must be recorded using a security agreement and financing statement. The recording of a financing statement gives notice to purchasers and mortgagees of the security interests in chattels and fixtures on the specific parcel of real estate.

REVIEW QUESTIONS

Please complete all of the questions before turning to the Answer Key on page 338.

1. In the process of defending a claim against an insured's property, the title insurance company may acquire certain rights that previously belonged to the insured through the concept of
   a. priority.
   b. subrogation.
   c. registration.
   d. defeasance.

2. Under the Torrens system,
   a. all original documents are retained by the grantor.
   b. a certificate of title is prepared by the registrar.
   c. all landowners in the state are required to register.
   d. property may not be simultaneously recorded under the county recorder system.

3. A prospective homeowner recently visited the county recorder's office and examined the records that pertained to the property she was considering purchasing. She has received
   a. notice of default.
   b. inquiry notice.
   c. actual notice.
   d. constructive notice.

4. A condensed history of all of the documents that affect a particular parcel of land is called
   a. a patent.
   b. a title insurance policy.
   c. a lawyer's opinion of title.
   d. an abstract of title.

5. The purpose of recording an interest in real estate in the public records is to provide
   a. constructive notice.
   b. actual notice.
   c. subrogation.
   d. caveat emptor.

6. The principal purpose of requiring title evidence is to show that the grantor is
   a. legally capable of ownership.
   b. competent and of minimum age.
   c. conveying marketable title.
   d. transferring the property unencumbered.

7. The chain of title provides a complete list of
   a. all recorded documents relating to the property.
   b. everyone registered under the Torrens system.
   c. all conveyances of the property from a certain starting point.
   d. established priority of rights.

8. A man gives a deed to a parcel of property to a woman. The woman does not record the deed, but does move onto the property. Later, the original owner gives another deed to the same parcel to a man, who does record that deed. Who owns the property?
   a. The woman
   b. The man who most recently received the deed
   c. Both the woman and the man equally
   d. The original owner

9. A couple is moving from Massachusetts to their new home in Wade County, North Carolina. The sellers of the Wade County property currently live in Orange County, Florida. All documents that affect property ownership on this property must be recorded in
   a. Massachusetts.
   b. Orange County, Florida.
   c. North Carolina.
   d. Wade County, North Carolina.

10. The Uniform Commercial Code would *NOT* apply to a
    a. conveyance of real estate.
    b. conditional sales agreement.
    c. security agreement or financing statement.
    d. chattel mortgage.

11. A title insurance policy with standard coverage will *NOT* protect the new owners against
    a. forged documents.
    b. incorrect marital statements.
    c. unrecorded rights of parties in possession.
    d. incompetent grantors.

12. The purchasers of a new home have been told that they will have to purchase a mortgagee's title policy that will provide protection from loss for
    a. the purchasers.
    b. the seller.
    c. the lender.
    d. both the mortgage company and the purchasers.

13. A sells a portion of her property to B. B promptly records the deed in the appropriate county office. If A tries to sell the same portion of her property to C, which of the following statements is *TRUE*?
    a. C has been given constructive notice of the prior sale because B promptly recorded her deed.
    b. C has been given actual notice of the prior sale because B promptly recorded her deed.
    c. Because C's purchase is more recent, it will have priority over B's interest.
    d. A cannot sell only a portion of her property, so neither conveyance is valid.

14. A purchaser went to the county building to check the land records, which showed that the seller was the grantee in the last recorded deed and that no mortgage was on record against the property. The purchaser may assume that
    a. all taxes are paid and no judgments are outstanding.
    b. the seller has good title.
    c. the seller did not mortgage the property.
    d. no one else is occupying the property.

15. The concept of caveat emptor, or buyer beware, that is interpreted today to mean that the buyer is responsible for making an inspection of the property and insuring that a search of public documents is made is based on
    a. English common law.
    b. the Uniform Commercial Code.
    c. the statute of frauds.
    d. the Torrens system.

16. What information does the law presume that the public knows by recording documents in the public record?
    a. Actual notice
    b. Constructive notice
    c. Caveat emptor
    d. Both actual and constructive notice

17. Which of the following statements about owners' title policies and lenders' title policies is *TRUE*?
    a. A lender's policy can be transferred.
    b. An owners' policy may be assumed by a new buyer.
    c. A lender's policy amount remains the same for the life of the loan.
    d. An owners' policy amount decreases during ownership.

18. When are title insurance premiums due?
    a. Annually
    b. Annually until the loan is satisfied
    c. Once at closing
    d. Every time that the loan is sold

19 A buyer was aware that the seller had given a deed to another party who did not record the deed. In this situation, what type of title insurance, if any, protects the buyer against the unrecorded claim?
    a. Standard coverage
    b. Extended coverage
    c. Both standard and extended coverage
    d. Neither standard nor extended coverage

20. Because a valid lien was unrecorded, no one was aware of it until after the sale. Which title insurance policy, if any, provides protection for this defect?
    a. Standard coverage
    b. Extended coverage
    c. Any policy issued by a title insurance company
    d. No policy protects against unrecorded liens

Real Estate Agency and Brokerage

LEARNING OBJECTIVES

When you finish reading this chapter, you will be able to

- list and describe the various parties involved in real estate brokerage,
- recognize that the intent of license law is to protect the public,
- differentiate between the agent's fiduciary and statutory responsibilities to the principal and third parties,
- describe various forms of agency representation,
- explain nonagency transactions,
- compare the activities of an employee versus an independent contractor,
- recognize that all compensation is paid to the broker who then pays affiliate licensees, and
- state that all commission rates are negotiable between broker and consumer.

agent	fiduciary relationship	puffing
antitrust laws	fraud	ready, willing, and able buyer
broker	general agent	real estate license laws
brokerage	independent contractors	salesperson
buyer-broker	latent defect	single agency
commingling	law of agency	special agent
commission	Megan's Law	statutory duties
conversion	National Do Not Call Registry	stigmatized property
designated agency	ostensible agency	subagency
dual agency	patent defect	single agency
errors and omissions (E&O) insurance	price-fixing	transaction brokers
employees	principal	trust (escrow) accounts
	procuring cause	

Real estate brokerage is the business of bringing buyers and sellers together in the marketplace. The nature of real estate brokerage services has changed significantly in recent years. Traditionally, a broker represented the seller's interest in a transaction, whether the broker was the listing broker or a co-broker working with the buyer. This meant that buyers were not represented. Today, laws and practices have changed so that buyers, as well as sellers, have access to representation.

REAL ESTATE BROKERAGE DEFINED

Brokerage is the business of bringing people together in a real estate transaction. A brokerage firm acts as a point of contact between two or more people in negotiating the sale, purchase, exchange, or rental of property. State law requires that persons conducting brokerage activities be licensed. There are typically two categories of state licensing with different experience, education, and testing requirements for each: brokers and salespersons.

A **broker** either can work as the firm's principal (or designated or sponsoring) broker or as a broker licensee affiliated with the office. In this text, *broker* indicates the licensee who is in charge of the brokerage office and the party who enters into contractual arrangements with buyers and sellers. The broker is ultimately responsible for the real estate activities of the affiliated licensees in the office who conduct brokerage activities on behalf of the firm and the firm's clients. Affiliate licensees may be licensed as either brokers or **salespersons**. They may work as employees or, more likely, as independent contractors.

The person who employs the broker is called a principal; the principal (client) may be a seller, a prospective buyer, an owner who wishes to lease property, or a person who seeks property to rent. The real estate broker acts as an agent of the **principal**, who usually compensates the broker in the form of a **commission**, usually an agreed-upon percentage of the sales or rental price. The commission is contingent upon the broker successfully performing the service for which the broker was employed—negotiating a transaction with a prospective purchaser, seller, lessor, or lessee who is ready, willing, and able to complete the contract.

REAL ESTATE LICENSE LAW

Licensing and Regulation

All states have a regulatory body that controls the activities of those licensed in real estate. Whether called commissions, councils, or boards, these governmental bodies issue rules and regulations to implement laws passed by state legislatures. The **real estate license laws** are designed to protect the public from incompetent brokers and salespeople through prescribing and enforcing standards and qualifications for the licensing of brokers and salespeople. Regulations govern criteria for obtaining and maintaining a license as well as the penalties for noncompliance.

License laws are not standardized, and although there are similarities among the states, the specifics for any licensing issue should be directed to the individual state. The Association of Real Estate License Law Officials (ARELLO) maintains a website (www.arello.org) with complete licensing information for each state.

Licensing categories.   The following activities, if offered or performed for compensation or the promise of such, generally require a license: sale, purchase, rental, exchange, or auction of real property. In most states, a person must be licensed as either a salesperson or a broker. Some states, such as South Carolina, have separate property management and time-share licenses.

- *Exemptions.* Each state lists those who are exempt from licensing, but the exemptions typically include owners who sell, purchase, or lease their own property, attorneys who are involved in real estate strictly as part of duties to a client, receivers or trustees of estates, and government agencies.

- *Assistants.* States also have regulations regarding what an unlicensed real estate assistant can do. Generally, assistants who act in any capacity other than as clerical support need to be licensed.

- *Single licensure.* Single licensure is legal in some states, such as Colorado and Oregon. With single licensing, all real estate licensees have the same license rather than the traditional method of licensing brokers and salespersons. Single licensure still requires supervision by a managing broker, but licensees (brokers) have more comprehensive prelicensing requirements and bear more responsibility for their activities.

Prelicensing education requirements.   Although most states require prelicensing education before an examination, the hours required vary widely. Some states require live classroom instruction, while others allow some form of distance education, such as correspondence or online for prelicensing. All states have examinations that test the applicant for minimum competency. Generally, additional hours and experience are required for those seeking a broker license.

Post-licensing and continuing education.   Almost all states impose an additional post-licensing education requirement. This may occur as additional hours required during the first year of licensure or as additional hours added to the normal continuing education requirements for maintaining a license. Most states require that licensees complete continuing education courses, often in prescribed topics, such as agency, contract law, fair housing, ethics, or trust accounts, to maintain the license.

Trust (escrow) accounts.   Client and customer monies are placed in special **trust (escrow)** accounts that are strictly regulated, including whether or not the accounts can earn interest and who may be the recipient of the interest. **Commingling**, the mixing of funds entrusted to a broker with office operating funds, is prohibited as is **conversion**, which is misappropriating trust funds. For more information about the handling of funds, see Chapter 8.

Licensure recognition and nonresidency.   It is not unusual for those licensees who live in a jurisdiction bordered by other states to hold licenses in those states. Each regulatory agency determines what, if any, education or additional testing is required, to obtain a nonresident license. The requirements can be as little as an application and letter of licensure from the applicant's current state or more education and testing.

Fee sharing.   Most states allow referral fees from one jurisdiction to another if the fee is paid through the employing broker. However, there are regulations about conducting sales transactions in a state without a real estate license issued by that state, and these must first be investigated prior to conducting licensing activities. Regulations about sharing or rebating fees to those who are unlicensed also vary from state to state.

Noncompliance. Each licensing and regulatory body has procedures for responding to complaints about a licensee's activities. Typical activities that might result in disciplinary action include misrepresentation, mishandling client funds, and nondisclosure of material facts. Penalties include additional education, fines, and/or license suspension or revocation.

Errors and omissions (E&O) insurance. Although **errors and omissions (E&O) insurance** is not mandated for salespersons or brokers in all states, it should be addressed in office policies. Most policies, with limitations, cover unintentional (not fraudulent) contractual errors and protect a broker in the event of litigation. E&O insurance will not protect a licensee from antitrust charges.

Recovery funds. Some states have established funds to protect consumers who may have lost money in a transaction due to the negligence or illegal activities of a licensee. The funds are usually maintained by fees paid by licensees, and an injured party can collect if a judgment against a licensee is uncollectible. Surety bonds are required in some states and must be posted before a license is issued.

Future considerations. With technology growing and consumers able to access information across state lines, regulatory agencies are facing new challenges, from national licensure recognition to regulation of internet sales and virtual offices. Protecting the public and still satisfying consumer demands may prove to be a daunting task.

AGENCY RELATIONSHIPS

The role of a broker as the agent of the principal may be established as either a **fiduciary relationship** or a brokerage relationship based on statutory duties, depending on the requirements for that state. The **law of agency** defines the relationship between the principal, the party who hires, and the agent, the one who is hired. In real estate sales, the principal may be the seller, the landlord, the buyer, or the tenant. Each party has certain rights and responsibilities, which will be further discussed.

Subagency

In the past, all licensees represented the seller under **subagency**, created when a broker, with the knowledge and consent of the principal, appointed other brokers to represent the same principal. These cooperating brokers become subagents of the principal and owed the same fiduciary obligations to the seller as did the listing broker. The listing broker was responsible for the actions of the subagent. No one represented the buyer. Today, subagency is no longer assumed in most multiple listing services and is rarely practiced.

It must be emphasized that the payment of a commission by one party does not create an agency relationship. Agency relationships are created by contract, regardless of who might be obligated to pay a commission.

Agent's Fiduciary Responsibilities to Principal

Under common law, agents have a fiduciary relationship with their principals, that is, a relationship of trust and confidence between an employer and employee. This confidential relationship carries with it certain duties that brokers must perform—*care, obedience, accounting, loyalty,* and *disclosure.* These duties may be more easily remembered by the acronym COALD (see Figure 7.1).

FIGURE 7.1   **Agent's Responsibilities**

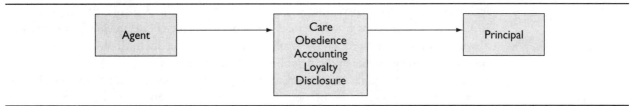

Care.   Brokers, as agents, must exercise a reasonable degree of care while transacting business entrusted to them by their principals. Brokers are liable to their principals for any loss resulting from negligence or carelessness.

Obedience.   Brokers are at all times obligated to act in good faith and in conformity with their principals' lawful instructions and authority. Again, a broker is liable for any losses incurred by the principal due to the broker's performance of acts that are not within the broker's scope of authority.

Accounting.   Brokers must be able to report the status of all funds entrusted to them by their principals. Most state real estate license laws require brokers to give accurate copies of all documents to all parties affected by them and to keep copies of such documents on file for a specified period.

All states forbid brokers or salespeople to buy property listed with them for their own accounts, or for accounts in which they have a personal interest, without first notifying and receiving the consent of the principal. Likewise, by law, neither brokers nor salespeople may sell property in which they have an interest without informing the purchaser of their personal interest.

Loyalty.   Brokers owe their principals 100% loyalty. Agents must always place a principal's interests above those of the other persons with whom they are dealing. Thus, agents cannot disclose such information as a principal's financial condition, the fact that a principal will accept a price lower than the listing price or that a principal may offer more, or any similar confidential facts that might damage the principal's bargaining position.

Disclosure.   Along with these four responsibilities is the duty of disclosure, or *notice*. Licensees are responsible for keeping their principals fully informed at all times of all facts the licensee obtains that could affect the transaction. A licensee who fails to disclose such information may be held liable for any damages that result.

Licensees may also be held responsible for facts they should have known and revealed to the principal. This duty of discovery includes both favorable and unfavorable facts, even if their disclosure might endanger the transaction.

Agency disclosure.   Today, most states require that the licensee explain brokerage representation options available to the consumer and the type of relationship the licensee has with others in the transaction. Such disclosure should be made as early as possible.

Stigmatized properties.   A stigmatized property is one that is psychologically impacted because buying decisions are based on negative emotional factors rather than economic factors. For example, stigmatized properties are often those that were the scene of a murder, suicide, rape, rumored to have ghosts, toxic wastes, or the previous occupant had HIV or AIDS.

Licensees must always disclose a physical defect, such as a sinking foundation or a leaking roof, to every party, whether represented or not. The Brownfields Law, discussed in Chapter 16, explains how licensees can work with buyers of previously stigmatized, abandoned properties. Federal law prohibits any discussion about disability, such as HIV or AIDS, or the presence in the neighborhood of group homes.

Disclosure of stigmas is not so clear. Most states, but not all, do not require any disclosure about stigmatized properties. If the licensee knows and/or if the property owner discloses the information, the licensee should advise the owner that the buyer is likely to discover the information. A seller who discloses such information from the onset can reduce the negative impact of the buyer's psychological reaction. However, under the duty of disclosure, buyer agents may have a responsibility to disclose this information, when known, since it may have an impact on their buyer client's decision to make an offer.

Megan's Law.   **Megan's Law** is the common name for a federal law, now passed in every state, that requires certain sex offenders, especially those involving children, to register with local law enforcement. Some states have enacted laws prohibiting such individual from living within a certain distance from day care centers and schools. Reporting varies from state to state, but generally, the basic list is posted on a state website. Real estate licensees are not required to discover or disclose this information, but they are encouraged to provide information about the websites to their buyer clients so they can conduct research if this is important to them.

Agent's Statutory Responsibilities to Principal

In some states, the common law of agency has been abrogated (abolished) and replaced with specific **statutory duties** owed to both a client and a customer. The exact wording of these duties varies from state to state, but the basic premise of providing protection and promotion of the client's best interests is paramount. In some states, the agent is required to provide fiduciary responsibilities in addition to the statutory duties outlined in the state law of agency.

Principal's Responsibilities to the Agent

An agency agreement is not one-sided. The principal must deal in good faith and comply with the agency agreement to compensate the agent according to the agency agreement.

Types of Agency

A licensed real estate broker is hired by a principal to become the principal's agent. An **agent** is one who is authorized by another to negotiate the interests for that person. An agent is classified as a *general agent* or a *special agent*, based on the extent of the agent's authority.

A general agent is authorized to perform any and all acts associated with a particular limited activity. For example, a property manager might be the **general agent** of the owner of an apartment building. A special agent, on the other hand, has extremely limited authority and is usually authorized to represent the principal in only one specific transaction or piece of business. Therefore, a real estate broker is a **special agent**, hired by either a seller or a buyer for a specific real estate transaction. As a special agent, the broker is not authorized to sell or buy the property or to bind the principal to any contract.

Creation of Agency

A broker-client relationship is created by a consensual agreement of the parties. Although a written contract of employment, commonly called a listing agreement (seller representation) or a buyer agency agreement (buyer representation), is preferred, it is not necessary in all states. However, most states require that the obligation to pay a fee be in writing. As discussed in the contracts chapter, there are different types of agency agreements. For a more detailed discussion of agency and sample agreements, see Chapter 8. Some states recognize agency relationships that are created by (1) *oral agreement*, (2) *implication*, or (3) *ratification*.

Oral agreement.   Some states have determined that an oral, open listing is binding. All that is technically necessary is that the client express willingness to be represented in a transaction by the broker and that the broker express willingness to carry out the client's directions.

Implication.   This relationship is created when one party gives another party reason to believe that the broker is the first party's agent. For example, suppose an owner knows that the broker is showing her unimproved property to prospective buyers without the authority to do so. If the owner does not stop the broker's unauthorized showings, the law says that all persons dealing with the broker have reason to believe—based on the actions of the broker and the seller—that an agency exists. Such an agency is called an **ostensible agency** (meaning it appears on the surface to exist). Once this agency is created, the law prevents the principal from denying its existence by the legal doctrine of *estoppel*, under which a person may not assert rights or facts contrary to that person's actions or silence.

Ratification.   This broker-seller relationship is created when the broker has acted without authority and without the seller's knowledge of the broker's acts, but the seller later approves all of the broker's previous unauthorized acts. For example, suppose the owner has no idea that the broker is showing her property to prospective buyers, but when an offer to purchase is presented by the broker to the owner, she accepts the offer and agrees to pay the broker a commission. By accepting the offer, the seller has accepted all of the broker's previously unauthorized acts and created an agency relationship with the broker through this ratification.

Because of the special nature of a real estate broker's responsibility, most states require that brokerage agreements be in writing when a commission will be paid for securing a person who is ready, willing, and able to buy, sell, or rent.

Again, remember that the payment of a commission by one party does not create an agency relationship. Agency relationships are created by contract, regardless of who might be obligated to pay a commission, or by the actions of the party.

Termination of Agency

An agency relationship may be terminated by the actions of either principal or agent or through the operation of law in a number of ways, as listed in Figure 7.2.

FIGURE 7.2   **Ways an Agency May Be Terminated**

Acts of the Parties	Operation of Law
• Full performance by agent	• Death of either party
• Expiration of the listing period	• Incapacity of either party
• Abandonment by the agent	• Destruction of the property
• Revocation by the principal	• Bankruptcy of either party
• Cancellation by the agent	• Condemnation of the property
• Mutual agreement by the parties	• Revocation of the agent's license

Abandonment by the listing agent occurs when neither time nor money has been spent to market the property. A principal who revokes the agency may be responsible for damages or expenses or both. In addition, the agent may cancel the listing if given illegal instructions by the principal.

Agent's Responsibilities to Third Parties

While an agent's primary responsibility is to the agent's principal, an agent also owes duties to non-represented third-parties. Duties to third parties include using reasonable care and skill, honesty and fair dealing, accounting, and disclosure of known and reasonably knowable material facts. Additionally, agents must abide by state licensing laws, fair housing laws, and ethical obligations when dealing with customers.

Broker-Seller Relationship

The broker can represent the seller and work with the buyer as a third party, or the broker can represent a buyer and work with the seller as a third party.

Seller as principal.   Historically, real estate brokers represented the seller under the terms of the listing agreement. The broker marketed the seller's property, found buyers, and was paid a commission from the seller's equity. Brokers are obligated to represent the seller by obtaining the best offer for the seller as reflected in the current market. Sellers typically paid brokers a percentage of the sale price. The seller is the broker's principal (client) and is owed the traditional duties of care, obedience, accounting, loyalty, and disclosure or statutory duties as discussed previously.

Seller as unrepresented third party.   The seller can also be the third party, who is not represented when the broker represents the buyer. In this situation, the broker owes the seller reasonable care and skill, honesty and fair dealing, accounting, and disclosure of known facts. The broker does not owe the seller confidentiality and loyalty.

Broker-Buyer Relationship

A buyer can be either the principal (the client) or a third party who is not represented, but with whom the broker works. Traditionally, the buyer is considered a customer of a broker.

Buyer as principal.   Today, state laws have developed rules and procedures to regulate **buyer-brokers**. Professional associations, such as the Real Estate Buyer's Agent Council

(REBAC) and the National Association of Exclusive Buyer's Agents (NAEBA), offer assistance, certification, training, and networking opportunities for buyer's agents.

An agency relationship is dependent not on payment of a fee, but on the terms of the agency agreements. Whether the buyer pays the broker an upfront fee for services or the buyer's broker accepts a split of the listing agent's commission, in both instances, the buyer is the broker's principal (client) and is owed the traditional duties of care, obedience, accounting, loyalty, and disclosure or statutory duties as discussed previously.

Buyer as third party (customer).   A broker who represents the seller owes the nonrepresented buyer honesty, reasonable care and skill, fair dealing, accounting and disclosure of known facts. The seller's agent does not owe the buyer customer confidentiality and loyalty. Brokers must use care in making statements about a parcel of real estate. Exaggerated statements of opinion, called **puffing**, are permissible as long as they are offered as opinions and without any intention to deceive. An example is the statement, "In my opinion, this house has the best view in the city." Statements of fact, however, must be accurate. Brokers must be alert to ensure that none of their statements in any way can be interpreted as involving fraud.

Fraud.   **Fraud** consists of all deceitful or dishonest practices intended to harm or take advantage of another person. Fraud also includes false statements about a property, and concealment or nondisclosure of important facts. If a contract to purchase real estate is obtained as a result of misstatements made by a broker or the broker's salespeople, the purchaser may disaffirm or renounce the contract in which case the broker will lose the commission. If either party suffers loss because of a broker's misrepresentations, the broker can be held liable for damages. However, if the broker's misstatements are based upon the owner's own inaccurate statements, the broker may be entitled to a commission even if the buyer rescinds the sales contract.

Latent defects.   Buyers are responsible for responding to **patent defects** (defects readily seen and understood by the buyer), but a seller is responsible for revealing to a buyer any hidden or **latent defects** in a property. A latent defect is one that is known to the seller, but not the buyer, and is not discoverable by ordinary inspection. When such information is withheld from the buyers, buyers have been able to rescind a sales contract and/or receive damages. The use of the phrase "as-is" in a sales contract has no effect on the duty to disclose latent defects but means the seller will not repair items.

Property condition disclosure.   Many states require seller property disclosure statements in residential transactions of one- to four-family dwelling units. Typically, the form must be given to a buyer before the signing of a contract, and if not, the buyer has opportunity to revoke the offer or rescind the contract. The seller, not the licensee, is responsible for completing the form. A broker representing a seller should ensure that the seller is aware of the legal obligation to honestly complete the form and to deliver the form to the buyer in a timely manner.

Other Forms of Agency Representation

Disclosed dual agency.   Some states allow a broker to represent both the seller and the buyer in a single transaction by both parties so long as both parties agree, in writing, to **dual agency**. Although representing both parties may be legal, dual agency is not always easy. The dual agent is limited to what may be disclosed, such as the seller will accept less, the buyer would offer more, and the confidential reasons why either is buying or selling. This situation occurs most frequently when a buyer client wishes to purchase a property listed with the agent's office. Compensation arrangements must also be disclosed in writing if the agent is receiving payment from both parties.

A charge of undisclosed dual agency may be filed when the agent has represented the seller and the buyer and not disclosed this to both parties. Undisclosed dual agency can result in a suit for fraud and/or rescission of the contract.

Designated agency.   To avoid the conflict of dual agency, some state laws allow **designated agency**. A broker can designate one affiliate licensee as the buyer's agent and another affiliate licensee as the seller's agent in a single in-house transaction. The role of the broker may vary in these instances, depending on the state statutes, from being totally removed from the transaction to being a dual agent.

The acceptance of dual and designated agency—where agents representing both the seller and the buyer may be located in the same office—has brought up an important issue. Both listing agents and buyer agents should take care to not reveal information that could be of benefit to someone on the other side of the transaction. Files must be securely maintained to protect the privacy of all parties to the transaction.

Single agency.   Another method of avoiding conflict with dual agency situations is for a broker to represent only the buyer or the seller, not both, in any single transaction. For example, under **single agency**, the broker will not sell an in-house listing to a buyer client.

Limited agency.   Several states have now developed limited agency representation where the agent is required to explain in detail exactly what duties will, and will not, be performed.

Nonrepresentation

Transaction broker.   A **transaction broker**, also called a *facilitator, nonagent, coordinator,* or *contract broker,* is not an agent of either of the parties and is limited to facilitating a real estate transaction between a buyer and a seller. A transaction broker is generally expected to treat all parties honestly and competently, to locate qualified buyers or suitable properties, to work with both the buyer and the seller to arrive at mutually acceptable terms, and to assist in the closing of the transaction. Because neither party's interest is being represented, a transaction broker is not bound by rules of confidentiality. Agency laws do not usually govern transaction brokers, but all parties should clearly understand the nature of the services being offered (see Figure 7.3).

FIGURE 7.3   **Types of Representation**

Agency	*Nonagency*
Sellers only	Transaction broker (facilitator)
Buyers only	
Single agency (buyers or sellers but never both in the same transaction)	
Disclosed dual agency	
Designated agency	
Subagency	

Agency Disclosure

Many unrepresented buyers believe that the listing agent at an open house represents them in subsequent negotiations. A For Sale by Owner (unrepresented seller) who is paying the commission may not understand that the agent who brought the buyer to the house is representing the buyer, not the seller.

To avoid these problems, all states have enacted statutes that require licensees to present an agency disclosure statement or form explaining the representation options available to the consumer. Although the timing varies, most require that the options be presented before the consumer (buyer or seller) enters into a contract that obligates them to payment of a fee. Real estate licensees must be knowledgeable about their state's particular disclosure requirements in order to provide effective representation and to avoid liability. Figure 7.4 shows one state's agency disclosure form.

NATURE OF THE REAL ESTATE BUSINESS

Real estate brokers are independent businesspeople who set the policies of their own offices. Brokers engage employees and salespeople, determine their compensation, and direct their activities. They are free to accept or reject agency relationships with principals. This is an important characteristic of the brokerage business: brokers have the right to reject agency contracts that, in their judgment, violate the ethics or standards of the office (taking care that no possible discrimination is involved). Once the brokerage relationship has been established, brokers represent the people who engaged them. Brokers owe those people, their principals (clients), the duty to exercise care, skill, and integrity in carrying out the agreed-upon activities.

Broker-Salesperson Relationship

A person licensed to perform any of the real estate activities discussed at the beginning of this chapter on behalf of a licensed real estate broker is most often licensed as a real estate salesperson or an associate broker. The licensee is responsible only to the broker under whom the person is affiliated and can carry out only those responsibilities assigned by that broker.

A broker is licensed to act as the principal's agent and can thus collect a commission for performing assigned duties. An affiliated licensee, on the other hand, has no authority to make contracts or receive compensation directly from a principal and performs as a subagent of the principal. Brokers pay commission to the affiliate licensees and are fully responsible for their acts. All of an affiliate licensee's activities must be performed in the name of that affiliate licensee's supervising broker.

Employee versus independent-contractor status. Affiliate licensees are engaged by brokers as either **employees** or **independent contractors**. The agreement between a broker and an affiliate licensee in a written contract defines the obligations and responsibilities of the relationship. Whether the affiliate licensee is employed by the broker or operates under the broker as an independent contractor affects the broker's relationship with the affiliated licensee and the broker's liability to pay and withhold taxes from that salesperson's earnings (see Figure 7.5).

FIGURE 7.4   **Agency Relationships in Real Estate Transactions**

DISCLOSURE OF BROKERAGE RELATIONSHIP

THIS IS NOT A CONTRACT; IT DOES NOT CREATE AN OBLIGATION

In connection with this transaction, whether purchase, sale, lease or option,
the client of the Broker/Firm is: *(check one)*

☐ Seller   ☐ Buyer

☐ Lessor (Landlord)   ☐ Lessee (Tenant)

☐ Optionor   ☐ Optionee

The duties of real estate licensees in Virginia are set forth in Section 54.1-2130 <u>et seq.</u> of the Code of Virginia and in the regulations of the Virginia Real Estate Board. You should be aware that in addition to the information contained in this disclosure pertaining to brokerage relationships, there may be other information relative to the transaction which may be obtained from other sources. Each party should carefully read all documents to assure that the terms accurately express his or her understanding and intent. Licensees can counsel on real estate matters, but if legal or tax advice is desired, you should consult an attorney or a financial professional.

Date   Name   Date   Name

Date   Name   Date   Name

Brokerage Firm   Sales Associate

IVAR - 1207 - 10/00

Source: Minnesota Association of REALTORS®

FIGURE 7.5   **Employees Versus Independent Contractors**

Employees	Independent Contractors
Must have income and Social Security taxes withheld from wages by broker	Assume responsibility for paying own income and Social Security taxes
May receive employee benefits from broker	Cannot receive any employee benefits whatsoever from broker

Employee.   The nature of the employer-employee relationship allows a broker to exercise certain controls over salespeople who are **employees**. The broker may require an employee to adhere to regulations concerning such matters as working hours, office routine, and dress or language standards. As an employer, a broker is required by the federal government to withhold Social Security tax and income tax from wages paid to employees. The broker is also required to pay unemployment compensation tax on wages paid to one or more employees, as defined by state and federal laws. In addition, a broker may provide employees with such benefits as health insurance and profit-sharing plans.

Independent contractor.   A broker's relationship with independent contractors is very different. Basically, the broker may control what the independent contractor does, but not how it is done. Independent contractors assume responsibility for paying their own income and Social Security taxes and must provide their own health insurance, if such coverage is desired. Independent contractors may not receive anything from their brokers that might be construed as an employee benefit.

The Internal Revenue Service (IRS) often investigates the independent contractor/employee situation in real estate offices. Under the qualified real estate agent category in the Internal Revenue Code, three requirements must be met to establish independent contractor status:

1. The individual must have a current real estate license.

2. The individual must have a written contract with the broker containing the following clause: "The salesperson will not be treated as an employee with respect to the services performed by such salesperson as a real estate agent for federal tax purposes."

3. Of the individual's income as a licensee, 90% or more must be based on sales production and not on the number of hours worked for the broker.

The broker should have a standardized agreement drawn up or reviewed by an attorney to ensure its compliance with these federal dictates. The broker should also be aware that written agreements mean little to an IRS auditor if the actions of the parties are contrary to the document's provisions.

Broker's Compensation

The broker's compensation is specified in the brokerage agreement with the principal and is always negotiable between broker and seller or buyer. In most real estate transactions, although the broker's commission is generally *earned* when a completed sales contract has been signed by a ready, willing, and able buyer and accepted by the seller, it is typically paid when the sale is consummated by delivery of the seller's deed.

To be entitled to a sales commission, a broker must (1) be a licensed broker, (2) be under a brokerage agreement with the consumer, (3) and complete the activities called for in the brokerage agreement. A brokerage agreement is not always an agency agreement; it could also call for payment of fee by an unrepresented seller for whom the broker provided a buyer or the agreement could call for ministerial services detailed in a transaction brokerage agreement (see Figure 7.6).

FIGURE 7.6   **Broker's Compensation**

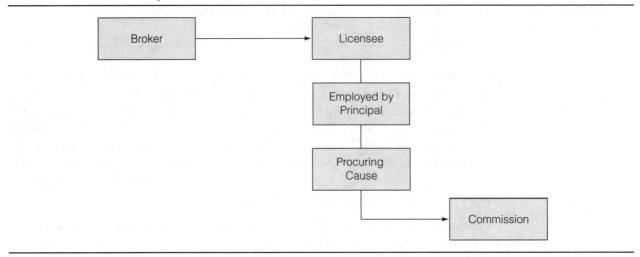

Procuring cause.   In order to be considered the **procuring cause**, the broker must have taken action that started or caused a chain of events that resulted in the sale. A broker who causes or completes an action without a promise or contract to be paid is termed a volunteer and has no legal claim for compensation. In order to collect a sales commission from a seller, a broker must be able to prove that the seller agreed to pay the broker a commission for the sale.

Ready, willing, and able buyer.   A **ready, willing, and able buyer** is one who is prepared to buy on the seller's terms and is ready to take positive steps toward consummation of the transaction. Once a seller accepts an offer from a ready, willing, and able buyer, the seller is technically liable for the broker's commission regardless of whether or not the buyer completes the purchase. Modern courts, however, tend to prevent a broker from seeking a commission from the seller if the broker knew or should have known that the buyer was not financially able to complete the purchase.

A broker who has produced a buyer who is ready, willing, and able to meet the listing terms is usually still entitled to a commission if the transaction is not consummated for any of the following reasons:

- The owner has second thoughts and refuses to sell.

- The owner's spouse refuses to sign the deed.

- The owner's title contains uncorrected defects.

- The owner commits fraud during the transaction.

- The owner is unable to deliver possession within a reasonable time.

- The owner insists on terms not in the listing, such as the right to restrict the use of the property.

- The owner and the buyer agree to cancel the transaction.

Broker's commission. The rate of a broker's commission is *negotiable* in every case. Any attempt by members of the profession, no matter how subtle, to impose uniform commission rates is a clear violation of state and federal antitrust laws, which will be discussed later in this chapter. If no amount or percentage rate of commission is stated in the listing contract, then the broker is not entitled to a commission. If such a case is taken to court, the court might assign a reasonable amount of commission based on the custom in that community.

Under many state license laws, it is illegal for a broker to share a commission with someone who is not licensed as a salesperson or broker. This has been defined to include personal property (for example, a broker giving a new television to "a friend" for providing a valuable lead) and other premiums (vacations and the like), as well as finder's fees and actual percentages of the commission paid to the broker.

The compensation of the affiliate licensees is set by agreement between the broker and affiliate licensees. Most brokers treat their affiliates as independent contractors, paying them a share of the commissions earned from the transactions originated by the affiliates who are then responsible for paying income taxes and contributions into Social Security.

National Do Not Call Registry

The **National Do Not Call Registry** is a federal registry that allows consumers to register their phone numbers to avoid calls from telemarketers. Telemarketers must search the registry at least once every 31 days and drop the numbers of those registered. Exempt organizations include many charitable organizations, certain nonprofits, and those soliciting political contributions. Telemarketers, including real estate licensees who are calling randomly to find prospects, may only call those with whom they have an established business relationship.

Real estate licensees may call anyone with whom they have had an existing business relationship for up to 18 months after the end of the transaction. If the consumer makes an inquiry, the licensee can call the person for up to three months after the inquiry.

A buyer's agent can contact an unrepresented seller (For Sale by Owner) on behalf of the agent's buyer client, even if the seller's name is on the registry. However, if the licensee is contacting the seller for the purpose of getting a listing, then the licensee should first consult the registry, and if the seller's number is there, should not call, but make the initial contact in person. When conducting an open house, licensees should include some kind of question/notice asking permission to follow up with a call.

Real estate offices should have in place written policies to emphasize compliance, provide training in those procedures, and monitor and enforce compliance with the procedures. The fine for calling someone whose name is on the registry is up to $16,000 per call.

Antitrust Laws

The real estate industry is subject to federal (e.g., Sherman Antitrust Act and Clayton Antitrust Law) and state **antitrust laws**. These laws prohibit monopolies and contracts, combinations, and conspiracies that unreasonably restrain trade. The most common antitrust violations in the real estate business are price-fixing and allocation of customers or markets.

Illegal **price-fixing** occurs when brokers conspire to set prices for the services they perform (sales commissions, management rates), rather than letting those prices be established through competition in the open market.

Allocation of customers or markets involves an agreement among brokers to divide their markets and refrain from competing for each other's business. Allocations might take place on a geographic basis, with brokers agreeing to specific territories within which they will operate exclusively. The division might also take place along other lines. For example, two brokers might agree that one will handle only residential properties under $150,000 in value, while another will handle only residential properties over $150,000 in value.

Under the Sherman Antitrust Act, individuals may be prosecuted by the Department of Justice. Those who fix prices or allocate markets may be found guilty of a misdemeanor punishable by a maximum $1 million and/or up to 10 years in prison. For corporations, the penalty may be as much as $100 million. In a civil suit, a person who has suffered a loss because of the antitrust activities of a guilty party may recover triple the value of the actual damages, plus attorney's fees and costs.

SUMMARY

Real estate brokerage is the bringing together, for a fee or commission, of people who wish to buy, sell, exchange, or lease real estate. A broker may hire affiliate licensees to assist in this work. The affiliate licensee works on the broker's behalf as either an employee or as an independent contractor.

Every state requires real estate brokers and their affiliate licensees to be licensed. Knowledge of the state's real estate license law is essential to the understanding of the legal authorities and responsibilities of brokers and salespeople. The purposes of such laws are to (1) protect the public from dishonest or incompetent brokers and salespeople, (2) prescribe standards and qualifications for the licensing of brokers and salespeople, and (3) maintain high standards in the real estate profession.

Real estate brokerage is regulated by the law of agency of complex inter-relationships of duties, rights, and liabilities among three people: the principal, the agent, and the third party with whom the agent deals. A real estate broker is a special agent normally authorized to act for the principal only in regard to one specific transaction. The broker may be hired by either a buyer or a seller of real estate to sell or find a particular parcel of real estate. The person who hires the broker is the principal. The principal and agent may have a fiduciary relationship, under which the agent owes the principal the duties of care, obedience, accounting, loyalty, and disclosure. A second type of brokerage relationship is one specified by law. Under this type of relationship, the agent has specific statutory duties to both the principal/client and to the third party/customer. Whether in a fiduciary or a statutory relationship, the third party (i.e., the person with whom the broker interacts in performing duties for the principal/client) is owed the obligation of accounting for monies received, fair and honest business practices, and disclosure of required facts.

The broker's compensation in a real estate sale generally takes the form of a commission, often a percentage of the real estate's selling price or an agreed-upon fee. The listing broker is considered to have earned a commission by procuring a buyer who is ready, willing, and able to buy under the seller's terms.

State and federal antitrust laws prohibit brokers from conspiring to fix prices or allocate customers or markets.

REVIEW QUESTIONS

Please complete all of the questions before turning to the Answer Key on page 339.

1. A real estate broker who is employed by a principal to market a specific parcel of property is classified as a
   a. general agent.
   b. special agent.
   c. subagent.
   d. client.

2. One type of real estate activity that does *NOT* require a person to have a real estate license is
   a. listing property.
   b. appraising property.
   c. selling property.
   d. leasing property.

3. A broker risks losing the right to receive a commission in a real estate transaction by
   a. not advertising the property every week.
   b. not being licensed when employed as an agent.
   c. not personally marketing and selling the listing.
   d. allowing a buyer agent to present the contract.

4. A licensee who works for a broker recently presented a contract from her buyer client. The contract was accepted by the sellers. By law, from whom may the licensee receive a commission check?
   a. The licensee's broker
   b. The listing broker
   c. The sellers
   d. The buyer client

5. The broker is employed by a listing contract with a seller. During the sales process, the buyer tells the broker how pleased he is with the way the broker negotiated the price. The broker allows the buyer to continue to think that he is represented by the broker, although there is no written contract or other agreement with the buyer. In this situation, the broker might be charged with
   a. puffing.
   b. misrepresentation.
   c. undisclosed dual agency.
   d. fraud.

6. A real estate salesperson who makes an exaggerated statement of opinion concerning a parcel of property is probably
   a. puffing.
   b. guilty of fraud.
   c. making a misrepresentation.
   d. liable to the buyer for damages.

7. A licensee hires an assistant who does not have a real estate license. This coming Sunday, in order to ensure that she is *NOT* violating any license law, the licensee should only allow her assistant to
   a. show a first-time buyer client three houses.
   b. design a brochure for the licensee's new million-dollar listing.
   c. answer questions about financing for one of the licensee's buyer clients.
   d. prepare an agreement of sale

8. A broker deposited his buyer client's earnest money check in his personal account because it was more convenient than making a trip downtown to deposit at the bank where he has an escrow account. The broker is guilty of
   a. dual agency.
   b. violation of fiduciary obligations.
   c. commingling.
   d. misrepresentation.

9. A real estate broker listed a home for a seller for $100,000. Later that same day, a buyer comes into the broker's office and asks for general information about homes for sale in the $90,000 to $120,000 price range. At this point,
   a. both the seller and the buyer are the broker's customers.
   b. both the seller and the buyer are the broker's clients.
   c. the seller is the broker's client; the buyer is the broker's customer.
   d. the broker is a dual agent.

10. A licensed salesperson acting as an independent contractor affiliated with a licensed broker is
    a. not responsible to the broker for what the salesperson does.
    b. responsible for paying all of his income taxes.
    c. allowed to receive employee benefits such as health insurance.
    d. told what specific hours he must work in the brokerage office.

11. One responsibility that is *NOT* included in the list of fiduciary responsibilities of the broker to the principal is that of
    a. care.
    b. loyalty.
    c. obedience.
    d. courtesy.

12. The real estate broker is generally considered to have earned a commission at the
    a. signing of the listing contract.
    b. presentation of the offer to purchase.
    c. acceptance of the offer to purchase.
    d. settlement table.

13. While in the employ of a real estate broker, an affiliate licensee has the authority to
    a. sign a listing contract with a seller.
    b. assume responsibilities assigned by the broker.
    c. accept a commission from another broker.
    d. advertise the property with only the salesperson's name and phone number.

14. The amount of real estate commission to be paid to a broker is
    a. fixed by law.
    b. set by local custom.
    c. determined by the real estate board.
    d. established through negotiation.

15. An individual hires a broker to market her property. The broker may refer to this individual by any of the following terms *EXCEPT*
    a. her client.
    b. the principal.
    c. a customer.
    d. the seller.

16. A broker is employed by a seller under a listing contract. It is *NOT* appropriate for the broker to disclose to any prospective buyer the
    a. lowest price that the seller will accept for the property.
    b. listing price that the seller will accept for the property.
    c. location of the nearest public and private schools.
    d. location of the nearest houses of worship.

17. When the seller listed his property with a broker, the seller specifically told the broker that he never had a water problem in the basement of his house. The broker repeated the statement to a buyer found by the broker. Before the closing, the buyer discovered that the basement floods with every rainstorm. If the buyer decides to void the contract, the broker may be entitled to a
    a. partial commission.
    b. full commission.
    c. half commission.
    d. no commission.

18. In a recent transaction, the broker was not acting as an agent of either the seller or the buyer, although he was still required to treat all parties honestly and competently. The broker was *MOST* likely acting as
    a. a disclosed dual agent.
    b. an undisclosed dual agent.
    c. a transaction broker.
    d. a procuring cause.

19. Two licensees work for the same broker. They agree to divide their town into two halves; one licensee will handle listings in the northern region, and the other licensee will handle listings in the southern region. Which of the following statements is *TRUE* regarding this agreement?
    a. The agreement between the two licensees does not violate antitrust laws.
    b. The agreement between the two licensees constitutes illegal price-fixing.
    c. The two licensees have violated the Sherman Antitrust Act and are liable for triple damages.
    d. The two licensees are guilty of group boycotting with regard to other licensees in their office.

20. After a particularly challenging transaction finally closes, the seller-client gives the listing salesperson a check for $500 for all the salesperson's extra work. Which of the following statements is accurate?
    a. While such compensation is irregular, it is appropriate for the salesperson to accept the check.
    b. A salesperson may only receive compensation from a broker.
    c. The salesperson should accept the check and deposit it immediately in a special escrow account.
    d. The salesperson's broker is entitled to a percentage of the check.

Real Estate Contracts

LEARNING OBJECTIVES

When you finish reading this chapter, you will be able to

- differentiate among expressed and implied contracts, bilateral and unilateral contracts, and executory and executed contracts;
- describe the essential elements of a valid contract;
- summarize how contracts are completed;
- explain how various agency contracts are created and terminated between broker and consumer;
- analyze the details of the sale contract between buyer and seller; and
- recognize how an option is used.

addendum	escrow account	option
amendment	exclusive-agency listing	parol evidence
assignment	exclusive-right-to-sell listing	protection clause
bilateral contract	executed contract	punitive damages
binder	executory contract	right of first refusal
breach of contract	expressed contract	specific performance
brokerage agreements	implied contract	statute of frauds
buyer agency agreement	liquidated damages	statute of limitations
compensatory damages	listing agreement	time is of the essence
consideration	management agreement	unenforceable contract
contingencies	multiple listing service (MLS)	unilateral contract
contract	net listing	valid contract
counteroffer	nominal damages	voidable contract
earnest money	novation	void contract
electronic signatures	offer and acceptance	
equitable title	open listing	

Brokers and salespeople use many types of contracts and agreements in the course of their business. Among these documents are agency contracts (both listing agreements and buyer agency agreements), sales contracts, option agreements, installment contracts, leases, and escrow agreements. State laws generally require that such agreements be in writing (see the discussions in Chapters 6 and 7). Before studying the specifics of each individual type of agreement, you must first understand the basic principles of contract law, the general body of law that governs the operation of such agreements.

Broker's Authority to Prepare Documents

As a rule, real estate brokers are not authorized to practice law—that is, to prepare legal documents such as deeds and mortgages or to give legal advice. Most states have specific guidelines that have been developed by agreement between broker and lawyer associations, by court decision, or by statute regarding the authority of real estate licensees to prepare documents for their clients and customers. In general, real estate licensees may be permitted to fill in the blanks of preprinted documents (such as sales contracts and leases) approved by the state bar association, local real estate association, or the real estate regulators. In other locations, licensees may only prepare a binder that is submitted to an attorney who prepares the sales agreement. Ask state officials or your local real estate association to determine the current authority of real estate licensees to prepare documents.

CONTRACT LAW

A **contract** is defined as a voluntary agreement between legally competent parties to perform or refrain from performing some legal act that is supported by legal consideration. Two parties exchange promises—one promises to do or not to do something in exchange for the promise of a second party to do or not to do something else.

Depending on the situation and the nature or language of the agreement, a contract may be (1) *expressed* or *implied*; (2) *bilateral* or *unilateral*; (3) *executory* or *executed*; and (4) *valid*, *void*, *voidable*, or *unenforceable*. These terms are used to describe the type, status, and legal effect of a contract.

Expressed and Implied Contracts

A contract may be expressed or implied, depending on how it was created. In an **expressed contract**, the parties state the terms and show their intentions in words, either orally or in writing. In an **implied contract**, the agreement of the parties is demonstrated by their conduct. Because the majority of real estate contracts must be in writing, they are considered express contracts.

Bilateral and Unilateral Contracts

Contracts may also be classified as either bilateral or unilateral. In a **bilateral contract**, both parties promise to do something; one promise is given in exchange for another. A real estate sales contract is a bilateral contract because the seller promises to sell a parcel of real estate and deliver the title to the property to the purchaser, who promises to pay a certain sum of money for the property.

In a one-sided, or **unilateral contract**, one party makes a promise in order to induce a second party to perform. The second party is not legally obligated to act. However, if the second party does comply, the first party is obligated to keep the promise. An option is a unilateral contract, discussed in more detail later in this chapter.

Executory and Executed Contracts

A contract may be classified as either executory or executed, depending on whether the agreement is completely performed. An **executory contract** exists when something remains to be done by one or both parties. A fully **executed contract** is one in which both parties have fulfilled their promises and thus performed the contract.

Validity of Contracts

The legal effect of any contract may be described as valid, void, voidable, or unenforceable, depending on the circumstances (see Figure 8.1).

FIGURE 8.1   **Legal Effects of Contracts**

Type of contract	Legal effect	Example
Valid	Binding and enforceable on both parties	Agreement complying with essentials of a valid contract
Void	No legal effect	Contract for an illegal purpose
Voidable	Valid but may be disaffirmed by one party	Contract includes a contingency
Unenforceable	Valid between the parties, but neither may force performance	Certain oral agreements

A **valid contract** complies with all the essentials of a contract and is binding and enforceable to both parties.

A **void contract** is one that has no legal force or effect because it does not meet the essential requirements of a contract. For example, one of the essential conditions for a contract to be valid is that it be for a legal purpose; thus, a contract to commit a crime is void.

A **voidable contract** is one that seems to be valid on the surface but may be rejected, or disaffirmed, by one of the parties. A contract agreed to under duress is voidable, as is any contract entered into with a minor. A minor is usually permitted to disaffirm a real estate contract within a reasonable period of time after reaching legal age. A voidable contract is considered to be valid if the party who has the option to disaffirm the agreement does not do so within a reasonable period of time, or as set by statute. A purchase agreement subject to financing is also a voidable contract; if the buyer cannot obtain financing, the buyer may disaffirm the agreement.

An **unenforceable contract** is also one that seems on the surface to be valid; however, neither party can sue the other to force performance. For example, in many states a listing or sales agreement is invalid, or unenforceable, unless it is in writing and signed by the parties. Unenforceable contracts are said to be "valid as between the parties" because once the agreement has been fully executed and both parties satisfied, neither would have cause to initiate a lawsuit to force performance.

ESSENTIAL ELEMENTS OF A VALID CONTRACT

The essential elements of a valid real estate contract vary somewhat from state to state. Those elements that are uniformly required are (1) *competent parties*, (2) *mutual assent*, (3) *consideration*, (4) *legality of object*, and (5) *legal form*.

Competent Parties

For a contract to be valid, all parties entering into it must have the legal capacity to contract. The buyer and the seller must be of legal age and not suffering from a mental disability that would make them incompetent. In most states, 18 is the legal age to enter into binding contracts. A contract entered into by someone who is under the influence of alcohol or drugs *may* be voidable; a contract with a person who is known to have been judged incompetent by the court is void.

Attorneys-in-fact. Persons acting under the dictates of a properly executed power of attorney may acquire the capacity to contract for another person, provided the power of attorney complies with state law. Such person would sign on behalf of another as an *attorney-in-fact*. Most states require that the power of attorney be in writing, signed and acknowledged by the principal, and recorded, if the act to be performed is the conveyance of title to real property. A power of attorney ceases to exist upon the death of its creator.

A corporation is considered legally capable of contracting. However, the individual signing on behalf of the corporation must have the authority from the board of directors; such authority is normally granted through a *resolution* by the directors. Plus, some states require that the corporate seal be affixed to all contracts entered into by the corporation.

Partnerships. In a general partnership, each general partner usually has the power to enter into agreements on behalf of the entire partnership. With a limited partnership, only the general partners may contract on behalf of the partnership because limited partners may have only a financial interest in the venture.

Mutual Assent

Mutual assent (also called reality of consent, mutual consent, and mutual agreement) requires that all parties must be mutually willing to enter into the contract and that the contract be signed as the free and voluntary act of each party. There must be a meeting of the minds between the two parties. The wording of the contract must express all of the agreed-upon terms and be clearly understood by the parties. The applicability of the mutual assent element to real estate contracts in particular is discussed later in this chapter.

To arrive at mutual assent, an **offer and acceptance** of that specific offer must be completed. An offeror makes an offer to an offeree, who then unconditionally accepts the offer and communicates that acceptance back to the offeror. If any terms of the original offer are changed, they constitute a total rejection of the original offer, relieve the original offeror of any liability under the original offer, and bring to life a *counteroffer*. A **counteroffer** is a new offer made as a reply to an offer received. It has the effect of rejecting the original offer, which cannot be accepted thereafter unless revived by the offeror.

Misrepresentation, fraud, and mistakes. To achieve mutual assent, both parties must agree to the same items without any misrepresentation, fraud, or mistake. *Misrepresentation* is an innocent misstatement of a material fact upon which someone relies and that causes that person to suffer damages. *Fraud* is a deliberate misstatement of a material fact with the intent to deceive, upon which someone relies and that causes that individual to suffer damages. Fraud may also result from failure to disclose vital information such as latent (hidden) defects. A *mistake* is not poor judgment, nor is it ignorance. It generally involves a mutual misunderstanding in negotiations between the parties or is a mistake of fact, such as a party being confused as to which property is under consideration. The practice called *puffing*, where the listing agent may over exaggerate certain features of the property, is allowed within reasonable limits.

Duress, menace, and undue influence. To be valid, every contract must be signed as the free and voluntary act of each party. *Duress*, *menace*, and *undue influence* cannot be used to obtain the signatures of the parties to the contract.

Consideration

For a contract to be valid, it must show **consideration**. In a few states, a seal is sufficient. The consideration given for the entering into of a contract can be either *good* or *valuable consideration*. *Good consideration* is generally recognized only in transactions between loved ones where it can be established that a relationship of love and affection exists. *Valuable consideration* is anything that can be expressed in terms of monetary value, such as money, notes, promises, labor, service, real property, or personal property. The amount of consideration is relatively unimportant; the consideration only needs to be stated to make the contract binding. With an option, the law does require that the stated consideration actually change hands.

Earnest money. Consideration should not be confused with earnest money. While consideration is a component of a contract, **earnest money** is given by the buyer with an offer to purchase to show sincerity and an intent to complete the contract if the seller accepts the offer. Earnest money is usually cash, but it may be any other item or items of value acceptable to the seller.

Seal. The sealing of a contract requires the placing of the word *seal* or the letters *L.S. (locus sigilli*, meaning place of the seal) on the signature lines following each party's signature. Under early common law, a seal took the place of the recital of consideration, but this has been abolished in all but a few states. It is still customary for a corporation to use its corporate seal to indicate that the contract is being executed by its authorized officers or agents.

Legality of Object

To be valid, a contract must have an intended purpose that is not illegal or against public policy.

Legal Form

Every state has enacted a **statute of frauds**. This law requires certain types of contracts to be in writing in order to be enforceable. The statute of frauds requires the following four formalities in order to prevent fraudulent proof of a fictitious oral contract (perjury):

1. The signatures of the buyers and sellers

2. A spouse's signature when necessary to release such marital rights as dower, curtesy, and homestead

3. An agent's signature for a principal if the agent has proper written authority (power of attorney)

4. The signatures of all co-owners selling the property

The courts hold that written contracts supersede oral contracts if there is a conflict between the two. The **parol evidence** rule states that oral agreements, promises, and inducements made by the parties prior to entering into a written contract may not be used in court to dispute or contradict some written provision expressed in the contract.

Description of the property.   In addition to the formalities listed above, a valid real estate sales contract must contain an accurate description of the property being conveyed. The property should be identified by street address as well as by a legal description.

PERFORMANCE OF CONTRACT

Each party has certain rights and obligations to fulfill under any contract. Contracts often call for a specific time at which or by which the agreed-upon acts must be completely performed. In addition, many contracts provide that "**time is of the essence**," an expression that means the contract must be performed within the limit specified, and any party who has not performed on time is guilty of a **breach of contract**.

When a contract does not specify a date for performance, the acts should be performed within a reasonable time. The interpretation of what constitutes a reasonable time will depend on the situation. Generally, if the act can be done immediately—such as payment of money—it should be performed immediately, unless the parties agree otherwise.

Assignment and Novation

Sometimes after a contract has been signed, one party may want to withdraw without actually terminating the agreement. This can be accomplished through either assignment or novation.

Assignment refers to a transfer of rights and/or duties under a contract. Generally speaking, rights may be assigned to a third party, unless the agreement forbids such an assignment. Obligations may also be assigned, but the original obligor remains secondarily liable for them (after the new obligor) unless specifically released from this responsibility by the other party to the contract. A contract that requires some personal quality or unique ability of one of the parties, such as a listing agreement, may not be assigned. Most contracts include a clause that either permits or forbids assignment.

Novation occurs when there is a substitution of a new contract for an existing agreement with the intent of extinguishing the old contract. The new agreement may be between the same parties, or a new party may be substituted for either. The parties' intent must be to discharge the old obligation. The new agreement must be supported by consideration and must conform to all the essential elements of a valid contract. For example, when a real estate purchaser assumes the seller's existing mortgage, the lender may choose to release the seller and substitute the buyer as the party primarily liable for the mortgage debt (see Chapter 12).

Discharge of Contract

A contract may be completely performed, with all terms carried out, or it may be breached (i.e., broken) if one of the parties defaults. In addition, there are various other methods by which a contract can be discharged (i.e., canceled). These methods include the following:

- *Partial performance* of the terms, along with a written acceptance by the person for whom acts have not been done or to whom money has not been paid

- *Substantial performance*, in which one party has substantially performed the contract but does not complete all the details exactly as the contract requires (such performance may be sufficient to force payment with certain adjustments for any damages suffered by the other party)

- *Impossibility of performance*, in which an act required by the contract cannot be legally accomplished

- *Mutual agreement* of the parties to cancel

- *Operation of law*, as in the voiding of a contract by a minor, as a result of fraud, the expiration of the statute of limitations, or a contract alteration without written consent of all parties involved

Default—Breach of Contract

A *breach* is a violation of any of a contract's terms or conditions without legal excuse, such as when a seller does not deliver title to the buyer under the conditions stated in the sales contract.

Damages.   When the contract terms are not met, one of the parties may feel harmed (damaged). Damages consist of monetary compensation to make up for the harm. Depending on the severity, courts can make the following awards:

- *Compensatory (actual) damages.* Injured parties must demonstrate in court that they suffered an actual injury or economic loss and the harm can be compensated by a certain amount of money.

- *Nominal damages.* A small amount of money, sometimes as little as $1 in **nominal damages**, is awarded to acknowledge that a wrong was committed, but no serious damage can be documented.

- *Punitive damages.* Awarded only in special cases, **punitive damages** are paid in excess of the actual damages. Punitive damages are meant to send a message to other potential wrong doers that such conduct will not be tolerated. They are not generally awarded for a breach of contract; however, a judge can award unlimited punitive damages for certain violations of the Fair Housing Act when the actions were made with malicious intent or gross negligence.

- *Liquidated damages.* When formulating the contract, the parties determine in advance the maximum amount that can be recovered for damages in the event of a default. Typically, in real estate purchase contracts, earnest money is designated as liquidated damages. With this clause, the nondefaulting party cannot obtain more, even if the damages sustained are greater than the designated amount.

If the actions of either party to a real estate sales contract clearly show an intent to breach the contract, or default, the defaulting party assumes certain burdens and the non-defaulting party has certain rights.

If the seller defaults, the buyer has the following three alternatives:

1. The buyer may *rescind*, or *cancel*, the contract and recover the earnest money.

2. The buyer may file a court suit, called an action for **specific performance**, to force the seller to perform the contract (i.e., convey the property).

3. The buyer may sue the seller for **compensatory damages**.

A suit for damages is seldom used in this instance, however, because in most cases, the buyer would have difficulty proving the extent of damages.

If the buyer defaults, the seller may pursue one of the following four courses:

1. The seller may declare the contract forfeited. The right to *forfeit* usually is provided in the terms of the contract, and the seller usually is entitled to retain the earnest money and all payments received from the buyer. The amount of total damages agreed to in a contract that one party will pay the injured party in the event of a breach of contract is called **liquidated damages**.

2. The seller may *rescind the contract*, that is, cancel or terminate the contract as if it had never been made. In this case the seller must return all payments the buyer has made.

3. The seller may *sue for specific performance*. This may require the seller to offer, or tender, a valid deed to the buyer to show the seller's compliance with the contract terms.

4. The seller may *sue for compensatory damages*.

Statute of limitations.   Laws in every state allow a specific time limit during which parties to a contract may bring legal suit to enforce their rights (for example, often within seven years). Parties who do not take steps to enforce their rights within this **statute of limitations** may lose the right to do so.

AGENCY CONTRACTS

Under the provisions of license laws in most states, only a broker can act as an agent to list, sell, buy, or rent another person's real estate for a fee. Although the broker's affiliate licensees are given the authority to conduct these activities, these activities may only be performed in the name of and on behalf of the broker.

Brokerage agreements are employment contracts that establish the relationship between the broker (and affiliate licensees) and the consumer. Although most establish agency relationships, others simply describe duties and responsibilities that do not rise to the level of representation, as in transaction brokerage. Before a broker can initiate a court action to collect a commission, most states require a written agreement, signed by the principal, which clearly states the commission amount.

The most common agency agreements include the following:

- The *listing agreement* in which the broker is hired to represent the seller

- The *buyer agency agreement* in which the broker is hired to represent the buyer

- The *management agreement* in which the broker is hired to represent the owner of a rental property

In most listing agreements and buyer agency agreements, the broker is a special agent, one who is authorized by a principal to perform a single act or transaction; the listing broker is to find a buyer, and the buyer's agent is to find a property. In the management agreement, the broker is most likely hired as a general agent, one who is authorized by a principal to represent the principal in a specific range of matters (also see Chapter 7).

All brokerage contracts should specify a definite period of time during which the broker is employed because the use of automatic extensions of time in exclusive listings has been discouraged by the courts and outlawed in many states. An example of an automatic extension is a listing that provides for a base period of 90 days and "continuing thereafter until terminated by either party by 30 days' notice in writing." Some contracts also contain a **protection clause** that protects the broker's interest for a stated period of time after the expiration of the original agreement as long as the client has not signed a new agreement with another broker.

Termination of an Agency Contract

An agency contract may be terminated by

- performance by the broker,

- expiration of the time period stated in it,

- abandonment by the broker who spends no time on it,

- the owner before the broker performs or spends time or money on it (although the owner may be liable for damages),;

- revocation by the broker before the broker performs or spends time or money on it (although the owner may be liable for damages),

- cancellation by the broker or by mutual consent,

- death or insanity of either party, or

- revocation, suspension, or expiration of the broker's license.

    In addition, a listing agreement may be terminated by

- destruction of the property,

- condemnation of the property, or

- transfer of title by operation of law, as in a bankruptcy.

Listing Agreements

Listing agreements are brokerage agreements in which the real estate broker is hired to legally represent a seller or landlord. See Figure 8.2 for an example of a typical listing agreement. The basic forms of listing agreements are (1) *open listing*, (2) *exclusive-agency listing*, and (3) *exclusive-right-to-sell listing*.

FIGURE 8.2   **Listing Contract: Exclusive Right to Sell**

This form provided to Kaplan Real Estate Education by the Minnesota Association of REALTORS® and is intended for educational purposes only.

LISTING CONTRACT:
EXCLUSIVE RIGHT TO SELL
This form approved by the Minnesota Association of REALTORS®, which disclaims any liability arising out of use or misuse of this form.
© 2013 Minnesota Association of REALTORS®, Edina, MN

1. Date _____

2. Page 1 of _____ pages

3. **DEFINITIONS:** This Contract involves the property located at _____ ,

4. legally described as _____

5. _____ ("Property").

6. Seller is _____ ("Seller").

7. Broker is _____ ("Broker").
    (Real Estate Company Name)

8. This Contract starts on _____ , 20 _____ , and ends at 11:59 p.m. on _____ ,

9. 20 _____ .

10. This Contract may only be canceled by written mutual agreement of the parties.

11. **PRICE:** Seller offers the Property for sale for the price of $ _____ , upon the following

12. terms: _____ .

13. **LISTING:** Seller gives Broker the exclusive right to sell the Property. In exchange, Broker agrees to list and market
14. the Property for sale. Broker may place a "For Sale" sign and a lock box with keys on the Property, unless prohibited by
15. governing authority. Seller understands this Contract DOES NOT give Broker authority to rent or manage the Property.
16. Seller understands Broker may be a member of a Multiple Listing Service ("MLS"), and if Broker is a member of MLS,
17. and where available, Broker may give information to the MLS concerning the Property. Broker may place information
18. on the Internet concerning the Property, including sold information (except as limited in the *Internet Display Options*
19. *Form*). If Broker sells the Property, Broker may notify the MLS and member REALTORS® of the price and terms of
20. the sale. Seller acknowledges that neither Broker, the MLS, the Minnesota Association of REALTORS®, nor any other
21. broker is insuring Seller or occupant against theft, loss or vandalism.

22. *(Initial)*

23. _____   _____   Seller acknowledges that Seller has received and has had the opportunity to review the *Internet*
    (Seller)   (Seller)
24. *Display Options* Form.

25. **LISTED FOR LEASE:** The Property ☐ **IS** ☐ **IS NOT** currently listed for lease. If **IS**, the listing broker is
    ----------*(Check one.)*----------

26. _____ . If **IS NOT**, Seller ☐ **MAY** ☐ **MAY NOT** list the Property for lease during the
    ----------*(Check one.)*----------
27. terms of this Contract with another broker.

28. Nothing in this Contract shall prohibit Broker and Seller from entering into a listing agreement for the lease of this
29. Property upon terms acceptable to both parties.

30. **SELLER'S OBLIGATION:** Seller shall notify Broker of relevant information important to the sale of the Property.
31. Seller shall cooperate with Broker in selling the Property. Seller shall promptly inform Broker about all inquiries Seller
32. receives about the Property. Seller agrees to provide and pay for any inspections and reports required by any
33. governmental authority. Seller agrees to provide unit owners' association documents, if required. Seller shall remain
34. responsible for security, maintenance, utilities and insurance during the term of this Contract, and for safekeeping,
35. securing and/or concealing any valuable personal property during Property showings or open houses. Seller shall
36. surrender any abstract of title and a copy of any owner's title insurance policy for this Property, if in Seller's possession
37. or control, to buyer or buyer's designated title service provider. Seller shall take all actions necessary to convey
38. marketable title by the date of closing as agreed to in a purchase agreement. Seller shall sign all documents necessary
39. to transfer to buyer marketable title to the Property. Seller has the full legal right to sell the Property.

40. Seller authorizes Broker, and any other broker authorized by Broker, to preview and show the Property at reasonable
41. times and upon reasonable notice and agrees to commit no act which might tend to obstruct Broker's performance
42. hereunder. If the Property is occupied by someone other than Seller, Seller shall comply with Minnesota law and any
43. applicable lease provisions of an existing lease and provide tenant with proper notice in advance of any Property
44. showing.

MN:LC:ERS-1 (8/13)

Source: Minnesota Association of REALTORS®

FIGURE 8.2   **Listing Contract: Exclusive Right to Sell (Cont.)**

LISTING CONTRACT:
EXCLUSIVE RIGHT TO SELL
45.   Page 2

46. Property located at _____ .

47. **SELLER CONTENT LICENSE:** In the event Seller provides content, including, but not limited to, any photos or videos
48. of the Property ("Seller Content") to Broker, Seller grants to Broker a nonexclusive, perpetual, world-wide, transferable,
49. royalty free license to sub-license (including through multiple tiers), reproduce, distribute, display, perform and create
50. derivate works of the Seller Content. Seller represents and warrants that Seller has authority to provide Seller Content
51. and Seller Content does not violate any restrictions regarding use including any third-party intellectual property rights
52. or laws. Seller agrees to execute any further documents that are necessary to effect this license.

53. **NOTICE:**   **THE COMPENSATION FOR THE SALE, LEASE, RENTAL OR MANAGEMENT OF REAL PROPERTY**
54.   **SHALL BE DETERMINED BETWEEN EACH INDIVIDUAL BROKER AND THE BROKER'S CLIENT.**

55. **BROKER'S COMPENSATION:**
56. Seller agrees to pay Broker a retainer fee of $ _____ at the commencement of this Contract, which
57. fee should be kept by Broker whether or not Seller sells the Property. The retainer fee will apply toward satisfaction of
58. any obligation to compensate Broker.

59. Seller shall pay Broker, as Broker's compensation, _____ percent (%) of the selling price or

60. $ _____ , whichever is greater, if Seller sells or agrees to sell the Property during the term of
61. this Contract.

62. Other: _____

63. In addition, if before this Contract expires Broker presents a buyer who is willing and able to buy the Property at the
64. price and terms required in this Contract, but Seller refuses to sell, Seller shall still pay Broker the same compensation.
65. Seller agrees to pay Broker's compensation whether Broker, Seller or anyone sells the Property. Seller hereby permits
66. Broker to share part of Broker's compensation with other real estate brokers, including brokers representing only the
67. buyer. Seller agrees to pay Broker's compensation in full upon the happening of any of the following events:

68.   1. the closing of the sale;
69.   2. Seller's refusal to close the sale; or
70.   3. Seller's refusal to sell at the price and terms specified above.

71. If, within _____ days *(not to exceed six (6) months)* after the expiration of this Contract, Seller sells or agrees to sell
72. the Property to anyone who:

73.   1. during this Contract made inquiry of Seller about the Property and Seller did not tell Broker about the inquiry;
74.   or
75.   2. during this Contract made an affirmative showing of interest in the Property by responding to an advertisement,
76.   or by contacting Broker or the licensee involved, or was physically shown the Property by Broker and whose
77.   name and address is on a written list Broker gives to Seller within 72 hours after the expiration of this Contract;

78. then Seller shall still pay Broker the compensation noted herein, even if Seller sells the Property without Broker's
79. assistance. Seller understands that Seller does not have to pay Broker's compensation if Seller signs another valid
80. listing contract or facilitator services agreement for this Property after the expiration or cancellation of this Contract,
81. under which Seller is obligated to compensate another licensed real estate broker.

82. To secure the payment of Broker's compensation, Seller hereby assigns to Broker the gross proceeds from the sale
83. of the Property in an amount equal to the compensation due to Broker under this Contract.

84. **COMPENSATION DISCLOSURE:** Broker's compensation to cooperating brokers shall be as specified in the MLS
85. unless Broker notifies Seller otherwise in writing.

86. **CLOSING SERVICES:**

87. **NOTICE:**   THE REAL ESTATE BROKER, LICENSEE REPRESENTING OR ASSISTING SELLER OR REAL ESTATE
88.   CLOSING AGENT HAS NOT EXPRESSED AND, UNDER APPLICABLE STATE LAW, MAY NOT EXPRESS
89.   OPINIONS REGARDING THE LEGAL EFFECT OF THE CLOSING DOCUMENTS OR OF THE CLOSING
90.   ITSELF.

91. After a purchase agreement for the Property is signed, arrangements must be made to close the transaction. Seller
92. understands that no one can require Seller to use a particular person in connection with a real estate closing and that
93. Seller may arrange for a qualified closing agent or Seller's attorney to conduct the closing.

MN:LC:ERS-2 (8/13)

Source: Minnesota Association of REALTORS®

FIGURE 8.2   **Listing Contract: Exclusive Right to Sell (Cont.)**

LISTING CONTRACT:
EXCLUSIVE RIGHT TO SELL
94.   Page 3

95.   Property located at _____ .

96.   Seller's choice for closing services. *(Initial one.)*

97.   _____ _____ Seller wishes to have Broker arrange for the closing.
         (Seller)   (Seller)

98.   _____ _____ Seller shall arrange for a qualified closing agent or Seller's attorney to conduct the closing.
         (Seller)   (Seller)

99.   **ADDITIONAL COSTS:** Seller acknowledges that Seller may be required to pay certain closing costs, which may
100. effectively reduce the proceeds from the sale.

101. Seller understands that mortgage financing services are usually paid for by buyer; however, certain insured government
102. loans may require Seller to pay a portion of the fees for the mortgage loan. Seller understands that Seller shall not be
103. required to pay the financing fees on any mortgage without giving Seller's written consent.

104. **WARRANTY:** There are warranty programs available for some properties which warrant the performance of certain
105. components of a property, which warranty programs Seller may wish to investigate prior to the sale of the Property.

106. **AGENCY REPRESENTATION:** If a buyer represented by Broker wishes to buy the Seller's Property, a dual
107. agency will be created. This means that Broker will represent both the Seller and the buyer, and owe the same
108. duties to the buyer that Broker owes to the Seller. This conflict of interest will prohibit Broker from advocating exclusively
109. on the Seller's behalf. Dual agency will limit the level of representation Broker can provide. If a dual agency should arise,
110. the Seller will need to agree that confidential information about price, terms, and motivation will still be kept
111. confidential unless the Seller instructs Broker in writing to disclose specific information about the Seller. All other
112. information will be shared. Broker cannot act as a dual agent unless both the Seller and the buyer agree to it. By
113. agreeing to a possible dual agency, the Seller will be giving up the right to exclusive representation in an in-house transaction.
114. However, if the Seller should decide not to agree to a possible dual agency, and the Seller wants Broker to represent
115. the Seller, the Seller may give up the opportunity to sell the Property to buyers represented by Broker.

116. Seller's Instructions to Broker:
117. Having read and understood this information about dual agency, Seller now instructs Broker as follows:
118. ☐   Seller will agree to a dual agency representation and will consider offers made by buyers represented by
119.   Broker.
120. ☐   Seller will not agree to a dual agency representation and will not consider offers made by buyers represented
121.   by Broker.

122. Real Estate Company Name: _____

123.   Seller: _____

124. By: _____   Seller: _____
                     (Licensee)

125.   Date: _____

126. **OTHER POTENTIAL SELLERS:** Seller understands that Broker may list other properties during the term of this
127. Contract. Seller consents to Broker representing or assisting such other potential sellers before, during and after the
128. expiration of this Contract.

129. **PREVIOUS AGENCY RELATIONSHIPS:** Broker or licensee representing or assisting Seller may have had a previous
130. agency relationship with a potential buyer of Seller's Property. Seller acknowledges that Seller's Broker or licensee
131. representing or assisting Seller is legally required to keep information regarding the ultimate price and terms the buyer
132. would accept and the motivation for buying confidential, if known.

133. **INDEMNIFICATION:** Broker will rely on the accuracy of the information Seller provides to Broker. Seller agrees
134. to indemnify and hold harmless Broker from and against any and all claims, liability, damage or loss arising from any
135. misrepresentation, misstatement, omission of fact or breach of a promise by Seller. Seller agrees to indemnify and hold
136. harmless Broker from any and all claims or liability related to damage or loss to the Property or its contents, or any
137. injury to persons in connection with the marketing of the Property. Indemnification by Seller shall not apply if the damage,
138. loss or injury is the result of the gross negligence or willful misconduct of the Broker.

MN:LC:ERS-3 (8/13)

Source: Minnesota Association of REALTORS®

FIGURE 8.2   **Listing Contract: Exclusive Right to Sell (Cont.)**

LISTING CONTRACT:
EXCLUSIVE RIGHT TO SELL
139.   Page 4

140. Property located at _____ .

141. **CERTIFICATION INDIVIDUAL TRANSFEROR: Section 1445 of the Internal Revenue Code provides that a**
142. **transferee (buyer) of a U.S. real property interest must be notified in writing and must withhold tax if the**
143. **transferor (Seller) is a foreign person and the sale price exceeds $300,000. In the event transferor (Seller) is a**
144. **foreign person and the sale price exceeds $300,000, requirements of the 1980 Foreign Investment in Real**
145. **Property Tax Act (FIRPTA) will be fulfilled.**

146. **Seller(s) states and acknowledges the following:** Seller is a citizen of the United States or, if a corporation, partnership
147. or other business entity, duly incorporated in the United States or, if a partnership or business entity, formed and
148. governed by the laws of the United States: ☐ Yes   ☐ No

149. If "No," please state country of citizenship, incorporation or the like: _____

150. Under the penalties of perjury Seller declares that Seller has examined this certification and, to the best of Seller's
151. knowledge and belief, it is true, correct and complete.

152. **FAIR HOUSING NOTICE:** Seller understands that Seller shall not refuse to sell, or discriminate in the terms, conditions
153. or privileges of sale, to any person due to his/her race, color, creed, religion, national origin, sex, marital status, status
154. with regard to public assistance, handicap (whether physical or mental), sexual orientation or family status. Seller
155. understands further that local ordinances may include other protected classes.

156. **ADDITIONAL NOTICES AND TERMS:** As of this date Seller has not received notices from any municipality, government
157. agency or unit owners' association about the Property that Seller has not informed Broker about in writing. Seller agrees
158. to promptly inform Broker, in writing, of any notices of such type that Seller receives during the term of this Contract.

159. This shall serve as Seller's written notice granting Broker permission to obtain mortgage information (e.g., mortgage
160. balance, interest rate, payoff and/or assumption figures) regarding any existing financing on the Property. A copy of
161. this document shall be as valid as the original.

162. **ELECTRONIC SIGNATURES:** The parties agree the electronic signature of any party on any document related to this
163. transaction constitute valid, binding signatures.

164. **CONSENT FOR COMMUNICATION:** Seller authorizes Broker and its representatives to contact Seller by mail, phone,
165. fax, e-mail or other means of communication during the term of this Agreement and anytime thereafter.

166. **OTHER:** _____
167. _____
168. _____
169. _____ .

170. **ACCEPTED BY:** _____
(Real Estate Company Name)

171. **BY:** _____   _____
(Licensee)   (Date)

172. **ACCEPTED BY:** _____   **ACCEPTED BY:** _____
(Seller)   (Seller)

173. _____   _____
(Date)   (Date)

174. _____   _____
(Address)   (Address)

175. _____   _____
(Phone)   (Phone)

176. _____   _____
(E-mail Address)   (E-mail Address)

177.   **THIS IS A LEGALLY BINDING CONTRACT BETWEEN SELLER AND BROKER.**
178.   **IF YOU DESIRE LEGAL OR TAX ADVICE, CONSULT AN APPROPRIATE PROFESSIONAL.**

MN:LC:ERS-4 (8/13)

Source: Minnesota Association of REALTORS®

Open listing. In an **open listing**, the seller retains the right to employ any number of brokers to act as the seller's agents. These brokers can act simultaneously, and the seller is obligated to pay a commission only to that broker who successfully produces a ready, willing, and able buyer. Most brokers avoid an open listing because the seller who personally sells the property without the aid of any of the brokers is not obligated to pay any of them a commission. A broker who was in any way a procuring cause in the transaction, however, may be entitled to a commission. A listing contract generally creates an open listing unless wording that specifically provides otherwise is included.

Exclusive-agency listing. In an **exclusive-agency listing**, only one broker is specifically authorized to act as the exclusive agent of the principal and seller retains the right to sell the property without obligation to the broker. In other words, the seller does not owe the broker a commission unless the broker was the procuring cause of the sale.

Exclusive-right-to-sell listing. In an **exclusive-right-to-sell listing**, one broker is appointed as the sole agent of the seller and is given the exclusive right, or authorization, to represent the seller in marketing the property and finding a purchaser. The seller gives up the right to find a buyer for the property. Regardless of who procures the buyer, the broker is entitled to receive a commission from the seller. The exclusive-right-to-sell listing is the preferred type of listing for most brokers and is sometimes required for entry into a multiple listing service.

Net listing. A **net listing** is based on the amount of money the seller will receive if the property is sold. A minimum sales price is agreed upon between the seller and the broker. The broker is then free to offer the property for sale at any price higher than that agreed upon. If the property is sold, the broker pays the seller only the net amount previously agreed upon. This type of listing is outlawed in most states and is not recommended in the others. The question of fraud is frequently raised because of the uncertainty over the sales price that is set or received by the broker. To avoid any hint of impropriety, the listing agreement should state a specific asking price and a specific commission rate.

Multiple Listing Agreements

A **multiple listing service (MLS)** is an organization of member brokers who agree to share information about their listings. By unilateral agreement, the member brokers agree to divide the commission between the listing broker and the selling broker upon the sale of the property. How the commission is divided is negotiated between the brokers. A multiple listing arrangement offers many advantages to sellers because the property is exposed to all members of the multiple listing service and their buyers.

In an exclusive-agency or exclusive-right-to-sell listing (usually the latter), the *multiple listing clause* includes additional authority and obligation for the listing broker to distribute information about the listed property within a certain time frame to member brokers. The length of time during which the listing broker can offer the property exclusively without notifying the other member brokers varies widely.

Buyer Agency Agreements

Buyer agency agreements are brokerage agreements used by the real estate broker to legally represent a buyer or tenant. See Figure 8.3 for an example of a typical buyer agency agreement. As with listing agreements, there are also three basic forms of buyer agency agreements. These forms, which mirror the forms of listing agreements in type and meaning, are (1) open right to represent buyer, (2) exclusive-agency right to represent buyer, and (3) exclusive right to represent buyer.

FIGURE 8.3   **Buyer Representation Contract: Exclusive**

This form provided to Kaplan Real Estate Education by the Minnesota Association of REALTORS® and is intended for educational purposes only.

BUYER REPRESENTATION CONTRACT: EXCLUSIVE
This form approved by the Minnesota Association of REALTORS®, which disclaims any liability arising out of use or misuse of this form.
© 2013 Minnesota Association of REALTORS®, Edina, MN

1.   Date _____

2.   Page 1 of _____ pages

3.   **DEFINITIONS:** Buyer is _____ ("Buyer").

4.   Broker is _____ ("Broker").
       _____(Real Estate Company Name)_____

5.   Buyer gives Broker the exclusive right to locate and/or to assist in negotiations for the purchase, exchange of or option to

6.   purchase ("Purchase") property at a price and with terms acceptable to Buyer. This Contract starts on

7.   _____ , 20 _____ , and ends at 11:59 p.m. on _____ , 20 _____ .

8.   This Contract may only be canceled by written mutual agreement of the parties.

9.   **BROKER'S OBLIGATION:** Broker shall make a reasonable effort to locate property acceptable to Buyer. Broker
10.   shall use professional knowledge and skills to assist in negotiations for the Purchase of property. Broker shall assist
11.   Buyer throughout the transaction. Broker shall act in Buyer's best interest at all times, subject to any limitations imposed
12.   by law or dual agency. Broker shall comply with all applicable fair housing and nondiscrimination regulations.

13.   **BUYER'S OBLIGATION:** Buyer shall work exclusively with Broker for the Purchase of property. Buyer shall promptly
14.   furnish to Broker accurate and relevant personal financial information to ascertain Buyer's ability to Purchase property,
15.   if requested. Buyer shall cooperate with Broker in finding a property to Purchase. After a purchase agreement has
16.   been accepted by seller, Buyer is legally obligated to Purchase the property. If Buyer refuses to close the Purchase for
17.   any reason other than the failure of seller to perform, subject to relevant contingencies, Buyer shall pay Broker all
18.   compensation due under this Contract.

19.   **NOTICE: THE COMPENSATION FOR THE PURCHASE, LEASE, RENTAL OR MANAGEMENT OF REAL**
20.   **PROPERTY SHALL BE DETERMINED BETWEEN EACH INDIVIDUAL BROKER AND THE BROKER'S**
21.   **CLIENT.**

22.   **BROKER'S COMPENSATION:** *(Fill in all blanks.):*
23.   If Buyer, or any other person acting on Buyer's behalf, agrees to Purchase any property during the term of this Contract,
24.   the following compensation will apply.
25.   1.   Buyer agrees to pay Broker a retainer fee of $ _____ at the commencement of this Contract,
26.   which fee shall be kept by Broker whether or not Buyer Purchases property. The retainer fee shall apply toward
27.   satisfaction of any obligation to compensate Broker.

28.   2.   Buyer shall pay Broker, as Broker's compensation, _____ percent (%) of the selling price or

29. $ _____ , whichever is greater, when Buyer closes the Purchase, if:

30.   A: Buyer Purchases or agrees to Purchase a property before the expiration of this Contract, even if Buyer does
31.   not use Broker's services; or

32.   B: within _____ days *(not to exceed six (6) months)* after the expiration of this Contract, Buyer Purchases
33.   property which either Broker or licensee representing or assisting Buyer has physically shown Buyer or in which
34.   Buyer has made an affirmative showing of interest to Broker or licensee representing or assisting Buyer before
35.   the expiration of this Contract, as long as Broker has identified this property on a written list Broker gives to
36.   Buyer within 72 hours after the expiration of this Contract.

37.   Broker is authorized to negotiate and receive compensation paid by seller, or broker representing or assisting seller, if
38.   Broker informs Buyer in writing before Buyer signs an offer to Purchase the property. Any compensation accepted by
39.   Broker from seller, or broker representing or assisting seller, ☐ **SHALL** ☐ **SHALL NOT** reduce any obligation of Buyer
       ----------------*(Check one.)*----------------
40.   to pay the compensation by the amount received by seller or broker.

41.   Buyer understands that Buyer does not have to pay Broker's compensation if Buyer signs another valid buyer
42.   representation contract or facilitator services agreement after the expiration or cancellation of this Contract, under
43.   which Buyer is obligated to compensate another licensed real estate broker.

MN:BRC:E-1 (8/13)

Source: Minnesota Association of REALTORS®

FIGURE 8.3 **Buyer Representation Contract: Exclusive (Cont.)**

**BUYER REPRESENTATION
CONTRACT: EXCLUSIVE**

44.   Page 2

45. **CAUTION: BUYER'S ACTIONS IN LOCATING A PROPERTY MAY AFFECT PAYMENT OF COMPENSATION BY**
46.   **SELLER(S) AND MAY THEREFORE OBLIGATE BUYER TO PAY ALL OR PART OF THE COMPENSATION**
47.   **IN CASH AT CLOSING. FOR EXAMPLE: THE ACT OF GOING THROUGH AN OPEN HOUSE**
48.   **UNACCOMPANIED BY BUYER'S BROKER OR LICENSEE REPRESENTING OR ASSISTING BUYER;**
49.   **OR SIGNING A PURCHASE AGREEMENT THROUGH ANOTHER BROKER OR WITH OWNER (FOR**
50.   **SALE BY OWNER) MAY REQUIRE BUYER'S PAYMENT OF THE FULL COMPENSATION TO BUYER'S**
51.   **BROKER.**

52. **GENERAL NATURE OF PROPERTY:** (Including the following property types: existing, new construction or to-be-built.)
53. *(Check all that apply.)*

54. ☐ Commercial/Industrial   ☐ Farm   ☐ Recreation
55. ☐ Residential/Investment   ☐ Residential/Personal   ☐ Vacant Land

56. **CLOSING SERVICES:**
57. **NOTICE:**   THE REAL ESTATE BROKER, LICENSEE REPRESENTING OR ASSISTING BUYER OR REAL ESTATE
58.   CLOSING AGENT HAS NOT EXPRESSED AND, UNDER APPLICABLE STATE LAW, MAY NOT EXPRESS
59.   OPINIONS REGARDING THE LEGAL EFFECT OF THE CLOSING DOCUMENTS OR OF THE CLOSING
60.   ITSELF.

61. After a purchase agreement for the property is signed, arrangements must be made to close the transaction. Buyer
62. understands that no one can require Buyer to use a particular person in connection with a real estate closing and that
63. Buyer may arrange for a qualified closing agent or Buyer's attorney to conduct the closing.

64. Buyer's choice for closing services. *(Initial one.)*

65. _____ _____   Buyer wishes to have Broker arrange for the closing.
        (Buyer)   (Buyer)

66. _____ _____   Buyer shall arrange for a qualified closing agent or Buyer's attorney to conduct the closing.
        (Buyer)   (Buyer)

67. **ADDITIONAL COSTS:** Buyer acknowledges that Buyer may be required to pay certain closing costs, which may
68. effectively increase the cash outlay at closing.

69. **PRIVATE INSPECTION/WARRANTY:** Broker recommends that Buyer obtain a private home inspection to satisfy
70. himself/herself with the physical condition of the property. Furthermore, there are warranty programs available for some
71. properties which warrant the performance of certain components of a property, which warranty programs Buyer may
72. wish to investigate prior to the Purchase of any specific property.

73. **AGENCY REPRESENTATION:** If the Buyer chooses to Purchase a property listed by Broker, a dual agency will be
74. created. This means that Broker will represent both the Buyer and the seller, and owe the same duties to the seller that
75. Broker owes to the Buyer. This conflict of interest will prohibit Broker from advocating exclusively on the Buyer's behalf.
76. Dual agency will limit the level of representation Broker can provide. If a dual agency should arise, the Buyer will need
77. to agree that confidential information about price, terms and motivation will still be kept confidential unless the Buyer
78. instructs Broker in writing to disclose specific information about the Buyer. All other information will be shared. Broker
79. cannot act as a dual agent unless both the Buyer and the seller agree to it. By agreeing to a possible dual agency,
80. the Buyer will be giving up the right to exclusive representation in an in-house transaction. However, if the Buyer should
81. decide not to agree to a possible dual agency, and the Buyer wants Broker to represent the Buyer, the Buyer may give
82. up the opportunity to Purchase the properties listed by Broker.

83. Buyer's Instructions to Broker:
84. Having read and understood this information about dual agency, Buyer now instructs Broker as follows:

85. ☐ Buyer will agree to a dual agency representation and will consider properties listed by Broker.

86. ☐ Buyer will not agree to a dual agency representation and will not consider properties listed by Broker.

87. Real Estate Company Name: _____

88.   Buyer: _____

89. By: _____   Buyer: _____
              (Licensee)

90.   Date: _____

MN:BRC:E-2 (8/13)

Source: Minnesota Association of REALTORS®

FIGURE 8.3   **Buyer Representation Contract: Exclusive (Cont.)**

**BUYER REPRESENTATION
CONTRACT: EXCLUSIVE**
91.   Page 3

92. **OTHER POTENTIAL BUYERS:** Buyer understands that other potential buyers may consider and/or make offers to
93. purchase through Broker the same or similar properties as Buyer is seeking to Purchase. Buyer consents to Broker
94. representing such other potential buyers before, during and after the expiration of this Contract.

95. **PREVIOUS AGENCY RELATIONSHIPS:** Broker or licensee representing or assisting Buyer may have had a previous
96. agency relationship with a seller of a property Buyer is interested in Purchasing. Buyer acknowledges that Buyer's
97. Broker or licensee representing or assisting Buyer is legally required to keep information regarding the ultimate price
98. and terms the seller would accept and the motivation for selling confidential, if known.

99.   **NOTICE REGARDING PREDATORY OFFENDER INFORMATION: Information regarding the predatory**
100. **offender registry and persons registered with the predatory offender registry under MN Statute 243.166 may**
101. **be obtained by contacting the local law enforcement offices in the community where the property is located**
102. **or the Minnesota Department of Corrections at (651) 361-7200, or from the Department of Corrections web site at**
103. **www.corr.state.mn.us.**

104. **ELECTRONIC SIGNATURES:** The parties agree the electronic signature of any party on any document related to this
105. transaction constitute valid, binding signatures.

106. **CONSENT FOR COMMUNICATION:** Buyer authorizes Broker and its representatives to contact Buyer by mail, phone,
107. fax, e-mail or other means of communication during the term of this Contract and any time thereafter.

108. **OTHER:** _____
109. _____
110. _____
111. _____

112. **ACCEPTED BY:** _____
                          (Real Estate Company Name)

113. **BY:** _____
          (Licensee)   (Date)

114. **ACCEPTED BY:** _____   ACCEPTED BY: _____
                          (Buyer)   (Buyer)

115. _____   _____
          (Date)   (Date)

116. _____   _____
          (Address)   (Address)

117. _____   _____
          (Phone)   (Phone)

118. _____   _____
          (E-mail Address)   (E-mail Address)

119.   **THIS IS A LEGALLY BINDING CONTRACT BETWEEN BUYER AND BROKER.**
120.   **IF YOU DESIRE LEGAL OR TAX ADVICE, CONSULT AN APPROPRIATE PROFESSIONAL.**

MN:BRC:E-3 (8/13)

Source: Minnesota Association of REALTORS®

The buyer agency agreement should state the duties of the broker, an agreement regarding compensation, and any other provisions mandated by state agency law or common business practice for the area. Ways to terminate the agreement and broker protection clauses are basically the same as shown under Agency Contracts.

Management Agreements

Management agreements are brokerage agreements establishing a general agency relationship between the broker and the owner of rental property. The management agreement should be for a certain amount of time, be in writing, be dated and signed by both parties, describe the property, and describe the relationship between the owner and the broker and the rights and responsibilities of each, including the basis on which the broker earns the management fee. It should clearly state the authority given to the broker by the owner and the responsibilities retained by the owner.

SALES CONTRACTS

A contract for the sale of real estate sets forth all details of the agreement between a buyer and seller for the purchase and sale of a parcel of real estate (see Figure 8.4 for an example). Depending on the state or locality, this agreement may be called an *offer to purchase, contract of purchase and sale, earnest money agreement, deposit receipt*, or other variation of these terms. Whatever the contract is called, when it has been prepared and signed by the purchaser, it is an offer to purchase the subject real estate. Later, if the document is accepted and signed by the seller, it then becomes a contract of sale.

Every sales contract requires at least two parties, a seller and a buyer. The same person cannot be both buyer and seller because individuals cannot legally contract with themselves. The contract of sale is the most important document in the sale of real estate because it sets out in detail the agreement between the buyer and seller and establishes both parties' legal rights and obligations.

FIGURE 8.4 **Purchase Agreement**

This form provided to Kaplan
Real Estate Education by the
Minnesota Association of
REALTORS® and is intended
for educational purposes only.

PURCHASE AGREEMENT
This form approved by the Minnesota Association of REALTORS®,
which disclaims any liability arising out of use or misuse of this form.
© 2014 Minnesota Association of REALTORS®, Edina, MN

1.   Date _____

2.   Page 1 of _____

3.   BUYER (S): _____

4.   _____

5.   Buyer's earnest money in the amount of_____

6.   _____ Dollars (\$ _____)

7.   shall be delivered to listing broker no later than two (2) Business Days after Final Acceptance Date of this Purchase

8.   Agreement. Buyer and Seller agree that listing broker shall deposit any earnest money in the listing broker's trust

9.   account within three (3) Business Days of receipt of the earnest money or Final Acceptance Date of this Purchase

10. Agreement, whichever is later.

11. Said earnest money is part payment for the purchase of the property located at

12. Street Address: _____

13. City of _____ , County of _____ ,

14. State of Minnesota, legally described as _____

15. _____

16. _____ .

17. Said purchase shall include all improvements, fixtures, and appurtenances on the property, if any, including but not

18. limited to, the following (collectively the "Property"): garden bulbs, plants, shrubs, trees, and lawn watering system;

19. shed; storm sash, storm doors, screens and awnings; window shades, blinds; traverse, curtain, and drapery

20. rods, valances, drapes, curtains, window coverings and treatments; towel rods; attached lighting and bulbs; fan fixtures;

21. plumbing fixtures; garbage disposals; water softener; water treatment system; water heating systems, heating systems;

22. air exchange system; radon mitigation system; sump pump; TV antenna/cable TV jacks and wiring/TV wall mounts;

23. wall/ceiling-mounted speakers and mounts; carpeting; mirrors; garage door openers and all controls; smoke detectors;

24. fireplace screens, door and heatilators; **BUILT-INS:** dishwashers; refrigerators; wine/beverage refrigerators; trash

25. compactors; ovens; cook-top stoves; warming drawers; microwave ovens; hood fans; shelving; work benches; intercoms;

26. speakers; air conditioning equipment; electronic air filter; humidifier/dehumidifier; liquid fuel tanks (and controls);

27. pool/spa equipment; propane tank (and controls); security system equipment; TV satellite dish; **AND** the following

28. personal property shall be transferred with no additional monetary value, and free and clear of all liens and encumbrances:

29. _____

30. _____ .

31. Notwithstanding the foregoing, leased fixtures are not included.

32. Notwithstanding the foregoing, the following item(s) are excluded from the purchase:

33. _____

34. _____ .

35. Seller has agreed to sell the Property to Buyer for the sum of (\$ _____)

36. _____ Dollars,

37. which Buyer agrees to pay in the following manner:

38. 1. **CASH** of _____ percent (%) of the sale price, or more in Buyer's sole discretion, which includes the earnest

39.   money; PLUS

40. 2. **FINANCING** of _____ percent (%) of the sale price, which will be the total amount secured against this

41.   Property to fund this purchase.

42. Such financing shall be (*check one*) ☐ **a first mortgage;** ☐ **a contract for deed;** or ☐ **a first mortgage with**

43. **subordinate financing,** as described in the attached *Addendum*:

44. ☐ *Conventional* ☐ *FHA* ☐ *DVA* ☐ *Assumption* ☐ *Contract for Deed* ☐ *Other:* _____ .
     \-(Check one.)\-\-\-\-\-\-\-\-\-\-\-\-\-\-

45. **The date of closing shall be** _____ **, 20** _____ .

MN:PA-1 (8/14)

Source: Minnesota Association of REALTORS®

FIGURE 8.4   **Purchase Agreement (Cont.)**

PURCHASE AGREEMENT

46.   Page 2 Date _____

47.   Property located at _____ .

48.   This Purchase Agreement ☐ **IS** ☐ **IS NOT** subject to an *Addendum to Purchase Agreement: Sale of Buyer's Property*
       -------(Check one.)-------

49.   *Contingency* for sale of Buyer's property. (If answer is **IS,** see attached *Addendum*.)

50.   (If answer is **IS NOT**, the closing of Buyer's property, if any, may still affect Buyer's ability to obtain financing, if financing

51.   is applicable.)

52.   This Purchase Agreement ☐ **IS** ☐ **IS NOT** subject to cancellation of a previously written purchase agreement
       -------(Check one.)-------

53.   dated _____ , 20 _____ . (If answer is **IS**, said cancellation shall be obtained no later than

54.   _____ , 20 _____ . If said cancellation is not obtained by said date, this Purchase Agreement

55.   is canceled. Buyer and Seller shall immediately sign a *Cancellation of Purchase Agreement* confirming said cancellation

56.   and directing all earnest money paid hereunder to be refunded to Buyer.)

57.   Buyer has been made aware of the availability of Property inspections. Buyer ☐ **Elects** ☐ **Declines** to have a
       -------------(Check one.)-------------

58.   Property inspection performed at Buyer's expense.

59.   This Purchase Agreement ☐ **IS** ☐ **IS NOT** subject to an *Addendum to Purchase Agreement: Inspection Contingency*.
       -------(Check one.)-------

60.   (If answer is **IS,** see attached *Addendum*.)

61.   **DEED/MARKETABLE TITLE:** Upon performance by Buyer, Seller shall deliver a *(check one)*:

62.   ☐ **Warranty Deed,** ☐ **Personal Representative's Deed,** ☐ **Contract for Deed,** ☐ **Trustee's Deed,** or

63.   ☐ **Other:** _____ **Deed** joined in by spouse, if any, conveying marketable title, subject to

64.   (a) building and zoning laws, ordinances, and state and federal regulations;

65.   (b) restrictions relating to use or improvement of the Property without effective forfeiture provisions;

66.   (c) reservation of any mineral rights by the State of Minnesota;

67.   (d) utility and drainage easements which do not interfere with existing improvements;

68.   (e) **rights of tenants as follows** (unless specified, not subject to tenancies): _____

69.   _____ ;and

70.   (f) others (must be specified in writing): _____

71.   _____ .

72.   **REAL ESTATE TAXES:** Seller shall pay on the date of closing all real estate taxes due and payable in all prior years

73.   including all penalties and interest.

74.   Buyer shall pay ☐ **PRORATED FROM DAY OF CLOSING** ☐ _____ **12ths OF** ☐ **ALL** ☐ **NO** real estate taxes due
       ---(Check one.)---

75.   and payable in the year 20 _____ .

76.   Seller shall pay ☐ **PRORATED TO DAY OF CLOSING** ☐ _____ **12ths OF** ☐ **ALL** ☐ **NO** real estate taxes due and
       -------------------------------------(Check one.)-------------------------------------

77.   payable in the year 20 _____ . If the closing date is changed, the real estate taxes paid shall, if prorated, be adjusted

78.   to the new closing date. If the Property tax status is a part- or non-homestead classification in the year of closing, Seller

79.   ☐ **SHALL** ☐ **SHALL NOT** pay the difference between the homestead and non-homestead.
       -----------------(Check one.)-----------------

80.   Buyer shall pay real estate taxes due and payable in the year following closing and thereafter, the payment of which

81.   is not otherwise herein provided. No representations are made concerning the amount of subsequent real estate taxes.

82.   **DEFERRED TAXES/SPECIAL ASSESSMENTS:**

83.   ☐ **BUYER SHALL PAY** ☐ **SELLER SHALL PAY** on date of closing any deferred real estate taxes (e.g., Green
       -------------------------(Check one.)-------------------------

84.   Acres) or special assessments, payment of which is required as a result of the closing of this sale.

85.   ☐ **BUYER AND SELLER SHALL PRORATE AS OF THE DATE OF CLOSING** ☐ **SELLER SHALL PAY ON**
       -------------------------------(Check one.)-------------------------------

86.   **DATE OF CLOSING** all installments of special assessments certified for payment, with the real estate taxes due and

87.   payable in the year of closing.

MN:PA-2 (8/14)

FIGURE 8.4   **Purchase Agreement (Cont.)**

PURCHASE AGREEMENT

88.   Page 3 Date _____

89.   Property located at _____ .

90.   ☐ **BUYER SHALL ASSUME** ☐ **SELLER SHALL PAY** on date of closing all other special assessments levied as
        ---(Check one.)--

91.   of the date of this Purchase Agreement.

92.   ☐ **BUYER SHALL ASSUME** ☐ **SELLER SHALL PROVIDE FOR PAYMENT OF** special assessments pending as
        --(Check one.)---

93.   of the date of this Purchase Agreement for improvements that have been ordered by any assessing authorities. (Seller's
94.   provision for payment shall be by payment into escrow of two (2) times the estimated amount of the assessments
95.   or less, as required by Buyer's lender.)

96.   Buyer shall pay any unpaid special assessments payable in the year following closing and thereafter, the payment of
97.   which is not otherwise herein provided.

98.   As of the date of this Purchase Agreement, Seller represents that Seller ☐ **HAS** ☐ **HAS NOT** received a notice
        ------------(Check one.)-----------

99.   regarding any new improvement project from any assessing authorities, the costs of which project may be assessed
100.   against the Property. Any such notice received by Seller after the date of this Purchase Agreement and before closing
101.   shall be provided to Buyer immediately. If such notice is issued after the date of this Purchase Agreement and on
102.   or before the date of closing, then the parties may agree in writing, on or before the date of closing, to pay, provide
103.   for the payment of or assume the special assessments. In the absence of such agreement, either party may declare
104.   this Purchase Agreement canceled by written notice to the other party, or licensee representing or assisting the other
105.   party, in which case this Purchase Agreement is canceled. If either party declares this Purchase Agreement canceled,
106.   Buyer and Seller shall immediately sign a *Cancellation of Purchase Agreement* confirming said cancellation and
107.   directing all earnest money paid hereunder to be refunded to Buyer.

108.   **POSSESSION**: Seller shall deliver possession of the Property no later than _____ after closing.
109.   Seller agrees to remove ALL DEBRIS AND ALL PERSONAL PROPERTY NOT INCLUDED HEREIN from the Property
110.   by possession date.

111.   **PRORATIONS**: All interest; unit owners' association dues; rents; and charges for city water, city sewer, electricity and
112.   natural gas shall be prorated between the parties as of date of closing. Buyer shall pay Seller for remaining gallons of
113.   fuel oil or liquid petroleum gas on the day of closing, at the rate of the last fill by Seller.

114.   **TITLE AND EXAMINATION:** As quickly as reasonably possible after Final Acceptance Date of this Purchase Agreement:
115.   (a) Seller shall surrender any abstract of title and a copy of any owner's title insurance policy for the Property, if
116.   in Seller's possession or control, to Buyer or Buyer's designated title service provider; and
117.   (b) Buyer shall obtain the title services determined necessary or desirable by Buyer or Buyer's lender, including
118.   but not limited to title searches, title examinations, abstracting, a title insurance commitment or an attorney's
119.   title opinion at Buyer's selection and cost and provide a copy to Seller.

120.   Seller shall use Seller's best efforts to provide marketable title by the date of closing. Seller agrees to pay all costs
121.   and fees necessary to convey marketable title including obtaining and recording all required documents, subject to the
122.   following:
123.   In the event Seller has not provided marketable title by the date of closing, Seller shall have an additional 30 days to
124.   make title marketable, or in the alternative, Buyer may waive title defects by written notice to Seller. In addition to
125.   the 30-day extension, Buyer and Seller may, by mutual agreement, further extend the closing date. Lacking such
126.   extension, either party may declare this Purchase Agreement canceled by written notice to the other party, or
127.   licensee representing or assisting the other party, in which case this Purchase Agreement is canceled. If either
128.   party declares this Purchase Agreement canceled, Buyer and Seller shall immediately sign a *Cancellation of*
129.   *Purchase Agreement* confirming said cancellation and directing all earnest money paid hereunder to be refunded
130.   to Buyer.

131.   **SUBDIVISION OF LAND, BOUNDARIES, AND ACCESS:** If this sale constitutes or requires a subdivision of land
132.   owned by Seller, Seller shall pay all subdivision expenses and obtain all necessary governmental approvals. Seller
133.   warrants that the legal description of the real property to be conveyed has been or shall be approved for recording as
134.   of the date of closing. Seller warrants that the buildings are or shall be constructed entirely within the boundary lines
135.   of the Property. Seller warrants that there is a right of access to the Property from a public right-of-way.

136.   **MECHANIC'S LIENS:** Seller warrants that prior to the closing, payment in full will have been made for all labor, materials,
137.   machinery, fixtures or tools furnished within the 120 days immediately preceding the closing in connection with
138.   construction, alteration or repair of any structure on, or improvement to, the Property.

MN:PA-3 (8/14)

FIGURE 8.4 **Purchase Agreement (Cont.)**

PURCHASE AGREEMENT

139.　Page 4　Date _____

140.　Property located at _____ .

141.　**NOTICES:** Seller warrants that Seller has not received any notice from any governmental authority as to condemnation
142.　proceedings, or violation of any law, ordinance or regulation. If the Property is subject to restrictive covenants, Seller
143.　warrants that Seller has not received any notice from any person or authority as to a breach of the covenants. Any
144.　such notices received by Seller shall be provided to Buyer immediately.

145.　**DIMENSIONS:** Buyer acknowledges any dimensions, square footage or acreage of land or improvements provided
146.　by Seller, third party, or broker representing or assisting Seller are approximate. Buyer shall verify the accuracy of
147.　information to Buyer's satisfaction, if material, at Buyer's sole cost and expense.

148.　**ACCESS AGREEMENT:** Seller agrees to allow reasonable access to the Property for performance of any surveys or
149.　inspections agreed to herein.

150.　**RISK OF LOSS:** If there is any loss or damage to the Property between the date hereof and the date of closing for any
151.　reason, including fire, vandalism, flood, earthquake or act of God, the risk of loss shall be on Seller. If the Property
152.　is destroyed or substantially damaged before the closing date, this Purchase Agreement is canceled, at Buyer's option,
153.　by written notice to Seller or licensee representing or assisting Seller. If Buyer cancels this Purchase Agreement,
154.　Buyer and Seller shall immediately sign a *Cancellation of Purchase Agreement* confirming said cancellation and
155.　directing all earnest money paid hereunder to be refunded to Buyer.

156.　**TIME OF ESSENCE:** Time is of the essence in this Purchase Agreement.

157.　**CALCULATION OF DAYS:** Any calculation of days begins on the first day (calendar or Business Days as specified)
158.　following the occurrence of the event specified and includes subsequent days (calendar or Business Days as specified)
159.　ending at 11:59 P.M. on the last day.

160.　**BUSINESS DAYS:** "Business Days" are days which are not Saturdays, Sundays or state or federal holidays unless
161.　stated elsewhere by the parties in writing.

162.　**RELEASE OF EARNEST MONEY:** Buyer and Seller agree that the listing broker shall release earnest money from the
163.　listing broker's trust account: 1) at or upon the successful closing of the Property; 2) pursuant to written agreement
164.　between the parties, which may be reflected in a *Cancellation of Purchase Agreement* executed by both Buyer and
165.　Seller; 3) upon receipt of an affidavit of a cancellation under MN Statute 559.217; or 4) upon receipt of a court order.

166.　**DEFAULT:** If Buyer defaults in any of the agreements herein, Seller may cancel this Purchase Agreement, and any
167.　payments made hereunder, including earnest money, shall be retained by Seller as liquidated damages and Buyer
168.　and Seller shall affirm the same by a written cancellation agreement.

169.　If Buyer defaults in any of the agreements hereunder, Seller may terminate this Purchase Agreement under the
170.　provisions of either MN Statute 559.21 or MN Statute 559.217, whichever is applicable. If either Buyer or Seller defaults
171.　in any of the agreements hereunder or there exists an unfulfilled condition after the date specified for fulfillment, either
172.　party may cancel this Purchase Agreement under MN Statute 559.217, Subd. 3. Whenever it is provided herein that
173.　this Purchase Agreement is canceled, said language shall be deemed a provision authorizing a Declaratory Cancellation
174.　under MN Statute 559.217, Subd. 4.

175.　If this Purchase Agreement is not canceled or terminated as provided hereunder, Buyer or Seller may seek actual
176.　damages for breach of this Purchase Agreement or specific performance of this Purchase Agreement; and, as to
177.　specific performance, such action must be commenced within six (6) months after such right of action arises.

178.　**BUYER HAS THE RIGHT TO A WALK-THROUGH REVIEW OF THE PROPERTY PRIOR TO CLOSING TO**
179.　**ESTABLISH THAT THE PROPERTY IS IN SUBSTANTIALLY THE SAME CONDITION AS OF THE DATE OF**
180.　**THIS PURCHASE AGREEMENT.**

181.　BUYER HAS RECEIVED A *(check any that apply):* ☐ *DISCLOSURE STATEMENT: SELLER'S PROPERTY* OR A
182.　☐ *DISCLOSURE STATEMENT: SELLER'S DISCLOSURE ALTERNATIVES* FORM.

183.　**DESCRIPTION OF PROPERTY CONDITION:** See *Disclosure Statement: Seller's Property* or *Disclosure Statement:*
184.　*Seller's Disclosure Alternatives* for description of disclosure responsibilities and limitations, if any.

185.　**BUYER HAS RECEIVED THE INSPECTION REPORTS, IF REQUIRED BY MUNICIPALITY.**

186.　BUYER IS NOT RELYING ON ANY ORAL REPRESENTATIONS REGARDING THE CONDITION OF THE PROPERTY
187.　AND ITS CONTENTS.

MN:PA-4 (8/14)

Source: Minnesota Association of REALTORS®

FIGURE 8.4 **Purchase Agreement (Cont.)**

PURCHASE AGREEMENT

188. Page 5   Date _____

189. Property located at _____ .

---

190. *(Check appropriate boxes.)*
191. SELLER WARRANTS THAT THE PROPERTY IS EITHER DIRECTLY OR INDIRECTLY CONNECTED TO:

192. **CITY SEWER** ☐ **YES** ☐ **NO** / **CITY WATER** ☐ **YES** ☐ **NO**

193. **SUBSURFACE SEWAGE TREATMENT SYSTEM**

194. SELLER ☐ **DOES** ☐ **DOES NOT** KNOW OF A SUBSURFACE SEWAGE TREATMENT SYSTEM ON OR
                    ----------------*(Check one.)*-----------------
195. SERVING THE PROPERTY. (If answer is **DOES,** and the system does not require a state permit, see *Disclosure*
196. *Statement: Subsurface Sewage Treatment System.*)

197. **PRIVATE WELL**

198. SELLER ☐ **DOES** ☐ **DOES NOT** KNOW OF A WELL ON OR SERVING THE PROPERTY.
                    ---------------------*(Check one.)*---------------------
199. (If answer is **DOES** and well is located on the Property, see *Disclosure Statement: Well.*)

200. THIS PURCHASE AGREEMENT ☐ **IS** ☐ **IS NOT** SUBJECT TO AN *ADDENDUM TO PURCHASE AGREEMENT:*
                               ----------*(Check one.)*----------
201. *SUBSURFACE SEWAGE TREATMENT SYSTEM AND WELL INSPECTION CONTINGENCY.*
202. (If answer is **IS**, see attached *Addendum.*)

203. **IF A WELL OR SUBSURFACE SEWAGE TREATMENT SYSTEM EXISTS ON THE PROPERTY, BUYER HAS**
204. **RECEIVED A** *DISCLOSURE STATEMENT: WELL* **AND/OR A** *DISCLOSURE STATEMENT: SUBSURFACE SEWAGE*
205. *TREATMENT SYSTEM.*

---

206. **NOTICE REGARDING PREDATORY OFFENDER INFORMATION: Information regarding the predatory offender**
207. **registry and persons registered with the predatory offender registry under MN Statute 243.166 may be obtained**
208. **by contacting the local law enforcement offices in the community where the Property is located or the Minnesota**
209. **Department of Corrections at (651) 361-7200, or from the Department of Corrections web site at**
210. **www.corr.state.mn.us.**

211. **HOME PROTECTION/WARRANTY PLAN:** Buyer and Seller are advised to investigate the various home protection/
212. warranty plans available for purchase. Different home protection/warranty plans have different coverage options,
213. exclusions, limitations and service fees. Most plans exclude pre-existing conditions. *(Check one.)*

214. ☐   A Home Protection/Warranty Plan will be obtained and paid by ☐ **BUYER** ☐ **SELLER** to be issued by _____
                                                          ---------------*(Check one.)*---------------
215. _____ at a cost not to exceed $ _____ .

216. ☐   No Home Protection/Warranty Plan is negotiated as part of this Purchase Agreement. However, Buyer may elect
217.   to purchase a Home Protection/Warranty Plan.

---

218.   **NOTICE**
219. _____   is ☐ Seller's Agent ☐ Buyer's Agent ☐ Dual Agent ☐ Facilitator.
            (Licensee)   -----------------------------------*(Check one.)*-----------------------------------

220. _____
        (Real Estate Company Name)

221. _____   is ☐ Seller's Agent ☐ Buyer's Agent ☐ Dual Agent ☐ Facilitator.
            (Licensee)   -----------------------------------*(Check one.)*-----------------------------------

222. _____
        (Real Estate Company Name)

223.   **THIS NOTICE DOES <u>NOT</u> SATISFY MINNESOTA STATUTORY AGENCY DISCLOSURE REQUIREMENTS.**

MN:PA-5 (8/14)

Source: Minnesota Association of REALTORS®

FIGURE 8.4   **Purchase Agreement (Cont.)**

PURCHASE AGREEMENT

224.   Page 6   Date _____

225.   Property located at _____ .

---

226.   **DUAL AGENCY REPRESENTATION**

227.   **PLEASE CHECK _ONE_ OF THE FOLLOWING SELECTIONS:**

228.   ☐ Dual Agency representation **DOES NOT** apply in this transaction. *Do not complete lines 229-245.*

229.   ☐ Dual Agency representation **DOES** apply in this transaction. *Complete the disclosure in lines 230-245.*

230.   Broker represents both the Seller(s) and the Buyer(s) of the Property involved in this transaction, which creates a
231.   dual agency. This means that Broker and its salespersons owe fiduciary duties to both Seller(s) and Buyer(s). Because
232.   the parties may have conflicting interests, Broker and its salespersons are prohibited from advocating exclusively for
233.   either party. Broker cannot act as a dual agent in this transaction without the consent of both Seller(s) and Buyer(s).
234.   Seller(s) and Buyer(s) acknowledge that
235.   (1) confidential information communicated to Broker which regards price, terms, or motivation to buy or sell will
236.   remain confidential unless Seller(s) or Buyer(s) instructs Broker in writing to disclose this information. Other
237.   information will be shared;
238.   (2) Broker and its salespersons will not represent the interest of either party to the detriment of the other; and
239.   (3) within the limits of dual agency, Broker and its salespersons will work diligently to facilitate the mechanics of
240.   the sale.

241.   With the knowledge and understanding of the explanation above, Seller(s) and Buyer(s) authorize and instruct Broker
242.   and its salesperson to act as dual agents in this transaction.

243.   Seller _____   Buyer _____

244.   Seller _____   Buyer _____

245.   Date _____   Date _____

---

246.   **CLOSING COSTS:** Buyer or Seller may be required to pay certain closing costs, which may effectively increase the
247.   cash outlay at closing or reduce the proceeds from the sale.

248.   **ENTIRE AGREEMENT:** This Purchase Agreement and any addenda or amendments signed by the parties shall
249.   constitute the entire agreement between Buyer and Seller. Any other written or oral communication between Buyer and
250.   Seller, including, but not limited to, e-mails, text messages, or other electronic communications are not part of this
251.   Purchase Agreement. This Purchase Agreement can be modified or canceled only in writing signed by Seller and
252.   Buyer or by operation of law. All monetary sums are deemed to be United States currency for purposes of this Purchase
253.   Agreement.

254.   **ELECTRONIC SIGNATURES:** The parties agree the electronic signature of any party on any document related to this
255.   transaction constitute valid, binding signatures.

256.   **FINAL ACCEPTANCE:** To be binding, this Purchase Agreement must be fully executed by both parties and a copy
257.   must be delivered.

258.   **SURVIVAL:** All warranties specified in this Purchase Agreement shall survive the delivery of the deed or contract
259.   for deed.

260.   **OTHER:** _____

261.   _____

262.   _____

263.   _____

264.   _____

265.   _____

266.   _____

267.   _____

MN:PA-6 (8/14)

Source: Minnesota Association of REALTORS®

FIGURE 8.4   **Purchase Agreement (Cont.)**

PURCHASE AGREEMENT

268.   Page 7   Date _____

269.   Property located at _____ .

270.   **ADDENDA AND PAGE NUMBERING: Attached addenda are a part of this Purchase Agreement.**
271.   **Enter total number of pages of this Purchase Agreement, including addenda, on line two (2) of page one (1).**

272.   **NOTE: Disclosures and optional Arbitration Agreement are not part of this Purchase Agreement and should**
273.   **not be part of the page numbering.**

274.   I, the owner of the Property, accept this Purchase
275.   Agreement and authorize the listing broker to withdraw
276.   said Property from the market, unless instructed
277.   otherwise in writing.
278.   **I have reviewed all pages of this Purchase Agreement.**

I agree to purchase the Property for the price and on
the terms and conditions set forth above
I have reviewed all pages of this Purchase
Agreement.

279.   ☐ **If checked, this Purchase Agreement is subject to**
280.   **attached** *Addendum to Purchase Agreement:*
281.   *Counteroffer.*

282.   **X** _____   **X** _____
           (Seller's Signature)   (Date)   (Buyer's Signature)   (Date)

283.   **X** _____   **X** _____
           (Seller's Printed Name)   (Buyer's Printed Name)

284.   **X** _____   **X** _____
           (Marital Status)   (Marital Status)

285.   **X** _____   **X** _____
           (Seller's Signature)   (Date)   (Buyer's Signature)   (Date)

286.   **X** _____   **X** _____
           (Seller's Printed Name)   (Buyer's Printed Name)

287.   **X** _____   **X** _____
           (Marital Status)   (Marital Status)

288.   **FINAL ACCEPTANCE DATE:** _____ The Final Acceptance Date
289.   is the date on which the fully executed Purchase Agreement is delivered.

290.   **THIS IS A LEGALLY BINDING CONTRACT BETWEEN BUYER(S) AND SELLER(S).**
291.   **IF YOU DESIRE LEGAL OR TAX ADVICE, CONSULT AN APPROPRIATE PROFESSIONAL.**

292.   **I ACKNOWLEDGE THAT I HAVE RECEIVED AND HAVE HAD THE OPPORTUNITY TO REVIEW THE** *DISCLOSURE*
293.   *STATEMENT: ARBITRATION DISCLOSURE AND RESIDENTIAL REAL PROPERTY ARBITRATION AGREEMENT,*
294.   **WHICH IS AN OPTIONAL, VOLUNTARY AGREEMENT AND IS NOT PART OF THIS PURCHASE AGREEMENT.**

295.   **SELLER(S)** _____   **BUYER(S)** _____

296.   **SELLER(S)** _____   **BUYER(S)** _____

MN:PA-7 (8/14)

Source: Minnesota Association of REALTORS®

The Contract and the Deed

The sales contract is more important than the deed itself because the contract, in effect, dictates the contents of the deed. Through the process of *merger*, the contract merges into the deed and ceases to exist when the deed is delivered from the grantor to the grantee. In different parts of the country, a sales contract may also be called a purchase and sale agreement, an escrow agreement, or an agreement of sale.

Details of the contract.   The real estate sales contract must state all the terms and conditions of the agreement and identify all contingencies. The contract must include the names of the parties, price, terms, legal description of the land, kind and condition of the title, form of deed the seller will deliver, kind of title evidence required, who will provide title evidence, and how defects in the title, if any, are to be eliminated. Any included items of personal property (e.g., drapes, carpeting, appliances, etc.) should be thoroughly identified.

Contingencies.   In the purchase agreement, the buyer often includes **contingencies**, certain conditions that must be met before the contract is binding. Until the contingency is met, the contract is voidable. The most common contingencies are subject to the buyer obtaining suitable financing, a satisfactory property inspection, the ability to obtain insurance within a certain amount, and the buyers' ability to sell their current home.

Binder.   In some areas, it is customary for the real estate licensee to prepare a shorter document, called a **binder**, for the purchaser to sign. A binder states the essential terms of the purchaser's offer and acknowledges receipt of the purchaser's deposit. It also provides that upon the seller's acceptance and signing of the binder, the parties agree to have a more formal and complete contract of sale drawn up by an attorney. A binder receipt may be used in any situation in which the details of the transaction are too complex for the standard sales contract form.

Contract in writing.   Under the statute of frauds of every state, any contract for the transfer of a real estate interest must be in writing and signed by the parties to the agreement. A written agreement establishes the purchaser's interest and rights to enforce that interest by court action and prevents the seller from selling the property to another person. The signed contract agreement also obligates the buyer to complete the transaction according to the terms agreed upon in the contract.

Offer and acceptance.   The process of offer and acceptance creates one of the essential elements of a valid contract of sale, that is, a meeting of the minds, whereby the buyer and seller agree on the terms of the sale. An *offer* is a stated promise to perform if the other party agrees. Typically, the buyer makes a written offer to the seller detailing the price and terms to which the buyer commits. If the seller agrees to the offer exactly as it was made and signs the offer, the offer has been *accepted*. A valid contract is created by the delivery of the accepted contract.

The seller may reject the original offer outright or create a *counteroffer*. A counteroffer relieves the buyer from the original offer. The buyer can accept the seller's counteroffer or reject it and possibly make another counteroffer. Any change in the last offer made results in a counteroffer until one party finally agrees to the other party's last offer and both parties sign the final contract.

An offer or counteroffer may be withdrawn at any time before it has been accepted, and an acceptance may be withdrawn at any time prior to the communication of such action to the offeror. When the parties are communicating through an agent or at a distance, questions may arise regarding whether an acceptance, rejection, or counteroffer has effectively taken place. *Delivery* is complex today; most preprinted purchase agreements now include a clause on how delivery may be completed: by email or fax to the party and/or delivery to the agent. In any case, the licensee should transmit all offers, acceptances, or other responses as soon as possible in order to avoid such problems.

Electronic signatures.   For a valid contract, the signatures on the contract must be the signatures of the parties who are entering into the contract; their agent, personal representative, or any other party may not sign for them. Now, the Uniform Electronics Transactions Act (UETA) defines the process by which an **electronic signature** is deemed as acceptable as one signed by pen and ink. The federal E-Sign Act of 2000 further clarifies the requirements. Every state now has similar laws.

Equitable title.   When both buyer and seller have signed a sales contract, the buyer acquires **equitable title**, an equitable right to obtain absolute ownership. While the rights associated with equitable title vary by state, equitable title may give the buyer the right to legally require that the seller transfer the property to the buyer. If the parties decide not to go through with the purchase and sale, the buyer may be required to give the seller a quitclaim deed to release the buyer's equitable interest in the land.

Amendments and addendums.   After the contract is signed and delivered, both parties must agree in writing to any change to the terms. A separate amendment form can be used if the changes are minor. For example, an **amendment** can be used to change the date of closing. The **addendum** is part of the original contract that further identifies and clarifies specific agreements. Usually, the contract specifies "see attached addendum" or similar language. For example, the addendum could specify that the seller drill a well if the property lacks potable (drinkable) water. The addendum must be signed by all parties.

Destruction of the premises.   When the buyer acquires equitable title, unless the contract provides otherwise, the buyer must bear the loss if any damage to or destruction of the property occurs by fire or other casualty. However, many states have adopted the Uniform Vendor and Purchaser Risk Act, an act that specifically provides that the seller (vendor) bear any loss that occurs before the title passes or the buyer (vendee) takes possession. Additionally, many purchase agreements include a clause that specifically assigns the risk to the seller.

Earnest money deposits.   In the purchase agreement, the buyer often includes a deposit, commonly called earnest money, to provide evidence of the buyer's intention to carry out the terms of the contract. The sales contract usually provides that the listing broker holds the deposit for the parties.

The amount of the deposit is negotiable, but in general the deposit should be sufficient to discourage the buyer from defaulting, compensate the seller for taking property off the market, and cover any expenses the seller might incur if the buyer defaults. Most contracts provide that the deposit become the seller's property if the buyer defaults. See liquidated damages discussed earlier in this chapter.

Most state laws require that the broker hold the earnest money in a special trust account or **escrow account**. This money cannot be commingled (mixed) with a broker's personal funds. Usually, one account for all such deposits is sufficient. A broker should maintain full, complete, and accurate records of all earnest money deposits in order to comply with strict state license laws covering these deposits.

OTHER AGREEMENTS

Options

An **option** is a contract by which an *optionor* (generally an owner) gives an *optionee* (prospective purchaser or lessee) the right to buy or lease the owner's property at a fixed price within a stated period of time. The *optionee* pays a fee (the agreed-upon consideration) for this option right and assumes no obligation to make any other payment until deciding, within the specified time, to either (1) exercise the option right (to buy or lease the property) or (2) allow the option right to expire. An option must meet all of the requirements for a contract and is an example of a unilateral contract, one that is enforceable only by the optionee.

At the time the option is signed by the parties, the owner does not sell, nor does the optionee buy. They merely agree that the optionee will have the right to buy and the owner will be obligated to sell if the optionee decides to exercise the right of option. Option contracts should always be recorded to provide constructive notice of the encumbrance against the property.

A common application of an option is a lease that includes an option for the tenant to purchase the property. Options on commercial real estate frequently are made dependent upon the fulfillment of specific conditions, such as obtaining a change in zoning or a building permit. The optionee is usually obligated to exercise the option if the conditions are met. Similar terms could also be included in a sales contract.

The **right of first refusal** gives the tenant a right to buy the real estate only if the owner decides to sell. The owner is not obligated to sell, but if the owner does sell, the owner must first offer the property to the tenant. The sales price may be a certain price set at the time the right of first refusal is given or may be the price the owner would ask in the future.

Leases

A *lease* is a contractual agreement in which the owner agrees to give possession of all or a part of the real estate to another person for a period of time in exchange for a rental fee. Leases are discussed in detail in Chapter 9.

Escrow Agreements

An escrow agreement is usually a separate agreement from the contract that sets forth the duties of the escrow agent and the obligations and requirements of the parties to the transaction. An escrow agreement may be used in closing such real estate transactions as a sale, mortgage loan, exchange of property, installment contract (contract for deed), or lease.

Escrow agreements as used in the closing of a real estate transaction will be further discussed in Chapter 17.

SUMMARY

Contract is defined as an agreement made by competent parties, with adequate consideration, to perform or not to perform some proper or legal action. The essentials of a valid real estate contract are (1) competent parties, (2) mutual assent, (3) seal or consideration, (4) legality of object, and (5) legal form.

Contracts may be classified according to whether the parties' intentions are expressly stated or implied by their actions. They may also be classified as bilateral if both parties have obligated themselves to act or unilateral if one party is obligated to perform only if the other party acts. Many contracts specify a deadline for performance. In any case, all contracts must be performed within a reasonable time. An executed contract is one that has been fully performed. An executory contract is one in which some act remains to be performed. In addition, contracts may be classified according to their legal enforceability as either valid, void, voidable, or unenforceable.

In a number of circumstances, a contract may be canceled before it is fully performed. Furthermore, in many types of contracts, either of the parties may transfer rights and obligations under the agreement by assignment of the contract or novation (i.e., substitution) by a new contract.

If either party to a real estate sales contract defaults, alternative methods of action are available. Contracts usually provide that the seller has the right to declare the contract canceled through forfeiture if the buyer defaults. In general, if either party has suffered a loss because of the other's default, that party may sue for damages to cover the loss. If one party insists on completing the transaction, that party may sue the defaulter for specific performance of the terms of the contract. In this way, a court can order the parties to comply with their agreement.

Contracts frequently used in the real estate business include listing agreements, buyer agency agreements, management agreements, sales contracts, options, leases, and escrow agreements.

A real estate sales contract binds a buyer and seller to a definite transaction, as described in detail in the contract, and provides the buyer with equitable title. The buyer is bound to purchase the property for the amount of consideration stated in the agreement. The seller is bound to deliver a good and marketable title, free from liens and encumbrances (except those allowed by the "subject to" clause of the contract). The purchase contract may be voidable until certain contingencies are met. Amendments and addenda may further explain or alter the original contract. Under most purchase agreements, the seller remains responsible for any losses prior to closing. The amount of earnest money is negotiable and is usually held by the listing broker.

Under an option agreement, the optionee purchases from the optionor, for a limited time period, the exclusive right to purchase or lease the optionor's property. For a potential purchaser or lessee, an option is a means of buying time to consider or complete arrangements for the transaction.

Any real estate transaction may be completed through an escrow, a means by which the parties to the contract carry out the terms of their agreement.

REVIEW QUESTIONS

Please complete all of the questions before turning to the Answer Key on page 340.

1. If both a written contract and an oral contract exist between two parties for the same purpose, the written contract will supersede the oral contract due to
   a. the parol evidence rule.
   b. the statute of limitations.
   c. laches.
   d. caveat emptor.

2. The buyers have a ratified contract to purchase 1200 Main Street with settlement scheduled for October 15. This contract is considered to be
   a. executed.
   b. executory.
   c. implied.
   d. void.

3. A couple is purchasing a property as an assumption. The lender will allow them to assume the existing loan, retaining all of the original terms, but the couple will now be assuming full liability for repayment of the loan. This is
   a. an assignment.
   b. an escrow.
   c. a novation.
   d. an estoppel.

4. The statute of frauds requires that
   a. legal actions be instituted within a reasonable period of time.
   b. real estate purchase contracts be in writing.
   c. a suit for specific performance be filed after any seller default.
   d. a suit to quiet title be used in every transaction.

5. The owner of a property has entered into an agreement with a buyer to convey the property to the buyer by a certain date only if the buyer still wants to acquire the property. This is an example of
   a. a bilateral contract.
   b. an unilateral contract.
   c. an expressed contract.
   d. an implied contract.

6. A seller deliberately gave a purchaser misinformation about planned zoning changes for the seller's property. In this case, the contract between them is
   a. still valid and binding on both parties.
   b. immediately void and without effect.
   c. voidable at the option of the buyer.
   d. voidable at the option of either party.

7. A woman makes an offer to purchase a man's property. The man changes the terms of the offer and returns it to the woman for her acceptance. This becomes a valid contract when the
   a. woman makes her original offer.
   b. man makes his counteroffer.
   c. woman accepts the man's counteroffer.
   d. woman repeats her original offer.

8. A contract is called a bilateral contract if
   a. all the parties to the contract are bound to act.
   b. only one party to the contract is bound to act.
   c. the contract has yet to be fully performed.
   d. one of the parties to the contract is a minor.

9. A seller has signed a listing contract with a licensee in which the broker is specifically authorized to act for the seller, but the seller retains the right to sell the property himself without an obligation to pay the licensee a commission. This is
   a. an exclusive-right-to-sell listing.
   b. an exclusive-agency listing.
   c. an open listing.
   d. a multiple listing.

10. All of the following items are essential elements of a valid contract *EXCEPT*
    a. consideration.
    b. competent parties.
    c. legal purpose.
    d. assignment.

11. A young man inherited a farm from his grandfather. Later, when he was 16, the young man sold it to his uncle. This contract is
    a. valid.
    b. void.
    c. voidable.
    d. executed.

12. A recent retiree has a contract for the purchase of an ocean-front condominium unit. Because of poor health, she has decided not to move to the beach, but would like for a granddaughter to be able to make the purchase under the same terms that are in the existing contract with the seller. This is
    a. a novation.
    b. an assignment.
    c. a substitution.
    d. a rescission.

13. A prospective purchaser has a buyer agency agreement with a broker under which he can work with as many brokers as he likes but only be obligated to pay a commission to the broker who locates a property he ultimately chooses to buy. This is
    a. an exclusive-right-to-represent buyer agreement.
    b. an exclusive-agency right-to-represent buyer agreement.
    c. an open right-to-represent buyer agreement.
    d. a multiple right-to-represent buyer agreement.

14. A man and a woman have a contract whereby the woman has the right to purchase the man's house anytime within the following year at an agreed-upon price. Under this agreement, the man cannot force the woman to go through the sale, but will have to execute the contract at any time of her choice. The woman has executed
    a. an option.
    b. a right of first refusal.
    c. a lease.
    d. a partial performance.

15. The money the buyer presents, along with an offer to purchase, that shows an intent to complete the terms of any contract that might be created with the seller is called
    a. commission.
    b. down payment.
    c. consideration.
    d. earnest money.

16. The type of listing contract that states that the seller wishes to receive a specific amount from the sale of the property and that any proceeds above that amount will be paid to the broker as commission is called
    a. an exclusive-agency listing.
    b. a net listing.
    c. a multiple listing.
    d. an open listing.

17. A man had a ratified contract with a couple for the purchase of their house. When the couple then decided not to move and refused to go to settlement, the man could have asked the court to force the couple to go through with the sale by filing a suit for
    a. quiet title.
    b. partition.
    c. specific performance.
    d. restitution.

18. The seller has agreed to a term in the contract that states that should the buyer breach the contract and refuse to go to settlement, the seller will accept the amount deposited as earnest money with no further obligation for damages. The amount of earnest money is called
    a. compensatory damages.
    b. specific performance.
    c. liquidated damages.
    d. forfeiture.

19. A prospective buyer signed a buyer agency agreement with a broker on July 1 when the broker showed the buyer a property that had been advertised in the local newspaper. It is now three months since that day, and the broker has made no further contact with the prospective buyer. The prospective buyer is able to terminate the buyer agency contract based on broker
    a. performance.
    b. abandonment.
    c. revocation.
    d. suspension.

20. The buyers offered in writing to purchase a house for $220,000, including its draperies, with the offer to expire on Saturday at noon. The sellers reply in writing on Thursday, accepting the $220,000 offer, but excluding the draperies. On Friday, while the buyers consider this counteroffer, the sellers decide to accept the original offer, draperies included, and state so in writing. At this point, the buyers

    a. are legally bound to buy the house.

    b. are not bound to buy the house.

    c. must buy the house and are not entitled to the draperies.

    d. must buy the house but may deduct the value of the draperies from the $220,000.

Leases

LEARNING OBJECTIVES

When you finish reading this chapter, you will be able to

- list and describe the effects of four different leasehold estates,
- identify standard lease provisions,
- discuss the legal principles of leases, and
- describe how rent is determined in the three primary types of leases.

actual eviction	exculpatory clause	lessor
cash rent	graduated lease	market rent
constructive eviction	gross lease	net lease
contract rent	ground lease	percentage lease
economic rent	index lease	sandwich lease
estate at sufferance	lease	sharecropping
estate at will	lease option	sublease
estate for years	lease purchase	
estate from period to period	lessee	

An owner of real estate who does not wish to personally use the property or wants to derive some measure of income from its ownership can allow another person to use it in exchange for valuable consideration. This is usually accomplished by means of an agreement called a **lease**. A lease is a contract between a property owner (called the **lessor**) and a tenant (the **lessee**) that transfers the right to exclusive possession and use of the landlord's property to the tenant for a specified period of time. This agreement sets forth the length of time the contract is to run, the amount to be paid by the lessee for the right to use the property, and other rights and obligations of the parties.

The lease agreement conveys an interest in the real property. The landlord-lessor grants the tenant-lessee the right to occupy the premises and use them for purposes stated in the lease. In return, the landlord retains the right to receive payment for the use of the premises plus a *reversionary right* to retake possession after the lease term has expired. The lessor's interest in leased property is called a leased fee plus reversionary right. The statute of frauds in most states requires that to be enforceable, a lease for a term of more than one year must be in writing and signed by both lessor and lessee.

LEASEHOLD ESTATES

As discussed in Chapter 3, when an owner of real property leases property to a tenant, the tenant's right to occupy the land for the duration of the lease is called a *leasehold*, or *less-than-freehold, estate*. Leasehold estates are *chattels real*. Although they give their owner (the tenant-lessee) an interest in real property, they are in fact personal property and are governed by laws applicable to personal property. When the contract is a lease for life or more than 99 years under which the tenant assumes many of the obligations of the landowner, certain states give the tenant some of the benefits and privileges of a property owner.

The four most important types of leasehold estates are (1) *estate for years*, (2) *estate from period to period*, (3) *estate at will*, and (4) *estate at sufferance* (see Figure 9.1).

FIGURE 9.1   **Leasehold Estates**

Type of estate	Distinguishing characteristics
Estate for years	For definite period of time
Estate from period to period	Automatically renews
Estate at will	For indefinite period of time
Estate at sufferance	Without landlord's consent

ESTATE FOR YEARS

An **estate for years** is a leasehold estate that continues for a definite period—one month, one year, five years, and so on. When a definite term is specified in a written or oral lease and that period of time expires, the tenant (lessee) is required to vacate the premise and surrender possession to the landlord (lessor), unless the parties agree to renew the lease for another specified term. No notice is required to terminate such an estate; the termination date was established in the lease. An estate for years is not terminated by the death of either the landlord or tenant or by the sale of the property.

Estate from Period to Period

An **estate from period to period** (or *periodic estate*) is created when the landlord and tenant enter into an agreement that continues for an indefinite number of definite periods. These estates are generally created by agreement or operation of law to run for a certain amount of time; for example, from month to month, quarter to quarter, or year to year. The agreement is automatically renewed for identical succeeding periods until one of the parties gives notice to terminate. The notice requirement for both tenant and landlord is governed by state law, and it is normally established by the length of the period. For example, a month-to-month periodic estate would require one month's notice from either the tenant or the landlord to terminate the estate. This type of tenancy is more common in residential than in commercial leases. It is not terminated by the death of either party or the sale of the property.

Estate at Will

An **estate at will** is an estate of indefinite duration. It is created at the will of the landlord and will continue to exist until either landlord or tenant serves proper notice to the other of a desire to terminate the estate. Most states have statutory notice requirements to terminate an estate at will. Death of either party, or sale of the property, automatically terminates an estate at will.

Estate at Sufferance

An **estate at sufferance** arises when a tenant who lawfully came into possession of real property continues to hold possession of the premises after those rights have expired, without the consent of the landlord. Because the tenant's original possession was legal, however, the tenant is not considered a trespasser. It is an estate of indefinite duration because the landlord can institute legal action to regain possession of the property at any time.

STANDARD LEASE PROVISIONS

In determining the validity of a lease, the courts apply the rules governing contracts. If the intention to convey temporary possession of a certain parcel of real estate from one person to another is expressed, the courts generally hold that a lease has been created. Most states require no special wording to establish the landlord-tenant relationship. Likewise, the lease may be written, oral, or implied, depending on the circumstances. However, the provisions of the statutes of the state where the real estate is located must be followed to ensure the validity of the lease. Figure 9.2 is an example of a typical residential lease.

Once a valid lease has been signed, the lessor, as the owner of the real estate, is usually bound by the implied covenant of quiet possession. Under this covenant, the lessor guarantees that the lessee may take possession of the leased premises and will not be evicted from these premises by any person who successfully claims to have a title superior to that of the lessor.

FIGURE 9.2   **Residential Lease Agreement**

This form provided to Kaplan Real Estate Education by the Minnesota Association of REALTORS® and is intended for educational purposes only.

RESIDENTIAL LEASE AGREEMENT
This form approved by the Minnesota Association of REALTORS®, which disclaims any liability arising out of use or misuse of this form.
© 2014 Minnesota Association of REALTORS®, Edina, MN

1. Date _____

2. Page 1 of _____

3. Lease Agreement (Lease), dated _____ , 20 _____ , pertaining to the lease of the property

4. located at Street Address: _____

5. _____ City of _____ ,

6. County of _____ , State of Minnesota (Premises), by and between

7. *(list all Tenants)* _____

8. _____ (Tenant)

9. and _____ (Owner). The

10. Premises include(s) a ☐ **garage** ☐ **storage unit** ☐ **parking stall** identified as garage/unit/stall number _____ .
    ----------------------*(Check all that apply.)*----------------------

11. 1. **TERMS OF LEASE:** The following provisions and definitions apply to this Lease. They are modified and supplemented
12.   by the remaining terms of this Lease.

13.   (a) **Term:** The term means *(check only one):*

14.   ☐ the period of _____ months commencing _____

15.   and terminating _____ .

16.   ☐ month-to-month lease commencing _____ .

17.   (b) **Rent:** The rent is $ _____ per month.

18.   (c) **Utilities** (see Paragraph 6):

19.   ☐ Paid by ☐ **Tenant** ☐ **Owner**.
                -----------*(Check one.)*-----------

20.   ☐ Paid in part by each with Tenant to pay for _____

21.   and Owner to pay for _____ .

22.   (d) **Security Deposit:** The security deposit is $ _____ .

23.   (e) **Late Fee:** The late fee is $ _____ (not to exceed eight percent
24.   (8%) of the overdue rent amount).

25.   (f) **Pets** (see Paragraph 14):

26.   ☐ Pets are not allowed.

27.   ☐ Pets are allowed and Tenant may have _____ cats and _____ dogs in the Premises and no pet

28.   may weigh more than _____ pounds. Tenant shall be allowed to have _____
29.   in the Premises.

30.   (g) **Occupants:** The occupants of the Premises are _____

31.   _____

32.   _____ .

MN:RLA-1 (8/14)

Source: Minnesota Association of REALTORS®

FIGURE 9.2 **Residential Lease Agreement (Cont.)**

RESIDENTIAL LEASE AGREEMENT

33.   Page 2   Date _____

34. Premises located at _____ .

35.   (h) **Common Interest Community (CIC):** The Premises ☐ **ARE** ☐ **ARE NOT** part of a CIC.
              ------------*(Check one.)*------------

36.   (i) **Notices:** Addresses for Notices:
37.   If to Owner: If to Tenant:
38.   _____   _____
39.   _____   _____
40.   _____   _____
41.   _____   _____
          (Phone)   (Phone)

42.   (j) **Lead-Based Paint:** The Premises ☐ **WERE** ☐ **WERE NOT** built before 1978. If "were" is checked,
              ---------------*(Check one.)*-----------------

43.   Tenant acknowledges receipt of a copy of the disclosure identified in Paragraph 27. _____
                                                                  (Tenant's initials.)

44. 2. **TERM:** This Lease is for the term set forth in Paragraph 1(a), unless sooner terminated as provided herein, or
45.   unless extended by written agreement by Tenant and Owner prior to the end of Lease term. If Owner and Tenant
46.   fail to agree to mutually acceptable extension/renewal terms, this Lease shall terminate according to its original
47.   term.

48. 3. **OCCUPANCY:** Only Tenant and the occupants listed in Paragraph 1(g) may reside in the Premises, unless otherwise
49.   permitted by law. The number of occupants is restricted in accordance with the Minnesota State Building Code
50.   and/or local building code.

51. 4. **USE OF THE PREMISES:** The Premises, and all utilities, shall be used by Tenant and occupants exclusively as a
52.   private, single family dwelling for residential purposes only. The Premises may not be used for transient, hotel,
53.   commercial, business or other non-residential purposes.

54. 5. **RENT:** During the term of this Lease, Tenant shall pay the rent specified in Paragraph 1(b). Rent shall be paid by
55.   Tenant to Owner on or before the first day of each and every month during the Lease term. Rent is considered
56.   paid when received by Owner. Each Tenant is individually responsible for payment of the full amount of the rent
57.   to Owner, including additional rent as defined in this Lease. Tenant's obligation to pay rent shall survive the
58.   termination of this Lease. Tenant must continue to pay all rent even if Tenant surrenders the Premises or is evicted
59.   by Owner. Rent for any partial month during the term of this Lease shall be prorated.

60. 6. **UTILITIES:** If the "Paid by Tenant" box is checked in Paragraph 1(c), then Tenant shall pay all utilities directly to the
61.   service provider, including water, sewer, gas, electricity, fuel oil, trash removal, recycling, telephone, cable and
62.   association dues. Tenant shall be responsible to Owner for any utilities payments that have not been paid, including
63.   late charges or fees imposed by the service provider.

64.   If the "Paid in part by each" box is checked in Paragraph 1(c), then Tenant shall pay directly to the service provider
65.   the utilities noted in Paragraph 1(c) to be paid for by Tenant and shall be responsible to Owner for any utilities
66.   payments that have not been paid, including late charges or fees imposed by the service provider, and Owner shall
67.   pay directly to the service provider the utilities noted in Paragraph 1(c) to be paid for by Owner. Tenant is responsible
68.   for contracting for and paying for any other utilities desired. No modification to the Premises to install or add utilities
69.   may occur without Owner consent in writing. Any utilities not specified to be paid by Owner shall be paid by Tenant.

70.   If utilities Tenant is to pay for are provided or paid for by Owner, then Tenant shall pay Owner for such utilities upon
71.   demand in the amounts due as identified in statements covering the period during which this Lease is in effect.

MN:RLA-2 (8/14)

Source: Minnesota Association of REALTORS®

FIGURE 9.2   **Residential Lease Agreement (Cont.)**

RESIDENTIAL LEASE AGREEMENT

72.   Page 3   Date _____

73.   Premises located at _____ .

74.   7.   **COMMON INTEREST COMMUNITY:** If the Premises are part of a CIC as noted in Paragraph 1(h), then the
75.   Premises are subject to the declaration, bylaws, rules and regulations and other governing documents of the CIC (the
76.   Governing Documents). Copies of the current Governing Documents have been provided to Tenant and Tenant
77.   acknowledges receipt of the Governing Documents. Tenant shall comply with the Governing Documents, including
78.   any modifications which may be made from time to time by the CIC. Tenant acknowledges that the CIC may have
79.   a right to evict Tenant for failure to comply with the terms of the Governing Documents.

80.   8.   **LATE FEES:** If Owner does not receive the rent on or before the fifth (5th) day of any month, Tenant shall pay
81.   a late fee in the amount stated in Paragraph 1(e) to compensate Owner for the time, expense and administrative
82.   burdens resulting from such late payment. In the event the amount in Paragraph 1(e) exceeds eight percent (8%)
83.   of the overdue rent payment, the late fee shall be eight percent (8%) of the overdue amount in order to comply
84.   with MN Statute Chapter 504B. The late fee shall be considered additional rent. Tenant shall be assessed a returned
85.   check fee in the amount of $40 as additional rent for each unpaid check which is returned by the Tenant's bank.

86.   9.   **SECURITY DEPOSIT:** Owner acknowledges receipt of the security deposit from Tenant in the amount set forth
87.   in Paragraph 1(d). Owner shall retain the security deposit for the entire term of this Lease, including any extensions.
88.   Owner may use the security deposit as permitted by Minnesota law, and shall, to the extent required by Minnesota
89.   law, return any remaining portion of the security deposit, as well as any required interest, to Tenant following the
90.   termination of this Lease. If Owner uses a portion of the security deposit during the Lease to cure a default by
91.   Tenant, Tenant shall replenish the security deposit to the full amount, upon request by Owner.

92.   10.   **DAMAGE TO THE PREMISES:** Tenant shall pay for all loss, damage, costs or expenses (including but not limited
93.   to problems with or damage to plumbing, electrical and appliances) caused by Tenant's willful or negligent conduct,
94.   or the conduct of any occupant, guest or person under Tenant's or any occupant's direction or control. Tenant
95.   shall promptly notify Owner of any conditions which may cause damage to the Premises or waste of utilities or other
96.   services provided by Owner. The Premises may not be modified, altered, improved or repaired without prior
97.   authorization from Owner, in writing. Modification includes but is not limited to modification of floor covering or wall
98.   covering, changing/replacing/adding fixtures or attachments, painting or anything which creates a hole or mark
99.   that cannot be remedied without expense to the Owner.

100.   11.   **INSPECTION OF THE PREMISES AND RIGHT OF ENTRY:** Owner, or Owner's designee, may enter upon the
101.   Premises for any reasonable business purpose, including to inspect the Premises from time to time. Owner
102.   shall make a reasonable effort to give reasonable notice to Tenant before entering the Premises, except in the case
103.   of an emergency. In the event Owner enters the Premises for emergency purposes, Owner shall provide written
104.   confirmation to Tenant of the emergency entry, which confirmation shall include the date, time and purpose of the
105.   emergency entry.

106.   12.   **COVENANTS OF OWNER:** Owner covenants and promises that:

107.   (i)   the Premises are fit for residential use as a single family dwelling;

108.   (ii)   Owner will make all necessary repairs to the Premises during the term of the Lease, except where damage is
109.   caused by Tenant, any occupant and/or any guest or person under Tenant's or any occupant's direction or
110.   control;

111.   (iii)   Owner shall keep the Premises up to applicable federal, state and local codes, except where a code violation
112.   is caused by Tenant, any occupant and/or any guest or person under Tenant's or any occupant's direction
113.   or control, in which case Tenant shall correct the code violation at Tenant's sole cost. Tenant shall notify
114.   Owner in writing of any necessary repairs before engaging in such repair.

MN:RLA-3 (8/14)

Source: Minnesota Association of REALTORS®

FIGURE 9.2 **Residential Lease Agreement (Cont.)**

RESIDENTIAL LEASE AGREEMENT

115.   Page 4   Date _____

116.   Premises located at _____ .

117.   13. **COVENANTS OF TENANT:** Tenant covenants and promises that:
118.   (i)   Tenant will not cause damage to the Premises or allow the Premises to be damaged by others;
119.   (ii)   Tenant will not make alterations or additions to the Premises (including but not limited to such issues as
120.   are identified in Paragraph 10) without the prior written consent of Owner;
121.   (iii) Tenant will not remove any of Owner's personal property from the Premises (including but not limited to
122.   appliances);
123.   (iv)   Tenant will maintain the Premises in a clean and habitable condition;
124.   (v)   Tenant will not disturb the peace and quiet of other tenants in the building and/or neighbors, or allow
125.   any occupant or guest to do so;
126.   (vi)   Tenant will not store hazardous or flammable substances on the Premises;
127.   (vii) Tenant will not use the Premises for illegal or unlawful activities, or in an illegal manner, or in a manner
128.   which would cause cancellation, restriction or increase in premiums for Owner's insurance, or such use
129.   as which would constitute a violation of applicable code or ordinance;
130.   (viii) Tenant shall not have water beds or any water-filled furniture in the Premises;
131.   (ix)   Tenant will not smoke in the Premises or permit smoking to occur in the Premises; and
132.   (x)   Tenant will not interfere with Owner in the management of the Premises or the property surrounding the
133.   Premises.

134.   14. **PETS:** If the "Pets are not allowed" box is checked in Paragraph 1(f), Tenant shall not have animals or pets of any
135.   kind in the Premises. If the "Pets are allowed" box is checked in Paragraph 1(f), Tenant may have in the Premises
136.   the pets noted in Paragraph 1(f).

137.   15. **VEHICLE STORAGE:** Neither Tenant nor any occupant shall store or park any unlicensed or inoperable vehicle,
138.   or any motor home, camper, trailer, boat or other recreational vehicle on or around the Premises. Neither Tenant
139.   nor any occupant shall store or park any commercial truck on or around the Premises. If, after three (3) days' notice
140.   to Tenant, Tenant fails to remove an unauthorized vehicle from on or around the Premises, Owner may remove
141.   and store the vehicle, and Tenant shall pay the removal and storage expenses as additional rent.

142.   16. **LOCKS:** Tenant may not add or change any locks on the Premises. At Tenant's request, Owner shall change or
143.   re-key the locks at Tenant's expense. Tenant shall pay a $150 fee for Owner to re-key the Premises, in the event
144.   a key is lost or missing.

145.   17. **TRANSFER OF LEASE:** Tenant may not sublet all or part of the Premises without Owner's prior written consent.
146.   Tenant may not assign or sell this Lease without Owner's prior written consent.

147.   18. **DAMAGE TO TENANT'S PROPERTY:** Owner shall not be responsible for any damage to Tenant's property, unless
148.   such damage is caused by Owner's willful or grossly negligent conduct.

149.   19. **HOLDING OVER:** Tenant may not continue to occupy the Premises after the initial term of this Lease unless this
150.   Lease has been renewed in writing, or unless Owner consents to Tenant holding over. If Owner consents to Tenant
151.   holding over without a written Lease extension, all provisions herein shall remain applicable except that the term of
152.   the Lease shall be month-to-month. If Lease becomes month-to-month, written notice to terminate is required by
153.   Owner or Tenant to end the Lease. Such written notice must end the Lease on the last day of a month, and must
154.   be received before the first day of that month (e.g., notice to terminate the Lease on July 31st must be given on
155.   or before the preceding June 30th).

156.   20. **MOVING OUT:** Tenant and occupants shall move out not later than 12:00 p.m. (noon) on the last day of the Lease
157.   term, or any extension thereof. Tenant must leave the Premises in the same condition as it was as of the date of
158.   commencement of the Lease term, ordinary wear and tear excepted. Tenant shall remove all personal property of
159.   Tenant and occupants, including trash, from the Premises (including any storage unit, garage or parking space).
160.   Tenant shall provide Owner with Tenant's forwarding address. If Tenant fails to return to Owner all keys and garage
161.   door openers within 24 hours of moving out, Tenant shall pay the costs of changing the locks and reprogramming
162.   the garage opener.

MN:RLA-4 (8/14)

Source: Minnesota Association of REALTORS®

FIGURE 9.2   **Residential Lease Agreement (Cont.)**

RESIDENTIAL LEASE AGREEMENT

163.   Page 5   Date _____

164.   Premises located at _____ .

165.   21. **DESTRUCTION OF PREMISES:** If the Premises are destroyed or become uninhabitable or unfit for occupancy, this
166.   Lease shall terminate upon reasonable written notice to Tenant, unless Owner, in Owner's reasonable discretion,
167.   believes Owner can complete necessary repairs to the Premises in a reasonable period of time. If the damage or
168.   destruction was not a result of any fault or negligence of Tenant, Tenant shall not be responsible for payment of
169.   rent for the period of time in which the Premises are uninhabitable or unfit for occupancy provided such determination
170.   has been agreed by Owner and Tenant or by a court of competent jurisdiction.

171.   22. **BREACH OF LEASE:** In the event of Tenant's breach of any term of this Lease, Owner has a right of re-entry and
172.   may pursue all remedies available by law, including but not limited to the following:
173.   (i)   bring an eviction action immediately to remove Tenant and occupant from the Premises; or
174.   (ii) demand in writing that Tenant immediately, or at some specified future date, surrender the Premises to
175.   Owner and if Tenant fails to do so, Owner may bring an eviction action; or
176.   (iii) terminate this Lease upon five (5) days written notice to Tenant. Owner's acceptance of rent or additional
177.   rent during the time Tenant continues to occupy the Premises shall not be construed as a waiver of Owner's
178.   right to evict Tenant. Tenant's obligation to pay rent shall continue after Tenant's eviction from the Premises,
179.   through the expiration of the Lease term.

180.   23. **ELECTION OF REMEDIES:** Either Owner or Tenant may exercise any or all of its legal rights and remedies at any
181.   time or from time to time, and the exercise of a particular remedy shall not be construed as a waiver of that party's
182.   right to exercise some other remedy or as an election of remedies.

183.   24. **MISCELLANEOUS:**
184.   (a) This Lease is subordinate to any mortgage on the Premises. Tenant shall sign any documents reasonably
185.   requested by Owner, and hereby appoints Owner as Tenant's attorney-in-fact to execute such documents
186.   as may be requested by a mortgagee.
187.   (b) Any attachments to this Lease, such as rules and regulations, are part of this Lease.
188.   (c) This Lease and any attachments comprise the entire agreement between Owner and Tenant. No oral
189.   representations have been made. This Lease may not be modified except by written agreement of the
190.   parties.

191.   25. **NOTICES:** All notices and communications from Owner or Tenant to the other, required or permitted hereunder,
192.   shall be in writing and shall be considered to have been duly given if personally delivered or if sent by first class
193.   mail, postage prepaid, to the other party at the address set forth in paragraph 1(i), or to such other address as
194.   such party may hereafter designate by notice to the other party. Notice given to one Tenant shall be considered
195.   given to all Tenants.

196.   26. **PROHIBITIONS AND STATUTORY NOTICES:** Owner and Tenant covenant and agree that neither will:
197.   (i)   unlawfully allow controlled substances in the Premises or in the common area and curtilage of the Premises;
198.   (ii) allow prostitution or prostitution-related activity as defined in MN Statute 617.80, Subd. 4, to occur on the
199.   Premises or in the common area and curtilage of the Premises;
200.   (iii) allow the unlawful use or possession of a firearm in violation of section 609.66, Subd. 1(a), 609.67 or
201.   624.713, on the Premises or in the common area and curtilage of the Premises; or
202.   (iv) allow stolen property or property obtained by robbery in the Premises or in the common area and curtilage
203.   of the Premises.

204.   Owner and Tenant further agree that neither they nor any person under their control will use the common area
205.   and curtilage of the Premises to manufacture, sell, give away, barter, deliver, exchange, distribute, purchase or
206.   possess a controlled substance in violation of any criminal provision of MN Statute Chapter 152. This covenant
207.   is not violated when a person other than the Owner or Tenant possesses or allows controlled substances in the
208.   Premises, common area or curtilage, unless the Owner or Tenant knew or had reason to know of that activity.

209.   The following notice is required by MN Statute 504B.305:
210.   A seizure under MN Statute 609.5317, Subd. 1, for which there is not a defense under MN Statute 609.5317,
211.   Subd. 3, constitutes unlawful detention by Tenant.

MN:RLA-5 (8/14)

Source: Minnesota Association of REALTORS®

FIGURE 9.2 **Residential Lease Agreement (Cont.)**

RESIDENTIAL LEASE AGREEMENT

212. Page 6   Date _____

213. Premises located at _____ .

214. 27. **LEAD-BASED PAINT DISCLOSURE:** If it is indicated in Paragraph 1(j) that the Premises were built before 1978,
215. then the Minnesota Association of REALTORS® Addendum to Lease Agreement Disclosure of Information on
216. Lead-Based Paint and Lead-Based Paint Hazards is attached to this Lease and is made a part of this Lease.

217. 28. **ADDENDA AND PAGE NUMBERING: Attached addenda are a part of this Residential Lease Agreement.**

218. **Enter total number of pages of this Residential Lease Agreement, including addenda, on line two (2) of**
219. **page one (1).**

220. 29. **ELECTRONIC SIGNATURES:** The parties agree the electronic signature of any party on any document related
221. to this transaction constitute valid, binding signatures.

222. 30. **RECEIPT OF COPY:** Tenant acknowledges receiving a copy of this Lease.

223. _____   _____
      (Owner)   (Date)   (Tenant)   (Date)

224. _____   _____
      (Owner)   (Date)   (Tenant)   (Date)

225.   _____
                                        (Tenant)   (Date)

226.   _____
                                        (Tenant)   (Date)

227.   **THIS MINNESOTA ASSOCIATION OF REALTORS® RESIDENTIAL LEASE AGREEMENT IS NOT**
228.   **DESIGNED TO BE AND IS NOT WARRANTED TO BE INCLUSIVE OF ALL ISSUES OWNER AND**
229.   **TENANT MAY WISH TO ADDRESS, AND EITHER PARTY MAY WISH TO MODIFY THIS LEASE TO**
230.   **ADDRESS STATUTORY OR CONTRACTUAL MATTERS NOT CONTAINED IN THIS FORM.**
231.   **BOTH PARTIES ARE ADVISED TO SEEK THE ADVICE OF AN ATTORNEY TO ENSURE**
232.   **THIS CONTRACT ADEQUATELY ADDRESSES THAT PARTY'S RIGHTS.**

MN:RLA-6 (8/14)

Source: Minnesota Association of REALTORS®

Requirements for a Valid Lease

The requirements for a valid lease are essentially the same as those for any other real estate contract. Specifically, the essentials of a valid lease are as follows:

- *Competent parties.* The parties must have the legal capacity to contract.

- *Mutual assent.* The parties must reach a mutual agreement on all the terms of the contract.

- *Legality of object.* The objectives of the lease must be legal.

Contract in writing. The statutes of frauds generally requires that leases that will not be fully performed within one year be in writing in order to be enforceable in court. When the statute of frauds applies but the provisions of the lease do not comply with its terms, the lease is considered unenforceable.

Valuable consideration. Every contract must be supported by valid, valuable consideration. In leasing real estate, rent is the usual consideration granted for the right to occupy the leased premises. Some courts have construed rent as being any consideration that supports the lease; for example, most ground leases and long-term leases provide that the tenant must pay all property charges—such as real estate taxes, insurance premiums, and the like—in addition to the rent.

The amount of rent the tenant must pay for use of the premises is set forth in the lease contract and is called the **contract rent**. The amount of rent the property would command in a fully informed competitive marketplace is called the **economic rent** or **market rent**. When the lease contract is negotiated, the contract rent and the economic rent are normally the same. But as the lease runs its term, the two may differ. In long-term lease situations, the lessor might provide for adjustments in the amount of rent throughout the term of the lease.

It is important to state specifically when the rent is to be paid to the lessor. If it is to be paid in advance or at any time other than the end of the term, the contract should state that fact. The law states that rent becomes due only at the end of the term (weekly, monthly, or yearly), unless it is specifically agreed to the contrary.

Description of the premises. A description of the leased premises should be clearly stated. If the lease covers land, the legal description of the real estate should be used. If the lease is for a part of the building, such as office space or an apartment, the space itself or the apartment designation should be clearly and carefully described. If supplemental space is to be included, the lease should clearly identify the space.

Signatures. To be valid, a lease must be signed by the landlord because the courts consider a lease to be a conveyance of an interest in real estate. When a married lessor holds interest in severalty, most states require the spouse to join in signing the lease in order to release any homestead or inheritance rights. The tenant's signature is usually not essential if the tenant has actually taken possession. Of course, it is considered better practice for both parties to sign the lease.

Use of Premises

A lessor may restrict a lessee's use of the premises through provisions included in the lease. For example, a lease may provide that the lease premises are to be used only for residential purposes and not for running a business or for the purpose of a real estate office and for no other. In the absence of such limitations, a lessee may use the premises for any lawful purpose.

Term of the Lease

The term of a lease is the period for which the lease will run and should be set out precisely. Good practice requires that the date of the beginning of the term and the date of its ending be stated together with a statement of the total period of the lease, for example, "for a term of 30 years beginning June 1, 2000, and ending May 31, 2030." Courts hold that a lease with an indefinite term is not valid, unless the language of the lease and the surrounding circumstances clearly indicate that a perpetual lease is the intention of the parties. Leases are controlled by the statutes of the various states and must be in accordance with those provisions. In some states, terms of agricultural leases are limited by statute. Also, the laws of some states prohibit leases of more than 99 years.

Security Deposits

Most leases require the tenant to provide some form of security. This security, which guarantees payment of rent and safeguards against a tenant's destruction of the premises, may be established by (1) contracting for a lien on the tenant's property, (2) requiring the tenant to pay a portion of the rent in advance, (3) requiring the tenant to post security, and/ or (4) requiring the tenant to have some third party guarantee the payment of the rent. Some states have laws that specify how security deposits must be handled and require that lessees receive annual interest on their security deposits.

Exculpatory Clauses

Landlords sometimes insert an **exculpatory clause** in the lease, which exculpates or excuses the landlord for any liability for negligence in maintaining the leased property. Some states allow this type of clause, while others do not.

LEGAL PRINCIPLES OF LEASES

Most states provide that leases can be filed for record in the county in which the property is located; however, unless the lease is for a relatively long term, it is not usually recorded. Possession of the property by the lessee is constructive notice to the world of the lessee's rights, and an inspection of the property will result in actual notice of the lessee's leasehold interest.

In some states, only a memorandum of lease is filed for record. The terms of the lease are not disclosed to the public by the filing; however, the objective of giving public notice of the rights of the lessee is still accomplished. The memorandum of lease must set forth the names of the parties and a description of the property leased.

Possession of the Leased Premises

Leases carry the implied covenant that the landlord will give the tenant possession of the premises and the right of *quiet enjoyment*. In most states, the landlord must give the tenant actual possession, or occupancy, of the leased premises. Thus, if the premises are occupied by a holdover tenant, or adverse claimant, at the beginning of the new lease period, it is the landlord's duty to bring whatever action is necessary to recover possession as well as to bear the expense of this action. However, in a few states, the landlord is only bound to give the tenant the right of possession. It is the tenant's obligation to bring any court action necessary to secure actual possession.

Maintenance of Premises

Most states require a lessor to maintain dwelling units in a habitable condition and to make any necessary repairs to common elements, such as hallways, stairs, or elevators. Constructive eviction, the tenant's right to terminate the lease if the landlord does not provide certain essential services, is discussed later in this chapter. The tenant does not have to make any repairs, but must return the premises in the same condition as they were when received, with certain allowances for ordinary use.

Improvements

The tenant may make improvements with the landlord's permission, but any such alterations in residential properties generally become the property of the landlord by accession; that is, they become fixtures. However, as discussed in Chapter 2, a commercial tenant may be given the right to install trade fixtures or chattel fixtures by the terms of the lease. Such trade fixtures may be removed by the tenant before the expiration of the lease, provided the tenant restores the premises to the condition they were in at the time of possession.

Assignment and Subleasing

A lessee may assign the lease or may sublease the premises as long as the terms of the lease contract do not prohibit these actions (see Figure 9.3). An *assignment* is the total transfer to another person (assignee) of all the tenant's (assignor's) right, title, and interest in the leasehold estate. After an assignment is completed, the assignee becomes called the tenant. The original tenant has no further interest in the leasehold estate, but does remain secondarily liable for the payment of rent. Under novation, the landlord releases the original tenant from all obligations and transfers all rights and obligations to the assignee.

FIGURE 9.3   Assignment Versus Subletting

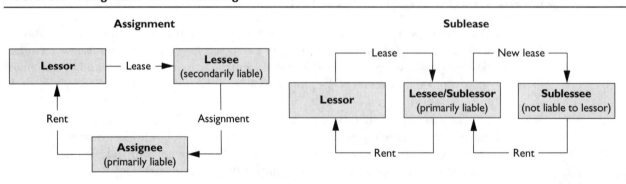

A **sublease** involves a transfer of only a portion of the rights held under a leasehold estate. Therefore, a sublease may concern only a portion of the leased premises or only a part of the lease term. The party acquiring the rights under a sublease is called the sublessee, while the original tenant becomes the sublessor. Generally, the sublessee pays rent to the sublessor, who in turn pays rent to the landlord. Because the interest of the original tenant is located between the interest of the property owner (landlord) and the end-user of the property (sublessee), it is also called a **sandwich lease**.

Options

Many leases contain an option that grants the lessee the privilege of renewing the lease but requires that the lessee give notice on or before a specific date of the intent to exercise the option. Some leases grant to the lessee the option to purchase the leased premises. The provisions for the option to purchase vary widely.

Destruction of Leased Premises

The state's residential landlord tenant law determines a tenant's obligation if the leased property is partially or completely destroyed. Residential tenants may be relieved of paying some or all of the rent, depending on the situation. In land leases involving agricultural land, the courts have held that damage or destruction of the improvements, even if it is not the tenant's fault, does not relieve the tenant from the obligation to pay rent to the end of the term. This ruling has been extended in most states to include ground leases upon which the tenant has constructed a building and, in many instances, leases that give possession of an entire building to the tenant.

In those cases where the leased premises are only a part of the building (such as office or commercial space), upon destruction of the leased premises, the tenant is not always required to continue to pay rent. Furthermore, in some states, if the property was destroyed as a result of the landlord's negligence, sometimes the tenant can recover damages from the landlord.

Termination of a Lease

A written lease for a definite period of time expires at the end of that time period; no separate notice is required to terminate the lease when it expires. Oral and written leases that do not specify a definite expiration date (such as a month-to-month or year-to-year tenancy or a tenancy at will) may be terminated by giving proper notice in advance as required by state law. Generally, the laws specify a minimum time period or number of days' notice that must be given by the party who wishes to terminate the lease.

When the conditions of a lease are breached (broken), a landlord may terminate the lease and evict the tenant. This kind of action must be handled through a court proceeding according to state law.

The parties to a lease may mutually agree to cancel the lease. The tenant may offer to surrender the lease and, if accepted by the landlord, will result in termination. A tenant who abandons leased property, however, remains liable for the terms of the lease—including the rent. In such cases, the terms of the specific lease usually dictate whether the landlord is obligated to try to rent the space.

In general, a lease does not terminate if either of the parties die. The heirs of a deceased landlord or tenant are bound by the terms of existing valid leases. Death only terminates a lease if either it is a tenancy or will or if the landlord has leased a life estate and the person on whose life the estate is based dies.

In addition, a lease does not terminate if a landlord sells the leased property. In such a case, the new owner takes the property subject to the rights of the tenants. However, a lease will be terminated in the event that the property is acquired by the government through condemnation, the landlord is declared bankrupt, or if the property is foreclosed upon by a lienholder. In some states, that lien must have predated the leases.

Breach of Lease

When a tenant breaches any lease provision, the landlord may sue the tenant to obtain a judgment to cover past due rent, damages to the premises, or other defaults. Likewise, when a landlord breaches any lease provision, the tenant is entitled to similar remedies.

Landlord's remedies/actual eviction.   When a tenant improperly retains possession of leased premises, the landlord may regain possession through a *suit for possession*. This process is called **actual eviction**. The law requires the landlord to serve notice on the tenant before commencing the suit. Depending on state laws, a five-day or ten-day notice must be given before filing a suit for possession based on a default in payment of rent. When a court issues a judgment for possession to a landlord, the tenant must peaceably vacate the premises and remove all belongings, or the landlord can have the judgment enforced by a bailiff or other court officer, who will forcibly remove the tenant.

Tenants' remedies/constructive eviction.   If a landlord breaches any clause of a lease agreement, the tenant has the right to sue, claiming a judgment for damages against the landlord. If an action or omission on the landlord's part results in the leased premises becoming uninhabitable for the purpose intended in the lease, the tenant may have the right to abandon the premises. This action, called **constructive eviction**, terminates the lease agreement if the tenant can prove that the premises have become uninhabitable because of the conscious neglect of the landlord. In order to claim constructive eviction, the tenant must actually vacate the premises while the uninhabitable condition exists. In some states, the tenant must remove all belongings as well.

For example, a lease requires the landlord to furnish heat in the winter. Because of the landlord's failure to repair a defective furnace, the heat is not provided. If this results in the leased premises being untenable, the tenant may abandon them. Some leases provide that if the failure to furnish heat is accidental and not the fault of the landlord, it does not constitute grounds for constructive eviction.

Tenants' Rights

For the most part, leases are drawn up primarily for the benefit of the landlord. Recent consumer awareness, however, has fostered the belief that a valid lease depends on both parties fulfilling certain obligations.

Uniform Residential Landlord and Tenant Act (URLTA).   To provide laws outlining such obligations, nearly two dozen states have adopted some variation of the Uniform Residential Landlord and Tenant Act (URLTA). This model law addresses such issues as the landlord's right of entry, maintenance of premises, response to tenant complaints, and disclosure of the property owners' names and addresses to the tenants. The act further sets down specific remedies available to both the landlord and the tenant if a breach of the lease agreement occurs. Even if the licensee is managing only one property, the licensee should be familiar with that particular state law.

Americans with Disabilities Act (ADA).   The Americans with Disabilities Act (ADA) (discussed further in Chapter 15) has a significant impact on commercial, nonresidential leasing practices. Any property in which public goods or services are provided must be free of architectural barriers or must accommodate individuals with disabilities so that they can enjoy access to those businesses or services.

Fair Housing Act. The Fair Housing Act (also discussed in Chapter 15) makes it illegal to discriminate against prospective tenants on the basis of any of the seven federally protected classes: race, color, religion, national origin, sex, familial status, and disability. State and local jurisdictions may have additional protected classes.

Tenants with disabilities must be permitted to make reasonable structural modifications (at their own expense) to units and public/common areas in a dwelling constructed prior to March 13, 1991, when those modifications may be necessary for a person with a disability to have full enjoyment of a dwelling. A landlord may require that rental premises be restored to their original condition at the end of the lease term. A landlord may require a tenant with a disability to place money in a separate trust account to cover the cost of restoring the unit. The act also dictates certain design standards for new construction of multifamily housing with four or more units, including accessibility arrangements in ground floor units and units served by an elevator.

Protecting Tenants at Foreclosure Act of 2009. In the past, most tenants lost their lease when a property was foreclosed. Under the Protecting Tenants at Foreclosure Act of 2009, leases survived a foreclosure, meaning that the tenant could stay at least until the end of the lease or for 90 days on a month-to-month lease. This act expired on December 31, 2014.

Some states have adopted laws requiring landlords to provide tenants with written notice of a mortgage default, notice of mortgage acceleration, or notice of foreclosure sale within five business days after the landlord receives written notice from the lender.

TYPES OF LEASES

The manner in which rent is determined indicates the type of lease in force. The three primary types of leases based on rentals are (1) *gross lease*, (2) *net lease*, and (3) *percentage lease* (see Figure 9.4).

FIGURE 9.4 **Types of Leases**

Type of lease	Lessee	Lessor
Gross lease (residential)	Pays basic rent	Pays property charges (taxes, repairs, insurance, etc.)
Net lease (commercial/industrial)	Pays basic rent plus all or most property charges	May pay some property charges
Percentage lease (commercial/industrial)	Pays basic rent plus percent of gross sales (may pay property costs)	May pay some or all property charges

Gross Lease

A **gross lease** provides for a fixed rental. The tenant is obligated to pay a fixed rental, and the landlord pays all property charges. This type of lease is most often used for rentals of residential properties, either single family or apartments.

Net Lease

The **net lease** provides that, in addition to the rent, the tenant pays all or part of the property charges except principal and interest on the owner's debt, which remain the owner's responsibility. In general, tenants are obligated to pay taxes, insurance, and maintenance for the property. The monthly rental paid to the landlord is in addition to these charges, so it is net income for the landlord after operating costs have been paid. Leases for entire commercial or industrial buildings (and the land on which they stand), long-term leases, and ground leases (discussed later in this chapter) are usually net leases.

Percentage Lease

A **percentage lease** bases the rent on a percentage of the gross income received by the tenant doing business on the leased property and is most often found in the rental of retail business locations. The percentage lease usually consists of a base rent plus a percentage of that portion of the tenant's business income that exceeds a stated minimum.

For example, a lease might provide for a minimum monthly rental of $1,200 with the further agreement that the tenant pay an additional monthly amount equivalent to 4% of all gross sales in excess of $30,000 (while the $1,200 rental represents 4% of $30,000 gross, the percentage feature of this lease will not actually begin to apply until after the tenant has grossed in excess of $30,000). The percentage charged in such leases varies widely with the nature of the business, and it is negotiable between landlord and tenant. A tenant's bargaining power is determined by the volume of business. Of course, percentages vary with the location of the property and general economic conditions.

Other Types of Leases

Several types of leases allow for changes in the fixed rental charge during the lease period.

Graduated lease.   A **graduated lease** begins with rent payments at a fixed, often low rate, with increases at set intervals during the term of the lease. For long-term commercial tenants, the advantage is the ability to avoid a heavy financial burden in the early years of business.

Index lease.   The **index lease** calls for an adjustment in the rent based on some designated index, such as the consumer price index or the wholesale price index.

Ground lease.   When a landowner leases the land to a tenant who agrees to erect a building on it, the lease is usually called a **ground lease**. Such a lease must be for a term long enough to make the transaction desirable to the tenant making the investment in the building. These leases are generally net leases that require the lessee to pay rent plus real estate taxes, insurance, upkeep, and repairs. Ground leases can run for terms of 50 years or longer, and a lease for 99 years is not impossible.

Oil and gas lease.   Special lease agreements are prepared when leasing subsurface minerals, such as gas, oil coal, and kaolin. Usually, the landowner receives a cash payment for executing the lease. The lease may expire if no action is taken within a time period stated in the lease. However, most oil and gas leases provide that the company may pay another flat rental fee to continue its rights. If oil and/or gas is found, the landowner usually receives a percentage of its value as royalty. In this case, the lease will continue for as long as oil and/or gas is obtained in significant quantities.

Lease option/right to purchase.   A **lease option** allows the tenant the right to purchase the leased property at a predetermined price for a certain period. Although it is not required, the owner will frequently give the tenant credit toward the purchase price for some of the rent paid. In a lease option, the lease is the primary consideration and the option is secondary.

Lease purchase.   A **lease purchase** is used when the tenant wants to purchase the property and is unable to do so presently yet still needs the use of the leased facility. Common reasons for using a lease purchase are current inability to obtain favorable financing or clear title or because of the unfavorable tax consequences of a current purchase. In this case, the purchase agreement is the primary consideration and the lease is secondary.

Agricultural lease.   Agricultural landowners often lease their land to tenant farmers, who provide the labor to produce and harvest the crop. The tenant can pay the owner in one of two ways: as an agreed-on rental amount in cash in advance (**cash rent**) or as a percentage of the profits from the sale of the crop when it is sold (**sharecropping**).

SUMMARY

A lease is an agreement that grants one person the right to use the property of another for a certain period in return for valuable consideration. The lease agreement is a combination of a conveyance creating a leasehold interest in the property and a contract outlining the rights and obligations of the landlord (lessor) and the tenant (lessee). A leasehold estate is generally classified as the personal property of the lessee.

The requirements for a valid lease include competent parties, mutual assent, legality of object, signatures, valuable considerations, and a description of the leased property. In addition, state statutes of frauds generally require that any lease that runs longer than one year must be in writing in order to be enforceable in court. Leases also generally include clauses relating to such rights and obligations of the landlord and tenant as the use of the premises, subletting, assignment, judgments, maintenance of the premises, and termination of the lease period.

Leases may be terminated by the expiration of the lease period, the mutual agreement of the parties (surrender), or a breach of the lease by either the landlord or the tenant. Neither the death of the landlord nor the landlord's sale of the rented property terminates a lease.

Upon a tenant's default on any of the lease provisions, a landlord may sue for a money judgment or for actual eviction when a tenant has improperly retained possession of the premises. If the premises have become uninhabitable due to the landlord's negligence, the tenant may have the right of constructive eviction, that is, the right to abandon the premises and refuse to pay rent until the premises are repaired.

Several basic types of leases, including gross leases, net leases, percentage leases, graduated leases, and index leases, are classified according to the method used in determining the rental rate of the property.

REVIEW QUESTIONS

Please complete all of the questions before turning to the Answer Key on page 340.

1. A lease can *ALWAYS* be terminated by
   a. mutual agreement of landlord and tenant.
   b. death of the landlord.
   c. sale of the property.
   d. unilateral rescission by either landlord or tenant.

2. A lease on an office building that allows for increases or decreases based on the 11th District Cost of Funds is
   a. an index lease.
   b. a gross lease.
   c. a ground lease.
   d. a percentage lease.

3. A young woman has a 99-year lease on farmland she inherited from her grandmother. This type of lease may take on the implication of being a
   a. leasehold interest.
   b. freehold interest.
   c. tenancy at sufferance.
   d. tenancy at will.

4. A tenant has a lease that runs from July 1 of this year to June 30 of the next year. A termination notice will *NOT* be required because this is an estate
   a. at will.
   b. for years.
   c. from period to period.
   d. at sufferance.

5. A landlord refuses to make the necessary repairs to a 60-year-old furnace in order for it to adequately heat his 12-unit apartment building. It is the middle of January and the average temperature in the area is –5 degrees. His tenants have the right to abandon the building based on
   a. a suit for possession.
   b. a judgment lien.
   c. an actual eviction.
   d. a constructive eviction.

6. A business pays a fixed amount of rent each month, but the landlord pays for all operating expenses connected with the property. The owner of the business has a
   a. gross lease.
   b. net lease.
   c. graduated lease.
   d. percentage lease.

7. A woman has been renting a garage apartment from a man with a one-year lease that has been renewed three times. The man now wants to convert that garage space into a recreation room and the lease is not renewed. The woman refuses to vacate the property, becoming a tenant
   a. in common.
   b. at sufferance.
   c. by the entirety.
   d. at will.

8. When calculating the property charges for a property under a net lease, the lessee could include all of the following *EXCEPT*
   a. maintenance expenses for the property.
   b. real estate taxes due on the property.
   c. mortgage payments required on the property.
   d. hazard and liability insurance for the property.

9. A business occupies rental space in a shopping mall. The owner pays $1,200 per month as base rent plus 10% of her gross profit each month. The business owner has
   a. a net lease.
   b. a gross lease.
   c. a percentage lease.
   d. an index lease.

10. A young couple has found a house they would like to buy, but they are not financially able to come up with a down payment and closing costs this year. They would like to rent the house for a year and then proceed with the purchase based on contract terms that can be agreed upon now. This is called
    a. a ground lease.
    b. a lease option.
    c. a lease purchase.
    d. sharecropping.

11. A new dentist is opening a new office and has agreed to a three-year lease that starts at $800 a month for the first year, increases to $900 a month the following year, and increases again to $1,000 per month for the third year. This is a
    a. percentage lease.
    b. index lease.
    c. graduated lease.
    d. gross lease.

12. A tenant who has a lease that automatically renews every week has an estate
    a. at will.
    b. for years.
    c. at sufferance.
    d. from period to period.

13. Which of the following statements concerning leasehold estates is *TRUE*?
    a. The property owner is called the lessee.
    b. The leasehold interest is personal property.
    c. The tenant's interest is called a leased fee.
    d. The tenant must record the lease for it to be valid.

14. A residential rental apartment building has been sold to a new owner, who feels that the current leases are underpriced. The new owner wants to negotiate new leases with the tenants immediately, rather than wait for each lease to expire. Can the new owner do this?
    a. Yes, a lease terminates if the property is sold to a new owner.
    b. Yes, as a condition of sale.
    c. No, leases are contracts, and the sale of property cannot change their previously negotiated terms.
    d. No, unless the leases contain a lease-purchase clause.

15. A woman has assigned her apartment lease to a man, and the landlord has agreed to the assignment. If the man fails to pay the rent, who is liable?
    a. The man is primarily liable; the woman is secondarily liable.
    b. The woman is primarily liable; the man is secondarily liable.
    c. Only the woman is liable.
    d. Only the man is liable.

16. Under what conditions may a lease be assigned?
    a. Any time, unless its terms prohibit assignment
    b. Only gross leases may be assigned
    c. Only if the owner consents
    d. When the owner feels that the new tenant is as financially stable as the original tenant

17. Who are the parties to a lease?
    a. Grantor and grantee
    b. Manager and owner
    c. Manager, owner, and tenant
    d. Lessor and lessee

18. A residential lease should contain all of the following *EXCEPT*
    a. the specific address.
    b. the date of possession.
    c. the use of the premises.
    d. the right to use as a business.

19. A landowner leases land to a tenant who agrees to erect a building on it. This is a
    a. lease purchase.
    b. ground lease.
    c. graduated lease.
    d. index lease.

20. The tenant has not paid rent for two months. How can the landlord regain possession of the rental unit?
    a. File for constructive eviction
    b. Start the process for actual eviction
    c. Change the locks when the tenant is not there
    d. Landlord has lost the right to evict because no action was taken after the first month's delinquency

Real Estate Taxation

LEARNING OBJECTIVES

When you finish reading this chapter, you will be able to

- differentiate between the general ad valorem taxes, special assessments, and the real estate transfer tax;
- explain the effects of federal income tax on real estate;
- list tax deductions available to home owners; and
- describe tax benefits to real estate investors.

adjusted basis	equitable right of redemption	special assessments
ad valorem tax	exchange	statutory redemption
appropriation	installment sale	statutory lien
basis	involuntary lien	transfer tax
capital gain	mill	voluntary lien
depreciation	mortgage tax	
equalization factor	redemption	

As discussed in Chapter 3, the ownership of real estate is subject to certain government powers. One of these powers is the right to levy taxes for the support of governmental functions. Because the location of real estate is permanently fixed, the government can levy taxes with a high degree of certainty that the taxes will be collected. State and local governments levy annual real estate taxes on all but certain exempt parcels of land within their jurisdictions. These taxes usually have priority over other previously recorded liens. Such liens may be enforced by the court sale of the real estate free of any other liens.

In addition to taxes on real estate ownership, the federal government and most state governments impose an income tax on all profits resulting from the ownership and/or sale of real estate. However, federal income taxes are generally reduced by certain provisions in the tax laws that are designed to encourage ownership of and investment in real estate.

STATE AND LOCAL PROPERTY TAXATION

Real estate taxes can be divided into two types: (1) *general real estate tax* or *ad valorem tax* and (2) *special assessments* or *improvement tax*. Both taxes are levied against specific parcels of property and automatically become liens on those properties. In addition, another category of state and local taxation that affects parcels of real estate when they are sold is called the real estate **transfer tax** or the *grantor tax*.

General Tax (Ad Valorem Tax)

General real estate taxes are levied for the support of the governmental agency authorized to impose the levy. These taxes are called **ad valorem taxes** (from the Latin, meaning "to value") because the amount of the tax varies in accordance with the value of the property being taxed.

The general real estate tax is made up of the taxes levied on real estate by various governmental agencies and municipalities. These include cities, towns, villages, and counties. Other taxing bodies are the school districts or boards (including local elementary and high schools, junior colleges, and community colleges), drainage districts, water districts, and sanitary districts. Municipal authorities operating recreational preserves, such as forest preserves and parks, are also authorized by the state legislatures to levy real estate taxes.

Exemptions from general taxes.   Many state laws also allow special exemptions to reduce real estate tax bills for certain property owners or land uses. Homeowners and senior citizens are frequently granted reductions in the assessed value of their homes. Some states offer real estate tax reductions to attract industry, and many states offer tax reductions for agricultural land.

State law may exempt certain real estate from real estate taxation. For example, property owned by cities, various municipal organizations (e.g., schools, parks, or playgrounds), the state and federal governments, and by religious organizations, hospitals, or educational institutions is tax exempt. Usually, the property must be used for tax-exempt purposes by the exempted group or organization, or it will be taxed.

Assessment.   Real estate is valued, or assessed, for tax purposes by county or township *assessors*. The land is usually appraised separately from the building. The building value is usually determined from a manual or set of rules covering unit-cost prices and rates of depreciation. Some states require assessments to be a certain percentage of market value. State laws may provide for property to be periodically reassessed.

Property owners who claim that errors were made in determining the assessed value of their property may present their objections to a local board of appeal or board of review. Protests or appeals regarding tax assessments may ultimately be taken to court. Such cases generally involve a proceeding whereby the court reviews the certified assessment records of the tax assessment official.

Equalization.   In some jurisdictions, when it is necessary to correct general inequalities in statewide tax assessments, uniformity may be achieved by use of an **equalization factor**. Such a factor may be provided for use in counties or districts where the assessments are to be raised or lowered. The assessed value of each property is multiplied by the equalization factor, and the tax rate is then applied to the equalized assessment. For example, the assessments in one county are determined to be 20% lower than the average assessments throughout the rest of the state. This can be corrected by the application of an equalization factor of 120% to each assessment in that county. Thus, a parcel of land assessed for tax purposes at $63,000 is taxed based on an equalized assessment of $75,600 in this county ($63,000 × 1.20 = $75,600).

Tax rates. The process of arriving at a real estate tax rate involves the following four steps:

1. The process begins with the adoption of a budget by each taxing body. The budget must include an estimate of all expenditures for the year and indicate the amount of income expected from all fees, revenue sharing, and other sources. The net amount remaining to be raised from real estate taxes is then determined from these figures.

2. The next step is **appropriation**, the action taken by each taxing body that authorizes the expenditure of funds and provides for the sources of such monies. Appropriation generally involves the adoption of an ordinance or the passage of a law setting forth the specifics of the proposed taxation.

3. The amount to be raised from the general real estate tax is then imposed on property owners through a tax *levy*, the formal action taken to impose the tax by a vote of the taxing district's governing body.

4. The *tax rate* for each individual taxing body is computed separately. To arrive at a tax rate, the total monies needed for the coming fiscal year are divided by the total assessments of all real estate located within the jurisdiction of the taxing body. For example, a taxing district's budget indicates that $300,000 must be raised from real estate tax revenues, and the assessment roll (assessor's record) of all taxable real estate within this district equals $10 million. The tax rate is computed as follows:

    $300,000 ÷ $10,000,000 = 0.03, or 3%

The tax rate may be expressed in a number of different ways. In many areas, it is expressed in mills. A **mill** is ¹⁄₁₀₀₀ of a dollar, or $0.001. The tax rate of the preceding example could be expressed as follows:

    $3 per $100 assessed value,

    or 30 mills,

    or $30 per $1,000 of assessed value

Tax bills. A property owner's tax bill is computed by applying the tax rate to the assessed valuation of the property. For example, on a property assessed for tax purposes at $90,000 at a tax rate of 3%, or 30 mills, the tax will be $2,700 ($90,000 × 0.030 = $2,700). If an equalization factor is used, the computation on a property with an assessed value of $75,000 and a tax rate of 2.5%, with an equalization factor of 120%, is as follows:

    $75,000 × 1.20 = $90,000 × 0.025 = $2,250 tax

Generally, one tax bill for each property incorporates all real estate taxes levied by the various taxing districts. In some areas, however, separate bills are prepared by different taxing bodies. Sometimes the taxing bodies operate on different fiscal years, so the taxpayer receives separate bills for various taxes at different times during the year.

Due dates for payment of taxes are usually set by statute. Often, taxes are payable in two installments. Collection procedures vary; in some areas, taxes become due during the current tax year; in others, they are payable in arrears during the year after the taxes are levied; and in still others, a partial payment is due in the year of the tax, with the balance due the following year. Knowledge of local tax-payment schedules is especially important in computing the proration of current taxes when the property is sold. Some states offer discounts to encourage prompt payment of real estate taxes. Penalties in the form of monthly interest charges are added to all taxes that are not paid when due. The due date is also called the *penalty date*.

Enforcement of tax liens. To be enforceable, real estate taxes must be valid, meaning that they must be (1) properly levied, (2) for a legal purpose, and (3) applied equitably to all affected property. Tax liens become involuntary **statutory liens** against the property and are generally given priority over all other liens against a property; that is, they must be satisfied before all of a property owner's other debts. Real estate taxes that are delinquent for a period of time specified by state law can be collected by either tax foreclosure (similar to mortgage foreclosure) or tax sale. While there are substantial differences in the methods and details of the various states' tax sale procedures, the results are the same.

Tax sales. A tax sale is usually held after a court has held that the tax and penalties are to be collected and has ordered that the property be sold and a notice of sale be published. The sale is usually conducted by the tax collector at an annual public sale. Because a definite amount of delinquent tax and penalty is to be collected, the purchaser must pay at least this amount. Because a defaulted owner has the right to redeem (i.e., buy back) the real estate, in many areas, bidding takes place on the percentage of interest the bidder may receive from the defaulted owner if and when the property is redeemed. In this type of bidding, the person bidding the lowest interest rate becomes the successful purchaser. The successful bidder receives a *certificate of sale* or similar document when paying the delinquent tax amount.

Redemption. Generally, the delinquent taxpayer can redeem the property at any time before the tax sale by paying the delinquent taxes plus interest and charges (e.g., court costs and attorney's fees); this is the **equitable right of redemption**. Most state laws also grant a period of **statutory redemption** after the tax sale during which the defaulted owner or other lienholders (i.e., creditors of the defaulted owner) may redeem the property by paying the amount paid at the tax sale plus interest and charges (including any taxes levied since the sale). If no **redemption** is made within this statutory redemption period, the certificate holder can apply for a *tax deed*. The quality of the title conveyed by a tax deed varies from state to state according to statutory provisions.

In some states, titles to tax-delinquent land are sold or conveyed to the state or a taxing authority. At the expiration of the *redemption period*, titles to these lands are then sold at auction to the highest bidder. The tax deeds issued to purchasers in such cases are regarded as conveying good title because they are considered conveyances of state-owned land. In some jurisdictions, tax-delinquent land that is not sold at a tax sale due to lack of buyers is forfeited to the state. The state may then either use the land for its own purposes or sell it to the highest bidder.

Special Assessments or Improvement Taxes

Special assessments are special taxes levied on real estate that require property owners to pay for improvements that benefit the real estate they own. Taxes are often levied to pay for improvements, such as streets, alleys, street lighting, and curbs, and are enforced in the same manner as general real estate taxes. The procedures for making a special assessment vary widely from state to state, but usually include the following steps.

- *Specific improvement recommended.* The authority to recommend or initiate the specific improvement is vested in either the property owners, who may petition for an improvement, or in a proper legislative authority, such as the city council or board of trustees, who may initiate the proposal for an improvement. Hearings are held and notices are given to the owners of the property affected.

- *Ordinance passed.* After the preliminary legal steps have been taken, the legislative authority authorized by statute to act in such cases adopts an ordinance that sets out the nature of the improvement, its cost, and a description of the area to be assessed.

- *Assessment roll spread.* The proper authority spreads the assessment (called the assessment roll) over the various parcels of real estate to benefit. The assessment for each parcel is determined by one of these methods: (1) the estimated benefit each tract will receive by reason of the assessment or (2) front footage. Regardless of the basis used, the assessment usually varies from parcel to parcel because all do not benefit equally from the improvement.

- *Petition and approval.* After hearing the benefits and nature of improvements to be made and hearing any objections from members of the local community affected by the improvements, the local authority, usually a court of record, either approves or rejects the proposal. This is called *confirming the assessment roll.*

- *Special assessment warrant.* Finally, the assessment becomes a lien on the land assessed. When the improvement has been completed, a warrant is usually issued by the clerk of the court that approved the roll. This warrant gives the local collector the authority to issue special assessment bills and begin collection.

- *Lien.* In most states, an assessment becomes a specific lien following the confirmation of the roll. If requested by the property owners, it is an example of a **voluntary lien**, and if imposed by the taxing body, it is an **involuntary lien**. Special assessments are usually due and payable in equal annual installments over a period of 5 to 10 years. Interest is also charged to each property owner on the total amount of that owner's assessment. The first installment generally becomes due during the year following confirmation. The bill includes yearly interest on the entire assessment. As subsequent installments are billed in subsequent years, each bill will include a year's interest on the unpaid balance. Property owners usually have the right to prepay any or all installments, thus stopping the interest charges. Special assessments remain a lien on the property until they are paid in full. Depending on the specific situation, buyers may or may not be able or willing to take title to the property with the liens still due. Licensees should be familiar with options and be able to explain these options to their clients.

Real Estate Transfer Tax

In many states, a *transfer tax* or a *grantor tax* is levied at the time the property is conveyed to a new owner. A tax rate is often an amount per $500 or fraction thereof and the amount is divided between the state, the county, and sometimes the municipality. To ensure enforcement and payment, transfer stamps must be purchased and affixed to the deed before the deed can be recorded. Although some state statutes dictate which party pays the tax, most often it is negotiated between the parties. When the buyer assumes the seller's mortgage, the tax is often based on the purchase price less the amount of the assumed mortgage.

Typically, both buyers and sellers (or, in some cases, their agents) must sign a transfer declaration form that is often filed with the tax office. The form details the full sales price of the property; the legal description of the property conveyed; the address, date, and type of deed; the type of improvement; and whether the transfer is between relatives or is a compulsory transaction in accordance with a court order.

Certain deeds may be exempted from the tax, such as gifts of real estate; deeds not made in connection with a sale , such as a change of joint tenants; conveyances to, from, or between governmental bodies; deeds by charitable, religious, or educational institutions; deeds securing debts or releasing property as security for a debt; partitions; tax deeds; deeds pursuant to mergers of corporations; correction deeds; and deeds from subsidiary to parent corporations for cancellation of stock.

Mortgage Tax

Nearly a dozen states levy a **mortgage tax** every time that a property is used as security for a loan, an acquisition, refinancing, and at the time a home equity line of credit is opened. Very often, the tax is assessed on the entire amount that could be potentially borrowed, not on the amount that is actually borrowed. The mortgage tax is a percentage of the loan amount, so licensees who are located in states that charge this fee should be well aware of the tax, which can add thousands to the buyers' closing costs.

FEDERAL INCOME TAX ON REAL ESTATE

Due to the complexity of federal tax laws, the following material is limited to the concepts that the real estate practitioner will be expected to recognize. The licensee must be current in all areas that can affect property and its value, such as zoning, land use, and tax implications of purchase and sale. As with potential legal problems, the practitioner should realize when customers or clients need to consult a tax advisor. The real estate professional should raise the issues but not offer opinions or make decisions concerning legal or accounting matters.

Federal Income Tax Lien

Unlike *ad valorem* tax liens, a *federal income tax lien* (one administered by IRS) does not attach to a specific parcel of real estate. An IRS tax lien resulting from a failure to pay federal income taxes (whether or not the tax pertains to real estate ownership) is a general lien that attaches to all real and personal property held by the delinquent taxpayer.

Capital Gains Tax on Real Estate

The federal government imposes a capital gains tax on profits resulting from the ownership and/or sale of real estate. However, both homeowners and real estate investors can take advantage of recent changes in the law to reduce the amount that must be paid.

Homeowner Benefits

Tax deductions.   Federal income tax is based on income; the greater a person's income, the greater the person's tax liability. Therefore, it is a tax benefit to reduce income through deductions because taxes are accordingly reduced. Federal tax law allows homeowners to deduct the following from their gross income:

- Mortgage interest payments on most primary residences and second homes (subject to limitation)

- Real estate taxes on primary residences

- Certain mortgage loan origination fees, discount points, and prepayment penalties

Items that homeowners may not use to reduce their taxable income (deductions) include payments into escrow to cover fire insurance or homeowners insurance premiums; insurance premiums paid other than through escrow; depreciation; utility or service fees and assessments; and amounts paid toward reducing the mortgage principal.

Exclusion of capital gain on sale.   Under tax regulations, a **capital gain** is the profit realized from the sale or exchange of any property, including real estate. More specifically, the capital gain on the sale of real estate is the difference between its *tax basis* (acquisition or construction cost of the home plus the cost of the lot) and the *adjusted sales price*. The adjusted sales price is the amount received minus the broker's commission and other sales expenses (such as legal fees or repairs needed to prepare a house for sale).

Married taxpayers who file jointly may exclude $500,000 in profits on the sale of a principal residence from capital gains tax (single filers are entitled to an exclusion of $250,000). This exemption may be used repeatedly, as long as the homeowners have occupied the property as their residence for at least two years out of the last five. Some provision is made for homeowners who do not meet the full 24-month requirements due to extenuating circumstances, as determined by the IRS.

For most homeowners, the net result of this new law is that they will never pay capital gains tax on the sale of their homes. Of course, sellers of high-bracket homes, or those who have accumulated profits that exceed $500,000, as well as sellers of second homes and rental properties, will continue to face capital gains taxation.

Withdrawals from IRAs for home purchase.   First-time homebuyers (or those who have not owned a qualified residence in the previous two years) may make penalty-free withdrawals from their tax-deferred individual retirement account (IRA) for use as a down payment. The limit on such withdrawals is $10,000. Income tax must still be paid on the $10,000, with the exception of a Roth IRA, where there is no penalty and no income tax due. The funds must be used within 120 days of withdrawal to pay qualified acquisition costs, include costs of buying, building, or rebuilding a home, and can include usual settlement, financing, or closing costs.

Homeowner Tax Relief

In 2008, the value of many homes throughout the United States decreased. In an effort to avoid an increase in home foreclosures, some states have subsidized low-income homeowners' tax bills. The federal government has also extended assistance by offering tax credits for first-time homebuyers and loan modification options for existing mortgages. Through these combined efforts, both federal and state governments have saved millions of homeowners from loss and helped the overall economy from a catastrophic collapse. This is discussed further in Chapter 12.

Investor Benefits

One of the main reasons real estate investments are so popular—and profitable—is that federal law allows investors to shelter portions of their incomes from taxation. Some of the more common methods of sheltering real estate profits are *exchanges, depreciation*, and *installment sales*.

The taxable gain on real estate held for investment is determined by two factors, the basis and the adjusted basis. **Basis** usually refers to the initial cost an investor pays for a parcel of real estate. Generally, the **adjusted basis** represents the basis, plus the cost of any physical improvements to the property, and less the costs of sale. The gain is the difference between the adjusted basis and the net selling price less any depreciation for tax purposes claimed on the property.

The discussions and examples used in this section are designed to introduce the reader to general tax concepts—a tax attorney or CPA should be consulted for further details on specific regulations. IRS regulations are subject to frequent change; again, a tax expert should be consulted for up-to-date information.

Exchanges.   A real estate investor can defer taxation of capital gains by making a property **exchange**, in other words, when exchanging the property for real estate of like kind with the same or greater selling value. This is officially called a *Section 1031 tax-deferred exchange*; the tax is deferred, not eliminated. An investor who ultimately sells the property (or subsequently exchanges properties) will be required to pay tax on the difference between the sales price and the carryover basis. Therefore, an investor can keep exchanging upward in value, adding to assets for a lifetime without ever having to pay any capital gains tax.

To qualify as a tax-deferred exchange, the properties involved must be of *like kind*—basically, property held for investment or production of income for a similar property. Any additional capital or personal property included with the transaction to even out the exchange is considered a boot and is taxed at the time of the exchange. In addition, the value of the boot is added to the basis of the property. To the extent that liabilities are given up in excess of liabilities assumed, the difference is taxed at the time of the exchange and the basis is increased by the gain.

Depreciation.   Also called cost recovery, **depreciation** is a statutory concept that allows an investor to recover in tax deductions the basis of an asset over the period of its useful life. Depreciation is an accounting concept and may have very little relationship to the actual physical deterioration of the real estate. Depreciation deductions may be taken only on improvements—not the total value of the real estate—and only if they are used in a trade or business or for the production of income. The value of land cannot be depreciated—technically, it never wears out or becomes obsolete. In addition, individuals cannot claim a depreciation deduction on their own personal residence. Depreciation on property can no longer be calculated on an accelerated basis but rather on a straight-line basis of 27.5 years for residential property and 39.5 years for commercial.

Installment sales.   Investors may defer federal income tax on a capital gain, provided they do not receive all cash for the asset at the time of sale, but instead receive payments in two or more periods. Such a transaction is an **installment sale**. This method of reporting is now automatic, unless the taxpayer elects not to use it. As the name implies, the seller receives payment in installments and pays income tax each year based only on the amount received during that year (this can be accomplished by selling through a contract for deed, purchase-money mortgage, or similar instrument). Besides avoiding tax payments on money not yet collected, the installment method often saves an investor money by spreading the gain over a number of years. The gain may be subject to a lower tax than if it were received in one lump sum. IRS regulations on installment sales are quite complicated, and the sale should be planned with the seller's tax advisor.

SUMMARY

Ad valorem real estate taxes are annually levied by local taxing authorities. Such tax liens are generally given priority over other liens. Payments are required before stated dates, after which penalties accrue. An owner may lose title to property for nonpayment of taxes because tax-delinquent property can be sold to pay the taxes. By equitable redemption, the owner can redeem the property prior to the sale by paying the delinquent amount plus penalties. Some states allow a redemption period after the sale for the delinquent owner to pay all amounts owed. Some states allow a time period during which an owner in default can redeem the real estate from a tax sale.

Special assessments are levied to spread the cost of improvements, such as new sidewalks, curbs, or paving, to the real estate that benefits from the improvements. Assessments are usually payable annually over a period of 5 to 10 years, together with interest due on the balance of the assessment. In addition, if required by state law, conveyances of real estate are subject to state transfer taxes; some states tax mortgages when they are filed.

One of the federal income tax benefits available to homeowners allows them to deduct mortgage interest payments and property taxes from their income tax returns. Income tax on the gain from the sale of a principal residence may be up to $500,000 for married filing jointly and $250,000 for single filers without paying any capital gains income tax.

By exchanging one property for another with an equal or greater selling value, an investor can defer paying tax on the gain realized until a sale is made. Depreciation or cost recovery is a statutory concept that allows an investor to recover in tax deductions the basis of an asset over the period of its useful life. Only costs of improvements to land may be recovered, not costs for the land itself. An investor may also defer federal income taxes on gain realized from the sale of an investment property through an installment sale. In this situation, the investor pays income tax only on the portion of the total gain received in any one year.

REVIEW QUESTIONS

Please complete all of the questions before turning to the Answer Key on page 341.

1. When it is necessary to correct general dissimilarities in statewide tax assessments, uniformity may be achieved with the use of
   a. a levy.
   b. an equalization factor.
   c. an appropriation.
   d. a mill.

2. A specific parcel of real estate has a market value of $80,000 and is assessed for tax purposes at 25% of market value. The tax rate for the county in which the property is located is 30 mills. The annual tax bill will be
   a. $300.
   b. $550.
   c. $600.
   d. $850.

3. Taxes levied based on the value of the property are called
   a. ad valorem taxes.
   b. special assessments.
   c. capital gain taxes.
   d. cost recovery.

4. An investor bought a factory as an investment. The property cost $405,000. He took out a loan of $365,000 and must pay annual property taxes of $13,200. After buying the property, he made various improvements totaling $35,000. The investor now hopes to resell the property for $485,000. The investor's original basis in the property is
   a. $365,000.
   b. $370,000.
   c. $405,000.
   d. $485,000.

5. For tax purposes, in an installment sale of real estate, the taxable gain is received and must be reported as income by the seller
   a. in the year that the sale is initiated.
   b. during the year in which the final installment payment is received.
   c. in each year during which the installment payments are being received.
   d. at any one time during the period that installment payments are being received.

6. What is the annual real estate tax on a property valued at $135,000 and assessed for tax purposes at $47,250 with an equalization factor of 125% and a tax rate of 25 mills?
   a. $1,181
   b. $1,477
   c. $3,375
   d. $4,219

7. After real estate has been sold by the state or county to satisfy a delinquent real estate tax lien, depending on state law, the former owner may have the right to
   a. refinance the parcel of property sold.
   b. remain indefinitely in possession of the property.
   c. redeem the property within the time period set by law.
   d. have the sale canceled by partial payment of the taxes due.

8. A couple has just sold their property. The type of tax based on the sales price of their property and charged as a cost of conveying the property is called the
   a. capital gains tax.
   b. cost recovery tax.
   c. transfer tax.
   d. special assessment.

9. A couple has just sold the home they have lived in for the past 25 years for a profit of $400,000. If they file their income taxes jointly, they will be able to take advantage of the capital gains tax exclusion of
   a. $125,000.
   b. $225,000.
   c. $250,000.
   d. $500,000.

10. The *MOST* likely recipient of an exemption from the payment of real estate taxes is a
    a. county courthouse.
    b. suburban shopping mall.
    c. private dance studio.
    d. country club.

11. A single woman bought her home 18 months ago and has found a new job in another city. A married couple who file jointly have owned their nine-bedroom home for only three years but now plan to move to a small condominium unit. A single man has owned his own home for 17 years and will use the proceeds from the sale of this house to purchase a larger house. Based on these facts, the individual(s) entitled to a full exclusion from capital gains on the sale is the
    a. married couple and the single man.
    b. married couple and the single woman.
    c. married couple only.
    d. single man only.

12. When calculating the depreciation on an apartment building that sits on a valuable piece of land, the person preparing the calculation must understand that
    a. only the building itself can be depreciated.
    b. both the building and the land can be depreciated.
    c. the building can be fully depreciated but the land can only be partially depreciated.
    d. the building and the land are depreciated in direct proportion to their value.

13. The initial cost of an investment property, plus the cost of any subsequent improvements, minus any depreciation, represents the investment's
    a. adjusted sales price.
    b. adjusted basis.
    c. basis.
    d. salvage value.

14. A local municipality is levying a tax for the installation of curbs and gutters along a road. The type of tax levied and collected from the homeowners who live along that road is called
    a. an ad valorem tax.
    b. a capital gain.
    c. a general assessment.
    d. a special assessment.

15. In their first year of homeownership, new homeowners will be able to deduct all of the following *EXCEPT*
    a. mortgage interest paid each month.
    b. real estate taxes paid twice during the year.
    c. homeowners insurance premiums annually.
    d. any discount points paid at settlement.

16. Who is usually exempt from paying real estate taxes?
    a. Senior citizens, if they have owned the property for at least five years
    b. Hospitals
    c. Military personnel, if posted in a war zone
    d. Farmers

17. What is the first step in the process of determining real estate taxes?
    a. Compute the tax rate
    b. Send the tax bills by a certain date
    c. Adopt a budget
    d. Apply an equalization factor

18. Because a property owner has not paid his property taxes for three years, a tax sale has been ordered. The owner has been told that he can redeem the property before the sale under
    a. the right of equitable title.
    b. no circumstances.
    c. statutory right of redemption.
    d. the equitable right of redemption.

19. All the property owners in a neighborhood have formed a group and asked the county to install street lights down their street. The county has agreed to make the improvements, but the property owners must pay for the installation. The county will raise the money through
    a. a special assessment.
    b. issuing a bond.
    c. ad valorem taxes.
    d. a tax sale.

20. A couple purchased their first and only home in 1971 for $35,000. They recently sold their home for $545,000 in order to move into an assisted-living facility. How much of this sale is subject to a capital gains tax?
    a. $10,000
    b. $35,000
    c. $510,000
    d. $500,000

Real Estate Appraisal

LEARNING OBJECTIVES

When you finish reading this chapter, you will be able to

- explain different meanings of value,
- name the external forces that influence value,
- describe the value principles,
- discuss the three valuation methods used by appraisers and when each is generally used,
- relate the process of reconciliation, and
- list the steps of the appraisal process.

anticipation	economic life	reconciliation
appraisal	external obsolescence	regression
assemblage	functional obsolescence	replacement cost
broker's price opinion (BPO)	gross income multiplier (GIM)	reproduction cost
capitalization rate	gross rent multiplier (GRM)	sales comparison approach
change	highest and best use	substitution
competition	income approach	supply and demand
comparative market analysis (CMA)	market data approach	value
conformity	market value	Uniform Residential Appraisal Report (URAR)
contribution	physical deterioration	Uniform Standards of Professional Appraisal Practice (USPAP)
cost approach	plottage	
depreciation	progression	

An **appraisal** is an estimate or opinion of value. Appraisals are frequently used for pricing, financing, protecting, or leasing property. The appraisal profession is now regulated separately from the real estate business. The Financial Institutions Reform, Recovery, and Enforcement Act of 1989 (FIRREA) requires that all appraisals performed as part of a federally related transaction must comply with state standards and be performed by state-licensed or state-certified appraisers. All states have implemented programs requiring that appraisal applicants meet certain education, experience, and examination criteria. State appraisal standards and appraiser licensing and certification requirements must meet at least the minimum levels set by the Appraisal Standards Board and the Appraiser Qualifications Board of The Appraisal Foundation, a national body composed of representatives of the major appraisal and related industry organizations.

Not all estimates of real estate value are made by professional appraisers, however. Everyone engaged in the real estate business should have at least a fundamental knowledge of real estate valuation. Listing agents prepare a **comparative market analysis (CMA)** to help the seller set a competitive asking price; buyer agents prepare a CMA to assist their buyers in making a reasonable offer. On the CMA, licensees list nearby properties, similar in size, that have sold recently to demonstrate what buyers have been willing to pay. They also list properties that are similar in size and location that will be competing with the seller's home. A third category, listings that expired, often indicates the prices that buyers have been unwilling to pay for a similar property. While a CMA is an excellent tool for an agent in helping a seller determine the best price for the home, the seller ultimately establishes the listing price and the buyer determines the offered price. Licensees should avoid the words *worth* or *value*. The CMA simply demonstrates what other buyers have been willing or not willing to pay for similar properties. A CMA must not be confused with a formal appraisal.

A broker may be asked to provide a **broker's price opinion (BPO)**. Depending on the state, the broker may or may not be able to perform a BPO for a fee. This is not a formal appraisal, but rather an opinion of value for a given property. This information is most often requested by a bank or a relocation company and is often used to verify that the property does, in fact, exist.

VALUE

Value may be defined as the relationship between a desired object and a potential purchaser. It is the power of a good or service to command other goods or services in exchange. In terms of appraisal, value may be described as the present worth of future benefits derived from the ownership of real property.

To have value in the real estate market, property must have these four characteristics:

1. *Demand*—the need or desire for possession or ownership, backed by the financial means to satisfy that need

2. *Utility*—the capacity to satisfy human needs and desires

3. *Scarcity*—a finite supply

4. *Transferability*—the relative ease with which ownership rights are transferred from one person to another

A given parcel of real estate may have many different kinds of value at the same time:

- *Market value*—often used to estimate selling price and determined by what buyers have paid for a similar property

- *Assessed value*—determined by the tax assessor for property taxes, often based on market value

- *Insured value*—the cost to rebuild a structure from the ground up

- *Book value*—on a balance sheet, the cost of the asset minus depreciation

- *Mortgage value*—the percentage of market value on which a lender will make a loan

- *Salvage value*—the remaining value after an asset has been depreciated

- *Condemnation value*—the value on which compensation is paid for property that is acquired by eminent domain

- *Depreciated value*—an accounting tool used to allocate costs, based on passage of time or level of activity

Market Value

Generally, the goal of an appraiser is to estimate **market value**—the most probable price that a property will bring in a competitive and open market, allowing a reasonable time to find a purchaser who knows all the purposes to which it can be adapted and for which it is capable of being used. Included in this definition are the following key points:

- Market value is the most probable price a property will bring—not the average price or the highest price.

- Payment must be made in cash or its equivalent.

- Buyer and seller must be unrelated and acting without undue pressure.

- A reasonable length of time must be allowed for the property to be exposed in the open market.

- Both buyer and seller must be well informed of the property's use and potential, including its assets and defects.

Market value versus market price.   Market value is an estimate based on an analysis of comparable sales and other pertinent market data. Market price, on the other hand, is what a property has actually sold for—its sales price. Theoretically, the market price is the same as market value. Market price can be taken as accurate evidence of current market value, however, only after considering all of the factors listed above. A sale from father to daughter, for example, might well have been designed to favor one of the parties.

Market value versus cost.   One of the most common errors made in valuing property is the assumption that cost represents market value. Cost and market value may be equal when the improvements on a property are new and represent the highest and best use of the land. More often, however, cost does not equal market value. For example, two homes are identical in every respect except that one is located on a street with heavy traffic, and the other is on a quiet residential street. The value of the former may be less than the latter, although the cost of each may be exactly the same.

External Forces That Influence Value

Real estate value is created, changed, and destroyed, in part, by the interaction of four forces: (1) *physical*, (2) *political*, (3) *economic*, and (4) *social*. Because these forces exist outside the property and are thus beyond the property owner's control, they are called externalities.

Physical externalities.   The climate, the topography of the land, the proximity to rivers and streams, the availability of water, and water quality are examples of physical forces that can influence property value.

Political externalities.   Government controls over money and credit, government-insured or government-guaranteed loan programs, health and safety codes, building codes, zoning ordinances, the availability of public housing, rent controls, the quality of schools and education, the quantity and quality of parks, and tax burdens are examples of government influences on property value.

Economic externalities.   The availability of employment, wage, and salary levels, the broadness of the economic base, or the dependence on one major industry for jobs are typical of economic externalities.

Social externalities.   These include population growth and decline, birth rates and death rates, attitudes toward marriage and family size, divorce rates, lifestyles, and life-style changes.

Principles of Value

Whether an appraiser observes them or not, a number of economic principles are always at work affecting the value of real estate. The more important principles are defined in this section.

Highest and best use.   The most profitable use to which the property can be adapted or the use that is likely to be in demand in the reasonably near future is its **highest and best use**. For example, a highest-and-best-use study may show that a parking lot in a busy downtown area should be replaced by an office building. To place a value on the property based on its present use is erroneous. In appraising a residential location, amenities and owner satisfaction become important.

Substitution.   The appraisal principle of **substitution** states that the maximum value of a property tends to be set by the cost of purchasing an equally desirable and valuable substitute property. Substitution is the basis of a comparative market analysis and the sales comparison approach.

Supply and demand.   The principle of **supply and demand** says that the value of a property will increase if the supply decreases and the demand either increases or remains constant (seller's market)—and vice versa (buyer's market). For example, the last available lot in a residential area where the demand for homes is high would probably sell for more than the first lot sold in the area.

Balance.   Balance is achieved when the addition of improvements to the land and structures increases the property value.

Conformity.   Maximum value is realized if the use of land conforms to existing neighborhood standards, the reason for zoning regulations. In areas of single-family houses, for example, buildings should be similar in design, construction, size, and age. Deed restrictions rely on the principle of **conformity** to assure maximum future value.

Regression and progression. When dissimilar properties exist in the same neighborhood, the worth of the better-quality properties is adversely affected by the presence of the lesser-quality properties. This is called **regression**. Conversely, **progression** states that the worth of a lesser property tends to increase if it is located among better properties.

Anticipation. Value can increase or decrease in **anticipation** of some future benefit or detriment affecting the property. For example, the value of a house may be affected if rumors are circulating that an adjacent property will be rezoned to commercial use in the near future.

Plottage. The **plottage** principle holds that the merging of adjacent parcels of property into one larger parcel may increase its utility and, thus, its value. For example, two parcels of land might be worth $20,000 each, but when combined, they might be worth $50,000 because more can be done with the larger parcel. The process of merging the parcels is called **assemblage**.

Increasing and decreasing returns. Improvements to land and structures eventually reach a point at which they have no effect on property values. If money spent on such improvements produces an increase in income or value, the law of increasing returns is applicable. Where additional improvements do not produce a proportionate increase in income or value, the law of decreasing returns applies. Owners might see decreasing returns if they add granite counter tops to their kitchen, a fifth bedroom, and an in-ground swimming pool in a neighborhood consisting of modest three-bedroom homes.

Contribution. The value of any component of a property consists of what its addition contributes to the whole value (**contribution**) or what its absence detracts from that value. For example, the cost of installing an air-conditioning system and remodeling an older office building may be greater than is justified by the rental increase that could result.

Competition. Excess profits attract **competition**, and too much competition sometimes destroys profits. For example, the success of a retail store may attract investors to open similar stores in the area. This could result in less profit for all stores concerned, unless purchasing power in the area increases substantially. However, in many cases more is better. Fast-food restaurants and gas stations are often found grouped around the same intersection. A large shopping mall may have 10 different clothing stores for women.

Change. No physical or economic condition remains constant. Real estate is subject to **change** from natural phenomena, such as tornadoes, fires, and routine wear and tear from the elements. The real estate business is also subject to the demands of its market, just as is any business. It is an appraiser's job to be knowledgeable about the effects of natural phenomena as well as about the vagaries of the marketplace.

VALUATION METHODS

To arrive at an accurate estimate of value, three basic approaches are used by appraisers: (1) the *sales comparison approach*, (2) the *cost approach*, and (3) the *income approach*. Each method serves as a check against the others and narrows the ranges within which the final estimate of value will fall. For specific types of property, one method is generally selected as the most reliable.

The Sales Comparison, or Market Data, Approach to Value

In the **sales comparison approach**, an estimate of value is obtained by comparing the *subject property* (the property under appraisal) with recent sales of *comparable properties* (properties similar to the subject). No two parcels of real estate are exactly alike, so each comparable property must be compared to the subject property and the sales prices adjusted for any dissimilar features. This approach, also called the **market data approach**, is most often used by brokers and salespeople helping a seller to set a price for residential real estate. The principal factors for which adjustments must be made fall into four basic categories:

1. *Sales or financing concessions.* This consideration becomes important if a sale is not financed by a standard mortgage procedure.

2. *Date of sale.* An adjustment must be made if economic changes have occurred since the comparable property was sold.

3. *Location.* An adjustment may be necessary to compensate for differences in location. For example, similar properties might differ in price from neighborhood to neighborhood, or even within the same neighborhood.

4. *Physical features and amenities.* Physical features that may cause adjustments include age of building, size of lot, landscaping, construction, number of rooms, square feet of living space, interior and exterior condition, presence or absence of a garage, fireplace, central air conditioning, and so forth.

After a careful analysis of the differences between comparable properties and the subject property, the appraiser assigns a dollar value to each of these differences. The value of a feature present in the subject property, but not in the comparable property, is added to the sales price of the comparable property. The value of a feature present in the comparable, but not in the subject property, is subtracted. The *adjusted sales price* represents the probable value range of the subject property. From this range, a single market value estimate can be selected. In this way, the properties, at least on paper, can be made equivalent.

The sales comparison approach is considered essential in almost every appraisal of real estate. It is thought to be the most reliable of the three approaches in appraising residential property, in which the intangible benefits are difficult to measure. An example of the sales comparison approach is shown in Figure 11.1.

FIGURE 11.1 **Sales Comparison Approach to Value**

	Subject property: 155 Potter Dr.	Comparables A	B	C	D	E
Sales price		$118,000	$112,000	$121,000	$116,500	$110,000
Financing concessions	none	none	none	none	none	none
Date of sale		current	current	current	current	current
Location	good	same	poorer +6,500	same	same	same
Age	6 years	same	same	same	same	same
Size of lot	60' × 135'	same	same	large −5,000	same	larger −5,000
Landscaping	good	same	same	same	same	same
Construction	brick	same	same	same	same	same
Style	ranch	same	same	same	same	same
No. of rooms	6	same	same	same	same	same
No. of bedrooms	3	same	same	same	same	same
No. of baths	1½	same	same	same	same	same
Sq. ft. of living space	1,500	same	same	same	same	same
Other space (basement)	full basement	same	same	same	same	same
Condition—exterior	average	better −1,500	poorer +1,000	better −1,500	same	poorer +2,000
Condition—interior	good	same	same	better −500	same	same
Garage	2-car attached	same	same	same	same	none +5000
Other improvements	none	none	none	none	none	none
Net adjustments		−1,500	+7,500	−7,000	-0-	+2,000
Adjusted value		$116,500	$119,500	$114,000	$116,500	$112,000

Note that the value of a feature that is present in the subject, but not in the comparable property, is added to the sales price of the comparable. Likewise, the value of a feature that is present in the comparable, but not in the subject property, is subtracted. The adjusted sales prices of the comparables represent the probable range of value of the subject property. From this range, a single market value estimate can be selected. Because the value range of the properties in the comparison chart (excluding comparables B and E) is close and comparable D required no adjustment, an appraiser might conclude that the indicated market value of the subject is $116,500. However, appraisers use a complex process of evaluating adjustment percentages and may consider other objective factors or subjective judgments based on research.

The Cost Approach to Value

The cost approach is based on the principle of *substitution*, which states that the maximum value of a property tends to be set by the cost of acquiring an equally desirable and valuable substitute property, assuming that no costly delay is encountered in making the substitution. It is most appropriate in the valuation of properties for which no comparable structures readily exist, such as schools, courthouses, churches, and cemeteries. The **cost approach** consists of five steps:

1. Estimate the value of the land as though it were vacant and available to be put to its highest and best use.

2. Estimate the current cost of constructing the building(s) and site improvements.

3. Estimate the amount of accrued depreciation resulting from physical deterioration, functional obsolescence, and/or external obsolescence.

4. Deduct accrued depreciation from the estimated construction cost of new building(s) and site improvements.

5. Add the estimated land value to the depreciated cost of the building(s) and site improvements to arrive at the total property value.

For example, assume the value of the land (step 1) is $75,000. The current cost of replacing the building and improving the site is $200,000, and the accrued depreciation is $40,000 (steps 2 and 3). Step 4 yields $200,000 – $40,000 = $160,000. The total property value (step 5) is $160,000 + $75,000 = $235,000.

Land value (step 1).   The sales comparison approach is used to estimate land value, which is the location and site improvements of the subject property compared to those of similar nearby sites with adjustments are made for significant differences. When the sales comparison approach is used to determine land value in the cost approach, a basis of comparison must be established. This is necessary because, unlike homes that are basically similar and easily compared, tracts of land might not share such similarity. Comparison of large tracts of land may be made by establishing a *per acre* value from comparables and applying it to the subject land, comparison of subdivided lots zoned for commercial or industrial usage may be made by establishing a *square foot* value from comparables and applying it to the subject lot, and comparison of land zoned for retail business usage may be made by establishing a *front foot* value from comparables and applying it to the subject land.

Reproduction cost and replacement cost (step 2).   Two different ways may be used to determine the construction cost of a building for appraisal purposes: reproduction cost or replacement cost. **Reproduction cost** is the dollar amount required to duplicate the subject building at current prices. Replacement cost of the subject property is the construction cost at current prices of a property that is not necessarily a duplicate, but it serves the same purpose or function as the original. Although the results are the same (keep rain out of the building), the cost of reproducing a roof with slate tiles is substantially more than replacing the tiles with asphalt shingles. **Replacement cost** is most often used in appraising because it eliminates obsolete features and takes advantage of current construction materials and techniques. An example of the cost approach to value is shown in Figure 11.2.

FIGURE 11.2   **Cost Approach to Value**

Subject property: 155 Potter Dr.

Land valuation: Size 60' × 135' @ $450 per front foot	=	$27,000
Plus site improvements: driveway, walks, landscaping, etc.	=	$8,000
Total		$35,000

Building valuation: Replacement cost

1,500 sq. ft. @ $85 per sq. ft.	= $127,500	

Less depreciation:

Physical depreciation

   Curable

(Items of deferred maintenance)		
Exterior painting	$4,000	
Incurable (structural deterioration)	$9,750	
Functional obsolescence	$2,000	
External depreciation	-0-	
Total	−15,750	
Depreciated value of building		$111,750
Indicated value by cost approach		$146,750

In determining the replaceme: f it were new, the appraiser generally uses one of the f

- *Quantity survey method.* An estir   w materials needed to replace the subject structure   th), as well as their current prices and installation   ndirect costs (such as building permits, surveys, pa   > arrive at the total replacement cost of the structure. This method is extremely detailed and time-consuming and usually is used only for historical and dedicated-use properties.

- *Unit-in-place method.* The replacement cost of the structure is estimated based on the construction cost per unit of measure of individual building components, such as materials, labor, overhead, and profit. Although some components are measured and costs are estimated in square feet, some, such as plumbing fixtures and heating and air-conditioning units, are estimated by unit cost.

- *Square-foot method.* The cost per square foot of a recently built comparable structure is multiplied by the number of square feet of the subject improvements. This is the most common method of cost estimation. For some properties, such as warehouses and industrial facilities, the cost per cubic foot of a recently built comparable structure is multiplied by the number of cubic feet of the subject structure.

- *Index method.* A factor representing a percentage increase in construction costs to the present time is applied to the original cost of the subject property. Because this method fails to account for individual property variables, it is useful only as a check of the estimate reached by one of the other methods.

Depreciation (step 3).   In a real estate appraisal, **depreciation** refers to any condition that adversely affects the value of an improvement. Land is never depreciated because it retains its value indefinitely, except in rare instances such as misused farmland. Depreciation is usually calculated by dividing the property value by the number of years allowed as its expected economic life. The **economic life** is based on the condition and utility of the structure and is generally lesser than the actual chronological age.

Depreciation for appraisal purposes is divided into the following three classes according to its cause:

1. *Physical deterioration.* **Physical depreciation** results from wear and tear due to everyday use and the action of natural elements such as sun, wind, rain, heat, and cold. Physical deterioration is within the property owner's control and is most often *curable*. This means that necessary repairs are economically feasible, considering the remaining years of life of the building. For example, a new roof is a justifiable expense, even on a 40-year-old brick building that is otherwise in good condition. When necessary repairs would not contribute a comparable value to a building—for example, near the end of a building's useful life—such deterioration is considered *incurable*.

2. *Functional obsolescence.* Functional depreciation results from outmoded function or poor design. An example is a four-bedroom, one-bath house, or a house with old-fashioned kitchen and bathroom fixtures and an inadequate electrical system. As with physical deterioration, **functional obsolescence** exists within the property, is within the property owner's control, and is often curable. Features that are no longer considered desirable by property buyers could be replaced or redesigned at reasonable cost. For example, outmoded plumbing fixtures are usually easily replaced. Room function might be redefined at no cost if the basic room layout allows for it, as in the case of a bedroom adjacent to a kitchen that might easily be converted to a family room. When currently undesirable physical or design features cannot be easily remedied because of cost or other factors, such obsolescence is considered incurable.

3. *External (economic) obsolescence.* This form of depreciation results from adverse factors outside the subject property and thus is beyond the property owner's control. Therefore, **external obsolescence** is always incurable. For example, proximity to a nuisance like a polluting factory or a noisy airport is an unchangeable factor that could not be cured by the owner of the subject property.

Depreciation is difficult to measure because much of functional obsolescence and all of locational obsolescence can be evaluated only by considering the actions of buyers in the marketplace.

The Income Approach to Value

The **income approach** is based on the present worth of the future rights to income. It assumes that the income derived from a property, to a large extent, will control the value of the property. The income approach is used primarily for valuation of income-producing properties—apartment buildings, shopping centers, and the like. In estimating value via the income approach, an appraiser must take the following five steps:

1. Estimate annual *potential gross income*, including both rental income and income from other sources, such as concessions and vending machines.

2. Based on market experience, deduct an appropriate allowance for vacancy and collection losses to arrive at *effective gross income*.

3. Based on appropriate operating standards, deduct the annual operating expenses of the real estate from the effective gross income to arrive at the annual *net operating income (NOI)*. Management costs are always included as operating expenses, even if the current owner also manages the property. Mortgage payments (including principal and interest), however , are debt service and *not* considered operating expenses, nor is depreciation.

4. Estimate the price a typical investor would pay for the income produced by this particular type and class of property (i.e., the rate of return, or yield) that an investor will demand for the investment of capital in this type of building. This rate of return is called the **capitalization rate** (or ***cap rate***) and is determined by comparing the relationship of net operating income with the sales prices of similar properties that have sold in the current market. For example, a comparable property that is producing an annual net income of $30,000 is sold for $300,000. The capitalization rate is $30,000 ÷ 300,000 = 10%. If other comparable properties sold at prices that yielded the same rate, the appraiser should apply a 10% capitalization rate to the subject property.

5. Finally, the capitalization rate is applied to the property's annual net income, resulting in the appraiser's estimate of the property value.

With the appropriate capitalization rate and the projected annual net income, the appraiser can obtain an indication of value by the income approach in the following manner:

> net income ÷ capitalization rate = value

For example,

> $15,000 income ÷ 10% capitalization rate = $150,000 value

This formula and its variations are important in dealing with income property:

> income ÷ rate = value

> income ÷ value = rate

> value × rate = income

A simplified version of the computations used in applying the income approach appears in Figure 11.3. Note the inverse relationship between the capitalization rate and market value. As the capitalization rate increases, market value decreases, and vice versa.

FIGURE 11.3   **Income Capitalization Approach to Value**

Potential gross annual income		$60,000
Market rent (100% capacity)		
Income from other sources		
(Vending machines and pay phones)		+600
		$60,600
Less vacancy and collection losses (estimated) @ 4%		−2,424
Effective gross income		$58,176
Expenses:		
Real estate taxes	$9,000	
Insurance	1,000	
Heat	2,500	
Maintenance	6,400	
Utilities, electricity, water, gas	800	
Repairs	1,200	
Decorating	1,400	
Replacement of equipment	800	
Legal and accounting	600	
Management	+3,000	
Total	$26,700	−$26,700
Annual net operating income		$31,476
Capitalization rate = 10% (0.10)		
		$31,476
		÷ 0.10
Indicated value by income approach =		$314,760

Gross rent multiplier (GRM).   Sometimes, single-family homes are purchased as an income-producing asset. As a substitute for the income approach, the **gross rent multiplier (GRM)** method is often used in appraising such properties. The GRM relates the sale price of a property to its rental price and can be determined by the following formula:

sale price ÷ monthly rental income = GRM

For example, a home recently sold for $180,000. The monthly rental income was $1,000. The GRM for the property is

$180,000 ÷ $1,000 = 180

To establish an accurate GRM, an appraiser must have recent sales and rental data from at least four properties that are similar to the subject property. The resulting GRM could then be applied to the estimated fair market rental of the subject property in order to arrive at its market value. The formula would then be

monthly rental income × GRM = estimated market value

Figure 11.4 shows some examples of GRM comparisons.

FIGURE 11.4   **Gross Rent Multiplier**

Comparable no.	Sales price	Monthly rent	GRM
1	$93,600	$650	144
2	78,500	450	174
3	95,500	675	141
4	82,000	565	145
Subject	?	625	?

Note that, based on an analysis of these comparisons, a GRM of 145 seems reasonable for homes in this area. In the opinion of an appraiser, then, the estimated value of the subject property is $625 × 145 = $90,625.

Gross income multiplier (GIM).   Generally, gross annual income is used in appraising industrial and commercial properties. The ratio to convert annual income into market value is then called a **gross income multiplier (GIM)**.

Much skill is required to use multipliers accurately because there is no fixed multiplier for all areas or all types of properties. Therefore, many appraisers view the technique simply as a quick way to check the validity of a property value obtained by the three accepted appraisal methods.

Reconciliation

When the three approaches are applied to the same property, they will usually produce three separate indications of value. **Reconciliation** is the art of analyzing and effectively weighing the findings from the three approaches.

Although each approach may serve as an independent guide to value, all three approaches should be used as a check on the final estimate of value. The process of reconciliation is more complicated than simply taking the average of the three value estimates. An average implies that the data and logic applied in each of the approaches are equally valid and reliable, and each should therefore be given equal weight. However, certain approaches are more valid and reliable with some kinds of properties than with others.

For example, in appraising a home, the income approach is usually given little weight, and the cost approach is of limited value, unless the home is relatively new. Therefore, the sales comparison approach is usually given the greatest weight in valuing single-family residences. In the appraisal of income or investment property, the income approach would normally be given the greatest weight. In the appraisal of churches, libraries, museums, schools, and other special-use properties where there is no income and few, if any, sales, the cost approach would usually be assigned the greatest weight. From this reconciliation, a single estimate of market value is produced. Reconciliation for a single-family residence might be weighted as follows:

Sales comparison approach	$150,000 × 70%	= $105,000
Cost approach	$144,000 × 20%	= $28,800
Income approach	$140,000 × 10%	= $14,000
Estimate of total market value		= $147,800

THE APPRAISAL PROCESS

The key to an accurate appraisal lies in the methodical collection of data. The appraisal process is an orderly set of procedures used to collect and analyze data to arrive at an ultimate value conclusion. The data are divided into two basic classes:

1. *General data,* covering the nation, region, city, and neighborhood. Of particular importance is the neighborhood, where an appraiser finds the physical, economic, social, and political influences that directly affect the value and potential of the subject property.

2. *Specific data,* covering details of the subject property, as well as comparative data relating to costs, sales, and income and expenses of properties similar to and competitive with the subject property.

Figure 11.5 outlines the steps an appraiser takes in carrying out an appraisal assignment. The numbers in the following list correspond to the numbers on the flowchart.

1. *State the problem.* The kind of value to be estimated must be specified, and the valuation approaches most valid and reliable for the kind of property under appraisal must be selected.

2. *List the data needed and the sources.* Based on the approaches the appraiser will be using, the types of data needed and the sources to be consulted are listed.

3. *Gather, record, and verify the necessary data.* Detailed information must be obtained concerning the economic, political, and social conditions of the nation, region, city, and neighborhood, and comments on the effects of these data on the subject property also must be obtained.

    Specific data about the subject site and improvements must be collected and verified. Depending on the approaches used, comparative information relating to sales, income, expenses, and construction costs of comparable properties must be collected. All data should be verified, usually by checking the same information against two different sources. In the case of sales data, one source should be a person directly involved in the transaction.

4. *Determine highest and best use.* The appraiser analyzes market forces, such as competition and current versus potential uses, to determine the reasonableness of the property's present use in terms of its profitability.

5. *Estimate land value.* The features and sales prices of comparable sites are compared to the subject to determine the value of the land alone.

6. *Estimate value by each of the three approaches.* The sales comparison, cost, and income approaches are used to estimate the value of the subject property.

7. *Reconcile estimated values for final value estimate.* The appraiser makes a definite statement of conclusions reached, usually in the form of a value estimate of the property.

8. *Report final value estimate.* After the three approaches have been reconciled and an opinion of value reached, the appraiser prepares a formal written report for the client. The report should

   - identify the real estate and real property interest being appraised;

   - state the purpose and intended use of the appraisal;

   - define the value to be estimated;

   - state the effective date of the value and the date of the report;

   - state the extent of the process of collecting, confirming, and reporting the data;

   - list all assumptions and limiting conditions that affect the analysis, opinion, and conclusion of value;

   - describe the information considered, the appraisal procedures followed, and the reasoning that supports the report's conclusions; if an approach was excluded, explain why;

   - describe (if necessary or appropriate) the appraiser's opinion of the highest and best use of the real estate;

   - describe any additional information that may be appropriate to show compliance with the specific guidelines established in the ***Uniform Standards of Professional Appraisal Practice (USPAP)*** or to clearly identify and explain any departures from these guidelines; and

   - include a signed certification, as required by *USPAP*.

FIGURE 11.5   **The Appraisal Process**

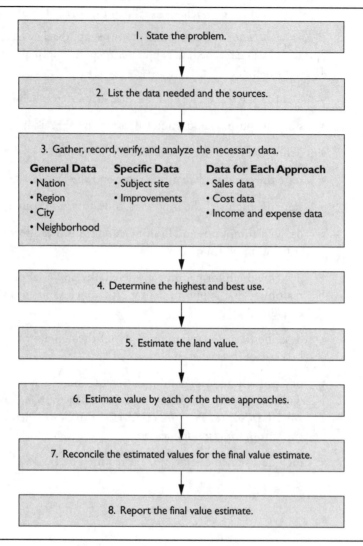

The **Uniform Residential Appraisal Report (URAR),** a form required by many government agencies, illustrates the types of detailed information required of an appraisal of residential property (see Figure 11.6).

FIGURE 11.6   **Uniform Residential Appraisal Report**

Uniform Residential Appraisal Report   File

The purpose of this summary appraisal report is to provide the lender/client with an accurate, and adequately supported, opinion of the market value of the subject property.

SUBJECT

Property Address		City	State	Zip Code
Borrower	Owner of Public Record		County	
Legal Description				

Assessor's Parcel #   Tax Year   R.E. Taxes $

Neighborhood Name   Map Reference   Census Tract

Occupant ☐ Owner ☐ Tenant ☐ Vacant   Special Assessments $ ☐ PUD   HOA $ ☐ per year ☐ per month

Property Rights Appraised ☐ Fee Simple ☐ Leasehold ☐ Other (describe)

Assignment Type ☐ Purchase Transaction ☐ Refinance Transaction ☐ Other (describe)

Lender/Client   Address

Is the subject property currently offered for sale or has it been offered for sale in the twelve months prior to the effective date of this appraisal? ☐ Yes ☐ No

Report data source(s) used, offering price(s), and date(s).

CONTRACT

I ☐ did ☐ did not analyze the contract for sale for the subject purchase transaction. Explain the results of the analysis of the contract for sale or why the analysis was not performed.

Contract Price $ Date of Contract   Is the property seller the owner of public record? ☐ Yes ☐ No   Data Source(s)

Is there any financial assistance (loan charges, sale concessions, gift or downpayment assistance, etc.) to be paid by any party on behalf of the borrower? ☐ Yes ☐ No
If Yes, report the total dollar amount and describe the items to be paid.

NEIGHBORHOOD

Note: Race and the racial composition of the neighborhood are not appraisal factors.

Neighborhood Characteristics			One-Unit Housing Trends			One-Unit Housing		Present Land Use %	
Location ☐ Urban ☐ Suburban ☐ Rural			Property Values ☐ Increasing ☐ Stable ☐ Declining			PRICE	AGE	One-Unit	%
Built-Up ☐ Over 75% ☐ 25–75% ☐ Under 25%			Demand/Supply ☐ Shortage ☐ In Balance ☐ Over Supply			$ (000)	(yrs)	2-4 Unit	%
Growth ☐ Rapid ☐ Stable ☐ Slow			Marketing Time ☐ Under 3 mths ☐ 3–6 mths ☐ Over 6 mths			Low		Multi-Family	%
Neighborhood Boundaries						High		Commercial	%
						Pred.		Other	%

Neighborhood Description

Market Conditions (including support for the above conclusions)

SITE

Dimensions   Area   Shape   View

Specific Zoning Classification   Zoning Description

Zoning Compliance ☐ Legal ☐ Legal Nonconforming (Grandfathered Use) ☐ No Zoning ☐ Illegal (describe)

Is the highest and best use of the subject property as improved (or as proposed per plans and specifications) the present use? ☐ Yes ☐ No   If No, describe

Utilities	Public	Other (describe)		Public	Other (describe)	Off-site Improvements—Type	Public	Private
Electricity	☐	☐	Water	☐	☐	Street	☐	☐
Gas	☐	☐	Sanitary Sewer	☐	☐	Alley	☐	☐

FEMA Special Flood Hazard Area ☐ Yes ☐ No   FEMA Flood Zone   FEMA Map #   FEMA Map Date

Are the utilities and off-site improvements typical for the market area? ☐ Yes ☐ No   If No, describe

Are there any adverse site conditions or external factors (easements, encroachments, environmental conditions, land uses, etc.)? ☐ Yes ☐ No   If Yes, describe

IMPROVEMENTS

General Description		Foundation		Exterior Description materials/condition		Interior materials/condition	
Units ☐ One ☐ One with Accessory Unit		☐ Concrete Slab ☐ Crawl Space		Foundation Walls		Floors	
# of Stories		☐ Full Basement ☐ Partial Basement		Exterior Walls		Walls	
Type ☐ Det. ☐ Att. ☐ S-Det./End Unit		Basement Area sq. ft.		Roof Surface		Trim/Finish	
☐ Existing ☐ Proposed ☐ Under Const.		Basement Finish %		Gutters & Downspouts		Bath Floor	
Design (Style)		☐ Outside Entry/Exit ☐ Sump Pump		Window Type		Bath Wainscot	
Year Built		Evidence of ☐ Infestation		Storm Sash/Insulated		Car Storage ☐ None	
Effective Age (Yrs)		☐ Dampness ☐ Settlement		Screens		☐ Driveway # of Cars	
Attic ☐ None		Heating ☐ FWA ☐ HWBB ☐ Radiant		Amenities ☐ Woodstove(s) #		Driveway Surface	
☐ Drop Stair ☐ Stairs		☐ Other Fuel		☐ Fireplace(s) # ☐ Fence		☐ Garage # of Cars	
☐ Floor ☐ Scuttle		Cooling ☐ Central Air Conditioning		☐ Patio/Deck ☐ Porch		☐ Carport # of Cars	
☐ Finished ☐ Heated		☐ Individual ☐ Other		☐ Pool ☐ Other		☐ Att. ☐ Det. ☐ Built-in	

Appliances ☐ Refrigerator ☐ Range/Oven ☐ Dishwasher ☐ Disposal ☐ Microwave ☐ Washer/Dryer ☐ Other (describe)

Finished area **above** grade contains: Rooms   Bedrooms   Bath(s)   Square Feet of Gross Living Area Above Grade

Additional features (special energy efficient items, etc.)

Describe the condition of the property (including needed repairs, deterioration, renovations, remodeling, etc.).

Are there any physical deficiencies or adverse conditions that affect the livability, soundness, or structural integrity of the property? ☐ Yes ☐ No   If Yes, describe

Does the property generally conform to the neighborhood (functional utility, style, condition, use, construction, etc.)? ☐ Yes ☐ No   If No, describe

FIGURE 11.6   **Uniform Residential Appraisal Report (Cont.)**

Uniform Residential Appraisal Report

File #

There are _____ comparable properties currently offered for sale in the subject neighborhood ranging in price from $ _____ to $ _____ .			
There are _____ comparable sales in the subject neighborhood within the past twelve months ranging in sale price from $ _____ to $ _____ .			

FEATURE	SUBJECT	COMPARABLE SALE # 1	COMPARABLE SALE # 2	COMPARABLE SALE # 3
Address				
Proximity to Subject				
Sale Price	$	$	$	$
Sale Price/Gross Liv. Area	$ sq. ft.	$ sq. ft.	$ sq. ft.	$ sq. ft.
Data Source(s)				
Verification Source(s)				

VALUE ADJUSTMENTS	DESCRIPTION	DESCRIPTION	+(-) $ Adjustment	DESCRIPTION	+(-) $ Adjustment	DESCRIPTION	+(-) $ Adjustment
Sale or Financing Concessions							
Date of Sale/Time							
Location							
Leasehold/Fee Simple							
Site							
View							
Design (Style)							
Quality of Construction							
Actual Age							
Condition							
Above Grade Room Count	Total Bdrms. Baths	Total Bdrms. Baths		Total Bdrms. Baths		Total Bdrms. Baths	
Gross Living Area	sq. ft.	sq. ft.		sq. ft.		sq. ft.	
Basement & Finished Rooms Below Grade							
Functional Utility							
Heating/Cooling							
Energy Efficient Items							
Garage/Carport							
Porch/Patio/Deck							
Net Adjustment (Total)		☐ + ☐ -	$	☐ + ☐ -	$	☐ + ☐ -	$
Adjusted Sale Price of Comparables		Net Adj. % Gross Adj. %	$	Net Adj. % Gross Adj. %	$	Net Adj. % Gross Adj. %	$

I ☐ did ☐ did not research the sale or transfer history of the subject property and comparable sales. If not, explain

My research ☐ did ☐ did not reveal any prior sales or transfers of the subject property for the three years prior to the effective date of this appraisal.

Data source(s)

My research ☐ did ☐ did not reveal any prior sales or transfers of the comparable sales for the year prior to the date of sale of the comparable sale.

Data source(s)

Report the results of the research and analysis of the prior sale or transfer history of the subject property and comparable sales (report additional prior sales on page 3).

ITEM	SUBJECT	COMPARABLE SALE # 1	COMPARABLE SALE # 2	COMPARABLE SALE # 3
Date of Prior Sale/Transfer				
Price of Prior Sale/Transfer				
Data Source(s)				
Effective Date of Data Source(s)				

Analysis of prior sale or transfer history of the subject property and comparable sales

Summary of Sales Comparison Approach

Indicated Value by Sales Comparison Approach $

Indicated Value by: Sales Comparison Approach $ _____   **Cost Approach (if developed)** $ _____   **Income Approach (if developed)** $ _____

This appraisal is made ☐ "as is", ☐ subject to completion per plans and specifications on the basis of a hypothetical condition that the improvements have been completed, ☐ subject to the following repairs or alterations on the basis of a hypothetical condition that the repairs or alterations have been completed, or ☐ subject to the following required inspection based on the extraordinary assumption that the condition or deficiency does not require alteration or repair:

Based on a complete visual inspection of the interior and exterior areas of the subject property, defined scope of work, statement of assumptions and limiting conditions, and appraiser's certification, my (our) opinion of the market value, as defined, of the real property that is the subject of this report is $ _____ , as of _____ , which is the date of inspection and the effective date of this appraisal.

Freddie Mac Form 70 March 2005	Page 2 of 6	Fannie Mae Form 1004 March 2005

FIGURE 11.6   **Uniform Residential Appraisal Report (Cont.)**

Uniform Residential Appraisal Report
File #

ADDITIONAL COMMENTS

COST APPROACH TO VALUE (not required by Fannie Mae)

Provide adequate information for the lender/client to replicate the below cost figures and calculations.

Support for the opinion of site value (summary of comparable land sales or other methods for estimating site value)

COST APPROACH		
ESTIMATED ☐ REPRODUCTION OR ☐ REPLACEMENT COST NEW	OPINION OF SITE VALUE .... = $	
Source of cost data	Dwelling Sq. Ft. @ $ .... =$	
Quality rating from cost service Effective date of cost data	Sq. Ft. @ $ .... =$	
Comments on Cost Approach (gross living area calculations, depreciation, etc.)		
	Garage/Carport Sq. Ft. @ $ .... =$	
	Total Estimate of Cost-New .... = $	
	Less Physical Functional External	
	Depreciation =$( )	
	Depreciated Cost of Improvements...........................=$	
	"As-is" Value of Site Improvements........................=$	
Estimated Remaining Economic Life (HUD and VA only) Years	Indicated Value By Cost Approach ....=$	

INCOME APPROACH TO VALUE (not required by Fannie Mae)

INCOME

Estimated Monthly Market Rent $ X Gross Rent Multiplier   = $ Indicated Value by Income Approach

Summary of Income Approach (including support for market rent and GRM)

PROJECT INFORMATION FOR PUDs (if applicable)

PUD INFORMATION

Is the developer/builder in control of the Homeowners' Association (HOA)? ☐ Yes ☐ No   Unit type(s) ☐ Detached ☐ Attached

Provide the following information for PUDs ONLY if the developer/builder is in control of the HOA and the subject property is an attached dwelling unit.

Legal name of project

Total number of phases   Total number of units   Total number of units sold

Total number of units rented   Total number of units for sale   Data source(s)

Was the project created by the conversion of an existing building(s) into a PUD? ☐ Yes ☐ No   If Yes, date of conversion

Does the project contain any multi-dwelling units? ☐ Yes ☐ No   Data source(s)

Are the units, common elements, and recreation facilities complete? ☐ Yes ☐ No   If No, describe the status of completion.

Are the common elements leased to or by the Homeowners' Association? ☐ Yes ☐ No   If Yes, describe the rental terms and options.

Describe common elements and recreational facilities

Freddie Mac Form 70   March 2005   Page 3 of 6   Fannie Mae Form 1004   March 2005

FIGURE 11.6   **Uniform Residential Appraisal Report (Cont.)**

Uniform Residential Appraisal Report   File

This report form is designed to report an appraisal of a one-unit property or a one-unit property with an accessory unit; including a unit in a planned unit development (PUD). This report form is not designed to report an appraisal of a manufactured home or a unit in a condominium or cooperative project.

This appraisal report is subject to the following scope of work, intended use, intended user, definition of market value, statement of assumptions and limiting conditions, and certifications. Modifications, additions, or deletions to the intended use, intended user, definition of market value, or assumptions and limiting conditions are not permitted. The appraiser may expand the scope of work to include any additional research or analysis necessary based on the complexity of this appraisal assignment. Modifications or deletions to the certifications are also not permitted. However, additional certifications that do not constitute material alterations to this appraisal report, such as those required by law or those related to the appraiser's continuing education or membership in an appraisal organization, are permitted.

SCOPE OF WORK: The scope of work for this appraisal is defined by the complexity of this appraisal assignment and the reporting requirements of this appraisal report form, including the following definition of market value, statement of assumptions and limiting conditions, and certifications. The appraiser must, at a minimum: (1) perform a complete visual inspection of the interior and exterior areas of the subject property, (2) inspect the neighborhood, (3) inspect each of the comparable sales from at least the street, (4) research, verify, and analyze data from reliable public and/or private sources, and (5) report his or her analysis, opinions, and conclusions in this appraisal report.

INTENDED USE: The intended use of this appraisal report is for the lender/client to evaluate the property that is the subject of this appraisal for a mortgage finance transaction.

INTENDED USER: The intended user of this appraisal report is the lender/client.

DEFINITION OF MARKET VALUE: The most probable price which a property should bring in a competitive and open market under all conditions requisite to a fair sale, the buyer and seller, each acting prudently, knowledgeably and assuming the price is not affected by undue stimulus. Implicit in this definition is the consummation of a sale as of a specified date and the passing of title from seller to buyer under conditions whereby: (1) buyer and seller are typically motivated; (2) both parties are well informed or well advised, and each acting in what he or she considers his or her own best interest; (3) a reasonable time is allowed for exposure in the open market; (4) payment is made in terms of cash in U. S. dollars or in terms of financial arrangements comparable thereto; and (5) the price represents the normal consideration for the property sold unaffected by special or creative financing or sales concessions* granted by anyone associated with the sale.

*Adjustments to the comparables must be made for special or creative financing or sales concessions. No adjustments are necessary for those costs which are normally paid by sellers as a result of tradition or law in a market area; these costs are readily identifiable since the seller pays these costs in virtually all sales transactions. Special or creative financing adjustments can be made to the comparable property by comparisons to financing terms offered by a third party institutional lender that is not already involved in the property or transaction. Any adjustment should not be calculated on a mechanical dollar for dollar cost of the financing or concession but the dollar amount of any adjustment should approximate the market's reaction to the financing or concessions based on the appraiser's judgment.

STATEMENT OF ASSUMPTIONS AND LIMITING CONDITIONS: The appraiser's certification in this report is subject to the following assumptions and limiting conditions:

1. The appraiser will not be responsible for matters of a legal nature that affect either the property being appraised or the title to it, except for information that he or she became aware of during the research involved in performing this appraisal. The appraiser assumes that the title is good and marketable and will not render any opinions about the title.

2. The appraiser has provided a sketch in this appraisal report to show the approximate dimensions of the improvements. The sketch is included only to assist the reader in visualizing the property and understanding the appraiser's determination of its size.

3. The appraiser has examined the available flood maps that are provided by the Federal Emergency Management Agency (or other data sources) and has noted in this appraisal report whether any portion of the subject site is located in an identified Special Flood Hazard Area. Because the appraiser is not a surveyor, he or she makes no guarantees, express or implied, regarding this determination.

4. The appraiser will not give testimony or appear in court because he or she made an appraisal of the property in question, unless specific arrangements to do so have been made beforehand, or as otherwise required by law.

5. The appraiser has noted in this appraisal report any adverse conditions (such as needed repairs, deterioration, the presence of hazardous wastes, toxic substances, etc.) observed during the inspection of the subject property or that he or she became aware of during the research involved in performing this appraisal. Unless otherwise stated in this appraisal report, the appraiser has no knowledge of any hidden or unapparent physical deficiencies or adverse conditions of the property (such as, but not limited to, needed repairs, deterioration, the presence of hazardous wastes, toxic substances, adverse environmental conditions, etc.) that would make the property less valuable, and has assumed that there are no such conditions and makes no guarantees or warranties, express or implied. The appraiser will not be responsible for any such conditions that do exist or for any engineering or testing that might be required to discover whether such conditions exist. Because the appraiser is not an expert in the field of environmental hazards, this appraisal report must not be considered as an environmental assessment of the property.

6. The appraiser has based his or her appraisal report and valuation conclusion for an appraisal that is subject to satisfactory completion, repairs, or alterations on the assumption that the completion, repairs, or alterations of the subject property will be performed in a professional manner.

FFIGURE 11.6 **Uniform Residential Appraisal Report (Cont.)**

Uniform Residential Appraisal Report   File

APPRAISER'S CERTIFICATION: The Appraiser certifies and agrees that:

1. I have, at a minimum, developed and reported this appraisal in accordance with the scope of work requirements stated in this appraisal report.

2. I performed a complete visual inspection of the interior and exterior areas of the subject property. I reported the condition of the improvements in factual, specific terms. I identified and reported the physical deficiencies that could affect the livability, soundness, or structural integrity of the property.

3. I performed this appraisal in accordance with the requirements of the Uniform Standards of Professional Appraisal Practice that were adopted and promulgated by the Appraisal Standards Board of The Appraisal Foundation and that were in place at the time this appraisal report was prepared.

4. I developed my opinion of the market value of the real property that is the subject of this report based on the sales comparison approach to value. I have adequate comparable market data to develop a reliable sales comparison approach for this appraisal assignment. I further certify that I considered the cost and income approaches to value but did not develop them, unless otherwise indicated in this report.

5. I researched, verified, analyzed, and reported on any current agreement for sale for the subject property, any offering for sale of the subject property in the twelve months prior to the effective date of this appraisal, and the prior sales of the subject property for a minimum of three years prior to the effective date of this appraisal, unless otherwise indicated in this report.

6. I researched, verified, analyzed, and reported on the prior sales of the comparable sales for a minimum of one year prior to the date of sale of the comparable sale, unless otherwise indicated in this report.

7. I selected and used comparable sales that are locationally, physically, and functionally the most similar to the subject property.

8. I have not used comparable sales that were the result of combining a land sale with the contract purchase price of a home that has been built or will be built on the land.

9. I have reported adjustments to the comparable sales that reflect the market's reaction to the differences between the subject property and the comparable sales.

10. I verified, from a disinterested source, all information in this report that was provided by parties who have a financial interest in the sale or financing of the subject property.

11. I have knowledge and experience in appraising this type of property in this market area.

12. I am aware of, and have access to, the necessary and appropriate public and private data sources, such as multiple listing services, tax assessment records, public land records and other such data sources for the area in which the property is located.

13. I obtained the information, estimates, and opinions furnished by other parties and expressed in this appraisal report from reliable sources that I believe to be true and correct.

14. I have taken into consideration the factors that have an impact on value with respect to the subject neighborhood, subject property, and the proximity of the subject property to adverse influences in the development of my opinion of market value. I have noted in this appraisal report any adverse conditions (such as, but not limited to, needed repairs, deterioration, the presence of hazardous wastes, toxic substances, adverse environmental conditions, etc.) observed during the inspection of the subject property or that I became aware of during the research involved in performing this appraisal. I have considered these adverse conditions in my analysis of the property value, and have reported on the effect of the conditions on the value and marketability of the subject property.

15. I have not knowingly withheld any significant information from this appraisal report and, to the best of my knowledge, all statements and information in this appraisal report are true and correct.

16. I stated in this appraisal report my own personal, unbiased, and professional analysis, opinions, and conclusions, which are subject only to the assumptions and limiting conditions in this appraisal report.

17. I have no present or prospective interest in the property that is the subject of this report, and I have no present or prospective personal interest or bias with respect to the participants in the transaction. I did not base, either partially or completely, my analysis and/or opinion of market value in this appraisal report on the race, color, religion, sex, age, marital status, handicap, familial status, or national origin of either the prospective owners or occupants of the subject property or of the present owners or occupants of the properties in the vicinity of the subject property or on any other basis prohibited by law.

18. My employment and/or compensation for performing this appraisal or any future or anticipated appraisals was not conditioned on any agreement or understanding, written or otherwise, that I would report (or present analysis supporting) a predetermined specific value, a predetermined minimum value, a range or direction in value, a value that favors the cause of any party, or the attainment of a specific result or occurrence of a specific subsequent event (such as approval of a pending mortgage loan application).

19. I personally prepared all conclusions and opinions about the real estate that were set forth in this appraisal report. If I relied on significant real property appraisal assistance from any individual or individuals in the performance of this appraisal or the preparation of this appraisal report, I have named such individual(s) and disclosed the specific tasks performed in this appraisal report. I certify that any individual so named is qualified to perform the tasks. I have not authorized anyone to make a change to any item in this appraisal report; therefore, any change made to this appraisal is unauthorized and I will take no responsibility for it.

20. I identified the lender/client in this appraisal report who is the individual, organization, or agent for the organization that ordered and will receive this appraisal report.

Freddie Mac Form 70 March 2005   Page 5 of 6   Fannie Mae Form 1004 March 2005

FIGURE 11.6   Uniform Residential Appraisal Report (Cont.)

Uniform Residential Appraisal Report   File

21. The lender/client may disclose or distribute this appraisal report to: the borrower; another lender at the request of the borrower; the mortgagee or its successors and assigns; mortgage insurers; government sponsored enterprises; other secondary market participants; data collection or reporting services; professional appraisal organizations; any department, agency, or instrumentality of the United States; and any state, the District of Columbia, or other jurisdictions; without having to obtain the appraiser's or supervisory appraiser's (if applicable) consent. Such consent must be obtained before this appraisal report may be disclosed or distributed to any other party (including, but not limited to, the public through advertising, public relations, news, sales, or other media).

22. I am aware that any disclosure or distribution of this appraisal report by me or the lender/client may be subject to certain laws and regulations. Further, I am also subject to the provisions of the Uniform Standards of Professional Appraisal Practice that pertain to disclosure or distribution by me.

23. The borrower, another lender at the request of the borrower, the mortgagee or its successors and assigns, mortgage insurers, government sponsored enterprises, and other secondary market participants may rely on this appraisal report as part of any mortgage finance transaction that involves any one or more of these parties.

24. If this appraisal report was transmitted as an "electronic record" containing my "electronic signature," as those terms are defined in applicable federal and/or state laws (excluding audio and video recordings), or a facsimile transmission of this appraisal report containing a copy or representation of my signature, the appraisal report shall be as effective, enforceable and valid as if a paper version of this appraisal report were delivered containing my original hand written signature.

25. Any intentional or negligent misrepresentation(s) contained in this appraisal report may result in civil liability and/or criminal penalties including, but not limited to, fine or imprisonment or both under the provisions of Title 18, United States Code, Section 1001, et seq., or similar state laws.

SUPERVISORY APPRAISER'S CERTIFICATION: The Supervisory Appraiser certifies and agrees that:

1. I directly supervised the appraiser for this appraisal assignment, have read the appraisal report, and agree with the appraiser's analysis, opinions, statements, conclusions, and the appraiser's certification.

2. I accept full responsibility for the contents of this appraisal report including, but not limited to, the appraiser's analysis, opinions, statements, conclusions, and the appraiser's certification.

3. The appraiser identified in this appraisal report is either a sub-contractor or an employee of the supervisory appraiser (or the appraisal firm), is qualified to perform this appraisal, and is acceptable to perform this appraisal under the applicable state law.

4. This appraisal report complies with the Uniform Standards of Professional Appraisal Practice that were adopted and promulgated by the Appraisal Standards Board of The Appraisal Foundation and that were in place at the time this appraisal report was prepared.

5. If this appraisal report was transmitted as an "electronic record" containing my "electronic signature," as those terms are defined in applicable federal and/or state laws (excluding audio and video recordings), or a facsimile transmission of this appraisal report containing a copy or representation of my signature, the appraisal report shall be as effective, enforceable and valid as if a paper version of this appraisal report were delivered containing my original hand written signature.

APPRAISER

Signature_____
Name _____
Company Name _____
Company Address _____
_____
Telephone Number _____
Email Address _____
Date of Signature and Report _____
Effective Date of Appraisal _____
State Certification #_____
or State License # _____
or Other (describe) _____ State # _____
State _____
Expiration Date of Certification or License _____

ADDRESS OF PROPERTY APPRAISED

_____
_____
APPRAISED VALUE OF SUBJECT PROPERTY $ _____
LENDER/CLIENT
Name _____
Company Name _____
Company Address _____
_____
Email Address _____

SUPERVISORY APPRAISER (ONLY IF REQUIRED)

Signature_____
Name _____
Company Name _____
Company Address _____
_____
Telephone Number _____
Email Address _____
Date of Signature _____
State Certification #_____
or State License # _____
State _____
Expiration Date of Certification or License _____

SUBJECT PROPERTY

☐ Did not inspect subject property
☐ Did inspect exterior of subject property from street
    Date of Inspection _____
☐ Did inspect interior and exterior of subject property
    Date of Inspection _____

COMPARABLE SALES

☐ Did not inspect exterior of comparable sales from street
☐ Did inspect exterior of comparable sales from street
    Date of Inspection _____

Freddie Mac Form 70   March 2005   Page 6 of 6   Fannie Mae Form 1004   March 2005

SUMMARY

An appraisal is an estimate of value. There are many different types of value, but the most common objective of a real estate appraisal is to estimate market value, which is the most probable sales price of a property.

Appraisals are concerned with values, costs, and prices. Value is an estimate of future benefits, cost represents a measure of past expenditures, and price reflects the actual amount of money paid for a property.

There are certain underlying economic principles basic to appraising, such as highest and best use, substitution, supply and demand, balance, conformity, regression and progression, anticipation, plottage, increasing and decreasing returns, contribution, competition, and change.

A professional appraiser analyzes a property through three approaches to value. In the sales comparison approach, the subject property is compared with others like it that have sold recently. Because no two properties are exactly alike, adjustments must be made to account for any differences. With the cost approach, an appraiser first sets aside the value of the land, then calculates the cost of building a similar structure on a similar site. The appraiser then subtracts depreciation (loss in value) that reflects the differences between new properties of this type and the subject property in its present condition and adds this value to the value of the land. The income approach is an analysis based on the relationship between the rate of return that an investor requires and the net income that a property produces.

Normally, the application of the three approaches results in three different estimates of value. In the process of reconciliation, the validity and reliability of each approach are weighed objectively to arrive at the single best and most supportable conclusion of value.

An offshoot of the income approach, the gross rent multiplier (GRM) may be used to estimate the value of single-family residential properties to be used as rental property. The GRM is computed by dividing the sales price of a property by its gross monthly rent. A gross income multiplier (GIM) uses gross annual income when appraising industrial and commercial properties.

REVIEW QUESTIONS

Please complete all of the questions before turning to the Answer Key on page 342.

1. A rental home rents for $15,000 per year in a community where the gross rent multiplier is 125. The value of the rental property is
   a. $125,000.
   b. $156,250.
   c. $187,500.
   d. $1,875,000.

2. An appraiser has used the market data, the cost, and the income approach to value to appraise an apartment building. The appraiser's analysis and effective weighing of the findings to develop the final value estimate is called
   a. reproduction.
   b. rehabilitation.
   c. reconsideration.
   d. reconciliation.

3. The owners of an old, four-story office building are having difficulty selling the property because the building does not have an elevator. This loss of property value is due to
   a. physical deterioration.
   b. physical obsolescence.
   c. functional obsolescence.
   d. external obsolescence.

4. An appraiser is using the cost approach to estimate the value of an historic property. The appraiser will *NOT* consider the
   a. reproduction or replacement cost.
   b. price the seller paid for the property.
   c. value of the land parcel.
   d. depreciation from all sources.

5. When determining the effective gross income of a property, the appraiser would consider all of the following items *EXCEPT*
   a. potential gross income.
   b. vacancies.
   c. management fees.
   d. collection losses.

6. A developer has purchased all the individual homes on one block in order to have a large contiguous property where the developer can build town houses. This action is called
   a. plottage.
   b. progression.
   c. reconciliation.
   d. regression.

7. When an improvement is new and represents the highest and best use of the property, the cost usually equals the
   a. mortgage value.
   b. salvage value.
   c. market value.
   d. assessed value.

8. A small shopping mall has a capitalization rate of 9% and a value of $270,000. If a capitalization rate of 10% were used instead, the value of the property would be
   a. $243,000.
   b. $270,000.
   c. $300,000.
   d. $315,000.

9. The appraisal value that holds the maximum value of a property tends to be set by the cost of purchasing an equally desirable and valuable property is
   a. plottage.
   b. contribution.
   c. substitution.
   d. anticipation.

10. A renovating company has a contract for work on an historic home. They will exactly duplicate the large fireplace in the kitchen area so that it can be used to both heat the home and to cook food. This duplication of both the function and the form of an improvement is called a
    a. reproduction.
    b. reconciliation.
    c. replacement.
    d. renovation.

11. The owner of a large piece of land would like to sell it. Unfortunately, the land is located adjacent to the city sewage treatment plant. The value of this property will be affected by the incurable type of depreciation called
    a. physical deterioration.
    b. physical obsolescence.
    c. functional obsolescence.
    d. external obsolescence.

12. The tenants who live in a 75-year-old apartment building have pleaded with the landlord to install central air-conditioning. After receiving three cost estimates for upgrading the electrical system for central air, the landlord realizes that the rents could never be increased enough to cover the cost. The landlord is *NOT* willing to comply with the tenant's request based on the principle of
    a. balance.
    b. competition.
    c. conformity.
    d. contribution.

13. An appraiser using the cost approach to value for a private boarding school will *MOST* likely use the most common method of cost estimation called the
    a. quantity survey method.
    b. unit-in-place method.
    c. square-foot method.
    d. index method.

14. One problem that occurs when a homeowner decides to add a 1,200 square-foot, two-story addition plus garage to the home in a neighborhood of small one-story ranch-style homes is that the value of this property will be harmed because of the impact of
    a. contribution.
    b. regression.
    c. increasing returns.
    d. progression.

15. The effective gross annual income for an office complex is $250,000. Total expenses for this year are $175,000. Using a capitalization rate of 10%, the property is valued at
    a. $250,000.
    b. $750,000.
    c. $1,750,000.
    d. $2,500,000.

16. Demand is necessary for a property to have
    a. value.
    b. substance.
    c. depreciation.
    d. functionality.

17. The market value of a newly constructed home is *MOST* likely very similar to its
    a. highest and best use.
    b. cost.
    c. depreciated value.
    d. worth.

18. The first few houses constructed in a subdivision were much smaller than those built at the end of the building phase. However, buyers are still willing to pay more for these smaller houses than for a larger one in a different subdivision. This is an example of
    a. highest and best use.
    b. conformity.
    c. progression.
    d. plottage.

19. Which of the following is considered an acceptable comparable sale?
    a. Son buys home from his father.
    b. Property purchased at a tax sale.
    c. Buyer knew that the seller was facing foreclosure.
    d. Out-of-town buyer chooses the home after viewing 10 homes.

20. A rumor is circulating that the largest employer in the area is planning to shut its doors. Sellers are finding it difficult to get their asking prices due to what principle of value?
    a. Anticipation
    b. Conformity
    c. Competition
    d. Change

Real Estate Financing

LEARNING OBJECTIVES

When you finish reading this chapter, you will be able to

- differentiate between a note and the security instruments;
- compare a fixed-rate amortized loan to an adjustable-rate mortgage (ARM);
- discuss the provisions of the mortgage document or deed of trust;
- describe different types of foreclosure methods;
- summarize the advantages and disadvantages of conventional, insured, or guaranteed loans; and
- name several specialized financing techniques.

acceleration clause

adjustable-rate mortgage

alienation clause

assumption of mortgage

balloon payment

buydown

conforming loan

construction loan

conventional loan

deed of trust

defeasance clause

deficiency judgment

discount points

equitable right of redemption

equity

FHA-insured loan

foreclosure

graduated-payment mortgage (GPM)

growing equity mortgage (GEM)

home equity loans

hypothecate

installment contract

interest

junior lien

lien theory

loan origination fee

loan-to-value ratio (LTV)

mortgage

mortgagee

mortgage insurance premium (MIP)

mortgagor

nonconforming loan

open-end loan

package loan

power-of-sale clause

prepayment penalty

principal

private mortgage insurance (PMI)

promissory note

purchase-money loan

real estate investment trust (REIT)

redemption

reverse annuity mortgage (RAM)

sale-and-leaseback

satisfaction of mortgage

shared-appreciation mortgage (SAM)

short sale

subordination

take-out loan

title theory

usury

VA loan

wraparound loan

F ew buyers bring cash to the closing table. Because most transactions involve some kind of financing, a general understanding of real estate financing is very important for all real estate licensees. In a typical transaction, the buyer borrows most of the purchase price by obtaining a loan and pledging the real property involved as *security* (collateral) for the loan. This is generally called a *mortgage loan*, even though in some states, a deed of trust is actually used to establish collateral. Many other types of real estate financing are available. Licensees who are aware of the various options can be very helpful to their sellers and buyers.

Many variations can be found in the terms used in either a mortgage or a deed of trust. Also, numerous types of alternative financing programs may be used in times of tight mortgage money. This chapter will discuss in detail the mortgage and deed of trust documents used to finance a typical real estate purchase. Chapter 13 details the various sources of mortgage money and addresses the government's role in the financing market.

MORTGAGE THEORY

From their inception, American courts of equity have considered a mortgage a voluntary lien on real estate, given to secure the payment of a debt or the performance of an obligation. Those states that interpret a mortgage purely as a lien on real property are called **lien theory** states, and the mortgagor/owner retains title and possession. In such states, if a mortgagor defaults, the lender may foreclose (generally through a court action), offer the property for sale, and apply the funds received from the sale to reduce or extinguish the obligation. As protection to the borrower, some states allow a statutory redemption period during which a defaulted mortgagor can redeem the property.

Yet other states recognize a lender as the owner of mortgaged land, an ownership subject to defeat upon full payment of the debt or performance of the obligation. These states are called **title theory** states. The lender holds the title, but the mortgagor has possession. Under title theory, a mortgagee (lender) has the right to possession of, and rents from, the mortgaged property immediately upon default by the mortgagor (borrower).

Today, a number of states have modified the strict interpretation of title and lien theories. These *intermediary* or *modified lien theory* states allow a lender to take possession of the mortgaged real estate upon default through the action of a trustee who initiates an auction for the sale of the property on behalf of the lender. No court action is required.

SECURITY AND DEBT

What Property May Be Mortgaged

Generally, any interest in real estate that may be sold may also be pledged as security for a debt. The basic principle of property law that insures that a person cannot convey greater rights in property than that person actually has applies equally to the right to mortgage. The owner of a fee simple estate can mortgage the fee, and the owner of a leasehold or subleasehold estate can mortgage that leasehold interest. For example, a large retail corporation renting space in a shopping center may mortgage its leasehold interest to finance remodeling work.

Loan Instruments

Loan instruments consist of two parts—the debt itself and the security for the debt. When a property is to be mortgaged, the owner must execute, or sign, two separate instruments:

1. The **promissory note**, or *financing document*, is the written promise to repay a debt in definite installments.

2. The *security document*, either the **mortgage**, or **deed of trust**, provides *security* for the debt.

In either situation, the borrower hypothecates the real estate to the lender in order to secure the loan. To **hypothecate** is to use the real estate as a security for the loan without giving up possession of the property.

Promissory note.   The promissory note, executed by the borrower (maker), is an unconditional promise to repay the debt. The note states the amount of the debt (principal) and the method of payment. If the note is used with a mortgage, it names the mortgagee as the payee; if it is used with a deed of trust, the note is usually made payable to the bearer. The promissory note refers to or repeats several of the clauses that appear in the mortgage document or deed of trust. Like the mortgage or deed of trust, all parties who have an interest in the property should sign the note. In states where dower and curtesy are in effect or homestead or community property is involved, both spouses have an interest in the property and must sign the note.

Mortgages.   By itself, a mortgage document is basically a pledge of property to secure a loan, that when recorded, becomes a lien against the property. Because a pledge of security is not legally effective, unless there is a debt to secure, the promissory note is fundamental to the transaction. Both documents must be executed to create an enforceable mortgage loan (see Figure 12.1). Note that the lender is the giver of the loan monies but the recipient of the mortgage. The *borrower*, therefore, is called the **mortgagor**, and the *lender*, the **mortgagee**.

FIGURE 12.1   **Mortgage and Deed of Trust**

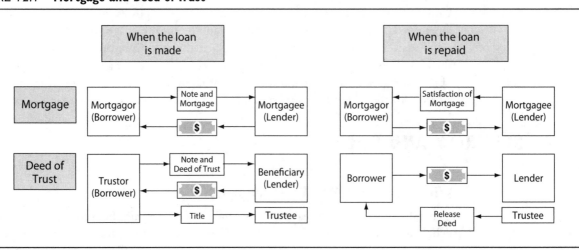

Deeds of trust.   In some states lenders use a three-party instrument called a *deed of trust*, or *trust deed*, rather than a mortgage. As with mortgages, deeds of trust involve two separate instruments: a note detailing the terms of the loan and a *trust deed*. A deed of trust conveys the real estate as a security for the loan to a third party, called the *trustee*.

The trustee then holds title on behalf of the lender, called the *beneficiary*, who is the legal owner and holder of the note (see Figure 12.1). The wording of the conveyance sets forth actions that the trustee may take if the borrower, called the *trustor*, defaults under any of the trust deed's terms. In states where deeds of trust are preferred, foreclosure procedures for defaulted deeds of trust are usually simpler and speedier than those for mortgage loans.

In most cases, the lender chooses the trustee and reserves the right of substitution if a trustee dies or is dismissed. In the financing of a commercial or industrial real estate venture that involves a large loan and several lenders, the borrower may execute a deed of trust rather than a mortgage because a deed of trust can be used to secure several notes, one note held by each lender.

PROVISIONS OF THE NOTE

A note is a *negotiable instrument*, that is, a written promise or order to pay a specific sum of money. Its holder, called the *payee*, may transfer the right to payment to a third party by assigning the document to the third party or by delivering the document to that individual. The transferee, or new holder of the note, is called a *holder in due course*. Other negotiable instruments include checks and bank drafts.

To be negotiable, or freely transferable, a document must meet certain requirements of the Uniform Commercial Code. The note must be in writing, made by one person to another, and signed by the maker. It must contain an unconditional promise to pay a sum of money on demand or at a set date in the future. In addition, the note must be payable to the order of a specifically named person or to the bearer (the person who has possession of the note). Notes that are payable to order must be transferred by endorsement; those payable to bearer must be transferred by delivery.

Components of a Loan

Principal. The **principal** is the amount of money borrowed. It is the amount on which interest is calculated.

Interest. **Interest** is a charge for the use of money. A lender charges a borrower a percentage of the principal as interest for each year the debt is outstanding. The amount of interest due on any one installment payment date is calculated by computing the total yearly interest based on the unpaid balance and dividing that figure by the number of payments made each year. For example, if the current outstanding loan balance is $150,000 with interest at the rate of 4.5% per annum and constant monthly payments of $836.03, the interest and principal due on the next payment are computed as follows:

> $150,000 × 4.5% = $6,000 annual interest
>
> $6,750 ÷ 12 = $562.50 one month's interest
>
> $836.03 − $562.50 = $273.53 this month's principal reduction

Interest is customarily due and charged at the end of each month or payment period; this is called *payment in arrears*. Because mortgage loan payments are customarily made at the beginning of each month, the interest portion of each payment covers the charge for using the borrowed money during the previous month. Some lenders, however, specify in the note that interest is charged in advance. In practice, the distinction between the two becomes important if the property is sold before the debt is repaid.

Usury. The maximum rate of interest that may be charged on loans may be set by state law. Charging interest in excess of this rate is called **usury**, and lenders may be penalized for making usurious loans.

Usury laws are state laws that were originally enacted to protect consumers from unscrupulous lenders. However, federal law exempts from state usury law interest paid on residential first mortgage loans made after March 31, 1980, if they were made by a federally chartered institution or were insured or guaranteed by a federal agency.

Amortized Loans

Most mortgage and deed of trust loans are *amortized loans*, in which the borrower makes regular payments consisting of principal and interest payments, over a specified term. By the end of the term, the full amount of the principal due is reduced to zero. As shown in Figure 12.2, the lender first credits each payment to the interest due and then applies the balance to reduce the principal of the loan. While each payment is the same, the portion applied toward repayment of the principal grows and the interest due declines as the unpaid balance of the loan is reduced.

FIGURE 12.2 **Fully Amortized Loan**

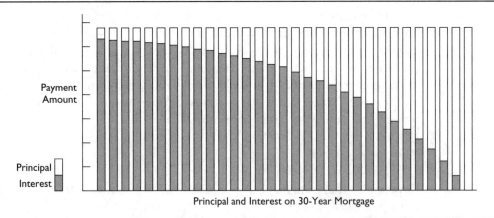

Payment Amount

Principal
Interest

Principal and Interest on 30-Year Mortgage

Fully amortized loan. Under a fully amortized loan, by the end of the term, the full amount of the principal due is reduced to zero.

Partially amortized loan. With a partially amortized loan, the periodic payments will not fully amortize the loan by the time the final payment is due. The final payment, called a *balloon payment*, is an amount larger than the others. Partially amortized loans are frequently used in second mortgages to keep installments low when paying off two loans at one time and in owner financing, where the seller needs to finance the property to expedite a sale, but does not want to be involved as a lender for more than a few years. With the latter, the seller expects that the buyer borrower will be able to get a different loan and pay off the balanced owed with a balloon payment.

Adjustable-Rate Mortgages (ARMs)

An **adjustable-rate mortgage (ARM)** is generally originated at one rate of interest, with the rate fluctuating up or down during the loan term based on economic indicators. Because the interest may change, so may the mortgagor's loan payments. Details of how and when the rate of interest on the loan will change are included in the provisions of the note. Common components of an ARM include the following:

- *Index.* The rate of the loan is tied to the movement of a financial indicator, such as the cost-of-funds *index* for federally chartered lenders. Many indexes are tied to U.S. Treasury securities.

- *Margin.* The interest rate on the loan is the index rate plus a premium called the *margin.* The margin represents the lender's cost of doing business. For example, the loan rate may be 2% over the U.S. Treasury bill rate.

- *Interest rate caps. Rate caps* limit the amount the interest rate may change. Most ARMs have both periodic rate caps, which limit the amount the rate may increase at any one time, and aggregate rate caps, which limit the amount the rate may increase over the entire life of the loan.

- *Interest rate floors.* An interest *rate floor* is the minimum interest rate that the borrower will be charged (i.e., a point below which the interest rate will not go). This protects the lender in the event that interest rates dramatically drop. Floors are less common than caps.

- *Payment cap.* The mortgagor is protected against the possibility of unaffordable individual payments by the *payment cap*, which sets a maximum amount for payments. However, with a payment cap, a rate increase could result in negative amortization—an increase in the loan balance.

- *Adjustment period.* This establishes how often the loan rate may be changed. Common adjustment periods are monthly, quarterly, and annually.

Figure 12.3 illustrates the effect interest rate fluctuations and periodic caps have on an adjustable-rate mortgage.

FIGURE 12.3 **Adjustable Rate Mortgage**

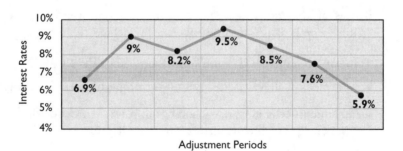

Without caps, the interest rate could fluctuate wildly, for example, if the figure changed from a low of 5.9% to a high of 9.5%. Such unpredictability makes personal financial planning difficult. If there were a rate cap of 7.5% and a floor of 6.5%, as shown in the shaded area in the figure, the borrower and lender would both be protected against dramatic changes in interest rates. Today's ARM loan products generally carry a 2% periodic rate cap with 6% for the life of the loan.

Prepayment

An amortized loan allows the borrower to make lower, affordable, payments over a long period of time, fifteen to thirty years for most residential loans. The longer that the borrower takes to repay the loan, the more the borrower pays in interest. Sometimes the interest payments exceed the amount borrowed.

When an amortized loan is paid off ahead of its full term, the lender does not receive the full interest. For this reason, many mortgage and trust deed notes include a **prepayment penalty** against the unearned portion of the interest when any payments are made ahead of schedule. Any penalty charged depends on the terms of the loan. If the loan is paid in full, the borrower may be charged a percentage of the principal paid in excess of that allowance.

However, many states either limit penalties or do not allow lenders to charge penalties on prepayment of residential mortgage or deed of trust loans. Federal law prohibits prepayment penalties on FHA, VA, and Fannie Mae/Freddie Mac conforming loans. These loans include a *repayment* privilege ("or more" clause), allowing the borrower to prepay the debt without penalty.

PROVISIONS OF THE MORTGAGE DOCUMENT OR DEED OF TRUST

The mortgage document or deed of trust refers to the terms of the note and establishes that the conveyance of land is security for the debt. It identifies the lender as well as the borrower, and it includes an accurate legal description of the property. It should be signed by all parties who have an interest in the real estate. In addition, the instrument sets forth the obligations of the borrower (mortgagor) and the rights of the lender (mortgagee).

When a mortgage document is used to convey real property as security, both the mortgage and the note must include the name of the mortgagee as the lender. The mortgage document must name as the mortgagee the same person who is named in the note as the payee. It cannot name a third party.

Duties of the mortgagor or trustor.   The borrower is required to fulfill many covenants (promises). Those covenants usually include

- payment of the debt in accordance with the terms of the note;

- payment of all real estate taxes on the property given as security;

- maintenance of adequate insurance to protect the lender if the property is destroyed or damaged by fire, windstorm, or other hazard;

- maintenance of the property in good repair at all times; and

- in some situations, the lender's authorization to make any major alterations on the property.

Failure to meet any of these obligations can result in a borrower's default. When this happens, the mortgage or deed of trust usually provides for a grace period (30 days, for example), during which the borrower can meet the obligation and cure the default. If the borrower does not do so, the lender has the right to foreclose the mortgage or deed of trust. The most frequent cause of default is the borrower's failure to make the monthly payments.

Provisions for Default

The provisions of a mortgage may include an *acceleration clause* to assist the lender in a foreclosure. If a borrower defaults, the lender has the right to accelerate the maturity of the debt—to declare the entire debt due and owing immediately—even though the terms of the mortgage allow the borrower to amortize the debt in regular payments over a period of years. Without the acceleration clause, the lender would have to foreclose the debt every time a payment became due and owing.

Other clauses in a mortgage or deed of trust enable the lender to take care of the property in the event of the borrower's negligence or default. If the borrower does not pay taxes or insurance premiums or make necessary repairs on the property, the lender may step in and do so to protect the real estate held as security. Any money advanced by the lender to cure such defaults is either added to the unpaid debt or declared immediately due and owing from the borrower.

Assignment

When a note is sold to a third party, the lender will endorse the note to the third party and also execute an *assignment of mortgage* or an *assignment of deed of trust*. The assignee becomes the new owner of the debt and security instrument. This assignment must be recorded. Upon payment in full, or satisfaction of the debt, the assignee is required to execute the satisfaction, or release, of the security instrument, as discussed in the following section. It is common practice for a lender to sell the note to an investor but retain the servicing of the loan. The lender services the loan by collecting monthly payments and interfacing with the borrower on behalf of the holder of the investor.

Release of the Lien

When all mortgage loan payments have been made and the note paid in full, the borrower wants the public record to show that the debt has been paid and the mortgage released. Under the provisions of the **defeasance clause** in the typical mortgage, the mortgagee is required to execute a **satisfaction of mortgage** when the note is fully paid. This document returns to the mortgagor all interest in the real estate that was transferred to the mortgagee by the original recorded mortgage document. Having this satisfaction entered into the public record shows that the debt has been paid and the mortgage released and canceled. If a mortgage has been assigned by a recorded assignment, the release must be executed by the assignee mortgagee.

When a real estate loan secured by a deed of trust has been completely repaid, the beneficiary requests in writing that the trustee convey the property back to the grantor. The trustee then executes and delivers to the grantor a *deed of reconveyance*. This deed reconveys the rights and powers that the trustee was given under the deed of trust. The deed should be acknowledged and recorded in the county where the property is located.

Recording

Mortgages or deeds of trust must be recorded in the recorder's office of the county in which the real estate is located. Recordation gives constructive notice to the world of the borrower's obligations and establishes the priority of the lien. If the property is registered in Torrens, notice of the lien must be entered on the original certificate of title on file at the registrar's office.

First and Second Priority

Mortgages and other liens normally have priority in the order in which they have been recorded. A mortgage or deed of trust on property that has no prior mortgage lien is a first mortgage or first deed of trust. When the owner of this property later executes another mortgage for additional funds, the new mortgage becomes a *second mortgage* (deed of trust), or **junior lien**, when recorded. The second mortgage is subject to the first; the first mortgage has prior claim to the value of the property pledged as security.

The priority of mortgage or deed of trust liens may be changed by the execution of a **subordination** agreement, in which the first lender subordinates the lien to that of the second lender. To be valid, such an agreement must be signed by both lenders. A subordination agreement is often used when the seller of raw land subordinates the original note in order for a new construction loan to take first priority.

Tax and Insurance Reserves

Many lenders require borrowers to provide a reserve fund, called an *impound* or *escrow account*, to meet future real estate taxes and insurance premiums. When the mortgage or deed of trust loan is made, the borrower starts the reserve by depositing funds to cover any amount of unpaid real estate taxes. When a new insurance policy has been purchased, the insurance premium reserve is started with an initial two-month deposit. A deposit of one-twelfth of the annual tax and insurance premium liability is then collected along with the required principal and interest in each monthly payment. Thereafter, the monthly loan payments required of the borrower will include principal, interest, and tax and insurance reserves (PITI).

The federal Real Estate Settlement Procedures Act (RESPA) limits the total amount of reserves that may be required by a lender. RESPA is discussed further in Chapter 13.

National Flood Insurance Program (NFIP). Property owners in certain flood-prone areas as identified by the Federal Emergency Management Agency (FEMA) are required to obtain flood-damage insurance. The National Flood Insurance Program (NFIP) requires flood insurance on properties financed by mortgages or other loans, grants, or guarantees obtained from all primary and secondary lending institutions that are regulated by federal law. Flood insurance is never included in a basic homeowners' insurance policy. The program seeks to improve future management and planning of floodplain areas through land-use and control measures. Visit www.fema.gov/national-flood-insurance-program and see the discussion in Chapter 1 for more information.

Comprehensive Loss Underwriting Exchange (CLUE). An increasingly significant problem with regard to obtaining homeowner insurance is the Comprehensive Loss Underwriting Exchange (CLUE) Home Seller's Disclosure Report. Some homebuyers today are making their purchase contract contingent on receipt of this CLUE report from the seller. The report provides information about any insurance losses in that home for the past five years and can only be obtained by the present homeowner from LexisNexis. An insurance company may not be willing to provide a homeowners' insurance policy for a home showing significant claims. Visit www.lexisnexis.com/risk/products/insurance/clue-home-seller.aspx for more information.

Assignment of Rents

The borrower may make an assignment of rents to the lender, to be effective upon the borrower's default. The rent assignment may be included in the mortgage or deed of trust, or it may be made as a separate document. In either case the rent assignment should be drafted in language that clearly indicates that the parties intend to assign the rents and not merely to pledge them as security for the loan. In title theory states, the lender is, in most cases, automatically entitled to any rents if the borrower defaults.

Buying Subject to or Assuming a Seller's Mortgage

A person who purchases real estate that has an outstanding mortgage or deed of trust may take the property subject to the mortgage or deed of trust or may *assume* it and agree to pay the debt (called **assumption of mortgage** or *assumption*). This technical distinction becomes important if the buyer defaults and the mortgage or deed of trust is foreclosed.

When the property is sold *subject to* the mortgage, the courts frequently hold that the purchaser is not personally obligated to pay the debt in full. The purchaser has bought the real estate knowing of the obligation to make the loan payments and that, upon default, the lender will foreclose and the property will be sold by court order to pay the debt. However, when the assumer not only purchases the property subject to the mortgage ,but assumes and agrees to pay the debt, then the assumer becomes personally obligated for the payment of the entire debt. If the mortgage is foreclosed, a deficiency judgment against both the assumer and the original borrower can be obtained for any unpaid balance of the note.

In certain cases, the lender will relieve the seller from continued liability by way of a *novation* (substituting new parties for an old obligation). This is an advantage to sellers as they are released from future liability on the loan. When a mortgage is assumed, most lending institutions charge a transfer or assumption fee to cover the costs of changing their records. This charge is customarily borne by the purchaser.

Alienation clause. Frequently, lenders wish to prevent some future purchaser from being able to assume real estate loans, particularly at old rates of interest. For this reason, many lenders include an **alienation clause** (also called a *due-on-sale clause*) in the note. If the borrower sells the property, the lender has the choice of declaring the entire debt immediately due or permitting a qualified buyer to assume the loan at current market interest rates.

UNDERWATER MORTGAGE LOANS

A loan is said to be underwater when it is larger than the current value of the property. There is no problem when property owners can continue to make their payments. However, the issue became especially acute in 2008 when many lost their jobs and were unable to make their mortgage payments. Some property owners found it difficult to refinance because most lenders require at least 20% equity, which was no longer there. Unless these sellers could bring cash to closing, they could not sell these properties. The following is a discussion about possible solutions instead of foreclosure.

Short Sale

A **short sale** is one that results from the lender agreeing to accept less than what is owed on the property (i.e., the proceeds are short, or not enough to repay the mortgage loan) and the seller does not have the funds to make up the difference. A short sale is not a foreclosure and it is not in the seller's control.

A lender may agree to a short sale to minimize its losses by avoiding the time and expense of foreclosure and avoiding all of the expenses of owning a vacant property. Sellers would like the lender to write off the unpaid balance of the loan; sometimes lenders do, but many require that the seller sign a promissory note to make up the difference.

Deed in Lieu of Foreclosure

An alternative to foreclosure is for the lender to accept a *deed in lieu of foreclosure* from the borrower. This is sometimes called a friendly foreclosure because it is by agreement rather than by civil action. The major disadvantage of this default settlement is that the mortgagee takes the real estate subject to all junior liens, while foreclosure eliminates all such liens. Also, by accepting a deed in lieu of foreclosure, the lender usually loses any rights pertaining to FHA insurance, VA guarantees, or private mortgage insurance and the right to sue for a deficiency judgment, which is discussed later in this chapter.

Government Initiatives

The housing crash of 2007 led to the 2008 great recession. On-going efforts to stimulate the economy focused on creating jobs and helping families stay in their homes.

Home Affordable Modification Program (HAMP). The Home Affordable Modification Program (HAMP) modifies current mortgages in order to make the monthly payments affordable. This program is set to expire December 31, 2015. The distressed loan must be owned, insured, or guaranteed by Fannie Mae, Freddie Mac, the Federal Housing Administration (FHA), the Department of Veterans Affairs (VA), or the Department of Agriculture.

To be eligible for this assistance,

- borrowers must be delinquent and/or face imminent risk of default;

- the property must be occupied as the borrower's primary residence;

- the mortgage must have originated before Jan. 1, 2009; and

- the loan must be less than $729,750 for a single-family dwelling.

The interest rate may be reduced to as low as 2% for eligible borrowers, the loan term may be extended to 40 years, and a portion of the principal can possibly be deferred until the loan is paid off.

Home Affordable Refinance Program (HARP). The Home Affordable Refinance Program (HARP) is available to homeowners whose loans are underwater and were sold to or guaranteed by Freddie Mac or Fannie Mae before May 31, 2009. Not all mortgage servicers participate in this program. To refinance for a more affordable loan,

- the borrower must be current with payments and have a good payment history for the preceding 12 months, and

- the current loan-to-value ratio (LTV) must be greater than 80%.

The HARP program is set to expire December 31, 2015.

FORECLOSURE

When a borrower defaults in making payments or fulfilling any of the obligations set forth in the mortgage or deed of trust, lenders can enforce their rights through foreclosure. A **foreclosure** is a legal procedure whereby the property that is pledged as security in the mortgage document or deed of trust is sold to satisfy the debt. The foreclosure procedure brings the rights of all parties to a conclusion and passes title in the subject property to either the person holding the mortgage document or deed of trust or to a third party who purchases the realty at a foreclosure sale. Property thus sold is free of the mortgage and all junior liens.

Methods of Foreclosure

The three general types of foreclosure proceedings are *judicial*, *nonjudicial*, and *strict*. The specific provisions of each vary from state to state.

Judicial foreclosure.   In a *judicial foreclosure* proceeding, the property pledged as security may be sold by court order after the mortgagee gives sufficient public notice. Upon a borrower's default, the lender may accelerate the due date of all remaining monthly payments. The lender's attorney then files a suit to foreclose the lien. After presentation of the facts in court, the property is ordered sold. A public sale is advertised and held, and the real estate is sold to the highest bidder.

Nonjudicial foreclosure.   Some states allow *nonjudicial foreclosure* procedures to be used when a **power-of-sale clause** is contained in the loan document. In those states that recognize deed of trust loans, the trustee is generally given the power of sale. In addition, some states allow a similar power of sale to be used with a mortgage loan. To foreclose, the trustee (or mortgagee) must record a notice of default at the county recorder's office within a designated period in order to give notice to the public of the intended auction. This official notice is generally accompanied by advertisements published in local newspapers that state the total amount due and the date of the public sale. After selling the property, the trustee (or mortgagee) may be required to file a copy of a notice of sale or affidavit of foreclosure.

Strict foreclosure.   Although the judicial and nonjudicial foreclosure procedures are the prevalent practices today, in some states it is still possible for a lender to acquire the mortgaged property by a *strict foreclosure* process. After appropriate notice has been given to the delinquent borrower and the proper papers have been prepared and filed, the court establishes a specific period during which the balance of the defaulted debt must be paid in full. If this is not done, the court usually awards full legal title to the lender.

Redemption

Most states give defaulting borrowers a chance to redeem their property. The **equitable right of redemption** provides that if, during the course of a foreclosure proceeding but *before the foreclosure sale*, the borrower or any other person who has an interest in the real estate (such as another creditor) pays the lender the amount currently due, plus costs, the debt will be reinstated. In some cases the person who redeems may be required to repay the accelerated loan in full. If some person other than the mortgagor or trustor redeems the real estate, the borrower becomes responsible to that person for the amount of the redemption.

Some states also allow defaulted borrowers a period in which to redeem their real estate *after the sale*. During this statutory redemption period (which may be as long as one year), the court may appoint a receiver to take charge of the property, collect rents, pay operating expenses, and so forth. The mortgagor or trustor who can raise the necessary funds to redeem the property within the statutory period pays the redemption money to the court. Because the debt was paid from the proceeds of the sale, the borrower then can take possession free and clear of the former defaulted loan. **Redemption** is illustrated in Figure 12.4.

FIGURE 12.4   **Redemption**

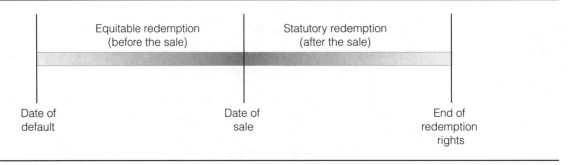

Equitable redemption (before the sale)	Statutory redemption (after the sale)	
Date of default	Date of sale	End of redemption rights

Deed to Purchaser at Sale

If redemption is not made, or if no redemption period is allowed by state law, then the successful bidder at the sale receives a deed to the real estate. This is a statutory form of deed (sheriff's, master's, or referee's deed) that may be executed by a sheriff or master in chancery to convey such title as the borrower had to the purchaser at the sale. There are no warranties with this deed; the title passes as-is but is free of the defaulted debt.

Deficiency Judgment

If the foreclosure or short sale does not produce enough cash to pay the loan balance in full after the deduction of expenses and accrued unpaid interest, the mortgagee may be entitled to a **deficiency judgment** against the signer of the note for the unpaid balance. It may be obtained against any endorsers or guarantors of the note and any owners of the mortgaged property who have assumed the debt by written agreement.

Whether the deficiency is due to a short sale or foreclosure, the IRS may still require the delinquent borrower to declare the forgiven funds as income on which the seller will owe taxes. The Mortgage Forgiveness Debt Relief Act of 2007 protected many debtors whose debt was incurred between 2007 and December 31, 2013. To date, the protection has not been renewed.

If any proceeds remain after expenses are deducted, they are paid to the borrower. As mentioned earlier, a lender who accepts a deed in lieu of foreclosure (as discussed earlier) cannot seek a deficiency judgment against the mortgagor.

CONVENTIONAL, INSURED, AND GUARANTEED LOANS

Mortgage and deed of trust loans are generally classified as *conventional*, insured, or guaranteed loans. The Federal Housing Administration (FHA) insures the full amount of an FHA loan. The Department of Veterans Affairs (VA) guarantees the top 25% of a VA loan. Anything other than a government loan is classified as conventional. A conventional loan relies on the ability of the borrower to repay the full amount due, with security provided by a mortgage or a deed of trust. Conventional loans with less than a 20% down payment generally require the borrower to purchase private mortgage insurance.

Conventional Loans

In making **conventional loans**, lenders rely primarily on their own appraisal of the security offered, credit reports, and other information concerning the reliability of the prospective borrower. Such loans are usually sold in the secondary market and must meet requirements established by the secondary market investor. The secondary market is discussed in more detail in Chapter 13.

Conventional loans are further classified as *conforming* or *nonconforming*. **Conforming loans** must meet the standards set by Fannie Mae and Freddie Mac, primary purchasers of mortgage loans on the secondary market. A **nonconforming loan** is any loan that does not meet the Fannie Mae/Freddie Mac qualifying standards. Visit www.fanniemae.com and www.freddiemac.com for more information.

Private Mortgage Insurance (PMI)

Previously, the ratio of the debt to the value of the property (loan to value) in conventional loans was generally lower than with insured and guaranteed loans. The **loan-to-value ratio (LTV)** did not usually exceed 80%. In contrast, the VA allowed 100% LTV loans, and FHA loans were at around 97%. The advent of **private mortgage insurance (PMI)** made it possible for homebuyers to obtain conventional mortgage loans for up to 95% of the appraised property value. More recently, conventional loans with LTVs of 97% and even 100% have become very popular on the market, thanks to **private mortgage insurance (PMI)**.

PMI insures lenders, not borrowers, against losses in case the borrower defaults on loan payments. The borrower is charged an annual premium based on a percentage of the loan amount that is divided by 12 and added to the monthly principal, interest, taxes, and insurance (PITI) payment (occasionally this premium is split into a partial payment at closing with the remainder paid along with the PITI payment). Because PMI insures only the top 20–25% of the loan, when the LTV drops below a certain percentage (usually 75% or 80%), the borrower can request that the lender terminate the coverage. PMI must terminate when the LTV reaches 78% (22% equity) based on the original value of the property.

Two options may be available to borrowers who want to avoid making monthly PMI payments:

1. *Lender paid.* The lender charges an approximately 0.5% higher interest rate and covers the PMI.

2. *Combination trusts.* The borrower places a first trust of 80%, plus a second trust, which in combination with a down payment adds up to 100%. For example, an 80/10/10 means 80% first, 10% second, and 10% down. The lender may also offer an 80/15/5 or even an 80/20.

FHA-Insured Loans

The FHA neither builds homes nor lends money. The common term, **FHA-insured loan**, refers to a loan that is made by an approved lending institution and insured by the agency. The FHA does not insure the property; it insures the lender against the borrower's default.

The most popular FHA program is Section 203(b); this program applies to loans on one- to four-family residences. Interest rates are competitive with other market loans. FHA requires the following:

- The borrower is charged a percentage of the loan amount as an up-front premium for the FHA insurance, which is generally financed as part of the loan. A monthly premium is also charged for all properties, except condominiums, and is usually added to the monthly payments. The mortgage insurance premium (MIP) is based on the amount of the loan, the down payment, and the length of the loan. The MIP remains for the life of the loan for loans originated after June 3, 2013.

- A minimum down payment of 3.5% of the sales price is required for all new FHA loans with the exception of HECM (reverse mortgage), Good Neighbor, and Hope for Homeowners loans.

- The mortgaged real estate must be appraised by an approved FHA appraiser. The maximum loan amount is based on local average home prices. For most parts of the United States, the upper limit is $271,050, but in high priced areas, the loan may be as much as $625,500.

- FHA regulations set general standards for type and construction of buildings, quality of neighborhood, and credit requirements of borrowers.

A buyer cannot assume, however, that if the FHA inspects, appraises, and agrees to insure the loan on a parcel of real estate, that the property is physically sound. HUD has approved a form encouraging the borrower to have a home inspection of the property. In some cases, FHA may insist that needed repairs be completed before the loan is approved. For the most current information on FHA loans, visit www.hud.gov.

Loan origination fee and discount points.   The FHA purchaser pays a *loan origination fee* equal to 1% of the loan amount. Any discount points required may be paid by either the buyer or the seller or shared between them. There is, however, a 6% ceiling on seller contribution toward closing costs or points; anything exceeding 6% is considered a reduction in sales price.

Prepayment privileges.   A borrower may repay an FHA-insured loan without penalty. For loans made before August 2, 1985, however, the borrower must give the lender at least 30 days written notice before the prepayment. No notice is required for loans made after that date.

Assumptions.   The assumption rules for FHA-insured loans vary as follows, depending on the date the loan was originated:

- FHA loans originated prior to December 1986 generally have no restrictions on their assumption.

- For FHA loans originated between December 1, 1986, and December 15, 1989, the person proposing to assume the loan must plan to occupy the property and be qualified by the lender.

- For FHA loans originated after December 15, 1989, assumptions require complete buyer qualification.

VA-Guaranteed Loans

Like the term *FHA loan*, a **VA loan** is something of a misnomer. The Department of Veterans Affairs (VA) does not usually lend money; it guarantees loans made by lending institutions approved by the agency. VA loans assist veterans in financing the purchase of homes with little or no down payments at competitive interest rates. The maximum guarantee is established in relationship to the current Fannie Mae/Freddie Mac conforming loan limits. Lenders will then loan four times the guaranteed amount with no money down. Rules and regulations are issued from time to time by the VA, setting forth qualifying standards, limitations, and conditions under which a loan may be guaranteed. Visit www.va.gov for the most current information.

Eligibility. The VA is authorized to guarantee loans to purchase or construct homes for eligible veterans and their spouses, including unremarried spouses of veterans whose death was service related. The VA also guarantees loans to purchase mobile or manufactured homes and the land on which to place them. A veteran who meets any of the following criteria is eligible for a VA loan:

1. Served 90 days of active service for veterans of designated war times

2. Served a minimum of 181 days of active service during non-war periods between July 26, 1947, and September 6, 1980

3. Served two full years of service during any peacetime period after September 7, 1980, for enlisted, and 1981 for officers

4. Served six or more years of continuous active duty as a reservist or National Guard

To determine what portion of a mortgage loan the VA will guarantee, the veteran must apply for a *certificate of eligibility*. This certificate does not mean that the veteran will automatically receive a mortgage. It merely sets forth the maximum guarantee that the veteran is entitled to.

Appraisal and other fees. The VA issues a *certificate of reasonable value (CRV)* for the property being purchased, stating its current market value based on a VA-approved appraisal. The CRV places a ceiling on the amount of a VA loan allowed for the property. If the purchase price is greater than the amount cited in the CRV, the veteran may pay the difference in cash (with VA approval).

The VA purchaser pays a loan origination fee to the lender, as well as a funding fee to the VA. Reasonable discount points may be charged on a VA-guaranteed loan, and either the veteran or the seller may pay them.

Assumptions. VA loans may be assumed by purchasers who are not veterans with prior approval from the VA for loans made after March 1, 1988. The original veteran borrower remains liable for the loan, unless a release of liability, which must be approved by the VA, is obtained. If the purchaser is a veteran, the seller may request the substitution of the buyer's entitlement, allowing the seller's entitlement to be reused in another home.

VA mortgage or deed of trust loans do not penalize borrowers for prepaying any portion of the loan balance at any time.

SPECIALIZED FINANCING TECHNIQUES

As discussed earlier in this chapter, a mortgage or deed of trust is nothing more than a string of individual clauses, the combination of which effects a desired result—a parcel of real estate is given as security for a loan. By altering the terms and provisions of a mortgage or deed of trust document, a borrower and a lender can tailor these financing instruments to best suit the type of transaction and the financial needs of both parties. In addition, these terms can be changed to reflect certain economic conditions in the marketplace. In times of tight mortgage money, creative financing becomes more popular. In addition, real estate can be financed using instruments other than mortgages and deeds of trust.

Purchase-Money Loan

A **purchase-money loan** is given at the time of purchase to facilitate the sale. The term is used most often to refer to the instrument given by the purchaser to a seller who takes back a note for part or all of the purchase price. It may be a first or second mortgage, and it becomes a lien on the property when the title passes. The term may also refer to any security instrument originating at the time of sale.

Blanket Loan

A *blanket loan* covers more than one parcel or lot and is usually used to finance subdivision developments. It usually includes a provision, called a *partial release clause*, allowing the borrower to obtain a release of any one lot or parcel from the lien by repaying a specified amount of the loan.

Package Loan

A **package loan** includes not only the real estate, but also all personal property in and appliances installed on the premises. This kind of loan is often used to finance furnished condominium units such as those found in resort areas.

Open-End Loan

The **open-end loan** secures a *note* executed by the borrower to the lender as well as any future *advances* of funds made by the lender to the borrower or to the borrower's successors in title. This type of loan is frequently used by farmers to enable them to purchase equipment, seed, and so forth, at a future time. The interest rate on the initial amount borrowed is fixed, but interest on future advances may be at the current market rate (see "Home Equity Loans" later in this chapter).

Another type of open-end loan is an equity line of credit, used by borrowers to obtain additional funds to improve their property. The borrower opens the mortgage or deed of trust loan to increase the debt beyond its original amount—after the debt has been reduced by payments over a period of time.

Construction Loan

A **construction loan** is made to finance the construction of improvements on real estate (homes, apartments, office buildings, and so forth). Under a construction loan, the lender commits the full amount of the loan but makes partial progress payments as the building is being constructed.

Progress payments (also called *draws*) are made to the general contractor for that part of the construction work that has been completed since the previous payment. The general contractor must provide the lender with adequate waivers of lien, releasing all mechanic's lien rights for the work covered by the payment. This type of short-term, or *interim,* financing generally bears a higher-than-market interest rate because of the risks assumed by the lender—inadequate releasing of mechanics' liens, possible delays in completing the building, or financial failure of the contractor or subcontractors. The borrower is expected to arrange for a permanent loan (also called an *end loan* or **take-out loan**) that will repay or take out the construction financing lender when the work is completed.

Straight Loan

A straight loan calls for periodic payments of interest, with the principal to be paid in full at the end of the loan term. Straight loans are nonamortizing and are also called term loans. They are often used for home improvement loans and second mortgages, rather than for residential first mortgage loans.

Wraparound Loan

A **wraparound loan**, also called an *overriding* or *all-inclusive mortgage* or *deed of trust*, enables a borrower who is paying off an existing mortgage or deed of trust loan to obtain additional financing from a second lender. The new lender assumes payment of the existing loan and gives the borrower a new, increased loan at a higher interest rate. The total amount of the new loan includes the existing loan as well as the additional funds needed by the borrower.

At a time when most mortgages loans were assumable, the wraparound mortgage was frequently used as a method of either refinancing or financing the purchase of real property. The majority of conventional mortgages today include a due on sale clause and are not freely assumable. Most real estate professionals agree that a wraparound loan should not be used as a way to circumvent a due on sale clause that may be in the senior mortgage that is to be wrapped. If so, the borrower is in default and the senior loan is subject to acceleration by the holder of the senior mortgage.

Shared-Appreciation Mortgage (SAM)

In a **shared-appreciation mortgage (SAM)** the lender originates a mortgage or deed of trust loan at a favorable interest rate that may be several points below the current rate in return for a guaranteed share of the gain (if any) the borrower will realize when the property is eventually sold. This type of loan was originally made to developers of large real estate projects, but in times of expensive mortgage money, it has appeared in the residential financing market. The specific details of the shared-appreciation agreement are set forth in the mortgage or deed of trust and note documents.

Reverse-Annuity Mortgage (RAM)

With a **reverse-annuity mortgage (RAM),** payments are made to the borrower, based on the equity the homeowner has invested in the property given as security for the loan. The payment may be in the form of one lump sum, monthly increments, or as a deed on a credit line. A reverse loan allows senior citizens at least 62 years of age to use the equity buildup in their homes without having to sell. The borrower is charged a fixed rate of interest, and the loan is eventually paid from the sale of the property or from the estate upon the borrower's death. The most popular of the RAMs is the FHA Home Equity Conversion Mortgage (HECM), which is available only through an FHA-approved lender.

Installment Contract

Real estate can be purchased under an installment contract, also called a *contract for deed*, *land contract*, or *agreement of sale*. Real estate is often sold on contract in one of two situations: (1) when mortgage financing is not available and (2) when the purchaser does not have a sufficient down payment.

Under an **installment contract**, the seller (vendor) retains fee ownership, while the buyer (vendee) secures possession and an equitable interest in the property. The buyer agrees to give the seller a down payment and pay regular monthly payments of principal and interest over a number of years. The buyer also agrees to pay real estate taxes and insurance premiums and for repairs and upkeep on the property. Although the buyer obtains possession when the contract is signed by both parties, the seller is not obligated to execute and deliver a deed to the buyer until the terms of the contract have been satisfied.

The installment contract is really another means of seller-financing. It is merely a sales contract without a mortgage or deed of trust. With this form of financing, the seller-vendor remains in strong control of the transaction with little protection for the buyer-vendee. Anyone considering making this type of purchase should consult first with a real estate attorney.

Sale-and-Leaseback

The owners of large commercial buildings or industrial plants often use a **sale-and-lease-back** arrangement as a method to acquire funds without taking out a loan. The fixed asset, used by the seller for business purposes, is sold to an investor or holding company. The buyer becomes the lessor, and the original owner becomes the lessee continuing to conduct business on the property as a tenant. The company can use the equity realized from the sale as working capital, and the lease payments reduce taxable income. The investor has a reliable source of income under a long-term lease.

Graduated-Payment Mortgage (GPM)

A flexible-payment plan, such as a **graduated-payment mortgage (GPM)**, allows a mortgagor to make lower monthly payments for the first few years of the loan (typically five years) and larger payments for the remainder of the term, when the mortgagor's income is expected to have increased. The problem is that the monthly payments are generally less than the interest due, resulting in negative amortization. As each payment is made, the unpaid interest is added to the principal balance, resulting in an increasing loan balance for the first few years. The GPM has been basically replaced with the adjustable-rate mortgage (ARM).

Balloon Payment Loan

As discussed earlier, when a mortgage or deed of trust loan requires periodic payments that will not fully amortize the amount of the loan by the time the final payment is due, the final payment is larger than the others. This is a *partially amortized loan* with a **balloon payment**. For example, a loan made for $180,000 at 7% interest is computed on a 30-year amortization schedule resulting in monthly payments of $1,190.60 for the first five years. At the end of five years, a final balloon payment for the amount of principal still owed becomes due. The lender has the option of extending the amortization period or requiring payment in full.

Growing-Equity Mortgage (GEM)

The **growing-equity mortgage (GEM)**, or *rapid-payoff mortgage*, makes use of a fixed interest rate, but payments of principal are increased according to an index or a schedule. The total payment thus increases, but the borrower's income is expected to keep pace, and the loan is paid off more quickly.

Buydown

In a **buydown** some of the mortgage loan interest is donated or prepaid in advance to the lender on the borrower's behalf for the purpose of temporarily reducing the interest rate. That is, the original interest rate is effectively bought down for a period of time by the advance payment. Typical buydown arrangements provide for a reduced interest rate of 1–3% over the first one to three years of the loan term.

Common sources of buydown funds include homebuilders who wish to sell their stock of houses by offering the lower rate, parents or other relatives wanting to assist the buyers in purchasing a home, and sellers seeking to help the buyers qualify for a loan at the lower interest rate, thus closing the sale on their property.

Home Equity Loan

Home equity loans are a source of funds for homeowners who wish to finance the purchase of expensive items; consolidate existing installment loans on credit card debt; or pay for medical, educational, home improvement, or any other expenses of their choice. They can draw on the equity that they have in their home. **Equity** consists of the difference between current market value and indebtedness. Equity builds up with every mortgage payment and when the value of the home increases. Drawing on a home's equity has become increasingly popular since the passing of tax laws in 1986 that ended the deductibility of interest on debts that are not secured by real estate. Home equity loans are secured by the borrower's residence, and the interest charged is deductible up to a loan limit of $100,000. Lenders generally allow for a total indebtedness of 75 or 80 LTV.

A home equity loan can be taken out as a fixed loan amount or as an equity line of credit, called a home equity line of credit (HELOC). The lender extends a line of credit that the borrowers can use whenever and for whatever purpose they choose. The borrowers can receive their money by a check sent to them, deposits to a checking or savings account, or a book of drafts the borrowers can use up to their credit limit.

Investment Group Financing

A real estate investment syndicate allows investors to pool capital to finance real estate investments they could not otherwise afford, thus stimulating the industry by providing a source of capital for all kinds of real estate projects. Syndicates purchase buildings and finance construction projects that might be considerably delayed if they were forced to wait for a single investor. Syndicates may range from a small group of investors who combine forces for a single project (joint venture) or a large group of investors who pool their assets in order to invest in a variety of projects.

The person who organizes the project and recruits the investors—usually a real estate broker, accountant, or lawyer who specializes in real estate—is called the *syndicator*. Private syndication, which involves a smaller group of investors, is distinguished from public syndication, which involves a much larger group of investors who may or may not be knowledgeable about real estate as an investment. The distinction between the two, however, is based on the nature of the arrangement between the syndicator and the investors and not on the type of syndicate. For this reason, any pooling of individuals' funds raises questions of definition and registration of securities under state security laws, commonly called blue sky laws. In addition, securities must be registered with the federal Securities and Exchange Commission (SEC) prior to public offering.

Syndication can take many different legal forms of ownership, from tenancy in common and joint tenancy to various kinds of partnerships, corporations, and trusts. As mentioned in Chapter 5, among the most popular kinds of syndicates are *limited partnerships* and *real estate investment trusts*.

Limited partnerships.   Limited partnerships are composed of general partners and limited partners. The general partners have complete charge of the operation and management of the partnership business, and they can bear extensive liability for the obligations of the partnership. The limited partners agree to contribute a definite amount of capital for which they can be held liable, but they have no voice in the actual operation of the business. They can share in the profits of the venture, if any, but their liabilities or potential losses are limited to the amount of their original subscription. The general partners assume all liability beyond the capital contributions of the limited partners.

Real estate investment trusts (REITs).   A **real estate investment trust (REIT)** (also called a *common law trust*) is unincorporated and involves 100 or more persons who make investments by purchasing shares. The capital is used to purchase, develop, and/or sell real estate. Title to the real estate is taken in the name of the trustees who conduct the business of the venture. REITs have grown in popularity, partly because they do not have to pay corporate income tax if they distribute 95% of their income to the shareholders. After the property is developed and sold, the trustees distribute any profits to the shareholders as return of capital or capital gains.

Discount Points

A lender may sell a mortgage to investors (as discussed in Chapter 13). However, the interest rate that the lender charges for a loan may be less than the rate of return that an investor demands. The lender may charge the borrower **discount points**, basically prepaid interest, which make up the difference between the amount the loan costs the lender and the amount the lender can expect to sell it for in the market.

For a borrower, one point equals 1% of the loan amount (not the purchase price). For example, two discount points charged on a $200,000 loan is $4,000 ($200,000 × 0.02). If a house sells for $180,000 and the borrower seeks a $160,000 loan, each point is $1,600, not $1,800.

The points can be paid to the lender with cash at the closing or financed as part of the total loan amount. Points may be paid by either the buyer or the seller.

Loan Origination Fees

The processing of a mortgage application is called loan origination. A **loan origination fee** is charged by lenders to cover the expenses involved in generating the loan. This fee is not prepaid interest; it is a charge that must be paid to the lender. Loan origination fees vary in amount and are usually figured in points (again, with one point equal to 1% of the loan amount).

The maximum loan origination fee allowed under an FHA or a VA loan is 1%. This fee is generally charged to the borrower on any loan, whether conventional, insured, or guaranteed and may be included as a tax deduction in the year of purchase.

SUMMARY

Most properties are acquired with borrowed money. Mortgage and deed of trust loans provide the security for the loans. Mortgage loans involve a borrower, called the mortgagor, and a lender, called the mortgagee. With a deed of trust loan, the borrower is the trustor and a third party, called the trustee, acts on behalf of the lender (beneficiary).

Some states, called title theory states, recognize the lender as the owner of mortgaged property. Others, called lien theory states, recognize the borrower as the owner of mortgaged property. A few intermediary states recognize modified versions of these theories.

After a lending institution has received, investigated, and approved a loan application, it issues a commitment to make the loan. The borrower is required to execute a note, agreeing to repay the debt, and a mortgage or deed of trust, which places a lien on the real estate to secure the note. The mortgage or deed of trust is recorded in the public record in order to give notice of the lender's interest.

The note for the amount of the loan usually provides for amortization under one of a number of plans. The note also sets the rate of interest at which the loan is made and which the mortgagor or trustor must pay as a charge for borrowing the money. Charging more than the maximum interest rate allowed by state statute is called usury and is illegal. The mortgage or deed of trust secures the debt and sets forth the obligations of the borrower and the rights of the lender. Payment in full by the note's terms entitles the borrower to a satisfaction, or release, that is recorded to clear the lien from the public records.

When the loan is underwater (the amount due is more than the current value of the property), borrowers may try to refinance or ask the lender to approve a short sale or a deed in lieu of foreclosure.

Default by the borrower may result in acceleration of payments, a foreclosure sale, and, after the redemption period (if provided by state law), loss of title. If the property is sold at foreclosure or in a short sale for an amount insufficient to cover the debt, the lender may seek a deficiency judgment against the borrower to cover the difference, plus costs.

Mortgage and deed of trust loans include conventional loans that may require private mortgage insurance and loans insured by the FHA or guaranteed by the VA. Conventional, FHA, and VA loans all set certain requirements that must be met by borrower in order to obtain the loan.

Specialized financing instruments include purchase-money, blanket, package, open-end, wraparound, shared-appreciation, and reverse-annuity mortgages, as well as construction, sale-and-leaseback, graduated-payment, balloon-payment, growing-equity, and home equity loans.

Other real estate financing is arranged through installment contracts (contracts for deed, land contracts), under which the seller retains title to the property until the full purchase price is received. Firms that own and operate large plants are able to release funds invested in such real estate for use in their businesses through sale-and-leaseback transactions.

Groups of investors may combine their assets to form a syndicate, joint venture, limited partnership, or real estate investment trust (REIT).

REVIEW QUESTIONS

Please complete all of the questions before turning to the Answer Key on page 343.

1. A legal document that may be used as security for a promissory note is a
   a. power of attorney.
   b. deed in lieu of foreclosure.
   c. deed of trust.
   d. personal check.

2. When a man purchased land to build his house, a mortgage lien was placed on the property and recorded on July 1, 2014. The man is now obtaining a construction loan. This will create a mortgage lien that will be dated October 10, 2015, but will take priority over the earlier lien. The first mortgage must have contained
   a. an acceleration clause.
   b. an alienation clause.
   c. a defeasance clause.
   d. a subordination clause.

3. A new homeowner has a mortgage loan in which the homeowner only pays the interest due on the $180,000 loan for 10 years. At the end of the 10 years, the homeowner will owe the entire principal balance of $180,000. This is a
   a. straight or term loan.
   b. fully amortized loan.
   c. subordinated loan.
   d. partially amortized loan.

4. Three discount points are being charged on a $250,000 mortgage loan. This $7,500 will
   a. be a credit to the seller.
   b. be considered as prepaid interest.
   c. decrease the effective yield.
   d. reduce the term of the loan.

5. A lender is able to make a nonjudicial foreclosure on a loan that is in default based on the power-of-sale clause contained in the
   a. certificate of reasonable value.
   b. deed of trust.
   c. promissory note.
   d. certificate of eligibility.

6. When the buyers went to settlement on their new home, they signed a deed of trust that conveyed their interest in the property to a trustee who would act on behalf of the lender. The new homeowners live in a state that recognizes
   a. title theory.
   b. intermediary theory.
   c. lien theory.
   d. modified lien theory.

7. A borrower is six months behind on mortgage loan payments, and the bank plans to foreclose in one week. If the borrower is able to bring the payments plus all other late fees and miscellaneous charges up to date before the foreclosure auction, the loan will be reinstated. The borrower lives in a state that allows for
   a. statutory right of redemption.
   b. equitable right of redemption.
   c. power of sale.
   d. power of attorney.

8. An adjustable-rate mortgage loan has an interest rate that can increase or decrease based on a specified U.S. Treasury security that has been designated as the
   a. interest rate cap.
   b. adjustment period.
   c. index.
   d. margin.

9. A man has bought a woman's house "subject to" the existing mortgage. This means that
   a. the man becomes fully responsible for the loan.
   b. if the man defaults, the woman will be held responsible for the loan.
   c. both the man and the woman share liability for the loan equally.
   d. the woman no longer has any liability for the loan.

10. With a VA mortgage loan, the market value of the property to be purchased is indicated by the
    a. certificate of reasonable value.
    b. certificate of eligibility.
    c. power of attorney.
    d. power-of-sale clause.

11. A homeowner became unemployed and was unable to make mortgage payments for a few months. The lender instituted a foreclosure proceeding and foreclosed on the property. The homeowner may still have a right to recover the property if the state allows a certain period for
    a. strict foreclosure.
    b. judicial foreclosure.
    c. equitable redemption.
    d. statutory redemption.

12. A buyer looking for a vacation property bought a lakeside house on an installment contract. With this type of financing, the buyer will receive title to the property when the
    a. sales contract is ratified.
    b. buyer completes paying for the property.
    c. seller decides it is time to convey the title.
    d. mortgage loan is recorded.

13. An elderly couple, both age 75, need funds to pay for full-time live-in help. Because their primary asset is their fully paid-for home, they are able to tap into their equity by obtaining
    a. an adjustable-rate loan (ARM).
    b. a graduated payment loan (GPM).
    c. a reverse-annuity mortgage (RAM).
    d. a shared-appreciation mortgage (SAM).

14. An investor bought an office building from a company and immediately leased the space back to the company for 10 years. In this arrangement, the
    a. company is the investor.
    b. investor can deduct rental payments from taxes as expense items.
    c. company can depreciate the building.
    d. investor has a reliable source of income.

15. In a mortgage loan that requires periodic payments that do *NOT* fully amortize the loan, the final payment would best be described as
    a. a balloon payment.
    b. an acceleration payment.
    c. a variable payment.
    d. an adjustment payment.

16. A condominium company is selling new fully furnished two-bedroom units complete with all kitchen appliances. The purchaser of one of these units would obtain a
    a. blanket loan.
    b. package loan.
    c. wraparound loan.
    d. shared-appreciation loan.

17. The term *interim financing* is *MOST* likely to be associated with
    a. sale-and-leasebacks.
    b. shopping center financing.
    c. take-out lending.
    d. construction financing.

18. A homeowner obtains a loan to make repairs to her property. The loan documents secure the loan, as well as any future funds advanced by the lender. The homeowner has
    a. a wraparound loan.
    b. a conventional loan.
    c. an open-end loan.
    d. a growing-equity loan.

19. When a lender offers a below-market interest rate in exchange for an equity position in the property, this is called
    a. a shared appreciation loan.
    b. a growing-equity loan.
    c. an open-end loan.
    d. an installment loan.

20. The asking price of a home is less than the amount that the homeowners owe. What is a possible solution for them to sell their home?
    a. Petition the lender to agree to a short sale
    b. Quickly refinance the home
    c. Take out a home equity loan to pay off the first loan
    d. Borrow from the buyers and give the buyers a 10-year promissory note

13

The Real Estate Financing Market

LEARNING OBJECTIVES

When you finish reading this chapter, you will be able to

- differentiate between the primary and secondary markets;
- discuss the effects of government participation in the finance market; and
- describe the effects of financing legislation, including the Dodd-Frank Wall Street Reform and Consumer Protection Act, Truth in Lending Act, Equal Credit Opportunity Act, Real Estate Settlement Procedures Act, Mortgage Disclosure Information Act, Fair Credit Reporting Act, and Community Reinvestment Act.

annual percentage rate (APR)	Fannie Mae	mortgage brokers
commercial banks	Federal Deposit Insurance Corporation (FDIC)	mutual savings banks
Community Reinvestment Act (CRA)		primary mortgage market
Consumer Financial Protection Bureau (CFPB)	Federal Home Loan Bank (FHLB)	qualified mortgage
	Federal Reserve System (the Fed)	Real Estate Settlement Procedures Act (RESPA)
Dodd-Frank Wall Street Reform and Consumer Protection Act	Freddie Mac	
	Ginnie Mae	Regulation Z
Equal Credit Opportunity Act (ECOA)	impound accounts	Rural Housing Service (RHS)
	kickbacks	savings associations
escrow account	loan servicing	secondary mortgage market
Fair Credit Reporting Act	mortgage banking companies	

The real estate finance market is one of the most important centers of monetary activity in the country. Buyers, sellers, lenders, developers, real estate licensees, and even federal and state governments participate in this important market. Chapter 12 described the basic instruments involved in real estate financing; the following pages examine mortgage lending from a marketplace perspective. This chapter discusses the various sources of real estate financing, the federal government's participation in the money market, the special creative lending plans that have evolved to address specific needs, and the various federal laws that affect the participants in the market for real estate finance.

SOURCES OF REAL ESTATE FINANCING

Most real estate purchases are financed by loans obtained from a variety of sources. Together, these sources are called the primary market, which works directly with borrowers. The primary market consists of savings associations, commercial banks, mutual savings banks, life insurance companies, mortgage banking companies, and mortgage brokers. This market sells its loans to the secondary market to raise capital to continue making loans directly to consumers. Governmental influences, especially the actions of the Federal Reserve System (the Fed), affect both of these markets.

The Primary Mortgage Market

The **primary mortgage market** consists of investors, companies, and banks that take applications from borrowers, analyze creditworthiness, assess the value of the real estate being used for security, work with underwriters, and originate the loans. Very few participants hold the notes until maturity. Most sell the loans in order to gain enough capital to continue to make loans.

The original lender may continue to collect the payments from the borrower, passing the receipts along to the investor who has purchased the loan and charging the investor a fee for loan servicing. Servicing charges are related to the day-to-day management of the loans. **Loan servicing** includes collecting and crediting monthly payments, collecting funds that are held in escrow (real estate taxes and hazard insurance), paying real estate taxes and insurance premiums, collecting late fees, and debt collection.

The following is a list of the lenders in the primary market and a brief description of their institutions.

Savings associations (thrifts).   Savings associations (once called savings and loan associations) are active participants in the home loan mortgage market, specializing in long-term residential loans, which are viewed as secure investments for the benefit of their depositors. Traditionally, savings associations, also called *thrifts*, are the most flexible of the lending institutions with regard to their mortgage lending procedures, and they are generally local in nature.

Although they primarily provide conventional loans, they do participate in FHA-insured and VA-guaranteed loans to a limited extent.

All savings associations must be chartered, either by the federal government or by the states in which they are located. Originally, the **Federal Home Loan Bank (FHLB)**, which was organized into 12 districts similar to the Federal Reserve's organization, was responsible for the supervision and regulation of the savings association. The Financial Institutions Reform, Recovery and Enforcement Act of 1989 (FIRREA), enacted in response to the savings and loan association crisis of the 1980s, was intended to ensure the continued viability of the savings association industry. FIRREA restructured the savings association regulatory system with the creation of the Office of Thrift Supervision (OTS) as well as the insurance system that protects its depositors. The Office of Thrift Supervision (OTS) regulates these associations and the **Federal Deposit Insurance Corporation (FDIC)** now manages the insurance funds for both savings associations and commercial banks.

The Federal Home Loan Bank system continues to supervise the savings associations and provides funding for its member banks.

Mutual savings banks. Although **mutual savings banks** do offer limited checking account privileges, they are primarily savings institutions that are highly active in the mortgage market, investing in loans secured by income property as well as residential real estate. State-chartered, they issue no stock and are mutually owned by their investors. Because mutual savings banks usually seek low-risk loan investments, they often prefer to originate FHA-insured or VA-guaranteed loans.

Commercial banks. Loan departments of **commercial banks** traditionally made short-term construction, home improvement, and mobile-home loans. In today's market, however, commercial banks are originating an increasing number of home mortgages—conventional, FHA, and VA loans. Like the savings associations, banks must be chartered by the state or federal government and are regulated by the Federal Reserve and the Office of the Comptroller.

Insurance companies. Insurance companies amass large sums of money from the premiums paid by their policyholders. Although some of this money is held in reserve to satisfy claims and cover operating expenses, more is invested in profit-earning enterprises, such as long-term real estate loans.

Most insurance companies prefer to invest their money in large long-term loans that finance commercial and industrial properties. They also invest in residential mortgage and deed of trust loans by purchasing large blocks of FHA-insured and VA-guaranteed loans from Fannie Mae and other agencies that warehouse such loans for resale in the secondary mortgage market (discussed later in this chapter).

Mortgage banking companies. **Mortgage banking companies** use their own funds or funds borrowed from other institutions to make real estate loans that may later be sold to investors. The mortgage company then receives a fee for the servicing of the loans. Mortgage bankers are involved in all types of real estate loan activities and often serve as intermediaries between investors and borrowers.

Mortgage banking companies are usually organized as stock companies. As a source of real estate financing, they are subject to considerably fewer lending restrictions than are commercial banks or savings associations. They are, however, regulated by state laws, and members belonging to the Mortgage Bankers Association are expected to follow its code of ethics.

Mortgage brokers. **Mortgage brokers** are not lenders, but rather individuals or firms that are licensed to act as an intermediary in bringing borrowers and lenders together. They locate potential borrowers, process preliminary loan applications, and submit the applications to lenders for final approval and receive a fee for these services. Frequently, they work with or for mortgage banking companies in these activities. They are not involved in servicing a loan once it is made.

Sometimes, mortgage brokers are also real estate brokers who offer these financing services in addition to their regular brokerage activities. However, strict regulations imposed by the Real Estate Settlement Procedures Act (RESPA) can affect such an arrangement.

Credit unions. Credit unions are cooperative organizations in which members place money in savings accounts. In the past, most credit unions made only short-term consumer and home improvement loans, but in recent years, legislation has made it possible for them to greatly increase their membership, giving them an opportunity to originate longer-term first and second mortgage and deed of trust loans.

Pension funds. Pension funds are active participants in financing real estate projects, perceived as low risk with a potential of higher income. Most of the real estate activity for pension funds is handled through mortgage bankers and mortgage brokers.

Other sources for funds. Many banks are trustees for endowments for educational institutions, hospitals, charitable foundation, and more. They also invest in real estate projects.

Funds are also raised through joint ventures, syndicates, partnerships, and real estate investment trusts to fund large real estate projects, such as high-rise apartment buildings, office complexes, and shopping centers (see Chapter 12).

Applications for Credit

The primary market consists of individuals who work directly with borrowers. A prospective borrower must submit personal information including employment, earnings, assets, and financial obligations. Details of the real estate securing the loan must be provided, including legal description, improvements, title, and taxes. The ratio of the loan to the value (LTV) determines whether or not mortgage insurance is necessary. Applications must be signed and must include a certificate that the information provided is true and complete.

Ability to pay. Additional information, including financial and operating statements, schedules of leases and tenants, and balance sheets, is required for loans on income property or loans made to corporations. Homebuyers must be able to afford to make monthly payments of principal, interest, $\frac{1}{12}$ of annual taxes, and $\frac{1}{12}$ of annual insurance premiums (PITI). As a rule of thumb, lenders also consider the ratio of debt to income. The best interest rates will be available to borrowers who make a 20% down payment and whose PITI is 28% or less of gross income. Total debt, household plus long-term car loans, student loans, and so on cannot exceed 36% of total gross income.

Credit scoring. The lender may access any or all of the three major credit-reporting agencies—Equifax, Experian, and Trans-Union—for a report of the applicant's credit history plus a numerical score. The commonly used FICO score is an analysis of the applicant's payment history, amounts owed, length of credit history, new credit, and the types of credit used. While the FICO score considers only information in the credit report, lenders also consider income, employment history, and the type of credit requested. Lenders offer their best interest rates to those with higher credits scores.

A loan officer carefully investigates the application information, using credit reports and an appraisal of the property to help decide whether to grant the loan. The lender uses a variety of forms to document the creditworthiness of the applicant, including a *verification of employment, verification of deposit,* and *tri-merged credit report*. When the loan is accepted, the applicant receives a loan commitment that creates a contract to make a loan, so long as the information remains the same.

Subprime loans. Those with lower credit scores can still borrow money. Such loans are called subprime loans. Because of the risk, subprime loans generally require a higher rate of interest, may be for a shorter term, and may require a larger down payment.

Predatory lending. Although there is a place for subprime loans in the real estate market, when a lender tries to force a borrower into a loan with a higher rate of interest than necessary or with other unfavorable terms, that lender is considered *predatory*.

The Secondary Mortgage Market

Mortgage lending takes place in both the primary market, where loans are originated, and the **secondary mortgage market**, where loans are bought and sold only after they have been funded. Secondary market activity provides a great stimulant to the housing construction market as well as to the mortgage market (see Figure 13.1).

FIGURE 13.1   **Primary and Secondary Mortgage Markets**

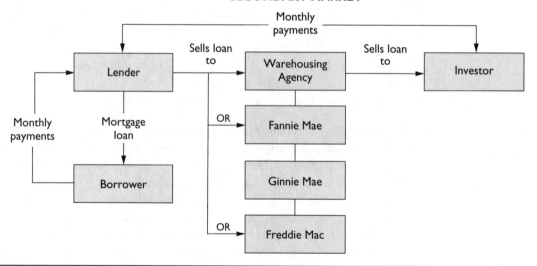

PRIMARY MARKET

SECONDARY MARKET

The major sources of secondary mortgage activity are the warehousing loan agencies that purchase a large number of mortgage loans, assemble them into packages of loans, and then issue bonds backed by these loans for resale to private investors. The proceeds from these sales are then reinvested into the housing market. These agencies are Fannie Mae, Freddie Mac, and Ginnie Mae.

Fannie Mae.   **Fannie Mae** (formerly the Federal National Mortgage Association, or FNMA) is a government-sponsored enterprise (GSE) and since 2008 has been under the conservatorship of the Federal Housing Finance Agency (FHFA). It is a privately owned corporation that issues its own common stock and provides a secondary market for mortgage loans, conventional as well as FHA and VA. Fannie Mae buys a block or pool of mortgages from a lender in exchange for cash or for *mortgage-backed securities* that the lender may keep or sell. For more information, visit www.fanniemae.com.

Freddie Mac. Formerly called the Federal Home Loan Mortgage Corporation (FHLMC), **Freddie Mac** is another GSE, also placed under the conservatorship of the Federal Housing Finance Agency (FHFA) in 2008. It provides a secondary market for mortgage loans, primarily conventional loans. Freddie Mac has the authority to purchase mortgages, pool them, and sell bonds in the open market with the mortgages as security. Note, however, that Freddie Mac does not guarantee payment of Freddie Mac mortgages. For more information, visit www.freddiemac.com.

Many lenders use the Fannie Mae/Freddie Mac standardized documents for loan applications, credit reports, and appraisal forms in order to be able to sell packages of their loans to those agencies. Although Fannie Mae and Freddie Mac are competitors in the secondary market, they have very similar guidelines for maximum loan amount, down payment, qualifying ratios, and other mandatory requirements for their various loan projects. Both GSEs are subject to government supervision and take an active role in providing affordable loan products to increase home ownership for all U.S. citizens.

Ginnie Mae. **Ginnie Mae** (Government National Mortgage Association, or GNMA) is a government-owned corporation within the Department of Housing and Urban Development (HUD). Ginnie Mae is designed to administer special assistance programs and works with Fannie Mae in secondary market activities. Ginnie Mae does not buy or sell loans or issue mortgage-backed securities (MBS).

Ginnie Mae guarantees investment securities issued by private offerors (such as banks, mortgage companies, and savings associations) that are backed by pools of FHA and VA mortgage loans. The Ginnie Mae *pass-through certificate* is a security interest in a pool of mortgages that provides for a monthly pass-through of principal and interest payments directly to the certificate holder. Such certificates are guaranteed by Ginnie Mae. For more information, visit www.ginniemae.gov.

Rural Housing Service (RHS). This Department of Agriculture agency offers programs to help purchase or operate family farms or ranches. **Rural Housing Service (RHS)** also provides loans to help purchase or improve single-family homes in rural areas (generally areas with a population of fewer than 10,000), through both guaranteed loans serviced by a private lender and insured loans made by the agency. For more information, visit www. rurdev.usda.gov.

GOVERNMENT PARTICIPATION IN FINANCING

Aside from FHA and VA loan programs, the federal government influences mortgage lending practices through the Federal Reserve System, as well as through various federal agencies such as the Department of Agriculture Rural Development Program, the Federal Home Loan Bank, and Ginnie Mae. The GSEs of Fannie Mae and Freddie Mac are influential in the secondary mortgage market.

Federal Reserve System (the Fed)

The **Federal Reserve System (the Fed)** operates to maintain sound credit conditions, to help counteract inflationary and deflationary trends, and to create a favorable economic climate. The system divides the country into 12 districts, each served by a Federal Reserve bank. All nationally chartered banks must join the Fed and purchase stock in its district reserve banks.

The Fed indirectly regulates the flow of money in the marketplace through its member banks by controlling their reserve requirements and discount rates. In addition, the Fed tempers the economy through its open-market operations.

Reserve requirements.   The Fed requires each member bank to keep a certain amount of its assets on hand as reserve funds that are unavailable for loans or any other use. This requirement was designed primarily to protect customer deposits, but it also provides a means of manipulating the flow of cash in the money market. By increasing its reserve requirements, the Fed limits the amount of money that member banks can use to make loans, thus causing interest rates to increase and slowing down an overactive economy. The opposite is also true: by decreasing the reserve requirements, the Fed can allow more money to be circulated in the marketplace, thereby boosting the economy.

Discount rates.   Member banks are permitted to borrow money from the district reserve banks to expand their lending operations. The interest rate that the district banks charge for the use of this money is called the *discount rate*. The discount rate is the basis on which the banks determine the rate of interest that they charge their loan customers. When the Fed discount rate is high, bank interest rates are high; therefore, fewer loans will be made and less money will circulate in the marketplace. Conversely, a lower discount rate results in lower interest rates, more bank loans, and more money in circulation.

Open market activities.   The Fed can buy or sell U.S. Treasury securities and, by so doing, change the money supply. If the Fed sells securities, the money supply decreases (money flows from investors to the government) and the economy slows. If the Fed buys securities, the money supply increases (money flows from the government to investors) and the economy expands.

FINANCING LEGISLATION

The federal government regulates the lending practices of mortgage lenders through the Dodd-Frank Wall Street Reform and Consumer Protection Act, the Truth in Lending Act (TILA), Equal Credit Opportunity Act (ECOA), and the Real Estate Settlement Procedures Act (RESPA).

Both the Truth in Lending Act (TILA) and the Real Estate Settlement Procedures Act (RESPA) will change as of August 1, 2015. To find out more about the changes, visit www.consumerfinance.gov/regulatory-implementation/tila-respa/.

Dodd-Frank Wall Street Reform and Consumer Protection Act

In response to the 2008 financial crisis, Congress passed the Dodd-Frank Wall Street Reform and Consumer Protection Act to prevent financial risk taking and to provide protections for the average consumer. The law affects many consumer protection laws, including the Equal Credit Opportunity Act, the Fair Credit Reporting Act, the Home Mortgage Disclosure Act, the Truth in Lending Act, and more. Several sections are relevant to real estate licensees.

Title X: Consumer Financial Protection Act.   Dodd-Frank created the Consumer Financial Protection Bureau (CFPB) to set clear rules to oversee payday lenders, credit card companies, mortgage lenders and others that had exploited consumers. The bureau has exclusive rulemaking authority over most consumer protection laws. It prohibits unfair, deceptive, or abusive acts or practices and requires that consumers have access to information when they are borrowing money.

Title XIV: Mortgage Reform and Anti-Predatory Lending Act. Title XIV provides rules for mortgage loan originators, minimum standards for mortgages, and information about high-cost mortgages, mortgage servicing, and appraisal activities. It also established the Office of Housing Counseling.

Know Before You Owe. The CFPB created the Know Before You Owe program to develop disclosure forms for consumers who are applying for a mortgage loan. These forms integrate disclosures required by the Truth in Lending Act (Regulation Z) and the Real Estate Settlement Procedures Act (RESPA). The two forms created by this program are the Loan Estimate, which must be given within three days of application, and the Closing Disclosure, given three business days before closing. The effective date for implementing the new disclosure rules is August 1, 2015. More information is available at www.consumerfinance.gov/knowbeforeyouowe/.

Federal rules concerning mortgages. The CFPB produces the *Shopping for a Mortgage? What You Can Expect Under Federal Rules* booklet, which provides in clear language what consumers should know as they shop for a mortgage loan. The booklet is available online at http://files.consumerfinance.gov/f/201401_cfpb_mortgages_consumer-summary-new-mortgage.pdf.

Qualified mortgages. Effective January 10, 2014, lenders are obligated to determine if the borrower is actually able to repay a consumer credit transaction secured by a dwelling before making the loan. Additionally, there are limits on prepayment penalties for these **qualified mortgages**. Qualified mortgages include the following:

- Debt-to-income ratio of 43% or less

- Loans that are eligible for purchase, guarantee, or insurance by the FHA, VA, USDA, or a GSE

- Loans held in portfolio under certain conditions, provided that the lender has considered and verified a borrower's debt-to-income ratio

  Mandatory features for qualified mortgages include the following:

- Points and fees are less than or equal to 3% of the loan amount (higher percentages are permitted for loan under $100,000)

- May not feature negative amortization, interest-only, or balloon loans (an exception is made for balloon loans originating prior to January 10, 2016)

- Maximum loan terms are 30 years or less

Truth in Lending Act (TILA) and Regulation Z

The National Consumer Credit Protection Act, called the Truth in Lending Act (TILA), is implemented under Regulation Z and is administered by the CFPB. TILA requires credit institutions to disclose to borrowers the true cost of obtaining credit versus paying cash. **Regulation Z** applies when credit is extended to individuals for personal, family, or household uses and the amount of credit is $25,000 or less. Regardless of the amount, Regulation Z always applies when a credit transaction is secured by a residence. The regulation does not apply to business or commercial loans of any amount or to agricultural loans over $25,000.

Annual percentage rate (APR).   The **annual percentage rate (APR)** is the total cost of financing a loan in percentage terms, as a relationship of the total finance charges to the total amount financed. It is often higher than the interest rate for the loan itself. Not all loan charges apply.

Creditor.   A *creditor*, for purposes of Regulation Z, is a person who extends consumer credit more than 25 times a year or more than 5 times a year if the transaction involves a dwelling as security. The credit must be subject to a finance charge or payable in more than four installments by written agreement.

Three-day right of rescission.   In the case of most consumer credit transactions covered by Regulation Z, the borrower has three days in which to rescind the transaction by merely notifying the lender. This *right of rescission* does not apply to residential purchase-money or first mortgage or deed of trust loans. In an emergency, the right to rescind may be waived in writing to prevent a delay in funding.

Advertising.   Regulation Z provides strict regulation of real estate advertisements that include mortgage financing terms. The act does not require creditors to advertise credit terms, but if they do advertise some credit terms, called *trigger terms*, they must include disclosure of all terms.

Trigger terms include the amount of the down payment, number of payments, amount of any payment, period of payments, and the amount of any finance charges. If an advertisement mentions one of these trigger items, then the following additional information must also be disclosed:

- Cash price or amount of the loan

- Amount of required down payment

- Number, amount, and frequency of payments

- Total of all payments (unless it refers to a first mortgage on property being purchased)

- APR

General phrases, such as "liberal terms available," may be used without triggering these additional disclosure requirements.

Penalties.   Regulation Z provides penalties for noncompliance. The penalty for violation of an administrative order enforcing Regulation Z is $10,000 for each day the violation continues. A fine of up to $10,000 may be imposed for engaging in an unfair or deceptive practice. In addition, a creditor may be liable to a consumer for twice the amount of the finance charge, plus court costs, attorney's fees, and any actual damages. Willful violation is a misdemeanor punishable by a fine of up to $5,000 or one year's imprisonment or both.

Equal Credit Opportunity Act (ECOA)

The **Equal Credit Opportunity Act (ECOA)** attempts to ensure fair and equal treatment of credit applications by lenders. It prohibits lenders and others who grant credit to consumers from discriminating against credit applicants on the basis of race, color, religion, national origin, sex, marital status, age (provided the applicant is of legal age), or dependence on public assistance. In addition, lenders and other creditors must now inform all rejected credit applicants in writing within 30 days of the principal reasons why credit was denied or, in some cases, terminated.

Real Estate Settlement Procedures Act (RESPA)

The **Real Estate Settlement Procedures Act (RESPA)** is a consumer protection law administered by the CFPB. It was created to ensure that buyers and sellers in residential real estate transactions are aware of all settlement costs and to eliminate kickbacks and referral fees that can increase the cost of some closing costs. RESPA requirements apply when a mortgage loan, secured by a one- to four-family dwelling, is funded by federally related money.

Federally related loans include those (1) made by banks, savings associations, or other lenders whose deposits are insured by federal agencies; (2) insured by the FHA or guaranteed by the VA; (3) administered by HUD; or (4) intended to be sold by the lender to Fannie Mae or Freddie Mac. In general, the regulations apply to a loan secured by a lien (first or subordinate position) on residential properties—home purchase loans, refinances, lender-approved assumptions, property improvement loans, equity lines of credit, time-shares, and reverse mortgages.

RESPA does not apply to a transaction financed solely by a purchase-money mortgage taken back by the seller, by an installment contract (land contract of sale, contract for deed), or a buyer's assumption of the seller's existing loan, and loans secured by a rental property, agricultural, or other business purpose transactions. Other excluded transactions include loans for construction and vacant land (unless a dwelling will be placed on it within two years).

By law, lenders and/or mortgage brokers must make certain disclosures at various times during a covered real estate transaction. At the time that the loan application is taken, or mailed within three business days, the applicant must be given HUD's special information booklet, a Good Faith Estimate (GFE), and the Mortgage Servicing Disclosure Statement. The lender is not required to supply these documents if the lender denies the loan within this time frame.

Special information booklet. *Shopping for Your Home Loan: HUD's Settlement Cost Booklet* is only required for loans to purchase and must be given to any mortgage loan applicant. The 48-page booklet, available on the HUD website in English and Spanish, explains the roles of a real estate licensee and an attorney; basic terms of the sale agreement; how to shop for a loan; the Good Faith Estimate (GFE) and HUD-1 forms; and what happens to loans after closing. It also includes additional information about home equity and refinancing.

Good Faith Estimate (GFE). The Good Faith Estimate (GFE) is a disclosure form that identifies the settlement costs the borrower is likely to incur (see Figure 13.2). The charges are grouped into three categories:

- *No tolerance.* Fees that cannot increase without triggering a new GFE include the lender's origination fee, points for the specific interest rate (after the rate is locked), adjusted origination fees (after the rate is locked), and transfer taxes.

- *Tolerance no more than 10%.* Fees that cannot increase by more than 10% are required settlement charges that are selected by the lender or used by the buyer from the lender's list, such as appraisal, title services, lender's title insurance, owner's title insurance, pest inspections, and government recording charges.

- *Charges that can increase.* These are required settlement charges from service providers chosen by the borrower, such as title services, lender and owner's title insurance, and initial deposit for the impound/escrow account.

FIGURE 13.2   **Good Faith Estimate (GFE)**

OMB Approval No. 2502-0265

Good Faith Estimate (GFE)

Name of Originator	Borrower
Originator Address	Property Address
Originator Phone Number	
Originator Email	Date of GFE

Purpose

This GFE gives you an estimate of your settlement charges and loan terms if you are approved for this loan. For more information, see HUD's *Special Information Booklet* on settlement charges, your *Truth-in-Lending Disclosures*, and other consumer information at www.hud.gov/respa. If you decide you would like to proceed with this loan, contact us.

Shopping for your loan

Only you can shop for the best loan for you. Compare this GFE with other loan offers, so you can find the best loan. Use the shopping chart on page 3 to compare all the offers you receive.

Important dates

1. The interest rate for this GFE is available through _____. After this time, the interest rate, some of your loan Origination Charges, and the monthly payment shown below can change until you lock your interest rate.

2. This estimate for all other settlement charges is available through _____.

3. After you lock your interest rate, you must go to settlement within ____ days (your rate lock period) to receive the locked interest rate.

4. You must lock the interest rate at least ____ days before settlement.

Summary of your loan

Your initial loan amount is	$
Your loan term is	years
Your initial interest rate is	%
Your initial monthly amount owed for principal, interest, and any mortgage insurance is	$ per month
Can your interest rate rise?	☐ No ☐ Yes, it can rise to a maximum of %. The first change will be in .
Even if you make payments on time, can your loan balance rise?	☐ No ☐ Yes, it can rise to a maximum of $
Even if you make payments on time, can your monthly amount owed for principal, interest, and any mortgage insurance rise?	☐ No ☐ Yes, the first increase can be in and the monthly amount owed can rise to $. The maximum it can ever rise to is $.
Does your loan have a prepayment penalty?	☐ No ☐ Yes, your maximum prepayment penalty is $.
Does your loan have a balloon payment?	☐ No ☐ Yes, you have a balloon payment of $ due in years.

Escrow account information

Some lenders require an escrow account to hold funds for paying property taxes or other property-related charges in addition to your monthly amount owed of $ _____ .
Do we require you to have an escrow account for your loan?
☐ No, you do not have an escrow account. You must pay these charges directly when due.
☐ Yes, you have an escrow account. It may or may not cover all of these charges. Ask us.

Summary of your settlement charges

A	Your Adjusted Origination Charges *(See page 2.)*	$
B	Your Charges for All Other Settlement Services *(See page 2.)*	$
A + **B**	Total Estimated Settlement Charges	$

Good Faith Estimate (HUD-GFE)   1

FIGURE 13.2 **Good Faith Estimate (GFE) (Cont.)**

Understanding your estimated settlement charges

Your Adjusted Origination Charges

1. Our origination charge
This charge is for getting this loan for you.

2. Your credit or charge (points) for the specific interest rate chosen

☐ The credit or charge for the interest rate of ⬚ % is included in "Our origination charge." (See item 1 above.)

☐ You receive a credit of $ ⬚ for this interest rate of ⬚ %. This credit **reduces** your settlement charges.

☐ You pay a charge of $ ⬚ for this interest rate of ⬚ %. This charge (points) **increases** your total settlement charges.

The tradeoff table on page 3 shows that you can change your total settlement charges by choosing a different interest rate for this loan.

A Your Adjusted Origination Charges | $

Your Charges for All Other Settlement Services

Some of these charges can change at settlement. See the top of page 3 for more information.

3. Required services that we select
These charges are for services we require to complete your settlement. We will choose the providers of these services.

Service	Charge

4. Title services and lender's title insurance
This charge includes the services of a title or settlement agent, for example, and title insurance to protect the lender, if required.

5. Owner's title insurance
You may purchase an owner's title insurance policy to protect your interest in the property.

6. Required services that you can shop for
These charges are for other services that are required to complete your settlement. We can identify providers of these services or you can shop for them yourself. Our estimates for providing these services are below.

Service	Charge

7. Government recording charges
These charges are for state and local fees to record your loan and title documents.

8. Transfer taxes
These charges are for state and local fees on mortgages and home sales.

9. Initial deposit for your escrow account
This charge is held in an escrow account to pay future recurring charges on your property and includes ☐ all property taxes, ☐ all insurance, and ☐ other ⬚ .

10. Daily interest charges
This charge is for the daily interest on your loan from the day of your settlement until the first day of the next month or the first day of your normal mortgage payment cycle. This amount is $ ⬚ per day for ⬚ days (if your settlement is ⬚).

11. Homeowner's insurance
This charge is for the insurance you must buy for the property to protect from a loss, such as fire.

Policy	Charge

B Your Charges for All Other Settlement Services | $

A + **B** Total Estimated Settlement Charges | $

Good Faith Estimate (HUD-GFE) 2

FIGURE 13.2   **Good Faith Estimate (GFE) (Cont.)**

Instructions

Understanding which charges can change at settlement

This GFE estimates your settlement charges. At your settlement, you will receive a HUD-1, a form that lists your actual costs. Compare the charges on the HUD-1 with the charges on this GFE. Charges can change if you select your own provider and do not use the companies we identify. (See below for details.)

These charges **cannot increase** at settlement:	The total of these charges **can increase up to 10%** at settlement:	These charges **can change** at settlement:
▪ Our origination charge ▪ Your credit or charge (points) for the specific interest rate chosen *(after you lock in your interest rate)* ▪ Your adjusted origination charges *(after you lock in your interest rate)* ▪ Transfer taxes	▪ Required services that we select ▪ Title services and lender's title insurance *(if we select them or you use companies we identify)* ▪ Owner's title insurance *(if you use companies we identify)* ▪ Required services that you can shop for *(if you use companies we identify)* ▪ Government recording charges	▪ Required services that you can shop for *(if you do not use companies we identify)* ▪ Title services and lender's title insurance *(if you do not use companies we identify)* ▪ Owner's title insurance *(if you do not use companies we identify)* ▪ Initial deposit for your escrow account ▪ Daily interest charges ▪ Homeowner's insurance

Using the tradeoff table

In this GFE, we offered you this loan with a particular interest rate and estimated settlement charges. However:

▪ If you want to choose this same loan with **lower settlement charges,** then you will have a **higher interest rate.**
▪ If you want to choose this same loan with a **lower interest rate,** then you will have **higher settlement charges.**

If you would like to choose an available option, you must ask us for a new GFE.

Loan originators have the option to complete this table. Please ask for additional information if the table is not completed.

	The loan in this GFE	The same loan with lower settlement charges	The same loan with a lower interest rate
Your initial loan amount	$	$	$
Your initial interest rate[1]	%	%	%
Your initial monthly amount owed	$	$	$
Change in the monthly amount owed from this GFE	No change	You will pay $ **more** every month	You will pay $ **less** every month
Change in the amount you will pay at settlement with this interest rate	No change	Your settlement charges will be **reduced** by $	Your settlement charges will **increase** by $
How much your total estimated settlement charges will be	$	$	$

[1] *For an adjustable rate loan, the comparisons above are for the initial interest rate before adjustments are made.*

Using the shopping chart

Use this chart to compare GFEs from different loan originators. Fill in the information by using a different column for each GFE you receive. By comparing loan offers, you can shop for the best loan.

	This loan	Loan 2	Loan 3	Loan 4
Loan originator name				
Initial loan amount				
Loan term				
Initial interest rate				
Initial monthly amount owed				
Rate lock period				
Can interest rate rise?				
Can loan balance rise?				
Can monthly amount owed rise?				
Prepayment penalty?				
Balloon payment?				
Total Estimated Settlement Charges				

If your loan is sold in the future

Some lenders may sell your loan after settlement. Any fees lenders receive in the future cannot change the loan you receive or the charges you paid at settlement.

 Good Faith Estimate (HUD-GFE) 3

If changes occur that require a new GFE, closing is delayed for three business days to allow the borrower to shop for alternatives. The fees and charges listed on the GFE must correspond to those actually listed on page three of the HUD-1 form. Loan originators are required to reimburse the borrower for any excess within 30 days after settlement.

Settlement Statement (HUD-1).   All settlements that must conform to RESPA requirements must be prepared on the Settlement Statement (HUD-1). The HUD-1 documents all costs and credits associated with the settlement. By law, upon the borrower's request, the closing agent must permit the borrower to inspect the settlement statement, to the extent that the figures are available, one business day before the closing.

All settlement charges are itemized on the second page, and those totals are brought forward to the first page. In the typical transaction, line 300 indicates the cash at settlement from/to the buyer and line 600 indicates the cash at settlement to/from the seller. The third page of the HUD-1 contains a comparison of the charges disclosed on the GFE and those charged at closing. As noted in the GFE discussion, many of the totals may not be different. The lender must specifically indicate the loan amount, loan term, interest rate, and more. A sample HUD-1 is shown in Figure 17.1.

Prohibited practices.   RESPA prohibits **kickbacks**, that is, receiving a fee for a referral or a fee for settlement services not actually performed involving a federally related loan. RESPA also prohibits fee splitting. Four sections are particularly important to real estate licensees and their clients and customers.

- *Section 6: Loan Servicing.* Loan servicers are required to notify borrowers within 15 days before the effective date of the loan transfer. The borrower may not be penalized so long as the borrower makes timely payments within 60 days of the loan transfer. The notice must include the name and address of the new servicer, toll-free telephone numbers, and the date that the new servicer will start accepting payments. Borrowers who are having problems are supposed to contact their servicer, in writing, with the details of their complaint; the servicer must acknowledge this complaint within 20 days and resolve the issue within 60 days. Borrowers may bring a private or class action lawsuit within three years and may obtain actual damages and additional damages if there is a pattern of noncompliance.

- *Section 8: Kickbacks, Referral Fees, and Unearned Fees.* RESPA explicitly prohibits the paying of kickbacks (i.e., unearned fees). Any referral must be based on quality of services received, not on what money (or thing of value) is paid for the referral. Violators are subject to criminal and civil penalties. A consumer may file a lawsuit and recover an amount equal to three times the amount paid for the service. In a criminal case, a person may be fined up to $10,000 and/or imprisoned up to one year. This prohibition does not, however, cover fee splitting between cooperating brokers, brokerage referral arrangements, or a broker's dividing commissions with salespeople.

- *Section 9: Seller-Required Title Insurance.* A seller may not require homebuyers to use a specific title insurance company; buyers are always free to choose their own. However, there is no RESPA violation if a builder chooses to pay the fees if using the builder's choice, but not if the buyers choose their own title services. A consumer may file a lawsuit and recover an amount equal to three times the amount paid for the service.

- *Section 10: Limits on Escrow/Impound Accounts.* Many government loan programs and some lenders require **escrow accounts** (also called **impound accounts**) as a condition of the loan for the purpose of ensuring that money is available to pay taxes, hazard insurance, and other charges related to the property. When such accounts are required, lenders may charge only one-twelfth of the estimated amounts during the year and maintain a cushion of no more than one-sixth of the total disbursements for the year. Lenders must audit these accounts once a year and refund any amount more than $50 to the borrower; they can also notify the borrower of any shortfalls. HUD can impose a civil penalty on loan servicers who do not submit either the initial or annual escrow account statements to borrowers.

Controlled business arrangements (CBAs).   Congress amended RESPA and created an exception to the prohibition against kickbacks between service providers. In a controlled business arrangement (CBA), if the party referring the buyer has a business relationship with the service provider, fees paid are not considered kickbacks if the business arrangements are disclosed to the buyer, a written estimate of charges is disclosed to the buyer, and the buyer is not required to use a particular service provider.

Fair Credit Reporting Act

The **Fair Credit Reporting Act** regulates the action of credit bureaus and the use of consumer credit. If a potential borrower is denied credit, the lender must make information in that person's credit file available to the borrower and must provide the name and address of the credit bureau that supplied the credit information. If requested by a person, a credit bureau must supply information included in that person's credit file. A person has the right to have an erroneous credit report corrected. Further, access to a person's credit file is limited.

Community Reinvestment Act (CRA)

In 1977, the **Community Reinvestment Act (CRA)** was passed to help prevent redlining and discrimination by lenders. The act was designed to ensure that banks "meet the credit needs of the community" where they conduct their lending business. To comply with the act, lenders must make a reasonable percentage of loans in their business area, and they must prepare community reinvestment statements that report on various details of their lending activities.

SUMMARY

The major sources of real estate financing in the primary mortgage market are savings associations, mutual savings banks, commercial banks, insurance companies, mortgage banking companies, credit unions, mortgage brokers, pension funds, and investment groups.

The federal government exercises its influence over the real estate finance market through the Federal Reserve Board as well as through various agencies, such as the Office of Thrift Supervision and the Federal Home Loan Bank. The Federal Reserve regulates the reserve requirements and discount rates of federally chartered banks and its member banks.

The secondary market is composed of the investors who ultimately purchase and hold the loans as investments. Fannie Mae and Freddie Mac take an active role in creating a secondary market by regularly purchasing mortgage and trust deed loans from originators and retaining them until investment purchasers are available. Ginnie Mae often acts in tandem with Fannie Mae and guarantees the payment of mortgage-backed securities composed of VA and FHA mortgage loans.

Syndication is the financing of real estate transactions and investments by groups of investors, including joint ventures, limited partnerships, and real estate investment trusts (REITs).

Regulation Z, the federal Truth in Lending Act, requires lenders to inform prospective borrowers who use their homes as security for credit of all finance charges involved in such a loan. Severe penalties are provided for noncompliance. The Real Estate Settlement Procedures Act (RESPA) requires lenders to inform both buyers and sellers in advance of all fees and charges required for the settlement or closing of a residential real estate transaction that is financed by a federally related mortgage or trust deed loan.

The Federal Equal Credit Opportunity Act prohibits creditors from discriminating against credit applicants on the basis of race, color, religion, national origin, sex, marital status, age, or dependency upon public assistance. Further, the Fair Credit Reporting Act regulates the action of credit bureaus and use of credit information.

The Community Reinvestment Act (CRA) helps with this antidiscrimination effort by ensuring that banks meet the credit needs of the community where they conduct their lending business.

REVIEW QUESTIONS

Please complete all of the questions before turning to the Answer Key on page 345.

1. The primary purpose of the Truth in Lending Act (Regulation Z) is to
   a. set maximum mortgage interest rates.
   b. disclose the costs of borrowing funds.
   c. protect lenders.
   d. allow fair credit reporting.

2. A mutual savings bank has the *MOST* in common with
   a. a commercial bank.
   b. Fannie Mae.
   c. a savings association.
   d. a credit union.

3. RESPA regulations do *NOT* require the lender to
   a. give the borrower a copy of *Shopping for Your Home Loan: HUD's Settlement Cost Booklet.*
   b. give the borrower a copy of the loan package submitted for underwriting.
   c. give the borrower a good-faith estimate of settlement costs.
   d. use the Settlement Statement (HUD-1).

4. A prime example of a government-sponsored enterprise (GSE) is
   a. FHA.
   b. Fannie Mae.
   c. Ginnie Mae.
   d. the OTS.

5. Freddie Mac participates in the secondary market by
   a. lending money to residential purchasers.
   b. buying FHA, VA, and conventional loans.
   c. insuring Freddie Mac loans.
   d. making loans to low-income rural borrowers.

6. One protected category that is included in the Equal Credit Opportunity Act but is *NOT* one of the seven classes designated in the Fair Housing Act is
   a. race.
   b. sex.
   c. source of income.
   d. familial status.

7. The Truth in Lending Act (Regulation Z) regulates
   a. personal loans for over $25,000.
   b. home improvement loans.
   c. business loans.
   d. loans secured by commercial real estate.

8. The secondary mortgage market is *BEST* described as the
   a. lenders who deal exclusively in second mortgages.
   b. market where loans are bought and sold after they have been originated.
   c. major lender for residential mortgages and deeds of trust.
   d. major lender for FHA-insured and VA-guaranteed loans.

9. The inclusion of which of the following phrases in a print advertisement would require full disclosure under the Truth in Lending Act (Regulation Z)?
   a. "Low monthly payments"
   b. "FHA and VA loans available"
   c. "Easy financing terms"
   d. "Pay off your loan in less than 15 years"

10. Under the provisions of the Truth in Lending Act (Regulation Z), the annual percentage rate (APR) includes all of the following components *EXCEPT*
    a. the discount points.
    b. the broker's commission.
    c. the loan origination fee.
    d. the loan interest rate.

11. Which of the following acts requires banks to meet the credit needs of the community they serve?
    a. Real Estate Settlement Procedures Act
    b. Equal Credit Opportunity Act
    c. Community Reinvestment Act
    d. Fair Housing Act

12. If the Federal Reserve wishes to slow down the economy, it might
    a. lower the discount rate.
    b. lower the reserve requirements.
    c. raise the discount rate.
    d. buy U.S. Treasury securities.

13. The Real Estate Settlement Procedures Act (RESPA) specifically prohibits
    a. brokerage referral arrangements.
    b. a broker's dividing commission with salespeople.
    c. fee splitting between cooperating brokers.
    d. kickbacks.

14. RESPA regulations apply to
    a. all recorded mortgage loans.
    b. first mortgage loans to be sold to Fannie Mae or Freddie Mac.
    c. only FHA and VA loans.
    d. any contract for deed.

15. The *MOST* commonly used method of credit scoring is
    a. Equifax.
    b. Experian.
    c. TransUnion.
    d. FICO.

16. At closing, the lender requires taxes and hazard insurance payments in addition to the principal and interest. If the hazard insurance costs $600 a year and the taxes are $1,800 a year, what is the maximum that the lender can require each month?
    a. $100
    b. $200
    c. $250
    d. $300

17. If hazard insurance costs $600 a year and taxes are $1,800 a year, what is the maximum cushion, if any, that the lender can accumulate during the year?
    a. $200
    b. $400
    c. $600
    d. No maximum

18. A mortgage broker asks a real estate licensee for the names of buyers who need a mortgage loan. For every five referrals, the mortgage broker will enter the licensee's name in a drawing for a vacation. Under RESPA rules, the mortgage broker's request is
    a. a good business practice.
    b. an opportunity for the real estate licensee to pick up some extra cash.
    c. an illegal request.
    d. is permitted because the licensee doesn't actually receive a fee.

19. What is the effect of the lender increasing the loan's interest rate just before closing?
    a. The borrower has to pay it.
    b. Closing will be delayed.
    c. The borrower can choose to pay extra points.
    d. The real estate licensee is expected to pay the extra points.

20. The buyer has approached a lender for a mortgage loan to buy his first home. Until the lender provides a good-faith estimate, which of the following may the lender charge this applicant?
    a. Appraisal fee
    b. Loan application fee
    c. Credit report fee
    d. All of these

14

The Control and Development of Land

LEARNING OBJECTIVES

When you finish reading this chapter, you will be able to

- discuss private ownership and development,
- name public land-use controls that affect private ownership and development,
- recognize the importance of the master plan, and
- discuss the constitutional issues regarding zoning.

buffer zone	Interstate Land Sales Full Disclosure Act	subdivision
building codes		taking
certificate of occupancy	master plan	transit-oriented development (TOD)
conditional-use permit	nonconforming use	variance
developer	planned unit development (PUD)	zoning ordinances
enabling acts	subdivider	

The control and development of land is accomplished in three ways: (1) *direct public ownership*, (2) *private ownership*, and (3) *public land-use controls*.

DIRECT PUBLIC OWNERSHIP

Over the years, the government's general policy has been to encourage private ownership of land. But the government must own a certain amount of land for such uses as municipal buildings, state legislative houses, schools, and military stations. Public ownership is also a means of land control.

There are other examples of necessary public ownership. Urban renewal efforts, especially government-owned housing developments, are one way that public ownership serves the public interest. Publicly owned streets and highways perform a necessary function for the entire population. In addition, public land is often used for recreational purposes. National and state parks and forests create areas for public use and recreation and, at the same time, help to conserve natural resources. Through direct public ownership, the government can put land to use in ways that will benefit all the people.

Interstate Land Sales Full Disclosure Act

To protect consumers from "overenthusiastic sales promotions" in interstate land sales, Congress passed the **Interstate Land Sales Full Disclosure Act**. The law requires those engaged in the interstate sale or leasing of 25 or more lots to file a statement of record and register the details of the land with HUD.

The seller is also required to furnish prospective buyers with a property report containing all essential information about the property, such as distance over paved roads to nearby communities, number of homes currently occupied, soil conditions affecting foundations and septic systems, type of title a buyer will receive, and existence of liens. The property report must be given to a prospective purchaser at least three business days before any sales contract is signed.

Any contract to purchase a lot covered by this act may be revoked at the purchaser's option until midnight of the seventh day following the signing of the contract. If the seller misrepresents the property in any sales promotion, a buyer induced by such a promotion is entitled to sue the seller for civil damages. Failure to comply with the law may also subject a seller to criminal penalties of fines and imprisonment.

Many state legislatures have enacted their own subdivided-land sales laws. Some affect only the sale of land located outside the state to state residents, while others affect sales of land located both inside and outside the state. Generally, these state land sales laws tend to be stricter and more detailed than the federal law.

PRIVATE OWNERSHIP AND DEVELOPMENT

Land use may be controlled by private parties as well as by governmental authorities. Land developers and subdividers, as well as individual owners, can dictate land use for future generations.

Subdividers and Developers

Land in large tracts must receive special attention before it can be converted into sites for homes, stores, or other uses. As cities and towns grow, additional land is required for their expansion. For new areas to develop soundly, the services of competent subdividers and developers working closely with city planners are required. A **subdivider** is someone who buys undeveloped acreage, divides it into smaller usable lots, and sells the lots. A **developer** or *builder* then builds homes or other buildings on the lots and sells them. Builders may use their personal sales organization or may act through local real estate brokerage firms. City planners, working with land developers, plan whole communities, which are later incorporated into cities or towns.

Subdivision

The process of **subdivision** generally involves three distinct stages of development: (1) initial planning; (2) final planning; and (3) disposition, or start-up.

During the *initial planning stage*, the subdivider seeks out raw land in a suitable area that can be profitably subdivided. Once the land is located, the property is analyzed for its highest and best use, and preliminary subdivision plans are drawn up. Close contact is initiated between the subdivider and local planning and zoning officials; if the project requires zoning variances, negotiations are initiated. The subdivider also locates financial backers and develops marketing strategies at this point. In many jurisdictions, it may be necessary to submit development proposals to a regional development authority in addition to a local authority when there are water or other issues.

The *final planning stage* is basically a follow-up of the initial stage—final plans are prepared, approval is sought from local officials, permanent financing is obtained, land is purchased, final budgets are prepared, and marketing programs are designed.

The *disposition*, or *start-up*, carries the subdividing process to a conclusion. Subdivision plans are recorded with local officials, and streets, sewers, and utilities are installed. Buildings, open parks, and recreational areas are constructed and landscaped. The marketing programs are implemented, and title to the individual parcels of subdivided land is transferred as the lots are sold.

Subdivision plans.   In plotting out a subdivision according to local planning and zoning controls, a subdivider determines the size as well as the location of the individual lots. The size of the lots, both in front footage and in depth, together with the total amount of square footage, is generally regulated by local ordinances and must be considered carefully. The land must be laid out with consideration of natural drainage and land contours along with *easements* (discussed in Chapter 3) for utilities and water and sewer mains.

Most subdivisions are laid out by the *lot and block system* (described in Chapter 2). An area of land is designated as a block that is then divided into lots.

Although subdividers customarily designate areas reserved for schools, parks, and shopping, once a subdivision has been recorded, the purchasers of the lots have a vested interest in those reserved areas. If, for any reason in the future, such a purpose becomes inappropriate, it will be difficult for the developer to abandon the original plan and use that property for residential purposes. To avoid this problem, many developers designate such areas as outlot A, outlot B, and so forth. Such a designation does not vest any rights in these outlots in the purchasers of the homesites. If one of these areas is to be used for a school, park, or church, it can be so conveyed later. If the outlot is not to be used for such a purpose, it can be resubdivided into residential properties without the burden of securing the consent of the lot owners.

Plat of subdivision.   The subdivider's completed *plat of subdivision* must contain all necessary approvals of public officials and must be recorded in the county where the land is located.

Because the plat will be the basis for future conveyances, the subdivided land should be measured carefully, with all lot sizes and streets noted by the surveyor and entered accurately on the document. Survey monuments should be established, and measurements should be made from these monuments, with the location of all lots carefully marked. See Figure 14.1 for an illustration of a subdivision plat.

FIGURE 14.1   **Subdivision Plat Map**

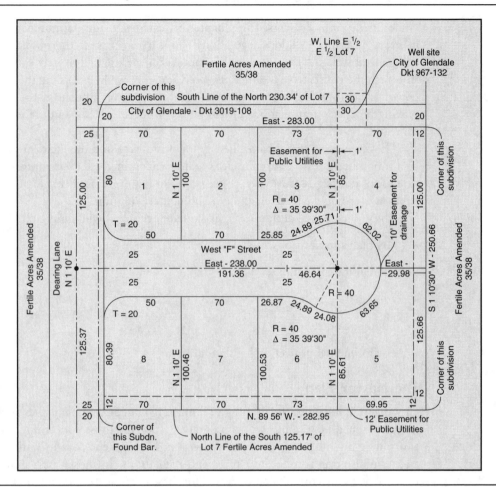

Covenants, conditions, and restrictions (CC&Rs).   Deed restrictions originated and recorded by a subdivider as a means of controlling and maintaining the desirable quality and character of the subdivision are commonly called *covenants, conditions, and restrictions (CC&Rs)*, which are discussed in Chapters 3 and 5. These restrictions can be included in the subdivision plat, or they may be set forth in a separate recorded instrument.

Development costs.   Most homeowners are not aware of the costs of developing land. The subdivider, developer, and builder frequently invest hundreds of thousands of dollars (and in larger developments, several millions of dollars) before the subdivision is even announced to the public. The difference between the raw land cost on a per-acre basis and the asking price per front foot of subdivided lot surprises the average homeowner. An analysis of development costs substantiates the sale price of a building lot in an average subdivision that is four to six times the cost of the raw land. These costs, of course, vary from area to area and according to the nature of the development.

A finished lot's sale price generally reflects such expenses as cost of land; installation of sewers, water mains, storm drains, landscaping, and street lights; earthworks (dirt removal, site grading, and similar operations); paving; engineering and surveying fees; brokers' commissions; inspections; bonding costs; filing and legal fees; sales costs; and overhead. In certain areas, a subdivider may also be required to give financial assistance to school districts, park districts, and the like, in the form of either donated school or park sites or a fixed subsidy per subdivision lot. If these further costs are incurred, they must be added proportionately to the sale price of each building site.

PUBLIC LAND-USE CONTROLS

Under *police power* (discussed in Chapter 3), each state and its municipalities have the inherent authority to adopt regulations necessary to protect the public health, safety, and general welfare. This includes limitations on the use of privately owned real estate. Although the courts have traditionally been conservative in extending the scope of police power, changing social and economic conditions have influenced the courts toward making broader interpretations of this power in recent years—and the trend is likely to continue.

Growing urban populations, new types of industry, and the increasing complexity of civilization make it necessary for cities and towns to increase their controls over the private use of real estate. Currently, police power in many areas is being increased to include controls over noise, air, water, and environmental pollution.

The governmental authorities that regulate privately owned real estate include

- city plan specifications,

- subdivision regulations,

- zoning,

- building codes, and

- environmental protection legislation.

The Master Plan

City planning includes the drafting of a **master plan**. Such a plan gives advice on planning and scheduling public works programs, especially those concerning traffic facilities and public buildings; controlling subdivision development; and preparing, modifying, and administering zoning ordinances and regulations. In most cases, a city, county, or regional planning commission is created for these purposes. A combination of residential, commercial, and industrial property is usually included in master plans to spread the tax base and provide employment for local residents.

City planning helps to meet the social and economic needs of ever-changing communities. Both economic and physical surveys are essential in preparing a master plan. Also, plans must include the coordination of numerous civic plans so that orderly city growth and stabilized property values can be assured.

Subdivision Regulations

Subdivision regulations have been adopted by most communities as part of a comprehensive master plan. These regulations usually provide for

- the location, grading, alignment, surfacing, and widths of streets, highways, and other rights of way;

- installation of sewers and water mains;

- building and setback lines;

- areas to be reserved or dedicated for public use, such as parks or schools; and

- easements for public utilities.

Subdivision regulations, like all other forms of land-use regulation, cannot be static. These regulations must remain flexible to meet the changing needs of society.

Zoning

Zoning ordinances are laws of local governmental authorities that regulate the use of land. Zoning powers are conferred on municipal governments by state **enabling acts**; there are no state or national zoning ordinances. The local ordinances usually regulate the height, size, and use of buildings, the use of land, and the density of population.

Zoning ordinances generally divide land use into three broad classifications: (1) residential, (2) commercial, and (3) industrial. A fourth use now included by many communities is called *cluster zoning*, or *multiple-use zoning*, that permits construction of *planned unit developments (PUDs)* (discussed later in this chapter).

To ensure adequate control, land-use areas are further divided into subclasses. For example, residential areas may be divided to provide for detached single-family dwellings, structures containing not more than four dwelling units, high-rise apartments, and so forth. Further, **buffer zones**, such as areas for landscaped parks and playgrounds, may be created to screen residential areas from nonresidential zones.

Constitutional issues.   Zoning ordinances must not violate the rights of individuals as property holders, as provided under the due process provisions of the Fourteenth Amendment of the U.S. Constitution or provisions of the constitution of the state in which the real estate is located. If the legislation used to regulate the use of property is destructive, unreasonable, arbitrary, or confiscatory, such legislation is usually considered void. Tests applied in determining the validity of ordinances require that the

- power be exercised in a reasonable manner;

- provisions be clear and specific;

- ordinances be free from discrimination;

- ordinances promote public health, safety, and general welfare under the police power concept; and

- ordinances must apply to all property in a similar manner.

Taking.   The concept of **taking** comes from the *takings clause* of the Fifth Amendment to the U.S. Constitution. The clause reads, "[N]or shall private property be taken for public use without just compensation." This means that when land is physically taken for public use through the government's power of eminent domain, the landowner must be compensated.

Courts have expanded this constitutional protection so that government regulation that is not an actual physical taking through eminent domain may also be considered a taking if a landowner's ability to use the property is severely limited. A series of U.S. Supreme Court cases have established tests for when regulation of property goes too far and is considered a taking. The *Kelo v. New London* case (discussed in Chapter 3) illustrates this point.

Planned unit development (PUD).   Zoning for a **planned unit development (PUD)** permits a higher density of dwellings, mixed uses, and greater use of open space. Because residential, shopping, office, and other uses are planned simultaneously, the result can be a harmonious combination that provides residents and workers with greater convenience and more green space. Occasionally, research facilities or light industrial uses are included, all with ready access to major highways and rail lines. A PUD can also be used for a resort area or shopping center. There may be one or more lot owner community organizations;

for example, one for homeowners and one for retailers. Provision for such associations is usually included in the recorded plat of subdivision.

The PUD concept is useful whenever variations on the setback or density regulations are desired, such as a development with zero lot lines where no setback from the lot line is necessary for structures. A PUD is similar to a condominium property in that there are generally common areas and more structures per acre than would normally be permitted. Condominium owners generally own a block of air, whether the condominium concept is for residential, office, or commercial purposes. However, the PUD owner owns the land underlying the structure plus a surrounding lot. The PUD common-area association is structured as a nonprofit corporation, and individual owners have no interest in the common areas.

A new variation is **transit-oriented development (TOD)**. A TOD is a type of urban development that focuses on walkable community design, mixing land uses to incorporate retail, residential, offices, open space, and public use with easy access to public transportation. The idea is to reduce dependence on automobiles for most everyday needs.

Nonconforming use.   In the enforcement of zoning, a frequent problem is a building that does not conform to the zoning because it was erected before the enactment of the zoning law. Such a building is not a violation because when it was built, there was no prohibitive zoning ordinance. This **nonconforming use** is often called a *grandfather clause*, and the use is allowed to continue. If the building is destroyed or torn down, any new structure must comply with the current zoning ordinance.

Zoning exceptions.   Each time a plan is created or a zoning ordinance enacted, some owners are inconvenienced and want to change the allowed uses of their properties. Generally, such owners may appeal for either a conditional-use permit or a variance to allow a use that does not meet zoning requirements.

A **conditional-use permit** may be granted to allow a special use of property that is in the public interest—for example, schools, hospitals, teen centers, and recreational facilities.

A **variance** is a permanent exception to zoning sought by a property owner who may suffer undue hardship as a result of a zoning ordinance. For example, if an owner's lot drops off to 30 feet below street level at the midpoint of the lot, the zoning board may be willing to allow a variance so the owner can build closer to the road than would normally be allowed. However, the board could refuse to allow a change if another use is available for the same parcel, and the only hardship that would result from using the alternative was a longer driveway that would cost more money.

A single parcel within a zone may be allowed for a different use than the zone surrounding it. Spot zoning is not a favored practice. However, if public opinion is in favor, for example, a small grocery store or a small public playground might be allowed on a parcel within a residential zone.

Zoning appeal boards.   Zoning appeal boards have been established in most communities to hear complaints about the effect of zoning ordinances on specific parcels of property. Petitions may be presented to the appeal board for changes or exceptions in the zoning law.

Building Codes

Most cities have enacted ordinances, called **building codes** that set requirements for the kinds of materials to be used plus standards for construction of all aspects of a building—for example, plumbing, electrical wiring, roofing, insulation, and fire prevention.

Most communities require a building permit to be issued by the city clerk (or other official) before a person can build, alter, or repair a structure on property within the corporate limits of the municipality. Through the permit requirement, city officials are made aware of construction or alterations and can verify compliance with both building codes and zoning ordinances by examination of the plans and inspection of the work. Once the completed structure has been inspected and found to be satisfactory, the city inspector issues a **certificate of occupancy**. A property may be conveyed without a certificate of occupancy, but no one is allowed to live in it. Real estate brokers should protect the best interests of their clients by insuring that a certificate of occupancy is included in the settlement documents.

If the construction or alteration of a building violates a deed restriction, the issuance of a building permit will not cure this violation. A building permit is merely evidence of the applicant's compliance with municipal regulations. When a conflict arises, rights of adjoining owners in a subdivision to enforce deed restrictions usually will prevail over the police power legislation of the community if the restrictions are more limiting.

SUMMARY

The control and development of land is accomplished through direct public ownership, such as municipal buildings, schools, and military facilities; through private ownership that is subject to subdivision regulations; and through police power that protects the public.

The process of subdivision includes dividing the tract of land and providing for utility easements as well as laying out street patterns and widths. A subdivider must record a completed plat of subdivision with all necessary approvals of public officials in the county where the land is located. Subdividers usually place restrictions upon the use of all lots in a subdivision as a general plan for the benefit of all lot owners.

Subdivided land sales are regulated on the federal level by the Interstate Land Sales Full Disclosure Act.

Effective control of land requires an overall master or comprehensive plan to be developed based upon a local economic survey of the community.

Subdivision regulations are necessary to maintain control of the development of expanding community areas so that growth will be harmonious with community standards. Zoning ordinances segregate residential areas from business and industrial zones and control not only land use but also height and size of buildings and density of population. Zoning enforcement issues that may be presented to a board of appeal include variances, exceptions, and nonconforming use permits.

Building codes are different from zoning ordinances. While zoning ordinances control use, building codes control construction of buildings by specifying standards for construction, plumbing, sewers, electrical wiring, and equipment.

In addition to land-use control on a local level, the state and federal governments have occasionally intervened to preserve natural resources through environmental legislation.

REVIEW QUESTIONS

Please complete all of the questions before turning to the Answer Key on page 346.

1. A homeowner wants to build a front porch on her house, but it is not allowed in that zone. In order to build the porch, she will first have to appeal for a
   a. variance.
   b. nonconforming use.
   c. building permit.
   d. certificate of occupancy.

2. A person who buys undeveloped acreage, splits it into smaller usable parcels, and then sells those parcels is called a
   a. land planner.
   b. developer.
   c. builder.
   d. syndicator.

3. Police power is the government's right to enact regulations to protect the public health, safety, and welfare. This power includes the right to create
   a. police stations.
   b. zoning regulations.
   c. covenants, conditions, and restrictions (CC&Rs).
   d. deed restrictions.

4. Local building codes are an important factor in the
   a. development of an area master plan.
   b. construction of a new structure.
   c. subdivision of a large tract of land.
   d. demolition of a partially destroyed building.

5. A town's municipal government receives the power to enact zoning ordinances through
   a. federal statutes.
   b. common law.
   c. court precedent.
   d. enabling acts.

6. The Interstate Land Sales Full Disclosure Act was enacted to
   a. protect the public from unscrupulous subdividers.
   b. encourage the interstate sales of land parcels.
   c. help the public purchase government-owned property.
   d. develop land for retirement and recreation purposes.

7. A building company submitted a request for zoning for a planned unit development (PUD). This will enable them to
   a. build high-rise residential buildings in an area zoned for agriculture.
   b. prohibit the building of shopping centers or offices on the property.
   c. make a greater use of open space.
   d. convert a rental to a condominium.

8. To protect the public, the Interstate Land Sales Full Disclosure Act requires that a developer involved in the interstate land sales of 25 or more lots
   a. provide each prospective buyer with a copy of the property report.
   b. pay the prospective buyer's expenses to see the property involved.
   c. provide preferential financing to such buyers.
   d. include the deed restrictions for such buyers.

9. A city may establish a board of appeal to hear complaints about
   a. deed restrictions.
   b. building codes.
   c. the effects of a zoning ordinance.
   d. the effects of public ownership.

10. A new zoning ordinance is enacted that prohibits barns from being built in a city. The owner of a previously existing barn on her property has been told that she does not need to tear it down. This is an example of
    a. inverse condemnation.
    b. eminent domain.
    c. a nonconforming use.
    d. a variance.

11. A couple are looking into buying some property to build a restaurant. To determine whether this property can be put to their intended use, they should examine the
    a. building codes for that location.
    b. zoning ordinances for that location.
    c. lists of permitted nonconforming uses.
    d. list of obtainable variances.

12. All of the following items are properly addressed by deed restriction *EXCEPT*
    a. types of buildings that may be constructed.
    b. minimum sizes of buildings to be constructed.
    c. activities prohibited on the property.
    d. permitted religious preferences of purchasers.

13. A local zoning authority that wants to grant an exception to zoning because it is in the public interest will grant a
    a. conditional-use permit.
    b. variance.
    c. nonconforming use.
    d. violation.

14. The Interstate Land Sales Full Disclosure Act requires
    a. compliance for those who sell or lease a minimum of 25 lots.
    b. a buyer to execute the contract within 30 days.
    c. every state to enact additional subdivided land policies.
    d. a 30-day rescission period after any contract is signed.

15. The plat map filed for a new subdivision will include all of the following *EXCEPT*
    a. easements for water and sewer lines.
    b. land to be dedicated for public facilities.
    c. land set aside for roadbeds and rights of way.
    d. prices of the available residential lots.

16. Plans prepared by a planning committee or commission that project 20 years or more into the future are called
    a. general development plans.
    b. master plans.
    c. wishful thinking.
    d. zoning ordinances.

17. A couple just purchased a home in a community so their children can walk to school and take swimming lessons in the community pool. In addition to the costs of maintaining their own home, they must also contribute to a general fund to maintain some of the public areas in their subdivision. In what type of community are they living?
    a. Mixed uses
    b. Small town
    c. Nonconforming uses
    d. Planned unit development (PUD)

18. A transit-oriented development (TOD) is *MOST* similar to
    a. a planned unit development (PUD).
    b. traditional suburbs.
    c. rural areas that lack zoning.
    d. a small town.

19. Which land use requirements can be enforced by local municipalities?
    a. Deed restrictions
    b. Covenants, conditions, and restrictions (CC&Rs)
    c. Zoning ordinances
    d. Restrictive covenants

20. How are building codes enforced?
    a. Building permits
    b. Certificate of occupancy
    c. Takings
    d. Planning commissions

Fair Housing Law

LEARNING OBJECTIVES

When you finish reading this chapter, you will be able to

- describe the history of federal fair housing laws,
- name discriminatory housing practices and exemptions,
- differentiate between blockbusting and steering, and
- discuss the legal requirements for the protection of the disabled.

Americans with Disabilities Act (ADA)	Fair Housing Amendments Act of 1988	Housing for Older Persons Act (HOPA)
blockbusting	familial status	protected class
Civil Rights Act of 1866	Federal Fair Housing Act of 1968	redlining
disability	Housing and Community Development Act of 1974	steering
Equal Credit Opportunity Act (ECOA)		testers

Real estate licensees who offer residential property for sale must be aware of the federal, state, and local laws pertaining to civil rights and nondiscrimination. These laws, under such titles as open housing, fair housing, and equal opportunity housing, prohibit undesirable and discriminatory activities. Their provisions affect every phase of the real estate sales process, from listing to closing, and all brokers and salespeople must comply with them.

The goal of legislators who have enacted these laws and regulations is to create an unbiased housing market—one in which all homeseekers have the opportunity to buy or rent any home they choose, provided the home is within their financial means. As a potential licensee, the student of real estate must be able to recognize illegal housing practices. Failure to comply with fair housing practices is not only grounds for license revocation, but also a criminal act.

FAIR HOUSING LAWS

Variations of the federal fair housing laws have been passed at state and local levels. While state and local laws might add protections, they can never remove any protection covered by federal law. Generally, when a discrepancy exists, the more restrictive prevails. Each of these laws can apply to different protected classifications (race, national origin, and families with minor children), different kinds of real estate (residential properties versus commercial properties), and different kinds of discriminatory practices (steering, discriminatory advertising, or blockbusting). A given act of discrimination (denial of an apartment rental because of race) can violate a number of different laws and may be enforceable in a federal court and in both a state and local agency, all at the same time.

Today, laws specifically prohibit discrimination based on being a member of a **protected class**. In this context, a protected class is one that has historically encountered discrimination not because of financial ability but rather on membership in a particular group.

History of Federal Fair Housing Laws

Although the first act was passed in 1866, little achievement in open housing was achieved until 1968 and later.

The **Civil Rights Act of 1866** prohibits any type of discrimination based on race. The law states, "All citizens of the United States shall have the same right, in every State and Territory, as is enjoyed by white citizens thereof to inherit, purchase, lease, sell, hold, and convey real and personal property."

The **Federal Fair Housing Act of 1968**, Title VIII of the Civil Rights Act of 1968, provides that it is unlawful to discriminate on the basis of race, color, religion, or national origin when selling or leasing residential property. The 1968 federal law exempts individual homeowners and certain groups.

However, in *Jones v. Alfred H. Mayer Company* (1968), the Supreme Court reaffirmed the Civil Rights Act of 1866, stating that the law "bars all racial discrimination, private as well as public, in the sale and rental of property." Despite any exemptions in the 1968 law, an aggrieved person may seek a remedy for racial discrimination under the 1866 law against any homeowner, regardless of whether or not the owner employed a real estate broker and/or advertised the property. Where race is involved, no exceptions apply.

The **Housing and Community Development Act of 1974** added sex as a protected class. In this context, sex is either male or female; it is not a protection for sexual orientation.

The **Fair Housing Amendments Act of 1988** added two more protected classes: those with mental or physical disabilities (originally called handicaps) and families with children (familial status).

Disability is defined as having a physical or mental impairment and/or as having a history of or being regarded as having an impairment that substantially limits one or more of an individual's major life activities. Persons who have AIDS and recovering drug addicts are protected under this classification. Current drug abusers are not protected, nor are those who pose a threat to the health or safety of others.

The act defines **familial status** as the presence of one or more individuals who have not reached the age of 18 living with either a parent or guardian. The term also includes a woman who is pregnant and any one in the process of securing legal custody. Unless a property qualifies as housing for older persons, all properties must be made available for families with children under the same terms and conditions as to anyone else. It is illegal to advertise properties "for adults only" or to indicate a preference for a certain number of children. Landlords cannot restrict the number of occupants to eliminate families with children.

Exempt housing.   HUD exempts certain housing from accepting children, providing that it meets any of the following requirements:

- The dwelling is specifically designed for and occupied by elderly persons under a federal, state, or local government program.

- The occupants are all 62 or older.

- It houses at least one occupant who is 55 or older in 80% of the units, and it must publish and follow policies that demonstrate an intent to be housing for those who are 55 and older.

Exempt properties may accept families with children, but they are not obligated to do so.

The **Housing for Older Persons Act (HOPA)** enacted in 1995 made several changes to the Fair Housing Act exemptions for the elderly. HOPA eliminated the requirement that the housing have "significant facilities and services" designed for the elderly and now does not prosecute those who have "good faith reliance" that the property meets the 55-and-older requirement.

The **Equal Credit Opportunity Act (ECOA)** prohibits discrimination in the granting of credit. The Fair Housing Act classifications of race, color, religion, national origin, and sex are protected; additionally, ECOA bars discrimination on the basis of marital status and age. It also prohibits lenders from discriminating against recipients of public assistance programs, such as food stamps and Social Security, on the basis of source of income. Figure 15.1 provides a summary of the federal fair housing laws and the classifications that each law protects.

FIGURE 15.1   **Summary of Federal Fair Housing Laws**

Law	Purpose
Civil Rights Act of 1866	Prohibits discrimination in housing based on race without exception
Executive Order No. 11063 (1962)	Prohibits discrimination in housing funded by FHA or VA loans
Civil Rights Act of 1964	Prohibits discrimination in federally funded housing programs
Title VIII of the Civil Rights Act of 1968 (Federal Fair Housing Act)	Prohibits discrimination in housing based on race, color, religion, or national origin, with certain exemptions
Housing and Community Development Act of 1974	Extends prohibitions to discrimination in housing based on sex
Fair Housing Amendments Act of 1988	Extends protection to cover persons with disabilities and families with children, with certain exemptions

State Fair Housing Laws

Many states have their own laws concerning fair housing. Most mirror the federal fair housing laws, but some states have added additional protected classes. Examples of additional classes that may be protected under state law include age, marital status, source of income, and sexual orientation. Real estate professionals need to be aware of any state and/or municipal law affecting housing practices in their area, in addition to the federal laws discussed in this text.

Whenever a state or municipality has a fair housing law that has been ruled "substantially equivalent to the federal law," all complaints in that state or locality, including those filed with the **Department of Housing and Urban Development (HUD)**, are referred to and handled by the local enforcement agencies. To be considered substantially equivalent, the local law and its related regulations must contain prohibitions comparable to the federal law. In addition, the state or locality must show that its local enforcement agency is taking sufficient affirmative action in processing and investigating complaints and in finding remedies for discriminatory practices.

DISCRIMINATORY HOUSING PRACTICES

The federal Fair Housing Act (along with the 1974, 1988, and 1995 acts) applies to houses, apartments, and vacant land acquired for the construction of residential buildings. These laws prohibit the following discriminatory acts:

- Refusing to sell, rent, or negotiate with any person or otherwise making a dwelling unavailable to any person

- Changing terms, conditions, or services for different individuals as a means of discrimination

- Practicing discrimination through any statement or advertisement that restricts the sale or rental of residential property

- Representing to any person, as a means of discrimination, that a dwelling is not available for sale or rental

- Making a profit by inducing owners of housing to sell or rent because of the prospective entry into the neighborhood of persons of a particular race, color, religion, national origin, disability, or familial status

- Altering the terms or conditions for a home loan to any one in any multiple listing service, real estate brokers' organization, or other facility related to the sale or rental of dwellings as a means of discrimination

- Denying people membership or limiting their participation in any multiple listing service, real estate brokers' organization, or other facility related to the sale or rental of dwellings as a means of discrimination

Exemptions. Based on the Supreme Court decision in *Jones v. Myers*, there can be no exemptions or exceptions based on race or color. However, the 1968 act permits the following five exemptions to the federal Fair Housing Act:

1. The sale or rental of a single-family home is exempted when the home is owned by an individual who does not own more than three such homes at one time, when a broker or salesperson is not used, and discriminatory advertising is not used. If the owner is not living in the dwelling at the time of the transaction or was not the most recent occupant, only one such sale by an individual is exempt from the law within any 24-month period.

2. The rental of rooms or units is exempted in an owner-occupied one- to four-family dwelling.

3. Dwelling units owned by religious organizations may be restricted to people of the same religion if membership in the organization is not restricted on the basis of race, color, religion, national origin, sex, disability, or familial status.

4. A private club that is not open to the public may restrict the rental or occupancy of lodgings to its members as long as the lodgings are not operated commercially.

5. Housing intended for older persons is exempt from the familial status classification if (1) it is occupied solely by persons 62 and older, or (2) 80% of its units are occupied by at least one person 55 or older.

Additional Prohibited Practices

Blockbusting, also called *panic selling*, means inducing homeowners to sell by making representations regarding the entry or prospective entry into the neighborhood of members of a protected class, usually a racial consideration. The blockbuster frightens homeowners into selling and makes a profit by buying the homes cheaply and selling them at considerably higher prices to minority group members. This practice is specifically prohibited by the federal Fair Housing Act.

Steering is the channeling of homeseekers to particular areas on the basis of race, religion, country of origin, or other protected class. On these grounds, it is prohibited by the provisions of the federal Fair Housing Act. Steering is often difficult to detect, however, because the steering tactics can be so subtle that the homeseeker is unaware that choices have been limited. Steering may be done unintentionally by agents who are not aware of their own prejudgment assumptions.

Refusing to make mortgage loans or issue insurance policies in specific areas without regard to the applicant's financial qualifications is called **redlining**. This practice, which often contributes to the deterioration of older, transitional neighborhoods, is frequently based on racial grounds rather than on any real objections to the applicant. However, a lending institution that refuses a loan solely on sound economic grounds cannot be accused of redlining.

Equal Housing Poster

An amendment to the federal Fair Housing Act of 1968 instituted the use of a fair housing opportunity poster (see Figure 15.2). This poster is available from HUD in many languages.

When HUD investigates a broker for discriminatory practices, it may consider failure to display the poster in the broker's place of business prima facie evidence of discrimination.

Advertising

No printed or published advertisement of property for sale or rent can include language that indicates any discriminatory preference or limitation, regardless of how subtle the choice of words. HUD's regulations cite examples of discriminatory and nondiscriminatory language (see Figure 15.3). For example, the phrases *master bedroom*, *mother-in-law suite*, and *walk-in closet* are not discriminatory, while *white neighborhood*, *nice Christian home*, and *no wheelchairs* suggest a discriminatory intent.

Pictures of people in advertisements should be as clearly representative of the entire population as reasonably possible and should not exclude anyone. The selective choice of media, whether by language or geographic coverage, may also be discriminatory. For example, advertising a property only in Spanish-language newspapers or over a cable service available only to white suburbanites may be construed as discriminatory.

FIGURE 15.2 **Fair Housing Poster**

U. S. Department of Housing and Urban Development

**EQUAL HOUSING
OPPORTUNITY**

We Do Business in Accordance With the Federal Fair Housing Law

(The Fair Housing Amendments Act of 1988)

It is illegal to Discriminate Against Any Person Because of Race, Color, Religion, Sex, Handicap, Familial Status, or National Origin

---

- In the sale or rental of housing or residential lots

- In advertising the sale or rental of housing

- In the financing of housing

- In the provision of real estate brokerage services

- In the appraisal of housing

- Blockbusting is also illegal

Anyone who feels he or she has been discriminated against may file a complaint of housing discrimination:

    1-800-669-9777 (Toll Free)
    1-800-927-9275 (TTY)
    www.hud.gov/fairhousing

**U.S. Department of Housing and Urban Development
Assistant Secretary for Fair Housing and Equal Opportunity
Washington, D.C. 20410**

Previous editions are obsolete

form HUD-928.1 (6/2011)

FIGURE 15.3   **Fair Housing Act Restrictions**

Prohibited by Federal Fair Housing Act	Example
Refusing to sell, rent, or negotiate the sale or rental of housing	A landlord owns an apartment building with several vacant units. When an Asian family asks to see one of the units, the landlord tells them to go away.
Changing terms, conditions, or services for different individuals as a means of discriminating	A Roman Catholic woman calls on a duplex and the landlord tells her the rent is $400 per month. When she talks to the other tenants, she learns that all the Lutherans in the complex pay only $325 per month.
Advertising any discriminatory preference or limitation in housing or making any inquiry or reference that is discriminatory in nature	A real estate agent places the following advertisement in a newspaper: "Just Listed! Perfect home for white family, near excellent parochial school!" A developer places this ad in an urban newspaper: "Sunset River Hollow–Dream Homes Just For You!" The ad is accompanied by a photo of several African American families.
Representing that a property is not available for sale or rent when in fact it is	A man who uses a wheelchair is told that the house he wants to rent is no longer available. The next day, however, the For Rent sign is still in the window
Profiting by inducing property owners to sell or rent on the basis of the prospective entry into the neighborhood of persons of a protected class	A real estate licensee sends brochures to homeowners in a predominantly white neighborhood. The brochures, which feature the licensee's past success selling homes, include photos of racial minorities, population statistics, and the caption, "The Changing Face of the Neighborhood."
Altering the terms or conditions of a home loan, or denying a loan, as a means of discrimination	A lender requires a divorced mother of two children to pay for a credit report. In addition, her father must cosign her application. After talking to a single male friend, the woman learns that he was not required to do either of those things, despite his lower income and poor credit history.
Denying membership or participation in a multiple listing service, a real estate organization, or another facility related to the sale or rental of housing as a means of discrimination	A real estate practitioners' association meets every week to discuss available properties and buyers. None of that area's black or female agents are allowed to be a member of the association.

Enforcement

A person who believes illegal discrimination has occurred has up to one year after the alleged act to file a charge with HUD or to bring a federal suit within two years. Complaints may be filed in English, Spanish, Arabic, Cambodian, Chinese, Korean, Russian, and Vietnamese. If HUD has reasonable cause to believe a discriminatory act has occurred, it generally refers complaints to state or local agencies whose fair housing laws are deemed to be substantially equivalent to federal law. The state statute of limitations is generally less than the federal statute of limitations.

HUD will investigate, and if the department believes a discriminatory act has occurred, it will litigate the case. Unless one of the parties requests a court procedure, an administrative law judge (ALJ) within HUD hears the charge. If the ALJ feels that discrimination has occurred, the ALJ can order any of the following of the respondent:

- Pay compensation to the complainant

- Provide injunctive relief (i.e., make the housing available to the complainant)

- Pay a civil penalty not to exceed $16,000 per violation for a first offense, up to $37,500 for a second offense within the previous five years, and up to $65,000 for a third violation within seven years

- Pay reasonable attorney's fees and costs

The complainant or HUD may choose to have the charge heard in a federal district court, and the attorney general will litigate on behalf of the complainant. The district court may offer relief and order payment of actual damages, attorney fees, and costs. The court can also order unlimited punitive damages.

In addition to offended parties filing suit, the Department of Justice may sue anyone who seems to show a pattern of illegal discrimination. Limits on penalties in such cases are set at $55,000, with a $110,000 penalty for subsequent violations.

Complaints brought under the Civil Rights Act of 1866 must be taken directly to a federal court. The only time limit for action is the state's statute of limitations for torts (injuries done by one individual to another).

Threats or Acts of Violence

The federal Fair Housing Act of 1968 contains criminal provisions protecting the rights of those who seek the benefits of the open housing law as well as owners, brokers, or salespeople who aid or encourage the enjoyment of open housing rights. Unlawful actions involving threats, coercion, and intimidation are punishable by civil action. In such cases, the victim should immediately report the incident to the local police and to the nearest office of the Federal Bureau of Investigation (FBI).

LEGAL REQUIREMENTS FOR THE PROTECTION OF THE DISABLED

Americans with Disabilities Act (ADA)

The **Americans with Disabilities Act (ADA)** is a civil rights law that guarantees individuals with certain disabilities an equal opportunity in the areas of employment, public accommodations, and telecommunications. Real estate brokers are often employers, and real estate brokerage offices are public spaces.

Title I of the ADA requires employers (including real estate brokers) to make *reasonable accommodations* that enable a person with a disability to perform essential job functions. Reasonable accommodations may include making the work site accessible, restructuring a job, providing part-time or flexible work schedules, and modifying equipment that is used on the job. The provisions of the ADA apply to any employer with 15 or more employees.

Title III of the ADA provides for accessibility to goods and services for people with disabilities. Real estate licensees who deal with nonresidential properties are significantly affected by the ADA. Building owners and property managers must ensure that any obstacles are eliminated. The Americans with Disabilities Act Accessibility Guidelines (ADAAG) contain detailed specifications for designing parking spaces, curb ramps, elevators, drinking fountains, toilet facilities, and directional signs to ensure maximum accessibility.

Federal Fair Housing Act

The federal Fair Housing Act makes it unlawful to discriminate against prospective buyers and tenants on the basis of disability. Landlords must make reasonable accommodations to existing policies, practices, and services to permit persons with disabilities to have equal access to the premises. For example, it is reasonable to permit a seeing-eye dog in a no-pets building. The interpretation of this law has been expanded to include all *service animals*; in other words, any animal that makes daily living safer, easier, or more comfortable for a disabled person.

Tenants with disabilities must be permitted to make reasonable modifications to rented premises at their own expense. Such modifications might include lowering door handles or installing bath rails to accommodate a person in a wheelchair. Failure to permit reasonable modifications constitutes discrimination. The landlord is allowed to require that the property be restored to its previous condition when the lease ends.

The law does not prohibit restricting occupancy exclusively to persons with disabilities in rental dwellings that are specifically designed for their accommodation.

Different rules apply to properties consisting of four or more units constructed before and after March 13, 1991. For example, since then, public and common areas must be accessible to anyone, include someone with a disability, and doors and hallways must be wide enough for wheelchairs. Anyone thinking of constructing multifamily housing should hire very knowledgeable architects and builders in order to comply with recent rules.

IMPLICATIONS FOR REAL ESTATE PROFESSIONALS

To a large extent, the laws place the burden of responsibility for effecting and maintaining fair housing on real estate professionals. The laws are clear and widely known. The complainant does not have to prove guilty knowledge or specific intent—only the fact that discrimination occurred.

When an allegation of discrimination occurs, real estate professionals cannot defend themselves by saying that the offense was unintentional or that they have always provided service to members of the same protected class in the past. The real estate professional's best course is to study fair housing law, develop sensitivity, and use consistent business practices designed to reduce the danger of unintentionally hurting any consumer regarding financial analysis, properties suggested, and properties shown. Using a standard written form for all qualifying interviews is helpful, as is being on time for appointments and promptly returning all phone calls. Besides helping to avoid civil rights violations, these practices are simply good business practices and should result in increased sales.

In addition, HUD offers guidelines for nondiscriminatory language and illustrations for use in real estate advertising to help licensees comply with the laws and make that policy known to the public. A complete discussion of this topic is available at www.hud.gov/offices/fheo/library/part109.pdf.

Testers. From time to time, real estate offices may be visited by **testers**, undercover volunteers who want to see whether customers and clients are being treated equally and are being offered the same free choice within a given price range without regard to any of the protected classes. The courts have held that such practice is permissible because it is the only way to test compliance with fair housing laws. Additionally, if asked by a seller or landlord to discriminate, real estate professionals must remove themselves from the situation by explaining what the law requires. Under no circumstances can a real estate professional be part of any discriminatory action.

National Association of REALTORS® (NAR) Code of Ethics

The National Association of REALTORS® (NAR) adopted the Code of Ethics for its members in 1913. NAR also publishes interpretations of the Code called Professional Standards. These are updated annually and may be found at www.realtor.org. The Code and Professional Standards provide practical applications of business ethics.

Many other professional organizations in the real estate industry have codes of ethics as well. In addition, many state real estate commissions are required by law to establish codes or canons of ethical behavior for state licensees.

SUMMARY

Federal regulations regarding equal opportunity in the sale or rental of residential property are contained in various acts of Congress. Of significant importance are the Civil Rights Act of 1866, which prohibits all racial discrimination, and the federal Fair Housing Act (Title VIII of the Civil Rights Act of 1968) that prohibits discrimination on the basis of race, color, religion, and national origin. Later acts or amendments added the protected classes of sex, disability, and familial status.

Discriminatory actions include refusing to deal with an individual or a specific group, changing any terms of a real estate or loan transaction, changing the services offered for any individual or group, making statements or advertisements that indicate discriminatory restrictions, or otherwise attempting to make a dwelling unavailable to any person or group because of membership in a protected class. Some exceptions apply to owners, but none to brokers and none when the discriminatory act is based on race.

Complaints under the federal Fair Housing Act may be reported to and investigated by the Department of Housing and Urban Development (HUD) and may be taken to a U.S. district court. Complaints under the Civil Rights Act of 1866 must be taken to a federal court. Fair housing law also prohibits steering, blockbusting, and redlining. Compliance is occasionally monitored by undercover testers.

The National Association of REALTORS® Code of Ethics mandates a set of ethical standards for all members to follow.

REVIEW QUESTIONS

Please complete all of the questions before turning to the Answer Key on page 347.

1. The primary goal of fair housing law is to
   a. create fair sales prices.
   b. encourage home purchases.
   c. create an unbiased housing market.
   d. promote discriminatory activities.

2. A licensee approaches homeowners in a popular section of town and tries to get them to sell by telling them that persons of a specific ethnic group are moving into the neighborhood. This is an example of
   a. steering.
   b. blockbusting.
   c. channeling.
   d. equal opportunity housing.

3. The Civil Rights Act of 1866 is unique because it
   a. has been broadened to protect the aged.
   b. adds welfare recipients as a protected class.
   c. contains choose your neighbor provisions.
   d. provides no exceptions to racial discrimination.

4. A licensee believes that he best assists clients by encouraging them to buy in an area where many other persons of the same nationality live. Although well-intentioned, he is still violating the fair housing prohibition against
   a. steering.
   b. blockbusting.
   c. redlining.
   d. testing.

5. Complaints brought under the Civil Rights Act of 1866 must be taken directly to
   a. federal court.
   b. state court.
   c. the secretary of HUD.
   d. the state enforcement agency.

6. A mortgage company has made it a practice to refuse to make mortgage loans in a specific area of town without regard to the economic qualifications of the applicant. The mortgage company is guilty of
   a. steering.
   b. redlining.
   c. blockbusting.
   d. channeling.

7. The Fair Housing Amendments Act of 1988 added the new protected classes of
   a. occupation and source of income.
   b. disability and familial status.
   c. political affiliation and country of origin.
   d. marital status and age.

8. The federal Fair Housing Act allows
   a. advertising property for sale only to a special group.
   b. altering the terms of a loan for a member of a minority group.
   c. refusing to sell a home to an individual because of poor credit history.
   d. telling an individual that an apartment has been rented when in fact it has not.

9. Undercover investigation to determine whether fair housing practices are being followed is sometimes made by
   a. testers.
   b. evaluators.
   c. operatives.
   d. appraisers.

10. An African American real estate professional's practice of offering a special discount to African American clients is
    a. satisfactory.
    b. illegal.
    c. legal but ill-advised.
    d. acceptable.

11. The Housing and Community Development Act of 1974 prohibits discrimination on the basis of
    a. disability.
    b. familial status.
    c. marital status.
    d. sex.

12. A seller who requests prohibited discrimination in the showing of a house should be told,
    a. "I'll need those instructions in writing to protect my company."
    b. "I'll do what I can, but I can't guarantee anything."
    c. "You'll have to clear that with my broker."
    d. "We're not allowed to obey such instructions."

13. The federal Fair Housing Act does *NOT* allow
    a. an apartment building to rent rooms to graduates of a specific university only.
    b. the owner of a 20-unit apartment building to rent to single women only.
    c. a Catholic convent to refuse to furnish housing for a Jewish man.
    d. an owner to refuse to rent the other side of a duplex home to families with children.

14. If a case brought under the federal Fair Housing Act is heard in a federal court, the maximum dollar amount that can be ordered for actual damages and punitive damages is
    a. $50,000.
    b. $100,000.
    c. $1,000,000.
    d. unlimited.

15. A property owner places a hand-painted sign in front of her 12-unit apartment building that says, "Rooms for rent—Christians only, and no lawyers." Under the federal Fair Housing Act of 1968, the owner may
    a. advertise as she pleases but must rent the rooms to anyone capable of paying the rent.
    b. restrict the rooms she rents by religion only.
    c. restrict the rooms she rents by occupation only, but she may not advertise her discriminatory preferences.
    d. restrict the rooms she rents by both religion and occupation.

16. A landlord is concerned about the safety of her tenants. Therefore, she shows only first floor apartments to families with children. This practice
    a. is a good business plan.
    b. should reduce her liability insurance.
    c. is an illegal practice of steering.
    d. is an illegal practice of blockbusting.

17. Which Supreme Court decision reaffirmed the Civil Rights Act of 1866, prohibiting all racial discrimination?
    a. *Jones v. Mayer*
    b. *Brown v. Board of Education*
    c. *Plessy v. Ferguson*
    d. *Shelly v. Kraemer*

18. Which of the following constitutes a family protected by fair housing rights?
    a. Elderly couple being cared for by their middle-aged son
    b. Brother and sister sharing an apartment since they were 35 and 40, respectively
    c. A couple with two foster children
    d. A married couple in their 20s

19. Which of the following may deny housing to a person who has a disability?
    a. Manager of a 20-unit apartment building
    b. Owner of a two-unit apartment building who lives in one of the units
    c. Property manager acting on behalf of the owner who does not want anyone with a disability renting
    d. Directors of condominium community

20. Which law prohibits discrimination based on receipt of public assistance?
    a. Federal Fair Housing Act
    b. Civil Rights Act of 1866
    c. Americans with Disabilities Act
    d. Equal Credit Opportunity Act

Chapter 16

Environmental Issues and the Real Estate Transaction

LEARNING OBJECTIVES

When you finish reading this chapter, you will be able to

- describe various hazardous substances that impact real estate transactions,
- summarize the effects of environmental protection legislation, and
- recognize the importance of always recommending professional discovery and disclosure of environmental hazards.

asbestos

brownfields

carbon monoxide (CO)

Comprehensive Environmental Response, Compensation, and Liability Act (CERCLA)

encapsulation

environmental impact statement (EIS)

environmental site assessment (ESA)

landfill

lead-based paint

mold

potentially responsible party (PRP)

radon

Small Business Liability Relief and Brownfields Revitalization Act

Superfund

underground storage tank (UST)

urea-formaldehyde foam insulation (UFFI)

People desire to live and work in an environment that does not put their health or safety at risk. Therefore, environmental issues have become important in the practice of real estate. Laws have been enacted at all levels that prohibit environmental pollution and hold property owners liable for cleanup. Disclosure of potential environmental problems in real estate transactions has become a substantial issue. Further, environmental problems negatively affect property values.

Purchasers are particularly concerned whether the property they are buying contains environmental hazards. Due to this concern, much of the legal burden for disclosure or elimination of hazards seems to arise when properties are transferred. This creates disclosure duties and potential legal liability for real estate agents involved in a real estate transaction. For these reasons, real estate licensees must be alert to environmental hazards, aware of their responsibilities regarding disclosure, and familiar with local, state, and federal environmental laws.

ENVIRONMENTAL HAZARDS

In general, real estate licensees are not expected to have the technical expertise necessary to determine whether an environmental hazard is present. However, they must be aware of what is considered an environmental hazard and why and to be able to direct their clients and customers to appropriate sources of information. Most states now require that sellers of most one- to four-family residential dwellings disclose any environmental concerns of which they have knowledge. These seller disclosures must be provided so that the buyers can make informed decisions.

Figure 16.1 depicts a number of common environmental hazards of which real estate agents should be aware. These hazards are briefly explained in the following paragraphs. More information is available at www.epa.gov.

FIGURE 16.1 **Environmental Hazards**

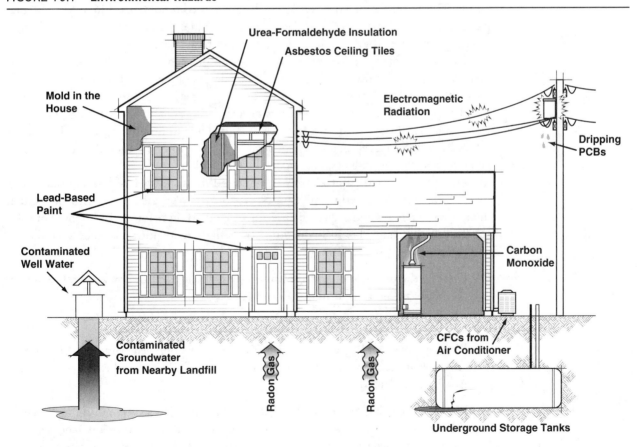

Asbestos

Asbestos is a mineral once commonly used as insulation in residential and commercial construction because of its fire-resistant and heat-containing qualities until 1978 when the use of asbestos insulation was banned. *Asbestos-containing materials (ACMs)* were used to cover pipes, ducts, and heating and hot water units in commercial and residential properties. Further, its fire-resistant properties made it a popular material for use in floor tile, exterior siding, and roofing products.

When asbestos is disturbed or exposed, as often occurs during renovation, remodeling, or aging, the asbestos fibers break down into tiny filaments and particles resulting in *friable* asbestos—microscopic airborne asbestos fibers that, when inhaled, can cause a variety of respiratory diseases. No safe level of asbestos exposure has been determined. If asbestos fibers in the indoor air of a building reach a certain level, the building becomes difficult to lease, finance, and insure. Intact asbestos is *nonfriable* and does not constitute a danger, unless it is disturbed and becomes airborne.

Only an engineer or home inspector skilled in this area should be consulted to determine the presence of asbestos. Asbestos removal is costly and requires state-licensed contractors, a specially sealed environment, and proper disposal. Removal may be dangerous because improper removal could create hazardous airborne asbestos. In certain circumstances, **encapsulation** (sealing off the disintegrating asbestos) may be preferable to removal.

Lead-Based Paint

Until 1978, when the practice was banned, lead was commonly used in alkyd oil-based paints for exterior and interior surfaces, in both residential and commercial buildings. Housing built after 1978 is unlikely to have a lead-based paint problem.

Essentially, intact **lead-based paint** causes no problems until it is disturbed. However, lead-based paint dust results from not only deteriorating or disturbed paint, but also from the normal wear and tear of intact paint (e.g., opening and shutting a window). A high level of lead in any person's system can cause serious neurological damage. However, children under the age of six are particularly vulnerable to negative effects of lead exposure. Excessive lead levels in a small child can result in damage to their developing brains and nervous systems, kidneys, hearing, and coordination.

Because lead-based paint is likely to be found in up to 75% of housing built prior to 1978, the federal government requires that owners of these properties make certain disclosures to tenants and buyers. Before any property built before 1978 is rented or sold, the Lead-Based Paint Hazard Reduction Act (LBPHRA) requires that sellers, landlords, and their agents do the following:

- Disclose the presence of any known lead-based paint and/or any known hazards on the HUD-formulated form (see Figure 16.2).

- Provide copies of any available reports.

- Provide buyers and tenants copies of the federally approved pamphlet *Protect Your Family From Lead in Your Home* (available in English, Spanish, Vietnamese, Russian, Arabic, and Somali).

- Provide buyers (but not tenants) with a period of up to 10 days (or any mutually agreeable time frame) for the buyer to conduct a risk assessment or inspection to determine if there is lead-based paint or lead-based paint hazards. Buyers may waive this opportunity.

- Purchase and lease agreements must include language that acknowledges that the sellers and the licensees have complied with these disclosures.

FIGURE 16.2   **Disclosure of Information on Lead-Based Paint and/or Lead-Based Paint Hazards**

Disclosure of Information on Lead-Based Paint and/or Lead-Based Paint Hazards

Lead Warning Statement

Every purchaser of any interest in residential real property on which a residential dwelling was built prior to 1978 is notified that such property may present exposure to lead from lead-based paint that may place young children at risk of developing lead poisoning. Lead poisoning in young children may produce permanent neurological damage, including learning disabilities, reduced intelligence quotient, behavioral problems, and impaired memory. Lead poisoning also poses a particular risk to pregnant women. The seller of any interest in residential real property is required to provide the buyer with any information on lead-based paint hazards from risk assessments or inspections in the seller's possession and notify the buyer of any known lead-based paint hazards. A risk assessment or inspection for possible lead-based paint hazards is recommended prior to purchase.

Seller's Disclosure

(a) Presence of lead-based paint and/or lead-based paint hazards (check (i) or (ii) below):

   (i) _____ Known lead-based paint and/or lead-based paint hazards are present in the housing (explain).

   _____

   (ii) _____ Seller has no knowledge of lead-based paint and/or lead-based paint hazards in the housing.

(b) Records and reports available to the seller (check (i) or (ii) below):

   (i) _____ Seller has provided the purchaser with all available records and reports pertaining to lead-based paint and/or lead-based paint hazards in the housing (list documents below).

   _____

   (ii) _____ Seller has no reports or records pertaining to lead-based paint and/or lead-based paint hazards in the housing.

Purchaser's Acknowledgment (initial)

(c) _____ Purchaser has received copies of all information listed above.

(d) _____ Purchaser has received the pamphlet *Protect Your Family from Lead in Your Home.*

(e) Purchaser has (check (i) or (ii) below):

   (i) _____ received a 10-day opportunity (or mutually agreed upon period) to conduct a risk assessment or inspection for the presence of lead-based paint and/or lead-based paint hazards; or

   (ii) _____ waived the opportunity to conduct a risk assessment or inspection for the presence of lead-based paint and/or lead-based paint hazards.

Agent's Acknowledgment (initial)

(f) _____ Agent has informed the seller of the seller's obligations under 42 U.S.C. 4852d and is aware of his/her responsibility to ensure compliance.

Certification of Accuracy

The following parties have reviewed the information above and certify, to the best of their knowledge, that the information they have provided is true and accurate.

Seller	Date	Seller	Date
Purchaser	Date	Purchaser	Date
Agent	Date	Agent	Date

The LBPHRA specifically mandates that real estate professionals ensure that all parties comply. The LBPHRA does not require that a home be tested for lead-based paint or that the hazards must be abated, but a state or municipality could possibly require such testing and abatement. Thus, real estate professionals must be knowledgeable about local requirements. Purchasers can make a contract contingent on receiving a satisfactory inspection report.

The EPA requires the use of lead-safe practices. All contractors performing renovation, repair, and painting projects that disturb lead-based paint in homes, child care facilities, and schools built before 1978 must be certified and follow specific work practices to prevent lead contamination. The ruling applies whenever more than six square feet of painted surface in an interior room or more than twenty square feet of exterior space is to be disturbed, including all window replacements or demolition.

EPA guidance pamphlets and other information about lead hazards are available at http://www2.epa.gov/lead/.

Other lead hazards.   Lead particles can be present in forms other than paint. Lead may also contaminate drinking water due to the water running through lead pipes or lead solder. Further, soil and groundwater may be contaminated by everything from lead plumbing in leaking landfills to discarded bullets from an old shooting range. High levels of lead have been found in the soil near waste-to-energy incinerators. Air and soil may be contaminated from leaded gasoline fumes or automobile exhausts. Lead from any source has the potential to be hazardous.

Radon

Radon is a colorless, odorless, tasteless, naturally occurring gas produced by the decay of natural radioactive minerals in the ground. It can occur anywhere. Radon is a known human carcinogen and is estimated to be a major cause of lung cancer. Opinions differ as to minimum safe levels of radon, though growing evidence suggests that radon may be the most underestimated cause of lung cancer, particularly for children, people who smoke, and those who spend considerable time indoors.

Radon levels vary, depending on the amount of fresh air that circulates through a house, the weather conditions, and the time of year. Radon is impossible to detect without testing. Home radon detection kits are available, although more accurate testing can be conducted by a home inspector or radon-detection professional. Radon is easily mitigated by installing ventilation systems or exhaust vans. A professional test may be required in a real estate transaction.

Urea-Formaldehyde

Urea-formaldehyde was first used in building materials, particularly insulation, in the 1970s. When incorrectly formulated, formaldehyde fumes are emitted from **urea-formaldehyde foam insulation (UFFI)** as it hardens. Formaldehyde gas may cause respiratory problems and eye and skin irritations. Further, formaldehyde is known to cause cancer in animals.

The Consumer Product Safety Commission has issued a warning regarding the use of UFFI, but has currently not banned its use. Some states, however, do prohibit the installation of UFFI. Tests can be conducted to determine the level of formaldehyde gas in a house.

Carbon Monoxide (CO)

Carbon monoxide (CO) is a colorless, odorless gas. Furnaces, water heaters, space heaters, fireplaces, and wood stoves all produce CO as a natural result of fuel combustion. Carbon monoxide emissions are not a problem when these appliances function properly and are ventilated. However, when improper ventilation or equipment malfunctions permit large quantities of CO to be released, it can cause dizziness, nausea, and death.

The presence of CO is difficult to detect. Carbon monoxide detectors are available, and their use is mandatory in some areas. Annual maintenance of heating systems helps mitigate CO exposure.

Mold

Fungi, including **mold** and mildew (bacillus), are natural phenomena, but their effect on human health has not been extensively examined until recently.

Among the thousands of types of mold, only a few are toxic. Molds reproduce spores that attach themselves to moist materials. In order to grow, they need oxygen, cellulose material, and moisture.

Molds produce allergens, irritants, and sometimes toxic substances (mycotoxins) into the indoor and outdoor environment. Due to higher concentrations of mold indoors, allergic reactions to toxic mold range from mild to severe when touched or inhaled and may cause tissue or immune system damage as well as cancer. Stachybotrys has become the most publicized toxic mold and the subject of much litigation.

The smell test is the easiest way of detecting the presence of mold because mold may exist in nonvisible areas of the home. Controlling sources of moisture, which often means reducing humidity and increasing air flow inside the property, is important. Leaky roofing and air-conditioning systems, poor ventilation in bathrooms and laundry rooms, and plumbing pipes are all common sources for mold problems, as are inadequate flashing or guttering and improperly sealed windows and doors. Cleaning and removing the mold is often not sufficient, unless the source of the moisture problem is remedied.

For professional advice on assessment and remediation, seek a home inspector who has the credentials to correctly test mold samples. Currently, there are no EPA or other federal limits on mold or mold spores, but some states have legislated disclosure requirements to include buyers, sellers, landlords, and tenants.

For more information on mold, visit www.epa.gov/mold/.

Groundwater Contamination

Contamination of underground water can threaten the supply of water for private wells and public water systems. Contamination can occur from a variety of sources, including underground storage tanks, septic systems, holding ponds, buried materials, and surface spills. Because water flows from one place to another, contamination can spread far from its source. Numerous state and federal laws have been enacted to preserve and protect the water supply.

Underground storage tanks (USTs). **Underground storage tanks (USTs)** are used to store petroleum products, including gasoline and heating oil, as well as manufacturing chemicals and hazardous waste. Some tanks are currently in use, but many are long forgotten. Tanks are considered a problem because over time they may leak hazardous substances into the environment. Leakage pollutes not only the soil around a tank, but also adjacent parcels and groundwater. Detection, removal, and cleanup of these contaminants can be very expensive.

State and federal laws impose very strict requirements on landowners to detect and correct UST leaks. Further, landowners in many states can be held liable for the clean-up costs and damage associated with a leak. Many states require sellers to disclose the presence of underground tanks to potential buyers, and some states and municipalities require the removal of older residential USTs. Real estate agents should be aware of these laws and be alert to any factors that would indicate the presence of a UST.

Waste Disposal Sites

Real estate professionals should be aware of how waste is disposed of because proximity to waste disposal sites may affect a property's desirability. Garbage and refuse mainly go to landfill operations. A **landfill** is an enormous hole that is lined with an impermeable membrane to prevent leakage into groundwater. Once the landfill is full, the site is capped with soil and vegetation plantings. A ventilation pipe runs from the landfill's base to the cap to vent off accumulated natural gases created by the decomposing waste. Hazardous and toxic materials go to hazardous waste disposal sites.

Federal, state, and local regulations govern the location, construction, content, and maintenance of landfill sites. Completed landfills have been used for such purposes as parks and golf courses, as well as residential and commercial development.

Brownfields

Economically depressed urban areas called **brownfields** are often stigmatized by the potential of being contaminated or thought to be contaminated by hazardous waste. Initially, the EPA insisted on permanent remedies for these sites, but no one wanted to take responsibility for the potential liability of cleaning them up. In 2002, the **Small Business Liability Relief and Brownfields Revitalization Act** was passed to allow some flexibility aimed at returning these sites to economic viability, which has happened. Essentially, current owners who did not cause or contribute to the contamination are not liable for the cleanup. Some states have also developed more flexible clean-up standards, protection for lenders, and financial incentives to open brownfields for redevelopment.

ENVIRONMENTAL PROTECTION LEGISLATION

Federal and state legislators have passed a number of environmental protection laws in an attempt to respond to the growing public concern over the improvement and preservation of America's natural resources. Figure 16.3 contains a brief summary of significant federal environmental legislation.

FIGURE 16.3 **Federal Environmental Legislation**

Law	Year Enacted	Purpose
National Environmental Policy Act	1970	Established a Council on Environmental Quality for land-use planning and created the Environmental Protection Agency (EPA) to enforce federal environmental legislation
Clean Air Amendment	1970	Created more stringent standards for automotive, aircraft, and factory emissions
Water Quality Improvement Act	1970	Strengthened water pollution standards
Resource Recovery Act	1970	Expanded the solid waste disposal program
Water Pollution Control Act Amendment	1972	Created standards for cleaning navigable streams and lakes by the mid-1980s
Clean Water Act	1974	Established standards for water suppliers
Resource Conservation & Recovery Act	1976	Regulated potentially dangerous water pollutants under the 1974 Clean Water Act
Clean Water Act Amendment	1977	Updated the list of potentially dangerous water pollutants under the Clean Water Act of 1974
Comprehensive Environmental Response, Compensation, and Liability Act (CERCLA)	1980	Provided large sums of money for hazardous waste disposal and charged clean-up costs to the parties responsible for the waste
Superfund Amendment and Reauthorization Act	1986	Clarified regulations regarding hazardous waste and limited liability for some parties, including real estate brokers

States have also responded to these issues by passing a variety of localized environmental protection laws regarding various types of pollution, including air, water, noise, and solid waste. For example, many states have enacted laws that prevent builders or private individuals from constructing septic tanks or other effluence disposal systems in certain areas, particularly near public bodies of water. In addition, cities and counties also pass environmental legislation of their own.

Any project funded by federal money is required by the EPA to produce a study that indicates the impact that the project will have on the environment. This **environmental impact statement (EIS)** can include comments about noise, air quality, public health and safety, wildlife, and vegetation. Other topics may include changes in population density, vehicle traffic, energy consumption, the need for sewer and water facilities, employment, and school enrollment that may require additional services from government agencies.

COMPREHENSIVE ENVIRONMENTAL RESPONSE, COMPENSATION, AND LIABILITY ACT (CERCLA)

The **Comprehensive Environmental Response, Compensation, and Liability Act (CERCLA)** established a fund, called the **Superfund**, to clean up hazardous waste sites and to respond to spills. The law also identifies **potentially responsible parties (PRPs)** who may be responsible for the costs of any clean-up action. CERCLA is administered and enforced by the EPA.

A landowner is liable under CERCLA when a release or threat of release of a hazardous substance has occurred on the landowner's property, regardless of whether the landowner caused the contamination. This liability includes the cleanup not only of the landowner's property, but also of any neighboring property that has been contaminated.

Previous owners, property managers, lenders who participate in the management of mortgaged property, and persons whose actions actually caused the contamination may all be PRPs.

The Superfund Amendment and Reauthorization Act of 1986 helped to limit the potential liability of real estate brokers to be considered a potentially responsible party.

Liability under the Superfund is considered to be strict, joint and several, and retroactive. *Strict liability* means that the owner is responsible to an injured party without excuse. *Joint and several liability* means that each of the PRPs is personally responsible for the total damages. If only one of the PRPs is financially able to handle the total damages, that person must pay the total and collect the proportionate shares from the other PRPs whenever possible. *Retroactive liability* means that the liability is not limited to the current owner, but includes people who have owned the site in the past.

There is a defense to CERCLA liability called the innocent landowner defense. A person is exempt from liability if they meet the following four criteria: (1) the pollution was caused by a third party; (2) the property was acquired after the contamination occurred; (3) the landowner had no knowledge of the contamination; and (4) the landowner made a reasonable search before purchasing the property to determine that there was no contamination (called *environmental due diligence*).

CERCLA now publishes on a two-year basis a list, in order of priority, of the substances that present the most potential threat to human health. A copy of the current list is available at www.atsdr.cdc.gov/SPL/.

LIABILITY OF REAL ESTATE PROFESSIONALS

Environmental hazards can create a significant problem for real estate transfer and ownership. It is important for real estate professionals and all others involved in the real estate transaction to be aware of both actual and potential liability.

Innocent landowners might be held responsible for clean-up costs, even though they did not create or know about an environmental hazard. Lenders may end up with worthless assets if owners default on loans rather than undertake expensive clean-up efforts. Sellers can face liability for not disclosing known hazards. Because real estate agents can also be held liable for improper or incomplete disclosure, they must be aware of potential environmental risks both on and off a property and to bring those risks to the attention of the purchaser.

There are additional liability exposures for professionals involved in other aspects of real estate transactions. For example, real estate appraisers must identify and adjust for environmental problems. Adjustments to market value typically reflect the clean-up costs plus a factor for degree of stigma.

Discovery of Environmental Hazards

Real estate professionals are not expected to have the technical expertise necessary to discover the presence of environmental hazards. However, because they are presumed by the public to have special knowledge about real estate, professionals should be aware both of possible hazards and of where to seek professional help. A professional should ask the seller of a property whether any environmental problems or hazardous conditions exist on the property. Further, a professional should always be alert for any physical conditions that may indicate that there is a potential problem.

To protect sellers, buyers, real estate professionals, and lenders, professionals should suggest a professional **environmental site assessment (ESA)** whenever the transaction involves raw land, industrial property, or anything other than a typical residential house with yard. An ESA is a due diligence audit done to determine the existence of any environmental issues that might affect the use of the property or impose future liability on the new owner. The ESA is not the same as the EIS, mentioned earlier. The EIS is required for government-funded projects; the ESA is simply good business.

Real estate professionals should encourage certified environmental engineers to conduct the ESA. The basic Phase I assessment simply looks for potential contamination of the site or any possible violation of an environmental law. If anything looks suspicious, the engineer will suggest further studies and testing.

To repeat, real estate professionals should always recommend that a property purchaser hire a home inspector, environmental auditor, and/or lead inspector who is a technical expert to provide a comprehensive study of the condition of the property. Not only can such experts detect environmental problems, they usually can offer guidance about how best to resolve any adverse conditions and at what cost.

Disclosure of Environmental Hazards

The laws in many states require that sellers of one- to four-family residential dwellings disclose known material facts regarding a property's condition to a potential purchaser. Most state laws do not require such disclosures for other types of properties. Real estate professionals involved with any other type of property should strongly encourage additional testing by experts. The presence of an environmental hazard is considered a material fact. A real estate professional may also be responsible for disclosing material facts that the agent knew of or should have known about. Property condition disclosures are discussed in Chapter 7.

SUMMARY

Environmental issues are important to real estate professionals because they may affect real estate transactions by raising issues of health risk, clean-up costs, and valuation. Some of the principal environmental hazards include asbestos, lead, radon, urea-formaldehyde, and mold.

Real estate professionals who are involved in the sale, leasing, management, financing, and appraisal of residential properties constructed before 1978 should be aware of the potential for lead-based paint hazards. Federal law requires that certain disclosures be given when selling or leasing pre-1978 housing; state and local laws may dictate when and how lead-based paint inspections and abatement are to occur.

CERCLA established the Superfund to finance the cleanup of hazardous waste disposal sites. Under the Superfund, many individuals and entities may be potentially responsible for clean-up costs.

REVIEW QUESTIONS

Please complete all of the questions before turning to the Answer Key on page 348.

1. Under the federal Lead-Based Paint Hazard Reduction Act,
   a. all residential housing built before 1978 must be tested for the presence of lead-based paint before being listed for sale or rent.
   b. a disclosure statement must be attached to all sales contracts and leases involving properties built before 1978.
   c. a lead-hazard pamphlet must be distributed to all prospective buyers, but not tenants.
   d. purchasers of housing built before 1978 must be given five days to test the property for the presence of lead-based paint.

2. Encapsulation refers to the
   a. process of sealing a landfill with three to four feet of topsoil.
   b. way in which insulation is applied to pipes and wiring systems.
   c. method of sealing disintegrating asbestos.
   d. way in which lead-based paint particles become airborne.

3. A licensee is showing a pre-World War I house to a prospective buyer who has a toddler and is worried about potential health hazards. Which of the following is *TRUE*?
   a. There is a risk that urea-foam formaldehyde insulation was used in the original construction.
   b. Because the salesperson is a licensed real estate professional, he can offer to personally inspect for lead and remove any lead risks.
   c. Because of the age of the house, there is a good likelihood of the presence of lead-based paint.
   d. Removal of lead-based paint and asbestos hazards is covered by standard title insurance policies.

4. One problem of having asbestos present in a building is that
   a. the removal of asbestos can further contaminate the building.
   b. asbestos causes health problems only when it is eaten.
   c. the level of asbestos in a building is affected by weather conditions.
   d. HUD requires all asbestos-containing materials to be removed from all residential buildings.

5. Potentially hazardous lead is usually *NOT* present in
   a. roofing tiles.
   b. plumbing pipes and solder.
   c. soil.
   d. interior paint.

6. A man discovers that his new house uses asbestos insulation around its hot water pipes. The insulation is in good condition. What should he do?
   a. Sue the seller and the buyer's agent for failure to disclose this fact.
   b. Devote an afternoon to removing the asbestos insulation and replacing it with other materials.
   c. Immediately call the EPA.
   d. Do none of these.

7. In the process of creating a landfill, waste is
   a. liquefied, treated, and pumped through pipes to tombs under the water table.
   b. layered with top soil in a pit, mounded up, then covered with dirt and plants.
   c. compacted and sealed into a container, then placed in a tomb designed to last several thousand years.
   d. buried in an underground concrete vault.

8. A large oil tank buried on a couple's property has caused extensive damage to a large area in their subdivision. They may find themselves held liable for damages as potentially responsible parties (PRPs) based on
   a. HUD.
   b. CERCLA.
   c. RESPA.
   d. AARP.

9. Radon poses the greatest potential health risk to humans when it is
   a. contained in insulation material used in residential properties during the 1970s.
   b. found in high concentrations in unimproved land.
   c. trapped and concentrated in inadequately ventilated areas.
   d. emitted by malfunctioning or inadequately ventilated appliances.

10. Asbestos contamination is *MOST* likely found in
    a. an elementary school built in 1980.
    b. a high school built in 1960.
    c. a private home built in 1970.
    d. a private home remodeled in 1990.

11. The *MOST* important consideration concerning mold is that
    a. mold is visible and easy to identify.
    b. most molds are toxic and harmful to humans.
    c. cleaning and removing mold is adequate.
    d. repairing the source of the moisture problem is necessary.

12. Which of the following is a hazardous substance that can cause serious neurological damage to children under the age of six?
    a. UFFI
    b. Lead-based paint
    c. Asbestos
    d. Radon

13. Dizziness, nausea, and death may be caused by colorless, odorless
    a. carbon dioxide.
    b. lead-based paint.
    c. carbon monoxide.
    d. mold.

14. With regard to discovery of environmental hazards, a real estate agent should do all of the following *EXCEPT*
    a. ask the sellers if they are aware of any environmental problems.
    b. be alert for physical conditions that might indicate a problem.
    c. recommend that a purchaser hire the appropriate inspector for a suspected environmental problem.
    d. attempt to correct the hazardous condition.

15. Which statement regarding mold is *TRUE*?
    a. All forms of mold are toxic.
    b. The smell test is not an adequate way to detect the presence of mold.
    c. Stachybotrys is a toxic mold that has been the subject of litigation.
    d. The EPA has established limits on the amount of mold spores allowable in buildings.

16. What environmental hazard may result from an improperly burning oil stove?
    a. Asbestos
    b. Radon
    c. Formaldehyde
    d. Carbon monoxide

17. Since 2010, contractors who are renovating an older apartment building must be certified in handling materials containing
    a. lead.
    b. formaldehyde.
    c. mold.
    d. electromagnetic fields.

18. Excessive moisture is a common reason for excessive
    a. radon levels.
    b. mold.
    c. carbon monoxide.
    d. urea formaldehyde.

19. What must be completed and discussed before starting a state-funded road?
    a. EPA overview assessment
    b. Phase I site assessment
    c. Environmental Impact Statement (EIS)
    d. Environmental Site Assessment (ESA)

20. What is the impact of the brownfields law?
    a. Renders some urban properties unsalable
    b. Enhances the value of these properties
    c. Has little impact on urban areas
    d. Brownfields are turned into residential properties

Closing the Real Estate Transaction

LEARNING OBJECTIVES

When you finish reading this chapter, you will be able to

- describe the closing concerns of the buyer, the seller, and the lender;
- differentiate between face-to-face closing and closing in escrow;
- identify RESPA requirements;
- explain how the closing statement works; and
- summarize the general rules for prorating.

accrued items	**debit**	**prepaid items**
affidavit of title	**escrow closing**	**prorations**
closing statement	**mortgage reduction certificate**	**Settlement Statement (HUD-1)**
credit	**payoff statement**	

Closing is the completion of the real estate transaction; in many cases, it actually consists of two events—the *title closing* and the *loan closing*. The title closing occurs when the seller transfers title to the real estate to the buyer and the buyer pays the seller the purchase price. If the buyer is borrowing money to purchase the real estate, the loan closing is also the time when the lender loans the purchase money to the borrower in exchange for the borrower giving a note and mortgage (or deed of trust) to the lender. The overall event is known by many names, including *settlement*, *passing papers*, *in escrow*, and *transfer (of title)*.

PRECLOSING PROCEDURES

Before the real estate title actually changes hands, there are a number of issues with which both the buyer and the seller must deal.

Buyer's Issues

The buyer wants to be sure that the seller delivers the title agreed upon in the purchase and sale contract. The buyer should also ensure that the property is in the agreed-upon physical condition. This involves inspecting

- the title evidence;

- the seller's deed;

- any documents demonstrating the removal of undesired liens and encumbrances;

- the survey;

- the results of required inspections, such as termite or structural inspections, or required repairs; and

- any leases if tenants reside on the premises.

Survey.   The buyer should inspect the property to determine the interests of any parties in possession or other interests that cannot be determined from inspecting the public record. The settlement attorney or title and escrow agent also protects the buyer's interest by conducting a title search of all recorded documents. A *survey* is frequently required so that the purchaser will know the exact location and size of the property. The survey normally spots the location of all buildings, driveways, fences, and other improvements located on the premises being purchased. The survey will also show any improvements located on adjoining property that may encroach on the premises being bought. Any existing easements and encroachments are shown. The contract should indicate whether the buyer or the seller is paying for the survey.

Final property inspection.   Shortly before the closing takes place, the buyer will usually make a final inspection of the property (often called the *walk-through*) with the broker. Through this inspection, the buyer can ensure that necessary repairs have been made, that the property has been well maintained (both inside and outside), that all fixtures are in place, and that there has been no unauthorized removal or alteration of any part of the improvements. However, the buyer's agent should remind the buyer that this is not the time to reopen negotiations.

Seller's Issues

Obviously, the seller's main interest is in receiving payment for the property. Sellers want to be sure that the buyer has obtained the necessary financing and has sufficient funds to complete the sale. The seller will also want to be certain that all requirements of the purchase and sale agreement have been met so that the transaction may be completed.

Both parties should carefully inspect the closing statement to make sure that all monies involved in the transaction have been accounted for properly.

Title Procedures

Both the buyer and the buyer's lender will want assurance that the seller's title complies with the requirements of the sales contract. This proof of ownership is usually accomplished by obtaining a certificate of title, opinion of title, and/or title insurance. Local custom or previous agreement in the sales contract generally dictates who pays title assurances.

Title commitment.   The seller is usually required to show proof of title by producing a current abstract or *title commitment* from a title insurance company. When an abstract of title is used, the purchaser's attorney examines it and issues an opinion of title. This opinion, like the title commitment, explains the status of the seller's title, including liens, encumbrances, easements, conditions, or restrictions that appear on the record and to which the seller's title is subject.

On the date when the sale is actually completed (the date of delivery of the deed), the buyer holds a title commitment or an abstract that was issued several days or weeks before the closing. For this reason, the title or abstract company is usually required to make two searches of the public records. The first shows the status of the seller's title on the date of the sales contract. The second search is made after the closing and covers the date when the deed is recorded to the purchaser. Payment for either or both of these searches varies depending on state law or local custom.

Affidavit of title.   At settlement, the seller is usually required to execute an **affidavit of title**. This is a sworn statement in which the seller assures the title insurance company (and the buyer) that since the date of the title examination there have been no judgments, bankruptcies, or divorces involving the seller; no unrecorded deeds or contracts made; no repairs or improvements that have not been paid for; and no defects in the title of which the seller is aware. Sellers also assure that they are in possession of the premises. This form is always required by the title insurance company before it will issue an owner's policy, particularly an extended-coverage policy, to the buyer. Through this affidavit, the title insurance company obtains the right to sue the seller if the statements in the affidavit prove to be incorrect.

In areas where real estate sales transactions are customarily closed through an escrow, the escrow instructions usually include provision for an extended-coverage policy to be issued to the buyer as of the date of closing. In such cases, there is no need for the seller to execute an affidavit of title.

Releasing existing liens.   The seller's existing loan(s) and liens must be paid in full and released of record. A current **payoff statement** provided by the seller's lender indicates the exact amount required to pay off the existing loan, including the unpaid amount of principal, interest due through the date of payment, the fee for issuing the certificate of satisfaction or release deed, credits (if any) for tax and insurance reserves, and penalties that may be due because the loan is being prepaid. The same procedure is followed for any other liens that must be released before the buyer takes title.

When the buyer assumes the seller's existing loan, the buyer requires a **mortgage reduction certificate** from the lender that states the exact balance due, the interest rate, and the date of the last payment made.

CONDUCTING THE CLOSING

At the closing, or settlement, the sellers receive their money and the buyers receive marketable title to and possession of the property. In the western part of the United States, settlements are generally done in escrow. There is no joint meeting of the parties involved; each party provides the required documents, funds, and so on, to the escrow agent who performs the closing, presents the deed to the buyer, and gives the appropriate funds to the seller. In the rest of the country, settlement (or closing) may be conducted by a real estate attorney, title and escrow agent, or even a real estate broker, and very often the buyers and sellers are present. In this chapter, the face-to-face closing will be discussed first, followed by closing in escrow.

Face-to-Face Closing

A face-to-face closing of a real estate transaction involves a gathering of interested parties at which the promises made in the real estate sales contract are kept, or executed. In many sales transactions, two closings actually take place at this time: the closing of the buyer's loan—the disbursement of mortgage funds by the lender—and the closing of the sale. The settlement attorney or agent does not represent either the buyer or the seller, but primarily serves to insure that all aspects of the contract have been met.

As discussed in Chapter 8, a sales contract is the blueprint for the completion of a real estate transaction. Before completing the exchange of documents and funds, the parties should assure themselves that the various stipulations of their sales contract have been met and that all of the buyer and seller issues discussed earlier in this chapter have been resolved. When the parties are satisfied that everything is in order, the exchange is made, and all pertinent documents are then recorded. The documents must be recorded in the correct order to avoid creating a defect in the title. For example, if the seller is paying off an existing loan and the buyer is obtaining a new loan, the seller's satisfaction of mortgage must be recorded before the seller's deed to the buyer. The buyer's new mortgage or deed of trust must then be recorded after the deed because the buyers cannot pledge the property as security for the loan until they own it.

Where closings are held and who attends. Face-to-face closings may be held at the offices of the title insurance company, the lending institution, one of the parties' attorneys, the broker, the county recorder (or other local recording official), or the escrow company. Those attending a closing may include any of the following interested parties:

- Buyer
- Seller
- Real estate licensees
- Attorney(s) for the seller and/or buyer
- Representatives of lending institutions involved with the buyer's new mortgage loan, the buyer's assumption of the seller's existing loan, or the seller's payoff of an existing loan
- Representatives of the title insurance company

Closing agent.   One person usually conducts the proceedings at a closing and calculates the official settlement, or division of incomes and expenses between the parties. In some areas, real estate brokers preside, but more commonly the closing agent is an escrow agent, the buyer's or seller's attorney, a representative of the lender, or a representative of a title company. Some title companies and law firms employ paralegal assistants, called *closers*, who conduct all closings for their firms. The closer is the person in such offices who arranges the closing with the parties involved; prepares the closing statements; compares figures with lenders; and orders title evidence, surveys, and other miscellaneous items needed.

Closing in Escrow

An **escrow closing** is a method of closing in which a disinterested third party is authorized to act as escrow agent and coordinates the closing activities. The escrow agent may also be called the *escrow holder*. The escrow agent may be an attorney, a title company, a trust company, an escrow company, or the escrow department of a lending institution. While many brokerages do offer escrow services, a broker cannot be a disinterested party in a transaction from which a commission is expected. Because the escrow agent is placed in a position of great trust, many states have laws regulating escrow agents and limiting who may serve in this capacity.

Escrow procedure.   When a transaction will be closed in escrow, the buyer and the seller choose an escrow agent and execute escrow instructions to the escrow agent after the sales contract is signed. Once the contract is signed, the broker turns over the earnest money to the escrow agent, who deposits it in a special trust, or escrow account.

The buyer and seller deposit all pertinent documents and other items with the escrow agent before the specified date of closing. The seller will usually deposit

- the *deed* conveying the property to the buyer;

- title *evidence* (abstract, title insurance policy, or Torrens certificate);

- existing *hazard insurance* policies;

- a letter from the lender and a *mortgage reduction certificate* stating the exact principal remaining if the buyer is assuming the seller's loan;

- *affidavits of title* (if required);

- a reduction certificate *(payoff statement)* if the seller's loan is to be paid off; and

- other instruments or documents necessary to clear the title or to complete the transaction.

The buyer will deposit

- the balance of the *cash needed* to complete the purchase, usually in the form of a certified check;

- *loan documents* if the buyer is securing a new loan;

- *proof of hazard insurance,* including flood insurance where required; and

- other documents required by the new lender.

Examining the title.   The escrow agent is given the authority to examine the title evidence. When marketable title is shown in the name of the buyer and all other conditions of the escrow agreement have been met, the agent is authorized to disburse the purchase price—minus all charges and expenses—to the seller and record the deed and mortgage or deed of trust (if a new loan has been obtained by the purchaser).

If the escrow agent's examination of the title discloses liens against the seller or a lien for which the seller is responsible, the escrow instructions usually provide that a portion of the purchase price can be withheld from the seller and used to pay such liens as are necessary to clear the title so the transaction can be closed.

If the seller cannot clear the title, or if for any reason the sale cannot be consummated and the buyer will not accept the title as is, then the escrow instructions usually provide that the parties be returned to their former status. To accomplish this, the purchaser reconveys title to the seller and the escrow agent restores all purchase money to the buyer. Because the escrow depends on specific conditions being met before the transfer becomes binding on the parties, the courts have held that the parties can be reinstated to their former status.

Internal Revenue Service (IRS) Reporting Requirements

The Internal Revenue Service (IRS) requires that the 1099-S—Proceeds from Real Estate Transactions be filed for reportable real estate, which includes the following:

- Improved or unimproved land, including air space

- Permanent structures, including residential, commercial, or industrial buildings

- Condominium units and their appurtenant fixtures and common elements, including land

- Stock in a cooperative housing corporation

However, no reporting is necessary for the sale or exchange of the principal residence (including stock in a cooperative) for $250,000 or less or $500,000 or less for married filing jointly. The person who closes the transaction is generally responsible for filing the 1099-S; if no one is responsible for closing, responsibility flows in this manner: mortgage lender, transferor's broker, transferee's broker, or the transferee. The required information includes the name and address of the transferor(s), tax identification numbers (TINs), date of closing, gross proceeds, legal description or address of the property, and the buyer's part of the real estate tax.

Broker's Role at Closing

Depending on local custom, the broker's role at a closing can vary from simply collecting the commission to conducting the proceedings. However, because real estate licensees are not authorized to give legal advice or otherwise engage in the practice of law, often a licensee's role is essentially finished when the sales contract is signed. Even so, many licensees continue their involvement after the contract is signed to ensure that all the details are taken care of so that the closing can proceed smoothly. On behalf of their clients, licensees often suggest sources of service providers for title evidence, surveys, appraisals, pest control inspections, and repairs.

Lender's Interest in Closing

Whether a buyer is obtaining new financing or assuming the seller's existing loan, the lender wants to protect its security interest in the property by ensuring that the buyer receives a good, marketable title with no liens with greater priority than the mortgage lien. Lenders often require additional information, such as a survey, a termite or other inspection report, and a certificate of occupancy (for newly constructed buildings).

The purchaser is also required to purchase a title insurance policy and a fire and hazard insurance policy. In most cases, the lender establishes a reserve, or escrow, account for tax and insurance payments, collecting one-twelfth of the total amount with each monthly principal and interest payment (PITI). Either a loan officer or an attorney represents the lender at closing.

RESPA REQUIREMENT

A full discussion of the Real Estate Settlement Procedures Act (RESPA) was covered in Chapter 13. Some of the requirements were in effect at the time of application; others are directly related to the closing.

The settlement agent is required to use the **Settlement Statement (HUD-1)** to itemize all charges and credits for both buyer and seller. A preliminary copy of this form should be available upon request to both parties 24 hours before closing. Page 3 of the HUD-1 must conform to certain amounts disclosed in the Good Faith Estimate (GFE). As discussed earlier, closing may be delayed if the lender must issue a new GFE, or the lender may proceed and issue refunds within 30 days.

PREPARATION OF CLOSING STATEMENTS

All **closing statements**, or settlement statements, are designed to achieve the same result: itemization of the expenses and credits for both buyers and sellers. Even if not mandated, many settlement agents use the HUD-1 statement. Many items must be prorated (adjusted or divided) between buyers and sellers, including items prepaid by sellers for which they must be reimbursed (such as prepaid taxes) and items of expense that sellers have incurred but for which buyers will be billed (such as mortgage interest paid in arrears when the buyer assumes the loan).

How the Closing Statement Works

The closing statement involves an accounting of the parties' debits and credits. A **debit** is a charge, an amount that the party being debited owes and must pay at the closing. A **credit** is an amount entered in a person's favor—either an amount that the party being credited has already paid, an amount that the party must be reimbursed for, or an amount the buyer promises to pay in the form of a loan.

To determine the actual amount that the buyer must bring to the closing, the total of the buyer's credits is subtracted from the total amount the buyer owes (debits). Usually the buyer is required to bring a cashier's or certified check. The buyer's debits include the purchase price and any expenses and prorated amounts for items prepaid by the seller. The buyer's credits include earnest money (already paid), the balance of the loan the buyer is obtaining or assuming, and the seller's share of any prorated items that the buyer will pay in the future.

To determine the amount that the seller will actually receive, the total of the seller's charges is subtracted from the total credits. Seller credits include the purchase price, plus the buyer's share of any prorated items that the seller has prepaid. The seller's debits include expenses, the seller's share of prorated items to be paid later by the buyer, and the balance of any mortgage loan or other lien that the seller is paying off.

Expenses

In addition to the payment of the sales price and the proration of taxes, interest, and the like, a number of other expenses and charges may be involved in a real estate transaction.

Broker's commission. The broker's commission is determined by prior agreements. In most cases, the seller has agreed to pay the listing broker, who in turn has agreed to split that commission with the broker working for the buyer. However, other parties, such as the buyer or a relocation company, can also be responsible.

Attorney's fees. If either of the parties' attorneys will be paid from the closing proceeds, that charge will be reflected in the expense in the closing statement.

Recording expenses. The charges for recording different types of documents are established by the local jurisdiction and are sometimes based on the number of pages.

The *seller* usually pays for recording charges (filing fees) to clear all defects necessary to furnish the purchaser with a marketable title, including recording of release deeds or satisfaction of mortgages, quitclaim deeds, affidavits, and satisfaction of mechanic's lien claims. The *purchaser* pays for recording charges incidental to the actual transfer of title, including recording the deed and a mortgage or deed of trust executed by the purchaser.

Transfer tax. Most states require some form of transfer tax, conveyance fee, or tax stamps on real estate conveyances. This expense is most often borne by the seller, although customs vary. This is sometimes called the *grantor's tax*.

Title expenses. The responsibility for title expenses varies according to local custom. In most areas, the seller is required to furnish evidence of good title and pay for the title search. If the buyer's attorney inspects the evidence or if the buyer purchases title insurance policies, the buyer is charged for these expenses. The type of deed (general warranty, bargain and sale, etc.) used to convey the property may influence which party is responsible for the title search.

Loan fees. The GFE must be coordinated with the fees actually charged and disclosed on the HUD-1. As discussed in Chapter 13, most fees associated with a new loan cannot increase without triggering a new disclosure and at least a three-day closing delay. If the loan closes and excess is charged, the lender must reimburse the borrower for the excess within 30 days after settlement.

Borrowers usually pay new loan fees at the time of closing. The buyer may have to pay an assumption fee if assuming the seller's existing loan. The seller may pay some of these fees, if agreed upon earlier. Under the terms of some loans, the seller may be required to pay a prepayment charge or penalty for paying off the existing loan in advance of its due date.

Tax and insurance reserves (escrows or impound accounts). A *reserve* is a sum of money set aside to be used later for a particular purpose. The mortgage lender usually requires the borrower to establish and maintain a reserve so that the borrower will have sufficient funds to pay real estate taxes and renew hazard insurance policies when these items become due. RESPA limits this reserve to two months. Thereafter, the borrower is required to pay an amount equal to one month's portion of the estimated tax and insurance premium as part of the monthly payment made to the mortgage company (a principal, interest, tax, and insurance [PITI] payment).

Appraisal fees.   Either the seller or the purchaser pays the appraisal fees, depending on who orders the appraisal. When the buyer obtains a mortgage, it is customary for the lender to require an appraisal, for which the buyer pays, usually during the loan application. If so, the fee is marked POC (paid outside of closing).

Survey fees.   The purchaser who obtains new mortgage financing customarily pays the survey fees. In some cases, the sales contract may require the seller to furnish a survey.

Additional fees.   The FHA borrower can make a lump sum payment for the mortgage insurance premium (MIP) at closing, although this is usually financed as part of the mortgage loan. A VA mortgagor pays the VA funding fee directly to the VA at closing. Private mortgage insurance on a conventional loan sometimes requires a partial annual premium payment at closing, but it is generally paid for on a monthly basis as part of the regular PITI payment.

Prorations

Most closings involve the division of financial responsibility between the buyer and seller for such items as loan interest, taxes, rents, and fuel and utility bills. These allowances are called **prorations**. Prorations are necessary to ensure that expenses are divided fairly between the seller and the buyer. For example, the seller may owe current taxes that have not been billed; the buyer should receive a credit for this at closing. In states where taxes must be paid in advance, the seller is entitled to a credit at closing. If the buyer assumes the seller's existing mortgage or deed of trust, the seller usually owes the buyer an allowance for accrued interest through the date of closing.

Accrued items are items to be prorated (such as water bills and interest on an assumed mortgage) that are owed by the seller but eventually will be paid by the buyer. The seller therefore gives the buyer credit for these items at closing.

Prepaid items are items to be prorated—such as fuel oil in a tank or homeowner or condominium association fees—that have been prepaid by the seller but which the buyer is now receiving the benefit of. They are therefore credits to the seller.

General rules for prorating.   The rules or customs governing the computation of prorations for the closing of a real estate sale vary widely from state to state and even within a given city, town, or county.

Following are some general rules regarding the closing procedure and closing statement:

- In most states, the seller owns the property on the day of closing, and prorations or apportionments are usually made to and including the day of closing. A few states specifically provide that the buyer owns the property on the closing date and that adjustments shall be made as of the day preceding the day on which title is closed.

- Mortgage interest, real estate taxes, insurance premiums, and similar expenses are usually computed by using 360 days in a year and 30 days in a month. However, some areas compute prorations on the basis of the actual number of days in the calendar month and year of closing. The methods for calculating prorations are explained in full later in this chapter.

- Accrued *real estate taxes* that are not yet due are usually prorated at the closing (see the following section). The proration is usually based on the last tax bill. *Special assessments* are usually paid in annual installments over several years. Unless the sales agreement requires that the special assessment be paid in full at time of closing, the seller pays the current installment and the buyer assumes all future installments.

- *Rents* are usually adjusted on the basis of the actual number of days in the month of closing. The seller is generally credited for the rent for the day of closing and pays all expenses for that day. If any rents for the current month are uncollected when the sale is closed, the buyer will often agree by a separate letter to collect the rents if possible and remit the pro-rata share to the seller.

- *Security deposits* made by tenants to cover the last month's rent of the lease or to cover the cost of repairing damage caused by the tenant are generally transferred intact by the seller to the buyer. Some leases may require the tenant's consent to such a transfer of the deposit.

Real estate taxes. Proration of real estate taxes varies widely, depending on how the taxes are paid in the area where the real estate is located. In some states, real estate taxes are paid *in advance*: if the tax year runs from January 1 to December 31, taxes for the coming year are due on January 1. In that case ,the seller, who has prepaid a year's taxes, should be reimbursed for the portion of the year remaining after the buyer takes ownership of the property. In other areas, taxes are paid *in arrears*, on December 31 for the year just ended. In that case, the buyer should be credited by the seller for the time the seller was occupying the property. Sometimes, taxes are due in two or more increments during the tax year, partly in arrears and partly in advance; sometimes they are payable in installments. To compound the confusion, city, state, school, and other property taxing bodies may start their tax years in different months. Whatever the case may be in a particular transaction, the licensee should understand how the taxes are to be prorated.

Mortgage loan interest. On almost every mortgage loan, the interest is paid in arrears, so buyers and sellers must understand that the mortgage payment due on June 1, for example, includes interest due for the month of May. The buyer who assumes a mortgage on May 31 and makes the June payment will be paying for the time the seller occupied the property and should be credited with a month's interest. On the other hand, buyers who place a new mortgage loan on May 31 may be pleasantly surprised to hear that they will not need to make a mortgage payment until July 1. In most cases, the buyers will pay for interest from the date of settlement until the end of the month, April 30. For example, settlement occurs on April 15. The buyer pays for interest from April 15 to the end of the month at closing; the next full mortgage payment is not due until June 1 (covering the interest for May).

Accounting for Credits and Debits

The items that must be accounted for in the closing statement fall into two general categories: prorations or other amounts due to either the buyer or seller (credit to) and paid for by the other party (debit to) and expenses or items paid by the seller or buyer (debit only).

Items shown as credits to the buyer.   Items that are shown only as a credit to the buyer are not prorated; they are entered in full. They are the following:

- *Buyer's earnest money.* The buyer, who already paid that amount toward the purchase price, receives a credit. Under the usual sales contract, the money is held by the broker or attorney until the settlement when it is included as part of the total amount due the seller.

- *Monies received from a new mortgage loan.* The buyer receives a credit for the amount of the new loan and the payoff amount on the old loan appears as a debit to the seller.

Items shown as credits to the buyer and debits to the seller.   The following items appear as a credit to the buyer and a debit to the seller:

- The unpaid principal balance of an outstanding mortgage loan being assumed by the buyer

- Interest on an existing assumed mortgage not yet paid (accrued)

- The unearned portion of current rent collected in advance (rental property)

- An earned janitor's salary and sometimes vacation allowance (rental or commercial property)

- Tenants' security deposits (rental property)

- Unpaid water and other utility bills

Items shown as credits to the seller.   These items include the following:

- The sales price

- Any fuel oil on hand, usually figured at current market price (prepaid)

- An insurance and tax reserve (if any) when an outstanding mortgage loan is being assumed by the buyer (prepaid)

- A refund to the seller of prepaid water charge and similar expenses

- Any portion of general real estate tax paid in advance

Accounting for expenses.   Expenses paid out of the closing proceeds are debited only to the party making the payment. Occasionally an expense item—such as an escrow fee, a settlement fee, or a transfer tax—may be shared by the buyer and the seller, and each party will be debited for half the expense.

THE ARITHMETIC OF PRORATING

Accurate prorating involves four considerations: (1) what the item is; (2) whether it is an *accrued item* that requires the determination of an earned amount; (3) whether it is a *prepaid item* that requires the unearned amount—a refund to the seller—to be determined; and (4) what arithmetic processes must be used. The information contained in the previous sections will assist in answering the first three questions.

The computation of a proration involves identifying a yearly charge for the item to be prorated, then dividing by 12 to determine a monthly charge for the item. It is usually also necessary to identify a daily charge for the item by dividing the monthly charge by the number of days in the month. These smaller portions are then multiplied by the number of months and/or days in the prorated time period to determine the accrued or unearned amount that will be figured in the settlement.

Using this general principle, there are two methods of calculating prorations:

1. The yearly charge is divided by a 360-day year (commonly called a banking year), or 12 months of 30 days each.

2. The yearly charge is divided by 365 (366 in a leap year) to determine the daily charge. Then the actual number of days in the proration period is determined, and this number is multiplied by the daily charge.

The final proration figure will vary slightly, depending on which computation method is used. The final figure will also vary according to the number of decimal places to which the division is carried. All the computations in this chapter are computed by carrying the division to three decimal places. The third decimal place is rounded off to cents, but only after the final proration figure is determined.

Accrued Items

When the real estate tax is levied for the calendar year and is payable during that year or in the following year, the accrued portion is for the period from January 1 to the date of closing (or to the day before the closing in states where the sale date is excluded). If the current tax bill has not yet been issued, the parties must agree on an estimated amount based on the previous year's bill and any known changes in assessment or tax levy for the current year.

For example, assume a sale is to be closed on September 17, current real estate taxes of $3,000 are to be prorated accordingly, and a 360-day year is being used. The accrued period, then, is 8 months and 17 days. First determine the prorated cost of the real estate tax per month and day:

$$\$3,600 \div 12 = \$300 \text{ per month}$$
$$\$300 \div 30 = \$10 \text{ per day}$$

Next multiply these figures by the accrued period and add the totals to determine the prorated real estate tax:

$300	$10	$2,400
× 8 months	× 17	+170
$2,400	$170	$2,570

Thus the accrued real estate tax for 8 months and 17 days is $2,570 (rounded off to two decimal places after the final computation). This amount represents the seller's accrued earned tax; it will be a *credit to the buyer* and a *debit to the seller* on the closing statement.

To compute this proration using the actual number of days in the accrued period, the following method is used: The accrued period from January 1 to September 17 runs 260 days (January's 31 days plus February's 28 days and so on). A tax bill of $3,600 ÷ 365 days = $9.863 per day; $9.863 × 260 days = $2,564.38.

Prepaid Items

Assume that the water is billed in advance by the city without using a meter. The six months' billing is $180 for the period ending October 31. The sale closes on August 3.

Because the water is paid to October 31, the prepaid time must be computed. Using a 30-day basis, the time period is the 27 days left in August plus two full months: $180 ÷ 6 = $30 per month. For one day, divide $30 by 30, which equals $1 per day. The prepaid period is 2 months and 27 days, so:

$$
\begin{array}{rcl}
2 \text{ months} \times \$30 & = & \$60 \\
27 \text{ days} \times \$1 & = & \$27 \\
& = & \$87
\end{array}
$$

This is a prepaid item and is *credited to the seller* and *debited to the buyer* on the closing statement.

To figure this on the basis of the actual days in the month of closing, the following process is used:

$$
\begin{array}{rcl}
\$30 \text{ per month} \div 31 \text{ days in August} & = & \$0.978 \text{ per day} \\
\text{August 4 through August 31} & = & 28 \text{ days} \\
28 \text{ days} \times \$0.978 & = & \$27.384 \\
2 \text{ months} \times \$30 & = & \$60.000 \\
& = & \$87.384, \text{ or } \$87.38
\end{array}
$$

SAMPLE CLOSING STATEMENT

As stated previously, there are many possible formats for settlement computations. The remaining portion of this chapter illustrates a sample transaction using the Settlement Statement (HUD-1) (see Figure 17.1) and also using separate buyer's and seller's closing statements.

Case Study

On May 3, the sellers list their home for sale with the ABC Company for $250,000 with possession offered within two weeks after contract signing. In the listing agreement, the sellers agreed to pay the broker a commission of 5% of the sales price.

On May 18, XYZ Realty submitted an offer to purchase from a buyer. The buyer offered the full price $250,000, with earnest money/down payment of $50,000 and the remaining $200,000 of the purchase price to be obtained through a new conventional loan. Because the loan-to-value ratio does not exceed 80%, private mortgage insurance is not required. The sellers signed the contract on May 29. Closing was set for June 15 at the lender's office.

The unpaid balance of the seller's mortgage as of June 1 was $184,921. Payments were $1,135.58 per month with interest at 5.5% per annum on the unpaid balance.

The sellers submitted evidence of title in the form of a title insurance binder at a cost of $75. The title insurance policy to be paid by the buyers at the time of closing cost an additional $1,135, which consists of $795 for lender's coverage and $340 for homeowner's coverage. Recording charges of $20 were paid for the recording of two instruments to clear defects in the sellers' title, and state transfer tax in the amount of $325 ($0.65 per $500 of sale price or fraction thereof) were affixed to the deed.

In addition, the sellers must pay an attorney's fee of $500 for preparation of the deed and for legal representation; this amount was paid from the closing proceeds.

The buyer must pay an attorney's fee of $450 for examination of the title evidence and legal representation, as well as $10 to record the deed. These amounts were also paid from the closing proceeds.

The real estate taxes are paid in arrears. Taxes for this year, estimated at last year's figure of $2,725, have not been paid. According to the contract, prorations are to be made on the basis of 30 days in a month.

Computing the prorations and charges. Following are illustrations of the various steps in computing the prorations and other amounts to be included in the settlement thus far:

1. *Closing date:* June 15

2. *Commission:* 5% × $250,000 (sales price) = $12,500

3. *Sellers' mortgage interest:*

    $184,921 × 5.5% (principal due after June 1 payment) = $10,170.655 interest per year
    $10,170.655 ÷ 360 days = $28.251 interest per day
    15 days of accrued interest to be paid by the sellers
    15 × $28.251 = $423.77 interest owed by the sellers
    $184,921 + $423.77 = $185,344.77 payoff of sellers' mortgage

4. *Real estate taxes* (estimated at $2,725):

    $2,725.00 ÷ 12 months = $227.083 per month
    $227.083 ÷ 30 days = $28.251 per day
    The earned period is from January 1 to and including June 15, and equals 5 months, 15 days:
    $227.083 × 5 months = $1,135.415
    $7.569 × 15 days = $113.535
    $1,135.415 + $113.535 = $1,248.95 seller owes buyer

5. *Transfer tax* ($0.65 per $500 of consideration or fraction thereof):

    $250,000 ÷ $500 = $500
    $500 × $0.65 = $325.00 transfer tax owed by sellers

The sellers' loan payoff is $184,921, and they must pay an additional $10 to record the mortgage release as well as $85 for a pest inspection and $375 for a survey, as negotiated between the parties.

The buyer's new loan is from A Savings Company in the amount of $200,000 at 5% interest. In connection with this loan, the buyer will be charged $350 to have the property appraised by The Appraisal Company and $60 for a credit report from a credit bureau. Because appraisal and credit reports are performed before loan approval, they are paid at the time of loan application, regardless of whether the transaction eventually closes. These items will be noted as POC—paid outside closing—on the settlement statement.

In addition, the buyer will pay for interest on his loan for the remainder of the month of closing—15 days at $27.777 per day, or $416.66. His first full payment (including July's interest) will be due August 1. He must deposit $1,589.58, or seven-twelfths of the anticipated county real estate tax ($2,725) into a tax reserve account. A one-year hazard insurance premium of $875 is paid to the insurance company. An insurance reserve to cover the premium for two months is deposited with the lender ($875 ÷ 12 × 2 = $145.83). The buyer will have to pay an additional $10 to record the mortgage and $375 for a survey. He will also pay a loan origination fee of $920 and two discount points.

Settlement Statement (HUD-1)

The Settlement Statement (HUD-1) is divided into Sections J, K, and L (see Figure 17.1). Section L is an explanation of all the settlement charges for the transaction; the buyer's expenses are listed in one column and the seller's expenses in the other.

FIGURE 17.1   **Settlement Statement (HUD-1)**

A. **Settlement Statement (HUD-1)**

B. Type of Loan				
1. ☐ FHA 2. ☐ RHS 3. ☐ Conv. Unins. 4. ☐ VA 5. ☐ Conv. Ins.	6. File Number:	7. Loan Number:	8. Mortgage Insurance Case Number:	

C. Note: This form is furnished to give you a statement of actual settlement costs. Amounts paid to and by the settlement agent are shown. Items marked "(p.o.c.)" were paid outside the closing; they are shown here for informational purposes and are not included in the totals.

D. Name & Address of Borrower:	E. Name & Address of Seller:	F. Name & Address of Lender:
G. Property Location:	H. Settlement Agent: Place of Settlement:	I. Settlement Date:

J. Summary of Borrower's Transaction		K. Summary of Seller's Transaction	
100. Gross Amount Due from Borrower		**400. Gross Amount Due to Seller**	
101. Contract sales price		401. Contract sales price	
102. Personal property		402. Personal property	
103. Settlement charges to borrower (line 1400)		403.	
104.		404.	
105.		405.	
Adjustment for items paid by seller in advance		Adjustment for items paid by seller in advance	
106. City/town taxes to		406. City/town taxes to	
107. County taxes to		407. County taxes to	
108. Assessments to		408. Assessments to	
109.		409.	
110.		410.	
111.		411.	
112.		412.	
120. Gross Amount Due from Borrower		**420. Gross Amount Due to Seller**	
200. Amount Paid by or in Behalf of Borrower		**500. Reductions In Amount Due to seller**	
201. Deposit or earnest money		501. Excess deposit (see instructions)	
202. Principal amount of new loan(s)		502. Settlement charges to seller (line 1400)	
203. Existing loan(s) taken subject to		503. Existing loan(s) taken subject to	
204.		504. Payoff of first mortgage loan	
205.		505. Payoff of second mortgage loan	
206.		506.	
207.		507.	
208.		508.	
209.		509.	
Adjustments for items unpaid by seller		Adjustments for items unpaid by seller	
210. City/town taxes to		510. City/town taxes to	
211. County taxes to		511. County taxes to	
212. Assessments to		512. Assessments to	
213.		513.	
214.		514.	
215.		515.	
216.		516.	
217.		517.	
218.		518.	
219.		519.	
220. Total Paid by/for Borrower		**520. Total Reduction Amount Due Seller**	
300. Cash at Settlement from/to Borrower		**600. Cash at Settlement to/from Seller**	
301. Gross amount due from borrower (line 120)		601. Gross amount due to seller (line 420)	
302. Less amounts paid by/for borrower (line 220)	( )	602. Less reductions in amounts due seller (line 520)	( )
303. Cash ☐ From ☐ To Borrower		**603. Cash** ☐ To ☐ From Seller	

The Public Reporting Burden for this collection of information is estimated at 35 minutes per response for collecting, reviewing, and reporting the data. This agency may not collect this information, and you are not required to complete this form, unless it displays a currently valid OMB control number. No confidentiality is assured; this disclosure is mandatory. This is designed to provide the parties to a RESPA covered transaction with information during the settlement process.

FIGURE 17.1   Settlement Statement (HUD-1) (Cont.)

L. Settlement Charges				Paid From Borrower's Funds at Settlement	Paid From Seller's Funds at Settlement
700. Total Real Estate Broker Fees					
Division of commission (line 700) as follows :					
701. $ to					
702. $ to					
703. Commission paid at settlement					
704.					
800. Items Payable in Connection with Loan					
801. Our origination charge		$	(from GFE #1)		
802. Your credit or charge (points) for the specific interest rate chosen		$	(from GFE #2)		
803. Your adjusted origination charges			(from GFE #A)		
804. Appraisal fee to			(from GFE #3)		
805. Credit report to			(from GFE #3)		
806. Tax service to			(from GFE #3)		
807. Flood certification to			(from GFE #3)		
808.					
809.					
810.					
811.					
900. Items Required by Lender to be Paid in Advance					
901. Daily interest charges from to @ $ /day			(from GFE #10)		
902. Mortgage insurance premium for months to			(from GFE #3)		
903. Homeowner's insurance for years to			(from GFE #11)		
904.					
1000. Reserves Deposited with Lender					
1001. Initial deposit for your escrow account			(from GFE #9)		
1002. Homeowner's insurance months @ $ per month $					
1003. Mortgage insurance months @ $ per month $					
1004. Property Taxes months @ $ per month $					
1005. months @ $ per month $					
1006. months @ $ per month $					
1007. Aggregate Adjustment -$					
1100. Title Charges					
1101. Title services and lender's title insurance			(from GFE #4)		
1102. Settlement or closing fee		$			
1103. Owner's title insurance			(from GFE #5)		
1104. Lender's title insurance		$			
1105. Lender's title policy limit $					
1106. Owner's title policy limit $					
1107. Agent's portion of the total title insurance premium to		$			
1108. Underwriter's portion of the total title insurance premium to		$			
1109.					
1110.					
1111.					
1200. Government Recording and Transfer Charges					
1201. Government recording charges			(from GFE #7)		
1202. Deed $ Mortgage $ Release $					
1203. Transfer taxes			(from GFE #8)		
1204. City/County tax/stamps Deed $ Mortgage $					
1205. State tax/stamps Deed $ Mortgage $					
1206.					
1300. Additional Settlement Charges					
1301. Required services that you can shop for			(from GFE #6)		
1302. $					
1303. $					
1304.					
1305.					
1400. Total Settlement Charges (enter on lines 103, Section J and 502, Section K)					

FIGURE 17.1   **Settlement Statement (HUD-1) (Cont.)**

Comparison of Good Faith Estimate (GFE) and HUD-1 Charrges		Good Faith Estimate	HUD-1
Charges That Cannot Increase	**HUD-1 Line Number**		
Our origination charge	# 801		
Your credit or charge (points) for the specific interest rate chosen	# 802		
Your adjusted origination charges	# 803		
Transfer taxes	# 1203		

Charges That In Total Cannot Increase More Than 10%		Good Faith Estimate	HUD-1
Government recording charges	# 1201		
	#		
	#		
	#		
	#		
	#		
	#		
	#		
	Total		
	Increase between GFE and HUD-1 Charges	$ or	%

Charges That Can Change		Good Faith Estimate	HUD-1
Initial deposit for your escrow account	# 1001		
Daily interest charges $ /day	# 901		
Homeowner's insurance	# 903		
	#		
	#		
	#		

Loan Terms

Your initial loan amount is	$
Your loan term is	years
Your initial interest rate is	%
Your initial monthly amount owed for principal, interest, and any mortgage insurance is	$ includes ☐ Principal ☐ Interest ☐ Mortgage Insurance
Can your interest rate rise?	☐ No ☐ Yes, it can rise to a maximum of %. The first change will be on and can change again every after . Every change date, your interest rate can increase or decrease by %. Over the life of the loan, your interest rate is guaranteed to never be **lower** than % or **higher** than %.
Even if you make payments on time, can your loan balance rise?	☐ No ☐ Yes, it can rise to a maximum of $
Even if you make payments on time, can your monthly amount owed for principal, interest, and mortgage insurance rise?	☐ No ☐ Yes, the first increase can be on and the monthly amount owed can rise to $. The maximum it can ever rise to is $.
Does your loan have a prepayment penalty?	☐ No ☐ Yes, your maximum prepayment penalty is $
Does your loan have a balloon payment?	☐ No ☐ Yes, you have a balloon payment of $ due in years on .
Total monthly amount owed including escrow account payments	☐ You do not have a monthly escrow payment for items, such as property taxes and homeowner's insurance. You must pay these items directly yourself. ☐ You have an additional monthly escrow payment of $ that results in a total initial monthly amount owed of $. This includes principal, interest, any mortgage insurance and any items checked below: ☐ Property taxes ☐ Homeowner's insurance ☐ Flood insurance ☐ ☐ ☐

Note: If you have any questions about the Settlement Charges and Loan Terms listed on this form, please contact your lender.

The total of the buyer's settlement costs itemized in Section L of the statement is entered on "Summary of Borrower's Transaction," Section J, line 103 as one of the buyer's charges. The buyer's credits are listed on lines 201 through 219 and totaled on line 220 (total paid by/for borrower). Then the buyer's credits are subtracted from the charges to arrive at the cash due from the borrower to close (line 303).

The HUD-1 includes a third page on which the buyer can compare the costs listed on the original Good Faith Estimate (GFE) with those on the HUD-1. As noted in Chapter 13, certain items have no tolerance; that is, if certain costs in connection with the loan are increased, either closing is delayed or the lender must issue a refund within 30 days.

In Section K, the "Summary of the Seller's Transaction," the seller's credits are entered on lines 400–412 and totaled on line 420 (gross amount due to seller). The seller's debits are entered on lines 501–519 and totaled on line 520 (total reduction amount due seller). The total of the seller's settlement charges is on line 502. Then, the debits are subtracted from the credits to arrive at the cash due the sellers in order to close (line 603).

Buyer's and Seller's Closing Statements

Figure 17.2 details a buyer's closing statement, and Figure 17.3 is a seller's closing statement for the Case Study that was previously described.

The upper half of the closing statement accounts for the transaction between buyer and seller; the lower part details each one's individual expenses.

SUMMARY

Closing a real estate sale involves both title procedures and financial matters. Real estate licensees, as agents for the sellers and the buyers, are often present at the closing to see that the sale is actually concluded and to account for the earnest money deposit.

The federal Real Estate Settlement Procedures Act (RESPA) requires disclosure of all settlement costs when a residential real estate purchase is financed by a federally related mortgage loan. RESPA requires lenders to use a Settlement Statement (HUD-1) to detail the financial particulars of a transaction.

The actual amount to be paid by the buyer at the closing is computed by preparation of a closing, or settlement, statement. This lists the sales price, earnest money deposit, and all adjustments and prorations due between buyer and seller. The purpose of this statement is to determine the net amount due to the seller at closing. The buyer reimburses the seller for prepaid items such as unused taxes or fuel oil. The seller credits the buyer for bills the seller owes that will be paid by the buyer (accrued items), such as unpaid water bills.

FIGURE 17.2   **Buyer's Closing Statement**

Buyer's Closing Statement
Closing on June 15

Buyer's credits

Deposits with Open Door Real Estate Company	$50,000.00	
Mortgage loan with Thrift Federal Savings	200,000.00	
Total credits		**$250,000.00**

Adjustments

Taxes

$2,725 per year ÷ 12 months = $227.083 per month, $7.569 per day

5 months, 15 days	1,248.95	
Total adjustments		**1,248.95**

Buyer's expenses

Purchase price	250,000.00	
Recording mortgage deed	20.00	
Loan origination fee	920.00	
Points	2,000.00	
Appraisal	POC	
Credit report	POC	
Interest		
15 days at 27.777 per day	416.66	
Insurance premium	875.00	
Tax escrow	1,589.58	
Insurance escrow	145.83	
Legal fees	450.00	
Total expenses	$256,417.07	**(256,417.07)**

Cash (paid) at closing   **$5,618.12**

FIGURE 17.3   **Seller's Closing Statement**

Seller's Closing Statement
Closing on June 15

Seller's credits

Purchase price $250,000.00

Total credits   **$250,000.00**

Adjustments

Taxes

$2,725 per year ÷ 12 months = $227.083 per month,
$7.569 per day

5 months, 15 days   1,248.95

Total adjustments   **(1,248.95)**

Seller's expenses

Real estate commission	12,500.00	
Title insurance binder	75.00	
Payoff mortgage	185,344.14	
Recording mortgage payoff	10.00	
Pest inspection	85.00	
Survey	375.00	
Conveyance tax	325.00	
Legal fees	500.00	
Total expenses	**$199,214.14**	**(199,214.14)**

Cash (received) at closing   **$49,536.91**

REVIEW QUESTIONS

Please complete all of the questions before turning to the Answer Key on page 349.

1. When an item to be prorated is owed by the seller and has not yet been paid for, the amount owed is figured as a
   a. credit to the seller only.
   b. debit to the buyer only.
   c. credit to the seller and a debit to the buyer.
   d. debit to the seller and a credit to the buyer.

2. One item that is *ALWAYS* prorated on a closing statement is the
   a. state transfer tax.
   b. earnest money.
   c. unpaid principal balance of the seller's mortgage loan that is assumed by the buyer.
   d. accrued interest on the seller's mortgage loan that is assumed by the buyer.

3. The Settlement Statement (HUD-1) must be used to illustrate all settlement charges for
   a. all real estate transactions.
   b. transactions financed with FHA and VA loans only.
   c. residential transactions financed with federally related mortgage loans.
   d. all transactions in which mortgage financing is involved.

4. Legal title passes from the seller to the buyer
   a. on the date of execution of the deed.
   b. when the deed is delivered.
   c. when the closing statement has been signed.
   d. when the deed is placed in escrow.

5. The earnest money given to the broker by the buyer is a
   a. credit to the buyer only.
   b. debit to the seller only.
   c. credit to the seller and a debit to the buyer.
   d. credit to the buyer and a debit to the seller.

6. One item that is *NOT* disclosed on the settlement statement is the
   a. APR on the mortgage loan.
   b. amount of money the seller will receive.
   c. amount of cash the buyer must bring to the closing.
   d. dollar amount of the down payment and closing costs.

7. The principal amount of the buyer's new mortgage loan is a
   a. credit to the seller.
   b. debit to the buyer.
   c. debit to the seller.
   d. credit to the buyer.

8. One benefit of closing a real estate transaction through escrow is that
   a. the buyer and seller can resolve walk-through issues at the table.
   b. both the buyer and the seller will be represented by their attorneys.
   c. there are no closing costs to be paid.
   d. neither party needs to be present at the closing.

9. All encumbrances and liens shown on the title report, other than those waived or agreed to by the buyer and listed in the contract, must be removed so that the title can be delivered free and clear. The removal of such encumbrances is the obligation of the
   a. buyer.
   b. seller.
   c. broker.
   d. title company.

10. One document that a lender generally requires to be produced at the closing is a
    a. title insurance policy.
    b. market value appraisal.
    c. buyer's application form.
    d. buyer's credit report.

11. When a transaction for a house built in 1945 is closing in escrow, the seller must deposit with the escrow agent all of the following *EXCEPT*
    a. the deed to the property.
    b. the property disclosure form.
    c. the lead-based paint disclosure form.
    d. the cash to complete the purchase.

12. Security deposits for rental property should be listed in a closing statement as a debit to the
    a. buyer.
    b. seller.
    c. tenants.
    d. escrow agent.

13. The seller collected the monthly rent of $550 from the tenant on September 1. At the September 15 closing, the
    a. seller owes the buyer $550.
    b. seller owes the buyer $275.
    c. buyer owes the seller $275.
    d. tenant owes the buyer $275.

14. The buyer of an $80,000 house has paid $5,000 as earnest money and has a loan commitment for 70% of the purchase price. How much more cash does the buyer need to complete the transaction?
    a. $5,000
    b. $19,000
    c. $24,000
    d. $29,000

15. A building was bought for $200,000 with 10% down and a loan for the balance. If the lender charged the buyer three discount points, how much cash did the buyer need to complete the transaction?
    a. $5,400
    b. $14,600
    c. $20,000
    d. $25,400

16. The buyers and the sellers are closing in escrow. What must the buyer deposit with the escrow agent?
    a. Deed to the property
    b. Affidavit of title
    c. Lead-based paint information booklet, if house was built before 1978
    d. Cash to complete the purchase

17. For *MOST* residential loans, what does the current payoff statement include?
    a. Remaining principal balance
    b. Interest owed until the day of closing
    c. Principal balance and interest owed
    d. Prepayment penalty

18. A couple sold the home they had lived in for 25 years. They paid $45,000 and sold it for $345,000. What must be filed with the IRS?
    a. Estimated tax on the gain of $300,000
    b. 1099-S form
    c. W-4 form
    d. Nothing

19. The seller has half a tank of fuel oil worth $325. How is this handled?
    a. Credit to seller, debit to buyer
    b. Debit the seller, credit to buyer
    c. Credit to seller
    d. Debit to buyer

20. Generally, who is responsible for the expenses of a rental property on the day of closing?
    a. Tenant
    b. Buyer
    c. Seller
    d. Prorated between buyer and seller

Real Estate Mathematics

LEARNING OBJECTIVES

When you finish reading this chapter, you will be able to

- differentiate between a calendar year and a banker's year,
- describe the process for calculating a broker's commission,
- explain how to arrive at a loan-to-value ratio, and
- state the difference between debit and credit.

area	**decimal**	**percentage**
banker's year	**fraction**	**volume**
calendar year	**front foot**	

Real estate involves working with numbers, from calculating commissions to determining loan payments to figuring out property taxes. Therefore, a real estate professional must have a working knowledge of math. This chapter will focus on the basic principles of math that a residential real estate licensee will use when working with a client or customer. These principles also are tested on licensing exams. Math used in commercial transactions becomes more complex and will not be covered here.

BASICS

Most real estate professionals use calculators or computers to assist them with math computations. Also, calculators are permitted when taking most state licensing exams. A basic calculator that adds, subtracts, multiplies, and divides is sufficient for most purposes. Financial calculators can offer additional functions, such as determining monthly loan payment amounts. Because each brand is different, consult the user's manual of your calculator.

Decimals

Calculators state numbers as **decimals**. Therefore, in order to use a calculator, all numbers must be expressed in decimal form.

Converting Fractions to Decimals

To convert a **fraction** to a decimal, divide the numerator (top number) by the denominator (bottom number).

$$\frac{1}{2} = 1 \div 2 = 0.50$$
$$\frac{3}{4} = 3 \div 4 = 0.75$$
$$\frac{5}{8} = 5 \div 8 = 0.625$$
$$\frac{9}{3} = 9 \div 3 = 3$$
$$5\frac{1}{4} = 5 + (1 \div 4) = 5 + 0.25 = 5.25$$

PERCENTAGES

Many real estate calculations use percentages. For example, a real estate broker's commission is usually stated as a **percentage** of the sales price. A percentage is a portion of a whole amount. The whole or total always represents 100%. For example, 20% means 20 parts of the possible 100 parts that comprise the whole.

$$20\% = 20 \text{ parts of } 100$$

Working with Percentage Rates

When working with a percentage rate, the percentage must first be converted to a decimal. To do this, move the decimal two places to the left and drop the percentage sign.

$$20\% \rightarrow 0.20$$

Another way to convert a percentage to a decimal is to divide the percentage by 100 and drop the percentage sign.

$$20\% \rightarrow 20 \div 100 \rightarrow 0.20$$

Most calculators will automatically change a number stated as a percentage into a decimal (usually by entering the percentage number and then pressing the percentage key), so that it can be used in a calculation.

Working with Decimals

Percentages are sometimes stated as decimals. In order to find the percentage rate, move the decimal two places to the right and add the percentage sign.

$$0.20 \rightarrow 20\%$$

Another way to convert a decimal to a percentage rate is to multiply the decimal by 100 and add the percentage sign.

$$0.20 \rightarrow 0.20 \times 100 = 20\%$$

Approaching a Percentage Problem

Keep in mind that there are always three components to a percentage problem. The first is the *percentage rate*; the second is the *whole amount*, or the number that you are usually trying to find a percentage of; and the third is the part of the *whole number*. If you are given two of these components, you can calculate the third.

whole × percentage rate = part
part ÷ whole = percentage rate
part ÷ percentage rate = whole

Calculating the part of a whole.   To calculate the part of a whole number, you multiply the whole by the percentage rate stated as a decimal.

■ **FOR EXAMPLE**   A broker is going to receive a commission of 20% of the sales price on a parcel of land. If the land sells for $230,000, what commission will the broker receive? Note that 20% is the percentage rate, $230,000 is the whole, and we are trying to find the commission, which is the part.

Convert the percentage to a decimal.
20% → 20 ÷ 100 → 0.20

Multiply the whole (here, sales price) by the decimal.
$230,000 × 0.20 = $46,000

The broker will receive a $46,000 commission.

Calculating the percentage rate.   Just as the part of a whole number can be calculated if the whole and the percentage rate are known, the percentage rate can be calculated if the part and the whole are known. To calculate the percentage rate, divide the part by the whole.

■ **FOR EXAMPLE**   Suppose a broker received a $46,000 commission on the sale of land where the sales price was $230,000. What percentage rate of the whole did the broker receive? Note that $230,000 is the whole and $46,000 is the part; we are trying to find the percentage.

Divide the part by the whole.
$46,000 ÷ $230,000 = 0.20

Convert the decimal to a percentage
0.20 → 0.20 × 100 → 20%

The broker received a 20% commission.

Calculating the whole or total amount. The whole or total amount can be found when the part and the percentage rate are known. To calculate the whole amount, divide the part by the percentage rate.

■ **FOR EXAMPLE** Suppose a broker received a $46,000 commission on the sale of land and the commission rate was 20%. What was the sales price? Note that $46,000 is the part and 20% is the percentage rate; we are trying to find the whole.

Convert the percentage to a decimal.
20% → 20 ÷ 100 → 0.20

Divide the part by the percentage rate.
$46,000 ÷ 0.20 = $230,000

The land sold for $230,000.

USING PERCENTAGE RATES

The following is a summary of some of the most commonly used types of percentage rates in real estate.

Broker's Commission

A broker's commission is usually set as a percentage of the sales price. Further, a salesperson's share of the commission is usually set as a percentage of the broker's commission.

■ **FOR EXAMPLE** A seller listed a home for $200,000 and agreed to pay the broker a commission rate of 5%. The home sold four weeks later for 90% of the list price. The listing broker paid the salesperson 50% of her share of the commission. How much commission did the salesperson receive?

90% of $200,000 = 0.90 × 200,000 = $180,000 sales price
5% of $180,000 = 0.05 × 180,000 = $9,000 broker's commission
50% of $9,000 = 0.50 × 9,000 = $4,500 = salesperson's commission

Earnest Money Deposits

Sellers typically require a buyer to put up a deposit at the time a contract is signed for the purchase of the property. The earnest money deposit may be a percentage of the purchase price or any other amount chosen by the buyer.

■ **FOR EXAMPLE** A buyer has contracted to buy a house for $140,000. The contract calls for the buyer to pay a deposit of 8% of the purchase price at the time the contracts are signed. How much should the buyer pay?

8% of $140,000 = 0.08 × 140,000 = $11,200 deposit

Property Taxes

Local property taxes are typically based on a percentage of the purchase price. The percentage is called the tax rate.

> ■ **FOR EXAMPLE**   The assessed value of a seller's house is $187,000. The property tax rate in the municipality where the property is located is 3.45%. What are the annual taxes on this property?
>
>   3.45% of $187,000 = 0.0345 × 187,000 = $6,451.50 taxes

Conveyance Taxes

When real estate is sold, the state and/or local government sometimes charges a conveyance tax based upon the purchase price. This tax is usually stated as a percentage.

> ■ **FOR EXAMPLE**   A seller is scheduled to close on his house. The purchase price is $234,500. If the seller's state charges a 0.055% conveyance tax, how much will the seller have to pay for this tax at closing?
>
>   0.055% of $234,500 = 0.00055 × 234,500 = $128.98 conveyance tax

> ■ **FOR EXAMPLE:**   You are interested in finding out what your neighbor paid for her house. You go to the land records and look up the deed, but the purchase price is not stated. There is, however, a stamp on the deed that states that $165 was paid in conveyance tax at the time of the transfer. If you know the conveyance tax rate is 0.11%, what was the purchase price? We know the percentage rate and the part, but don't know the whole.
>
> $165 part ÷ 0.11% percentage rate = 165 ÷ 0.0011 = $150,000 purchase price

Loan-to-Value Ratio (LTV)

Lenders are typically concerned about the amount of money they are lending out for the purchase of property, as compared to the value of property. They would like the value to be greater than the loan amount, in case they need to foreclose on the property and have it sold to pay off the outstanding loan amount. In analyzing the relationship between the loan amount and the value of the property, lenders compute a percentage rate, which is called the loan-to-value ratio (LTV). This rate is calculated by dividing the loan amount by the value of the property.

> ■ **FOR EXAMPLE**   A borrower is taking out a $150,000 loan to buy a $187,500 property. What is the LTV? We know the part and the whole and are trying to find out the rate.
>
> $150,000 part ÷ $187,500 whole = 0.80 = 80% LTV

Interest

Interest is the cost associated with borrowing money. It is usually stated as a percentage of the amount of money borrowed. The percentage is called the interest rate. The amount of interest paid (a part) is determined by multiplying the loan amount (whole) by the interest rate.

■ **FOR EXAMPLE** A lender charges 7.5% interest a year. If a borrower takes out a loan for $335,000, how much interest will the borrower pay in the first year?

7.5% of $335,000 = 0.075 × 335,000 = $25,125 interest

Note that computing interest can be complicated by compounding periods and amortization. A full discussion on interest and loan repayment schedules is beyond the scope of this book.

Points

Points are monies charged by a lender for making a loan. One point equals 1% of the loan amount.

■ **FOR EXAMPLE** A lender charges two points to make a mortgage loan. The buyer plans on buying a $200,000 house and needs to take out a loan for 80% of the purchase price. How many points will the buyer have to pay?

80% of $200,000 = 0.80 × 200,000 = $160,000 loan amount
2% of $160,000 = 0.02 × 160,000 = $3,200 points

Appreciation and Depreciation

Appreciation is an increase in value. Depreciation is a decrease in value. Both are expressed in terms of percentage rates. In real estate, we usually use the terms to describe increases and decreases in property values.

■ **FOR EXAMPLE** Five years ago, a woman bought a house for $123,000. How much has her house value increased if appreciation has been 5%? What is the current value of her house?

5% × $123,000 = 0.05 × 123,000 = $6,150 increase in value
$6,150 increase in value + $123,000 original cost = $129,150 current value

MEASUREMENTS

In order to determine the area of a parcel of land or space in a house, real estate professionals must know how to use and calculate measurements.

Linear Measurements

Linear measurement is a line measurement. It is typically used to determine the length of something, such as the length of a lot line or width of a room. Common types of linear measurements are

- inches,

- feet (12 inches),

- yards (3 feet), and

- miles (5,280 feet).

Sometimes the term **front foot** is used; front foot refers to the linear measurement on the frontage of the property.

Area Measurements

Area is the two-dimensional surface of an object. Area is quoted in square units or in acres. Common types of area measurements are

- square feet,

- square yards (9 square feet),

- acres (43,560 square feet), and

- square miles (640 square acres).

Volume Measurements

Volume is the space inside a three-dimensional object. Volume is quoted in cubic units. Common types of volume measurements are

- cubic feet, and

- cubic yards (27 cubic feet).

Converting One Unit of Measurement to Another

One unit of measurement can easily be converted to another unit of measurement (a known to an unknown). If the known unit is smaller than the unknown unit (for example, when the number of feet is known and you are trying to calculate the number of yards), divide the known unit by how many known units there are in the unknown unit (such as three feet in a yard). If the known unit is larger than the unknown unit (for example, when you know the number of inches and are trying to calculate the number of feet), multiply the known unit by how many known units there are in the unknown unit (such as 12 inches to a foot).

■ **FOR EXAMPLE**   A lot is 150 feet wide. How many yards wide is it?
150 feet ÷ 3 feet per yard = 50 yards

■ **FOR EXAMPLE**   A house is 3,000 feet from a fire hydrant. How many miles is this?
3,000 feet ÷ 5,280 feet per mile = 0.5682 miles

■ **FOR EXAMPLE**   A room consists of 18 square yards. How many square feet is that?
18 square yards × 9 square feet per square yard = 162 square feet

Calculating the Area of a Square or Rectangle

Squares and rectangles are four-sided objects. All four sides of a square are the same. Opposite sides of a rectangle are the same.

To determine the area of a square or a rectangle, multiply the length by the width.

■ **FOR EXAMPLE**   A room is 10 feet wide and 13 feet long. How many square feet are there?

10 feet long × 13 feet wide = 130 square feet

■ **FOR EXAMPLE:**   A lot is 120 feet wide and 175 feet deep. How many square feet are there? How many acres?

120 feet long × 175 feet wide = 21,000 square feet
21,000 square feet ÷ 43,560 square feet per acre = 0.4821 acres

Generally, the square footage of a building is based on its outside measurements and usually (but not always) includes heated/cooled areas and finished areas both above and below grade. Unfinished areas and garage space are typically not included.

Calculating the Area of a Triangle

A triangle is a three-sided object. The three sides of a triangle can be the same length or different lengths. If a triangle has a right (90 degree) angle in one corner, it is called a right triangle. One side of the right angle is called the base, and the other side is called the height. To calculate the area of this type of triangle, multiply the base times the height and then divide by two.

■ **FOR EXAMPLE**   A right angle triangle has a base of 50 feet and a height of 20 feet. What is the square footage?

(50 feet on base × 20 feet wide) ÷ 2 = 1,000 feet ÷ 2 = 500 square feet

Calculating the Area of an Irregular Shape

To calculate the area of an irregular shape, divide the shape into regular shapes. Calculate the area of each regular shape and add the areas together.

Calculating the Volume of a Cube or Rectangular Box

To calculate the volume of a cube or rectangular box, multiply the length by the width by the height.

■ **FOR EXAMPLE**   A building is 500 feet long, 400 feet wide, and 25 feet high. How many cubic feet of space are in this building?

500 feet long × 400 feet wide × 25 feet high = 5,000,000 cubic feet

Think of a room as a rectangular box so that the volume of a room is equal to the length times the width times the height. The ability to calculate volume is useful in determining heating and air-conditioning needs, warehouse space, and the amount of water in a pool.

PRORATIONS

To *prorate* means to divide proportionately. In real estate, prorations are used to divide income and expenses of a property between buyer and seller at closing. Salesperson licensing exams seldom ask questions on prorations, although such questions do appear on broker licensing exams. Refer to Chapter 17 for an introduction of when and how prorations are used at closing, and for further examples.

Different Calendars Used for Prorating

When prorating, calculate the number of days owed for the income or expense. In calculating the number of days, different versions of counting days within years may be used, depending on local custom. A **calendar year** contains 12 months, with 28 to 31 days in each month. There are a total of 365 days in a calendar year. Remember that a leap year contains 366 days.

The **banker's year** (or statutory year) contains 12 months, with 30 days in each month. The total number of days in a banker's year is 360 days.

Unless specified otherwise, a calendar year is typically used.

Prorating Through or To the Day of Closing

When prorating, you will be told whether to prorate *through* or *to* the day of closing. This is an important distinction. When prorating *through* the day of closing, the seller is responsible for the day of closing. When prorating *to* the day of closing, the buyer is responsible for the day of closing.

Prepaid Versus Accrued Expense

A prepaid expense is one that the seller has already paid. The buyer owes the seller for any prepaid expenses. An accrued item is one that is due but not yet paid. The seller owes the buyer for accrued items, also called paid in arrears.

Calculating Prorations

When calculating prorations, two things should be known: (1) the number of days owed, and (2) the amount of the expense or income per day. To find the number of days owed, determine how many days one party has paid for an expense that the other party is responsible for (or how many days one party has received income that is owed to the other party). To find the per day rate, divide the annual amount by the number of days in the year, or the monthly amount by the number of days in the month, being careful to use the right type of year. To then calculate the proration, multiply the per day rate by the number of days.

> ■ **FOR EXAMPLE**   A seller paid $155 in advance in condominium common charges for the month of December. The closing is set for December 15. At closing, the buyer will reimburse the seller for this expense. If prorations are made through the day of closing and a calendar year is used, how much will the buyer reimburse the seller?
>
>   31 days in December − 15 days = 16 days owed
> $155 per month ÷ 31 days = $5 per day rate
> $5 per day rate × 16 days owed = $80 credit to seller, debit to buyer

Difference Between "Debit" and "Credit"

Debit takes money from a person. Credit gives money to a person. When the prorated item involves both the buyer and the seller, there will always be a double entry on the closing statement. If the seller owes the buyer, the prorated amount will be debited to the seller and credited to the buyer. If the buyer owes the seller, the prorated item will be debited to the buyer and credited to the seller. When the prorated item involves the buyer and someone other than the seller, there will be only a single entry. Likewise, when the prorated item involves the seller and someone other than the buyer, there will be only a single entry.

Using Prorations

Prorations are necessary to ensure that expenses associated with a property are fairly divided between a buyer and a seller at the closing of the property. The rules or customs governing the computation of prorations vary widely from state to state and even between areas within a state. A case study on prorations can be found in Chapter 17.

Taxes

Proration of real estate taxes will vary, depending on how the taxes are paid in the area where the real estate is located. In some states, real estate taxes are paid in advance, in which case, the buyer owes the seller. In other states, taxes are paid in arrears, in which case the seller owes the buyer. Tax years may run from January 1 to December 31, October 1 to September 30, or any other period; sometimes taxes are due in installments.

> ■ **FOR EXAMPLE** Property tax on a piece of property is $3,400 a year, which is paid in arrears (meaning seller will owe buyer for accrued taxes). The property is scheduled to close on March 15. If a banker's year is used and prorations are made to the date of closing, what is the proration, and how is it credited and debited?
>
> 30 days in January + 30 days in February + 14 days in March = 74 days owed
> $3,400 per year ÷ 360 days = $9.44 per day tax
> $9.44 per day tax × 74 days owed = $698.56 credit to buyer, debit to seller

Rents

Tenants typically pay landlords rent in advance at the beginning of the month. This means that if there is a closing mid-month, the seller will owe the buyer for a portion of that month's rent already received.

> ■ **FOR EXAMPLE** A buyer is purchasing an apartment complex that consists of 15 units that rent for $450 per month. The sale is to be closed on May 20, and the May rent has been received by the seller for all units. Compute the rent proration by prorating through the day of closing. To whom is the rent credited and debited?
>
> 31 days in May − May 20 = 11 days of rent owed to the buyer
> $450 rent per unit × 15 units = $6,750 per month rent
> $6,750 per month rent ÷ 31 = $217.74 per day rent
> $217.74 per day rent × 11 days = $2,395.14 credit to buyer, debit to seller

Other Common Prorations

Other items typically prorated between the buyer and seller at closing include prepaid items, such as insurance, fuel oil, and rent, and accrued items, such as taxes, water, gas, and electricity.

SUMMARY

Real estate professionals can expect to encounter mathematical problems in their day-to-day activities. Calculators and computers greatly help with any needed computations, so licensees should become familiar with operating a calculator and/or computer. When using a calculator, all numbers must first be converted to decimal form.

The three most common types of math computations that come up in residential real estate are (1) working with percentages, (2) figuring measurements, and (3) estimating prorations.

A percentage is a portion of a whole number. The whole, or total, always represents 100%. To calculate the part of the whole number, multiply the whole by the percentage rate stated as a decimal. Percentages are used in calculating commissions, property and conveyance taxes, financing points and interest, and appreciation and depreciation.

Measurements are used to determine the area of a parcel of land or space in a house. Linear measurements, such as feet, are single-dimension measurements that can be used to measure the perimeter of a room or lot. Area measurements, such as square feet, are two-dimensional measurements that can be used to measure the floor area of a room or acreage of a lot. Volume measurements, such as cubic feet, are three-dimensional measurements that can be used to measure the total amount of space in a room or building.

Prorations are used to divide income and expenses of a property between the buyer and seller at closing. The manner and process of proration depends on local customs. In general, when calculating prorations, you need to know to whom the proration is to be debited and credited, the number of days owed, and the amount of the expense or income per day. Items such as property taxes, rent, insurance, and fuel oil are typically prorated.

REVIEW QUESTIONS

Please complete all of the questions before turning to the Answer Key on page 350.

1. A buyer is purchasing a house for $223,000. The lender will give the buyer a mortgage loan for 95% of the purchase price. How much cash must the buyer have for the down payment?
   a. $1,230
   b. $11,150
   c. $12,300
   d. $116,000

2. Two brokers split a 6% commission equally on a $173,000 home. The selling salesperson was paid 70% of his broker's share. The listing salesperson was paid 30% of her broker's share. How much did the listing salesperson receive?
   a. $1,557
   b. $3,114
   c. $3,633
   d. $7,266

3. A seller is selling a house for $195,000. At closing, in her state, she will be responsible for paying a state conveyance tax of 0.11% of the sales price and a town conveyance tax of 0.05% of the sales price. How much total conveyance tax will she need to pay?
   a. $312
   b. $2,140
   c. $21,450
   d. $31,200

4. A prospective buyer is interested in making an offer on a house and would like to know what the owners paid for it. He looks up the owners' deed in the land records. The deed does not state the purchase price, but does have a stamp on it that states that $448.50 in conveyance tax was paid at the time of that sale. If the conveyance tax rate is 0.13%, how much did the owners pay for the property one year ago?
   a. $34,500
   b. $58,305
   c. $345,000
   d. $583,050

5. If a borrower is taking out a $356,000 mortgage loan to pay for a property that she is buying for $445,000, what is the loan-to-value ratio?
   a. 12.5%
   b. 60.0%
   c. 75.0%
   d. 80.0%

6. A borrower is buying a house for $205,000. To finance the purchase, he is taking out a mortgage loan with an LTV of 85%. If his lender is charging him two points for this loan, how much money will he owe for points?
   a. $615.00
   b. $1,742.50
   c. $3,485.00
   d. $4,100.00

7. Over the past year, a local residential area has been experiencing a decrease in real estate value of approximately 3%. If a house sold last year for $176,000, what would it *MOST* likely sell for this year?
   a. $5,280
   b. $170,873
   c. $173,000
   d. $181,280

8. A lot purchased five years ago for $15,000 has appreciated by 75% over that time. What is it worth today?
   a. $11,250
   b. $18,740
   c. $22,500
   d. $26,250

9. A couple bought a house five years ago for $40,000. Its value went up, and today they sold it for $50,000. What percentage of profit did they make on their investment?
   a. 20%
   b. 25%
   c. 33%
   d. 80%

10. What is the square footage of a lot with a frontage of 75 feet, 6 inches, and a depth of 140 feet, 9 inches?
    a. 216.25
    b. 10,626.63
    c. 10,652.04
    d. 25,510.81

11. A fence is being built to enclose a lot that is 125 feet by 350 feet. If there is going to be one 10-foot gate, how many running feet of fence will it take?
    a. 465
    b. 600
    c. 940
    d. 960

12. If a 125-foot by 150-foot lot was purchased for $34,000, what price was paid per square foot?
    a. $0.55
    b. $1.81
    c. $63.75
    d. $226.67

13. A warehouse is 400 feet long, 250 feet wide, and 40 feet high. How many cubic feet are there?
    a. 100,000
    b. 400,000
    c. 1,000,000
    d. 4,000,000

14. Homeowners owe $1,282 per year in property tax on their house, which is paid in arrears. They have contracted to sell the home, with closing on April 23. How much will the tax proration be, using a calendar year with the seller responsible for the day of closing. Assume this is *NOT* a leap year.
    a. $393.38
    b. $396.86
    c. $885.11
    d. $888.62

15. A contract has been ratified with closing set for March 20. This year's water bill, paid in arrears, is $120. Using a banker's year and prorating through the closing, what will the proration be for the water bill, and to whom will this amount be credited?
    a. $26.66 credit to the buyer
    b. $26.66 credit to the seller
    c. $26.27 credit to the buyer
    d. $26.27 credit to the seller

16. The broker receives 5.5% commission of $10,500 for the sale of the property. How much did the property sell for?
    a. $175,000
    b. $190,909
    c. $210,000
    d. $213,000

17. A broker received a $15,000 commission on the sale of the home for $250,000. What commission rate did the broker charge?
    a. 5%
    b. 5.5%
    c. 6%
    d. 6.5%

18. A lender charges 5.5% interest a year. If the borrower takes out a loan for $435,000, how much interest will the buyer pay for the first month?
    a. $1,812.50
    b. $1,993.75
    c. $21,750
    d. $23,925

19. The property tax is $3,000 per year, which is paid in arrears. The property is expected to close on March 14, using a banker's year. Using a banker's year, calculate the tax that must be accounted for.
    a. Debit seller $616.64, credit buyer $616.64
    b. Credit seller $616.64, debit buyer $616.64
    c. Debit seller $2,383.36, credit buyer $616.64
    d. Credit seller $616.64, debit buyer $2,383.36

20. The seller has collected rents from all 20 rental units, which average $535 each. On the day of closing, April 15, the air conditioner broke down, and the repair was $1,500. Compute the rent proration by prorating through the day of closing.
    a. Debit seller $9,200, credit buyer $9,200
    b. Debit seller $5,350, credit buyer $5,350
    c. Debit seller $10,700, credit buyer $10,700
    d. Debit seller $4,600, credit buyer $4,600

Practice Examination

Please complete all of the questions before turning to the Answer Key on page 350.

1. A seller wants to net $165,000 from the sale of her house after paying a 6% commission. Her sales price will have to be
   a. $164,500.
   b. $171,000.
   c. $174,900.
   d. $175,532.

2. Under joint tenancy,
   a. a maximum of two people can own a property.
   b. the fractional interests can be different amounts.
   c. additional owners can be added later.
   d. there is usually a right of survivorship.

3. According to the statute of frauds, an oral three-year lease is
   a. illegal.
   b. unenforceable.
   c. renewable.
   d. a long-term lease.

4. A qualified veteran offers to purchase a home for $167,000 using a VA-guaranteed loan. After the offer was accepted, a certificate of reasonable value (CRV) was issued on the property for $164,500. In this situation, the veteran may
   a. purchase the property with a $2,500 down payment.
   b. withdraw from the sale after paying a 1% penalty.
   c. withdraw from the sale after paying a 2% penalty.
   d. not withdraw from the sale.

5. A cloud on the title to a property may be cured by
   a. bringing an action to repudiate the title.
   b. paying cash for the property at the settlement.
   c. obtaining quitclaim deeds from all interested parties.
   d. bringing an action to register the title.

6. Real property includes all of the following rights *EXCEPT*
   a. air rights.
   b. water rights.
   c. mineral rights.
   d. chattels.

7. Which of the following items is usually prorated between the seller and the buyer at the closing?
   a. Recording charges
   b. Real estate taxes
   c. Earnest money deposit
   d. Amount of new mortgage loan

8. For a deed to be valid, it must be signed by the
   a. grantor.
   b. grantee.
   c. grantor and the grantee.
   d. grantee and two witnesses.

9. A seller, who wants to sell his house, enters into a listing agreement with a broker. Another broker obtains a buyer for the property, and the first broker does not receive a commission. The listing agreement between the seller and the first broker was probably
   a. an exclusive-right-to-sell listing.
   b. an exclusive-agency listing.
   c. an open listing.
   d. a multiple listing.

10. The listing broker has been offering a house for sale at the price of $198,750. An African American couple saw the house and was interested in buying it. When they asked the price of the house, the broker told them it was $210,000. According to the federal Fair Housing Act of 1968, such a statement is
    a. illegal because the difference in the offering price and the quoted price was greater than 10%.
    b. illegal because the terms of the potential sale were changed for the African American couple.
    c. legal because all that is important is that the couple was given the opportunity to buy the house.
    d. legal because the representation was made by the broker and not directly by the owner.

11. A real estate loan that includes both personal property and real property as collateral is called a
    a. package loan.
    b. blanket loan.
    c. growing-equity loan.
    d. shared-appreciation loan.

12. The local power company wishes to convert the present electric pole lines that run in front of the houses to a buried system that will cross through the backyards of 50 houses. The power company will need to obtain
    a. an easement appurtenant.
    b an easement in gross.
    c. an easement by necessity.
    d. a party wall easement.

13. A portion of a building that was inadvertently built on another person's land is called an
    a. accretion.
    b. license.
    c. encroachment.
    d. easement.

14. The special form of joint tenancy called tenancy by the entirety is appropriate for
    a. two business partners buying a new office building.
    b. an unmarried couple purchasing a house together.
    c. newlyweds purchasing their first home.
    d. a single woman buying a condominium unit.

15. A young stockbroker sold the home she purchased three years ago and now rents an apartment. She had originally purchased the home for $177,800 and sold it for $306,100. In computing her income tax, she will pay capital gains taxes on
    a. $11,320.
    b. $16,980.
    c. $28,300.
    d. nothing.

16. Which of the following items is a lien on real estate?
    a. A recorded easement
    b. A recorded mortgage
    c. An encroachment
    d. A deed restriction

17. A residence with outdated plumbing is suffering from
    a. functional obsolescence.
    b. external obsolescence.
    c. curable physical deterioration.
    d. incurable physical deterioration.

18. The current value of a vacant lot is $40,000. For real estate tax purposes, the property is assessed at 40% of its current value, with an equalization factor of 1.5 applied to the assessed value. If the tax rate is $4 per $100 of assessed valuation, what is the amount of tax due on the property?
    a. $640
    b. $960
    c. $1,600
    d. $2,400

19. A contract signed under duress is
    a. discharged.
    b. void.
    c. breached.
    d. voidable.

20. Several years after a five-story building was completed, a city ordinance was passed prohibiting any structure taller than three stories. In this situation, the structure
    a. is a nonconforming use.
    b. has to be demolished.
    c. requires a variance.
    d. requires a conditional-use permit.

21. The document that shows the record of ownership from the time the property was granted to the first owner is the
    a. abstract of title.
    b. chain of title.
    c. evidence of title.
    d. Torrens certificate.

22. The duties of care, obedience, accounting, loyalty, and disclosure to a principal are specified as part of a
    a. fiduciary relationship.
    b. brokerage relationship.
    c. statutory agency relationship.
    d. transaction broker relationship.

23. An insurance company agreed to provide a developer with financing for a shopping center at a below-market interest rate in exchange for an equity position in the property. This type of arrangement is called
    a. a package loan.
    b. a blanket loan.
    c. an open-end loan.
    d. a shared appreciation loan.

24. A real estate transaction had a closing date of November 15. The seller, who was responsible for the costs up to and including the date of the settlement, had paid the property taxes of $1,116 for the calendar year (not a leap year). On the closing statement, the buyer is
    a. debited for $140.67.
    b. debited for $975.38.
    c. credited for $140.67.
    d. credited for $975.38.

25. What is the role of the Federal Housing Administration (FHA)?
    a. It builds homes for deserving citizens.
    b. It lends money for the purchase of homes to qualified applicants.
    c. It insures real estate loans made by approved lending institutions.
    d. It provides hazard and liability insurance for real property owners.

26. If a storage tank that measures 8 feet by 9 feet by 12 feet was designed to store natural gas and the cost of the gas is $1.82 per cubic foot, what does it cost to fill the tank to one-half its capacity?
    a. $685
    b. $786
    c. $864
    d. $1,572

27. On Monday, a seller offers to sell his residence to a buyer for $152,000. On Tuesday, the buyer counteroffers to buy the property for $150,500. On Friday, the buyer withdraws his counteroffer and accepts the seller's original price of $152,000. Under these circumstances, there is
    a. a valid agreement because the buyer accepted the seller's offer exactly as it was made, regardless that it was not accepted immediately.
    b. a valid agreement because the buyer accepted before the seller advised him that the offer was withdrawn.
    c. no valid agreement because the seller's offer was not accepted within 72 hours of its having been made.
    d. no valid agreement because the buyer's counteroffer was a rejection of the seller's offer, and once rejected, it cannot be accepted later.

28. The law that requires lenders to inform both sellers and buyers of all closing fees and charges is the
    a. Equal Credit Opportunity Act.
    b. Real Estate Settlement Procedures Act.
    c. Truth in Lending Act (Regulation Z).
    d. Real Estate Investment Trust Act.

29. A mortgage loan that requires monthly payments of $639.05 for 20 years and a final payment of $49,386.63 is called
    a. a wraparound loan.
    b. an accelerated loan.
    c. a balloon loan.
    d. an adjustable-rate loan.

30. Real estate salespeople may
    a. write checks from their broker's trust account.
    b. advertise the property in their own name.
    c. collect a commission directly from the principal.
    d. act under the supervision of the employing broker.

31. After a snowstorm, a property owner offers to pay $10 to anyone who will shovel her driveway. This is an example of
    a. a unilateral contract.
    b. an executed contract.
    c. an implied contract.
    d. a void contract.

32. A buyer is purchasing a home under the terms of a land contract. Until the contract is completed, the buyer has
    a. legal title to the premises.
    b. no interest in the property.
    c. a legal life estate to the premises.
    d. equitable title in the property.

33. The Equal Credit Opportunity Act makes it illegal for lenders to refuse credit or otherwise discriminate because an applicant is
    a. an unemployed person.
    b. a single person.
    c. a new homebuyer who does not have adequate credit history.
    d. a single parent who receives public assistance and cannot afford the payments.

34. The important economic principles that affect the value of a property include all of following *EXCEPT*
    a. highest and best use.
    b. supply and demand.
    c. substitution.
    d. demographics.

35. Which of the following leasehold estates automatically renews itself?
    a. Estate for years
    b. Estate from period to period
    c. Estate at will
    d. Estate at sufferance

36. A landlord has sold a building to the state so that a freeway can be built. The tenant's lease has expired, but the landlord is letting the tenant remain until the building is torn down. The tenant continues to pay the same rent as indicated in the original lease. This is a
    a. holdover tenancy.
    b. month-to-month tenancy.
    c. tenancy at sufferance.
    d. tenancy at will.

37. A default party who pays her debt after a foreclosure sale has the right to regain the property under which of the following concepts?
    a. Reversionary rights
    b. Equitable right of redemption
    c. Remainder rights
    d. Statutory right of redemption

38. Which of the following situations would *NOT* be a violation of the fair housing laws?
    a. The refusal of a property manager to rent an apartment to an otherwise-qualified Mormon couple
    b. The general policy of a loan company to avoid granting home improvement loans to individuals living in transitional neighborhoods
    c. The intentional neglect of a broker to show an Asian family any property listings of homes in all-white neighborhoods
    d. The insistence of a widowed woman on renting her spare bedroom only to another widowed woman

39. When a person dies without leaving a will but does have heirs, the state determines the disposition of the estate according to the
    a. statute of frauds.
    b. statute of descent and distribution.
    c. right of prior appropriation.
    d. reversionary rights.

40. When the title to real estate passes to a third party upon the death of a life tenant, the third party's interest in the property is a
    a. remainder interest.
    b. reversionary interest.
    c. pur autre vie interest.
    d. preemptory interest.

41. The approach to value used *MOST* often for residential properties is the
    a. gross rent multiplier.
    b. cost approach.
    c. sales comparison approach.
    d. income approach.

42. At the settlement, the lender requires the borrower to pay $345, which will be kept in an escrow account. This money is *MOST* likely held
    a. as a security deposit.
    b. for taxes and insurance.
    c. to ensure against borrower default.
    d. to cover the expense of discount points.

43. The type of hazardous substance that has the greatest effect on very young children is
    a. asbestos.
    b. lead-based paint.
    c. radon.
    d. mold.

44. In a sale-and-leaseback arrangement, the
    a. buyer becomes the lessor of the property.
    b. seller retains title to the real estate.
    c. buyer gets possession of the property.
    d. seller obtains a mortgage interest deduction.

45. Two licensees are affiliated with the same realty. One has a new listing, and the other has a buyer-client interested in purchasing it. Both licensees have full responsibility to promote and protect the best interests of their separate clients. Apparently, their state allows for
    a. single agency.
    b. dual agency.
    c. designated agency.
    d. facilitated agency.

46. An appraiser has been asked to appraise a health store located in a small strip shopping mall. By comparing other similar businesses that have sold in that area, the appraiser has determined that a capitalization rate of 8% is reasonable. The owner of the health store has provided figures showing that total receipts for the year were $72,000. Total expenses, including rent, salary, and operating expenses, were $60,000. The appraised value is
    a. $150,000.
    b. $165,000.
    c. $750,000.
    d. $900,000.

47. A buyer signs a buyer's brokerage agreement under which the broker will help the buyer find a three-bedroom house in the $85,000–$100,000 price range. A seller comes into the broker's office and enters into a listing agreement with the broker to sell the seller's two-bedroom condominium for $70,000. Based on these facts, which statement is *TRUE*?
    a. The buyer is the broker's client; the seller is the broker's customer.
    b. The buyer is the broker's customer; the seller is the broker's client.
    c. While both the buyer and the seller are clients, the broker owes the fiduciary duties of an agent only to the seller.
    d. Because both the buyer and the seller are the broker's clients, the broker owes the fiduciary duties of an agent to both.

48. What type of lease establishes a set rental payment and requires the lessor to pay for the taxes, insurance, and maintenance on the property?
    a. Percentage lease
    b. Net lease
    c. Graduated lease
    d. Gross lease

49. A parcel of ground over which an easement runs is called the
    a. dominant tenement.
    b. servient tenement.
    c. prescriptive tenement.
    d. eminent tenement.

50. A borrower defaulted on home mortgage loan payments, and the lender obtained a court order to foreclose on the property. At the foreclosure sale, however, the property sold for only $144,000, while the unpaid balance of the loan at the time of the foreclosure was $164,000. The lender can make an attempt to recover the $20,000 that the borrower still owes by
    a. suing for specific performance.
    b. suing for damages.
    c. seeking a judgment by default.
    d. seeking a deficiency judgment.

51. The difference between a general lien and a specific lien is that a
    a. general lien cannot be enforced in court, while a specific lien can.
    b. specific lien is held by only one person, while a general lien is held by two or more people.
    c. general lien is a lien against personal property, while a specific lien is a lien against real estate.
    d. specific lien is a lien against a certain parcel of real estate, while a general lien covers all of the debtor's property.

52. In an option to purchase real estate, the optionee
    a. must purchase the property but may do so at any time within the option period.
    b. is limited to a refund of the option consideration if the option is exercised.
    c. has no obligation to purchase the property during the option period.
    d. cannot obtain third-party financing on the property until after the option has expired.

53. A couple entered into a purchase contract to buy a house for $184,500. They provided $4,000 as earnest money and obtained a new mortgage for $166,050. The purchase contract provides for a March 15 settlement. The buyers and the sellers will prorate the previous year's real estate taxes of $1,880, which have been prepaid by the seller. The buyers have additional closing costs of $4,250, and the sellers have other closing costs of $13,850. How much cash must the buyers bring to the settlement?
    a. $20,288
    b. $23,042
    c. $23,042
    d. $24,188

54. A broker took a listing and later discovered that a client had previously been declared incompetent by the court. The listing is now
    a. unaffected because the broker was acting in good faith as the owner's agent.
    b. of no value to the broker because the contract is void.
    c. the basis for recovery of a commission.
    d. renegotiable between the broker and the client.

55. A broker receives a check for earnest money from a buyer and deposits it in an escrow or trust account to protect herself from the charge of
    a. commingling.
    b. novation.
    c. conversion.
    d. embezzlement.

56. What is steering?
    a. Leading prospective homeowners to or away from certain areas
    b. Refusing to make loans to persons residing in certain areas
    c. A requirement to join a multiple listing service
    d. Illegally setting commission rates

57. An estate (or tenancy) for years is a tenancy
    a. with the consent of the landlord.
    b. that expires on a specific date.
    c. created by the death of the owner.
    d. created by a testator.

58. If a house was sold for $140,000 and the buyer obtained an FHA-insured mortgage loan for $138,500, how much money is paid in discount points if the lender charged four points?
    a. $1,385
    b. $1,400
    c. $5,540
    d. $5,600

59. The Civil Rights Act of 1866 prohibits in all cases discrimination based upon a person's
    a. sex.
    b. race.
    c. religion.
    d. familial status.

60. A building was sold for $260,000, with the buyer making a 10% down payment and financing the balance. The lender charged a 1% loan origination fee. What was the total fee paid to the lender?
    a. $2,340
    b. $2,600
    c. $26,000
    d. $28,340

61. An individual seeking to be excused from the dictates of a zoning ordinance should request a
    a. building permit.
    b. certificate of alternate usage.
    c. variance.
    d. certificate of nonconforming use.

62. A borrower's real estate loan documents indicate that if she sells her property, she must immediately pay her lender in full. This clause is called
    a. an acceleration clause.
    b. an alienation clause.
    c. a subordination clause.
    d. a habendum clause.

63. The hazardous substance that has created the biggest problem in schools and office buildings is
    a. asbestos.
    b. lead-based paint.
    c. radon.
    d. mold.

64. In the deed of conveyance, the seller's only guarantee was that the property was not encumbered during the time he owned it, except as noted in the deed. The type of deed used in this transaction was a
    a. general warranty deed.
    b. special warranty deed.
    c. bargain and sale deed.
    d. quitclaim deed.

65. In the appraisal of a building constructed in the 1930s, the *MOST* difficult part of the cost approach to value is
    a. estimating changes in material costs.
    b. obtaining 1930s building codes.
    c. estimating changes in labor costs.
    d. estimating accrued depreciation.

66. Which of the following occurrences is *NOT* a violation of the Real Estate Settlement Procedures Act (RESPA)?
    a. Recommending a particular lender to a buyer
    b. Accepting a kickback on a loan subject to RESPA requirements
    c. Requiring the use of a particular title insurance company
    d. Accepting a fee or charging for services that were not performed

67. A man willed his estate as follows: 54% to his wife, 18% to his daughter, 16% to his son, and the remainder to his church. If the church received $79,000, how much did the daughter receive?
    a. $105,333
    b. $118,500
    c. $355,500
    d. $658,333

68. An example of external obsolescence is
    a. numerous pillars supporting the ceiling in a store.
    b. roof leaks making premises unusable and therefore unrentable.
    c. an older structure with massive cornices.
    d. vacant and abandoned buildings in the area.

69. The type of loan where the monthly payment may increase or decrease in each adjustment period depending on fluctuations in a selected economic indicator is
    a. a growing-equity mortgage.
    b. a shared-appreciation mortgage.
    c. an adjustable-rate mortgage.
    d. a graduated-payment mortgage.

70. When the buyer signs a purchase offer and the seller accepts it, the buyer acquires in the property an immediate interest called
    a. legal title.
    b. statutory title.
    c. defeasible title.
    d. equitable title.

71. Assuming that the listing broker and the seller broker in a transaction split their commission equally, what was the sales price of the property if the commission rate was 6.5% and the listing broker received $2,593.50?
    a. $39,900
    b. $56,200
    c. $79,800
    d. $88,400

72. The owner of a large single-family home decided to sell it and move into a small apartment in a cooperative building. Under the cooperative form of ownership, she will
    a. become a stockholder in the corporation.
    b. hold a fee simple interest in her unit.
    c. receive a fixed-term lease for her unit.
    d. have an undivided interest in the common elements.

73. The monthly rent on a warehouse is set at $1 per cubic yard. If the warehouse is 36 feet by 200 feet by 12 feet high, what is the annual rent?
    a. $3,200
    b. $9,600
    c. $38,400
    d. $115,200

74. A broker would *NOT* have to prove that he was the procuring cause under which of the following types of listing agreements?
    a. Net listing
    b. Open listing
    c. Exclusive-agency listing
    d. Exclusive-right-to-sell listing

75. A man moved into an abandoned home, made extensive repairs, and installed cabinets in the kitchen for his convenience. When the owner discovered the occupancy, he had the man ejected. What is the status of the cabinets?
    a. The man cannot get the cabinets back.
    b. The cabinets remain because they are trade fixtures.
    c. While the cabinets stay, the man is entitled to the value of the improvements.
    d. The man can recover the cabinets if they can be removed without damaging the real estate.

76. When placed in a printed advertisement, which phrase complies with the requirements of the Truth in Lending Act (Regulation Z) with regard to interest rates?
    a. "10% interest"
    b. "10% annual percent"
    c. "10% annual interest"
    d. "10% annual percentage rate"

77. On the settlement statement, the cost of the lender's title insurance policy that is required for a new mortgage loan is usually a
    a. credit to the seller.
    b. credit to the buyer.
    c. debit to the seller.
    d. debit to the buyer.

78. If a home that originally cost $142,500 three years ago is now valued at 127% of its original cost, what is its current value?
    a. $142,627
    b. $180,975
    c. $195,205
    d. $384,750

79. A broker listed a parcel of raw land at an 8% commission. After the property was sold and settlement had occurred, the owner discovered that the broker had been listing similar properties in the area at a 6% commission rate. Based on this information, the
    a. broker has done nothing legally wrong.
    b. broker can lose his license.
    c. owner can cancel the transaction.
    d. owner is entitled to a refund.

80. If the legal description of a property includes the phrase "W½ of the NW¼ of the NW¼" of a section, how many acres are in the property?
    a. 20
    b. 40
    c. 160
    d. 320

81. Which statement regarding underground storage tanks is *TRUE*?
    a. A leaking underground storage tank only affects the property on which it is located.
    b. A landowner will not be held responsible if the underground tank was already in place prior to the purchase of the property.
    c. Landowners can be held responsible for clean-up costs plus all damages.
    d. An underground storage tank is automatically covered by the Superfund.

82. A property manager is *LEAST* likely to
    a. handle new leases.
    b. arrange for repairs and improvements.
    c. resolve tenant disputes as to property use.
    d. prepare depreciation schedules for tax purposes.

83. A veteran wants to refinance his home mortgage loan with a new VA-guaranteed loan. The lender is willing but insists on three and a half discount points. In this situation, the veteran
    a. can refinance with a VA-guaranteed loan, provided that there are no discount points.
    b. can refinance with a VA-guaranteed loan, provided that the discount points do not exceed two.
    c. will not be required to pay a funding fee.
    d. can proceed with the refinance loan and pay the discount points.

84. The requirements of the Real Estate Settlement Procedures Act (RESPA) apply to any residential real estate transactions that involve
    a. a federally related mortgage loan.
    b. those taking place in a state that has adopted RESPA.
    c. any mortgage financing less than $100,000.
    d. any purchase price less than $100,000.

85. Which document is always available when searching the public record?
    a. Encroachments
    b. Rights of parties in possession
    c. Rights of mechanics who have recently done work
    d. Recorded mortgages

86. Capitalization rates are
    a. determined by the gross rent multipliers.
    b. the rates of return that a property will produce.
    c. mathematical values determined by the sales prices.
    d. determined by the amount of depreciation in properties.

87. The definition of *market value* includes all of the following *EXCEPT*
    a. buyer and seller are typically motivated.
    b. both parties are well informed.
    c. a reasonable time is allowed for exposure in the open market.
    d. the sales price is affected by creative financing or sales concessions.

88. With regard to offer and acceptance, which statement is *TRUE*?
    a. A counteroffer is a rejection of the original offer.
    b. A counteroffer cannot be withdrawn prior to acceptance.
    c. An offer cannot be withdrawn prior to acceptance.
    d. A counteroffer cannot be countered.

89. A borrower made the final payment on a mortgage loan to the bank. Regardless, the lender will still hold a lien on the mortgaged property until which document is recorded?
    a. A satisfaction
    b. A reconveyance
    c. A novation
    d. An estoppel

90. Discount points on a real estate loan are a potential cost to either the seller or the buyer. Such points are
    a. set by the FHA and the VA for their loan programs.
    b. charged only on conventional loans.
    c. limited by government regulations.
    d. prepaid interest to the lender.

91. One important rule for a metes-and-bounds legal description is that
    a. the boundary must return to the point of beginning.
    b. U.S. Geological Survey benchmarks must be used.
    c. only natural monuments may be used.
    d. no survey will be required.

92. All of the following situations are exemptions to the federal Fair Housing Act of 1968 *EXCEPT*
    a. the listing of a single-family residence where the listing broker does not advertise the property.
    b. the restriction of noncommercial lodgings by a private club to members of the club.
    c. the rental of a unit in an owner-occupied three-family dwelling.
    d. the restriction of residency in a monastery.

93. Which statement regarding adverse possession is *TRUE*?
    a. The person taking possession of the property must do so with the consent of the owner of the property.
    b. Occupancy of the property by the person taking possession must be continuous over a specified period of time.
    c. The person taking possession of the property must compensate the owner at the end of the adverse possession period.
    d. The person taking possession of the property can never end up as the legal owner.

94. What will it cost to put new carpeting in a den measuring 15 feet by 20 feet if the cost of the carpeting is $6.95 per square yard and the cost of laying it is an additional $250?
    a. $232
    b. $482
    c. $610
    d. $2,335

95. If the landlord of an apartment building breaches a lease with a tenant and the tenant's unit becomes uninhabitable, which event is the *MOST* likely result?
    a. Suit for possession
    b. Tenancy at sufferance
    c. Constructive eviction
    d. Covenant of quiet enjoyment

96. The rescission provisions of the Truth in Lending Act (Regulation Z) apply to
    a. business financing.
    b. construction lending.
    c. consumer credit.
    d. real estate loans.

97. A house is sold for $84,500 and the commission rate is 7%. If the commission is split 60/40 between the selling broker and the listing broker, respectively, and each broker splits his share of the commission evenly with his salesperson, how much will the listing salesperson receive from this sale?
    a. $1,183
    b. $1,775
    c. $2,366
    d. $3,549

98. A man was given the personal right to cut through a woman's yard to reach the beach and has used this right throughout his life. Before the man dies, he sells this easement to his nephew. What type of interest does the nephew have in the woman's property?
    a. No interest
    b. Easement in gross
    c. Appurtenant easement
    d. Dominant estate

99. Fannie Mae and Ginnie Mae are both
    a. involved as primary market lenders.
    b. involved in the secondary market.
    c. federal agencies.
    d. privately owned entities.

100. A young college graduate is applying for a mortgage loan in order to buy a condominium unit. While in college, she was consistently late making credit card and car payments. She also tended to run over the credit limits on two credit cards and was frequently charged penalty fees. She is now starting a new job at an annual salary of $80,000, with good chances for future advancement. Her parents have agreed to provide a $20,000 down payment on the property. The lender is offering a 15-year loan at 8% with 20% down payment. This is an example of a
    a. predatory loan.
    b. subprime loan.
    c. low-doc loan.
    d. FICO loan.

Glossary

abstract of title The condensed history of a title to a particular parcel of real estate, consisting of a summary of the original grant and all subsequent conveyances and encumbrances affecting the property and a certification by the abstractor that the history is complete and accurate.

acceleration clause The clause in a mortgage or deed of trust that can be enforced to make the entire debt due immediately if the borrower defaults on an installment payment or other covenant.

accession Acquiring title to additions or improvements to real property as a result of the annexation of fixtures or the accretion of alluvial deposits along the banks of streams.

accretion The increase or addition of land by the deposit of sand or soil washed up naturally from a river, lake, or sea.

accrued items On a closing statement, items of expense incurred, but not yet payable, such as interest on a mortgage loan or taxes on real property.

acknowledgment A formal declaration made before a duly authorized officer, usually a notary public, by a person who has signed a document.

actual damages Monetary loss that can be documented by the nonbreaching party to a contract.

actual eviction The legal process that results in the tenant's being physically removed from the leased premises.

actual notice Express information or fact; that which is known; direct knowledge.

addendum A document that was not part of the original contract that may contain additional terms for the contract; also called a rider.

adjustable-rate mortgage (ARM) A loan characterized by a fluctuating interest rate, usually one tied to a bank or savings association cost-of-funds index.

adjusted basis *See* basis.

adjusted sales price Sales price after costs of sale are deducted.

adjustment period The period of time that the interest rate remains constant on an adjustable-rate mortgage; rate may go up or down with each adjustment period.

administrator Person appointed to settle estate of someone who dies intestate.

ad valorem Latin phrase meaning "to the value."

ad valorem tax A tax levied according to value, generally used to refer to real estate tax. Also called the *general tax*.

adverse possession The actual, open, notorious, hostile, and continuous possession of another's land under a claim of title. Possession for a statutory period may be a means of acquiring title.

affidavit of title A written statement, made under oath by sellers or grantors of real property and acknowledged by a notary public, in which the grantors (1) identify themselves and indicate marital status, (2) certify that since the examination of the title on the date of the contracts no defects have occurred in the title, and (3) certify that they are in possession of the property (if applicable).

agency The relationship between a principal and an agent, usually a property owner and a real estate broker.

agency coupled with an interest   An agency relationship in which the agent is given an estate or interest in the subject of the agency (the property).

agent   One who acts or has the power to act for another. A fiduciary relationship is created under the law of agency when a property owner, as the principal, executes a listing agreement or management contract authorizing a real estate broker to be the agent.

agricultural   A category of real estate that includes farms, timberland, ranches, and orchards.

air lot   A designated airspace over a piece of land. An air lot, like surface property, may be transferred.

air rights   The right to use the open space above a property, usually allowing the surface to be used for another purpose.

alienation   The act of transferring property to another. Alienation may be voluntary, such as by gift or sale, or involuntary, as through eminent domain or adverse possession.

alienation clause   The clause in a mortgage or deed of trust stating that the balance of the secured debt becomes immediately due and payable at the lender's option if the property is sold by the borrower. In effect, this clause prevents the borrower from assigning the debt without the lender's approval.

allodial system   A system of land ownership in which land is held free and clear of any rent or service due to the government; commonly contrasted to the feudal system. Land is held under the allodial system in the United States.

amendment   A change to the original contract.

American Land Title Association (ALTA) policy   A title insurance policy that protects the interest in a collateral property of a mortgage lender who originates a new real estate loan.

Americans with Disabilities Act (ADA)   A federal law that prohibits illegal discrimination against someone with a disability in employment, access to state and local governmental offices, telecommunications, and transportation.

amortized loan   A loan in which the principal as well as the interest is payable in monthly or other periodic installments over the term of the loan.

annual percentage rate (APR)   Discloses total amount being received by lender; interest, points, and other fees.

anticipation   The appraisal principle holding that value can increase or decrease, based on the expectation of some future benefit or detriment produced by the property.

antitrust laws   Laws designed to preserve the free enterprise of the open marketplace by making illegal certain private conspiracies and combinations formed to minimize competition. Most violations of antitrust laws in the real estate business involve either price-fixing (brokers conspiring to set fixed compensation rates) or allocation of customers or markets (brokers agreeing to limit their areas of trade or dealing to certain areas or properties).

appraisal   An estimate of the quantity, quality, or value of something. The process through which conclusions of property value are obtained; also refers to the report that sets forth the process of estimation and conclusion of value.

appreciation   An increase in the worth or value of a property due to economic or related causes, which may prove to be either temporary or permanent; opposite of depreciation.

appropriation   An action taken by a taxing body that authorizes the expenditure of funds and provides for the sources of money. Appropriation generally involves the adoption of an ordinance or the passage of a law setting forth the specifics of the proposed taxation.

appurtenant   Appended or annexed to something.

area   The space inside a two-dimensional shape; area equals length times width.

asbestos   A mineral once used in insulation and other products that can cause respiratory diseases.

assemblage   The combining of two or more adjoining lots into one larger tract to increase their total value.

assignment   The transfer in writing of interest in a bond, mortgage, lease, or other instrument.

assumption of mortgage   Acquiring title to property on which there is an existing mortgage and agreeing to be personally liable for the terms and conditions of the mortgage, including payments.

attachment   The act of taking a person's property into legal custody by writ or other judicial order to hold it available for application to that person's debt to a creditor.

attorney-in-fact   A person who performs one or more acts for another person according to the authority granted to them in a document called a power of attorney.

attorney's opinion of title   An abstract of title that an attorney has examined and certified to be, in the attorney's opinion, an accurate statement of the facts concerning the property's ownership.

automatic extension A clause in a listing agreement stating that the agreement will continue automatically for a certain period of time after its expiration date. In many states, use of this clause is discouraged or prohibited.

avulsion The sudden tearing away of land, as by earthquake, flood, volcanic action, or the sudden change in the course of a stream.

balance The appraisal principle stating that the greatest value in a property will occur when the type and size of the improvements are proportional to each other, as well as the land.

balloon payment A final payment of a mortgage loan that is considerably larger than the required periodic payments because the loan amount was not fully amortized.

banker's year Statutory year that contains 12 months, with 30 days in each month; total number of days in a banker's year is 360 days.

bargain and sale deed A deed that carries with it no warranties against liens or other encumbrances but does imply that the grantor has the right to convey title. The grantor may add warranties to the deed at the grantor's discretion.

base line The main imaginary line running east and west and crossing a principal meridian at a definite point, used by surveyors for reference in locating and describing land under the rectangular (government) survey system of legal description.

basis The financial interest that the Internal Revenue Service attributes to an owner of an investment property for the purpose of determining annual depreciation and gain or loss on the sale of the asset. If a property was acquired by purchase, the owner's basis is the cost of the property plus the value of any capital expenditures for improvements to the property, minus any depreciation allowable or actually taken. This new basis is called the *adjusted basis*.

benchmark A permanent reference mark or point established for use by surveyors in measuring differences in elevation.

beneficiary (1) The person for whom a trust operates or in whose behalf the income from a trust estate is drawn; (2) a lender in a deed of trust loan transaction.

bilateral contract *See* contract.

binder Used to bind parties until a formal contract can be prepared.

blanket loan A mortgage covering more than one parcel of real estate, providing for each parcel's partial release from the mortgage lien upon repayment of a definite portion of the debt.

blockbusting The illegal practice of inducing homeowners to sell their properties by making representations regarding the entry or prospective entry of persons of a particular race or national origin into the neighborhood.

blue-sky laws Common name for those state and federal laws that regulate the registration and sale of investment securities.

boot Money or property given to make up any difference in value or equity between two properties in an exchange.

branch office A secondary place of business apart from the principal or main office from which real estate business is conducted. A branch office usually must be run by a licensed real estate broker working on behalf of the broker who operates the principal office.

breach of contract Violation of any terms or conditions in a contract without legal excuse (for example, failure to make a payment when it is due).

broker One who acts as an intermediary on behalf of others for a fee or commission.

broker's price opinion (BPO) An estimate of value, prepared by a real estate licensee, most often requested by a lender to determine that the property actually exists; a BPO is not an appraisal, which may only be done by an appraiser.

brokerage The bringing together of parties interested in making a real estate transaction.

brokerage agreements A written agreement between a brokerage firm and a consumer that defines exclusivity and payment of fees; examples include the listing agreement between a broker and a seller, a buyer agency representation agreement between broker and buyer, and a management agreement between broker and landlord.

brownfields A site that may or may not be contaminated with toxic contamination; often located in urban areas.

buffer zone A strip of land, usually used as a park or designated for a similar use, separating land dedicated to one use from land dedicated to another use (e.g., residential from commercial).

builder One who actually builds improvements on land.

building code   An ordinance that specifies minimum standards of construction for buildings to protect public safety and health.

building permit   Written governmental permission for the construction, alteration, or demolition of an improvement that shows compliance with building codes and zoning ordinances.

bulk transfer   *See* Uniform Commercial Code.

bundle of legal rights   The concept of land ownership that includes ownership of all legal rights to the land (for example, possession, control within the law, and enjoyment).

buydown   A financing technique used to reduce the monthly payments for the first few years of a loan. Funds in the form of discount points are given to the lender by the builder or seller to buy down, or lower, the effective interest rate paid by the buyer, thus reducing the monthly payments for a set time.

buyer agency agreement   A contract between a buyer (as principal) and a real estate broker (as agent) by which the broker is employed by the buyer to find a property for the buyer, on the buyer's terms, for which service the buyer agrees to pay the broker compensation. Under this agreement, the broker represents the buyer, with fiduciary responsibilities to the buyer.

buyer-broker   A broker who has entered into a buyer agency agreement with a buyer.

buyer's market   An economic condition occurring when the supply of a good exceeds the demand, resulting in a decrease in price.

caisson   Foundation supports for a building.

calendar year   The 365-day year with 12 months and 28 to 31 days in each month.

capital gain   The taxable profit derived from the sale of a capital asset. It is the difference between the sales price and the basis of the property after making adjustments for closing costs, capital improvements, and allowable depreciation.

capitalization   A mathematical process for estimating the value of a property using a proper rate of return on the investment and the annual net income expected to be produced by the property. The formula is income ÷ rate = value.

capitalization rate   The rate of return a property will produce on the owner's investment.

carbon monoxide (CO)   A colorless and odorless gas that occurs as a byproduct of burning certain types of fuels. CO poses a significant health hazard if not properly ventilated.

cash flow   The net spendable income from an investment, determined by deducting all operating and fixed expenses from the gross income. If expenses exceed income, a negative cash flow is the result.

cash rent   In an agricultural lease, the amount of money given as rent to the landowner at the outset of the lease, as opposed to sharecropping.

caveat emptor   A Latin phrase meaning "let the buyer beware."

certificate of eligibility   Document showing the amount that the government will guarantee for a veteran.

certificate of reasonable value   An opinion of value made by a VA appraiser establishing amount of mortgage loan that can be obtained.

certificate of occupancy   Granted by government agency when property determined to be in compliance with building codes and ready for occupancy.

certificate of sale   The document generally given to the purchaser at a tax foreclosure sale. A certificate of sale does not convey title; normally, it is an instrument certifying that the holder received title to the property after the redemption period passed and that the holder paid the property taxes for that interim period.

certificate of title   A statement of opinion on the status of the title to a parcel of real property based on an examination of specified public records.

chain of title   The succession of conveyances, from some accepted starting point, whereby the present holder of real property derives title.

change   The appraisal principle that holds that no physical or economic condition remains constant.

chattel   *See* personal property.

Civil Rights Act of 1866   The first civil rights act passed in the United States, this law prohibits any type of discrimination based on race. The constitutionality of this law was upheld by the Supreme Court in 1968 when it rendered its decision in the case of *Jones v. Mayer Company*.

closing statement   A detailed cash accounting of a real estate transaction showing all cash received, all charges and credits made, and all cash paid out in the transaction.

cloud on title   Any document, claim, unreleased lien, or encumbrance that may impair the title to real property or make the title doubtful; usually revealed by a title search and removed by either a quitclaim deed or suit to quiet title.

clustering The grouping of homesites within a subdivision on smaller lots than normal, with the remaining land used as common areas.

codicil A supplement or an addition to a will, executed with the same formalities as a will, that normally does not revoke the entire will.

coinsurance clause A clause in insurance policies covering real property that requires the policyholder to maintain fire insurance coverage generally equal to at least 80% of the property's actual replacement cost.

commercial A category of business real estate that includes office space, shopping centers, stores, theaters, hotels, and parking facilities.

commercial banks Institutional lenders with the following lending characteristics: small loans for short terms, such as construction, home improvement, and mobile-home loans; relatively low loan-to-value ratios; regulated by the Federal Reserve Banking System; and deposits insured by the Federal Deposit Insurance Corporation (FDIC).

commingling The illegal act by a real estate broker of placing client or customer funds with personal funds. By law, brokers are required to maintain a separate trust account for other parties' funds held temporarily by the broker.

commission Payment to a broker for services rendered, such as in the sale or purchase of real property; usually a percentage of the selling price of the property.

common elements Parts of a property that are necessary or convenient to the existence, maintenance, and safety of a condominium or are normally in common use by all of the condominium residents. Each condominium owner has an undivided ownership interest in the common elements.

common law The body of law based on custom, usage, and court decisions.

Community Reinvestment Act (CRA) A law passed to ensure that banks meet the lending needs in communities where they are located and to prevent redlining.

community property A system of property ownership based on the theory that each spouse has an equal interest in the property acquired by the efforts of either spouse during marriage. A holdover of Spanish law, found predominantly in western states, this system was unknown under English common law.

comparables Properties used in an appraisal report that are substantially equivalent to the subject property.

competition The appraisal principle that states that excess profits generate competition.

comparative market analysis (CMA) A comparison of the prices of recently sold homes that are similar to a listing seller's home in terms of location, style, and amenities.

Comprehensive Environmental Response, Compensation, and Liability Act (CERCLA) A law establishing a Superfund to clean up hazardous waste sites and to collect the costs from certain defined responsible persons associated with the sites.

condemnation A judicial or administrative proceeding to exercise the power of eminent domain, through which a government agency takes private property for public use and compensates the owner.

conditional-use permit Written governmental permission allowing a use inconsistent with zoning but necessary for the common good, such as locating an emergency medical facility in a predominantly residential area.

condominium The absolute ownership of a unit in a multiunit building based on a legal description of the airspace the unit actually occupies, plus an undivided interest in the ownership of the common elements that are owned jointly with the other condominium unit owners.

conforming loan A loan that conforms to the Fannie Mae/Freddie Mac guidelines.

conformity The appraisal principle holding that the greater the similarity among properties in an area, the better they will hold their value.

consideration (1) That received by the grantor in exchange for the deed; (2) something of value that induces a person to enter into a contract.

Consumer Financial Protection Act (Title X) A section of the Dodd-Frank Wall Street Reform and Consumer Protection Act that created the Bureau of Consumer Financial Protection to regulate consumer financial products and services.

Consumer Financial Protection Bureau (CFPB) Created by the Dodd-Frank Wall Street Reform and Consumer Protection Act and regulates loan underwriting and mortgage originators.

construction loan A short-term loan usually made during the construction phase of a building project.

constructive eviction Actions of a landlord that so materially disturb or impair a tenant's enjoyment of the leased premises that the tenant is effectively forced to move out and terminate the lease without liability for any further rent.

constructive notice Notice given to the world by recorded documents. All people are charged with knowledge of such documents and their contents, whether or not they have actually examined them.

contingency A provision in a contract that requires a certain act to be done or a certain event to occur before the contract becomes binding.

continuing education Required in most states for real estate license renewal.

contract A legally enforceable promise or set of promises that must be performed and for which, if a breach of the promise occurs, the law provides a remedy. A contract may be either unilateral, by which only one party is bound to act, or bilateral, by which all parties to the instrument are legally bound to act as prescribed.

contract rent The amount of rent the tenant must pay the landlord for the use of the leased premises as specified in the lease contract.

contribution The appraisal principle that states that the value of any component of a property is what it gives to the value of the whole or what its absence detracts from that value.

conventional loan A loan that is not insured or guaranteed by a government source.

conversion The illegal act of a broker misusing or misappropriating trust funds.

cooperating broker *See* listing broker.

cooperative A residential multi-unit building in which title is held by a trust or corporation that is owned by and operated for the benefit of persons living within the building, who are the beneficial owners of the trust or stockholders of the corporation, each possessing a proprietary lease.

co-ownership When title to one parcel of real estate is owned by two or more persons or organizations, such persons or organizations are said to be co-owners, or concurrent owners, of the property.

corporation An entity or organization, created by operation of law, whose rights of doing business are essentially the same as those of an individual. The entity has continuous existence until it is dissolved according to legal procedures.

correction lines Provisions in the rectangular survey (government survey) system made to compensate for the curvature of the earth's surface. Every fourth township line (at 24-mile intervals) is used as a correction line on which the intervals between the north and south range lines are remeasured and corrected to a full six miles.

cost approach The process of estimating the value of a property by adding to the estimated land value the appraiser's estimate of the reproduction or replacement cost of the building, less depreciation.

cost recovery An Internal Revenue Service term for depreciation.

counteroffer A new offer made as a reply to an offer received. It has the effect of rejecting the original offer, which cannot be accepted thereafter unless revived by the offeror.

covenant A written agreement between two or more parties in which a party or parties pledge to perform or not perform specified acts with regard to property; usually found in such real estate documents as deeds, mortgages, leases, and contracts for deed.

covenant of quiet enjoyment The covenant implied by law by which a landlord guarantees that a tenant may take possession of leased premises and that the landlord will not interfere in the tenant's possession or use of the property.

covenants, conditions, and restrictions (CC&Rs) Private restrictions on use of real property found in a subdivision or condominium project.

credit On a closing statement, an amount entered in a person's favor—either an amount the party has paid or an amount for which the party must be reimbursed.

creditor One extending credit.

credit union Cooperative organization where members deposit savings and obtain loans; recent entry into mortgage financing.

curtesy A life estate, usually a fractional interest, given by some states to the surviving husband in real estate owned by his deceased wife.

damages Money that is paid to the nonbreaching party to a contract in compensation for a loss, see also actual, nominal and punitive damages.

datum A horizontal plane from which heights and depths are measured.

debit On a closing statement, an amount charged; that is, an amount that the debited party must pay.

decedent A person who has died.

decimal Part of the whole expressed as a power of 10 (e.g., 0.20 is the same as ²⁄10).

dedication The voluntary transfer of private property by its owner to the public for some public use, such as for streets or schools.

deed A written instrument that, when executed and delivered, conveys title to or an interest in real estate.

deed in lieu of foreclosure Lender accepts the deed rather than foreclosing on property.

deed in trust An instrument that grants a trustee under a land trust full power to sell, mortgage, and subdivide a parcel of real estate. The beneficiary controls the trustee's use of these powers under the provisions of the trust agreement.

deed of reconveyance Conveys all interests in a property from the trustee to the borrower when debt is paid; used with deed of trust.

deed of trust *See* trust deed.

deed of trust lien *See* trust deed lien.

deed restriction Clause in a deed limiting the future uses of the property. Deed restrictions may impose a vast variety of limitations and conditions—for example, they may limit the density of buildings, dictate the types of structures that can be erected, or prevent buildings from being used for specific purposes or even from being used at all.

default The nonperformance of a duty, whether arising under a contract or otherwise; failure to meet an obligation when due.

defeasance clause A clause used in leases and mortgages that cancels a specified right upon the occurrence of a certain condition, such as cancellation of a mortgage upon repayment of the mortgage loan.

defeasible fee estate *See* fee estate defeasible.

deficiency judgment A personal judgment levied against the borrower when a foreclosure sale does not produce sufficient funds to pay the mortgage debt in full.

delivery and acceptance Required before a sales contract is ratified.

demand The amount of goods people are willing and able to buy at a given price; often coupled with supply.

demographics Refers to the characteristics of a population, such as age and economic status.

denial, suspension, or revocation of license The potential penalties for licensees who violate real estate statutes or rules and regulations.

density zoning Zoning ordinances that restrict the maximum average number of houses per acre that may be built within a particular area, generally a subdivision.

Department of Housing and Urban Development (HUD) Federal agency active in national housing programs—HUD has jurisdiction over the Federal Housing Administration (FHA), Ginnie Mae, and Interstate Land Sales Registration; oversees Fannie Mae and Freddie Mac; administers Community Block Grant program, Housing Voucher Program (formerly Section 8), and Indian Housing; is also active in urban renewal and public housing. Responsible for enforcing regulations of the Federal Fair Housing Act and the Real Estate Settlement Procedures Act.

depreciation (1) In appraisal, a loss of value in property due to any cause, including physical deterioration, functional obsolescence, and external obsolescence; (2) in real estate investment, an expense deduction for tax purposes taken over the period of ownership of income property.

descent Acquisition of an estate by inheritance in which an heir succeeds to the property by operation of law.

designated agency When a brokerage represents both parties equally in a transaction by the broker appointing a seller agent and a separate buyer agent.

developer One who attempts to put land to its most profitable use through the construction of improvements.

devise A gift of real property by will. The donor is the devisor, and the recipient is the devisee.

disability A long-lasting physical, emotional, or mental impairment that renders a person unable to engage in or is limited in normal day-to-day activities, such as walking, climbing stairs, dressing, bathing, and learning.

disclosed dual agent An agent who has received the informed, written consent of a buyer and seller to represent both parties to a transaction.

discount point A unit of measurement used for various loan charges; one point equals 1% of the amount of the loan.

discount rate The rate the Federal Reserve charges its member banks.

Dodd-Frank Wall Street Reform and Consumer Protection Act A federal law enacted in 2010 that significantly changed financial regulation. Title X created the Bureau of Consumer Financial Protection to regulate consumer financial products and services. Title XIV focuses on underwriting and mortgage originators.

dominant estate A property that includes in its ownership the appurtenant right to use an easement over another person's property for a specific purpose; also called dominant tenement.

dower The legal right or interest, recognized in some states, that a wife acquires in the property her husband held or acquired during their marriage. During the husband's lifetime the right is only a possibility of an interest; upon his death, it can become an interest in land.

draw The periodic advancing of funds on a construction loan; also, the advancing of funds toward future commissions.

dual agency Representing both parties to a transaction. This is unethical, unless both parties agree to it, and it is illegal in many states. *See* disclosed dual agent.

duress Unlawful constraint or action exercised upon a person whereby that person is forced to perform an act against the person's will. A contract entered into under duress is voidable.

earnest money Money deposited by a buyer under the terms of a contract; forfeited if the buyer defaults but applied to the purchase price if the sale is closed.

easement A right to use the land of another for a specific purpose, such as for a right-of-way or utilities; an incorporeal interest in land.

easement appurtenant An easement that is annexed to the ownership and used for the benefit of another's land.

easement by necessity An easement allowed by law as necessary for the full enjoyment of a parcel of real estate; for example, a right of ingress and egress over a grantor's land.

easement by prescription An easement acquired by continuous, open, and hostile use of the property for the period of time prescribed by state law.

easement in gross An easement that is not created for the benefit of any land owned by the owner of the easement, but that attaches personally to the easement owner. For example, a right granted by a woman to a man to use a portion of her property for the rest of his life is an easement in gross.

economic life The number of years during which an improvement will add value to the land.

economic rent The amount of rent the property would command in a fully informed competitive marketplace; the going market rate for rental space.

effective gross income Gross income minus percentage for vacancies.

elective share Replaces dower and curtesy rights in some states.

electromagnetic fields (EMFs) Fields generated by the movement of electrical currents, created by both the use of electrical appliances and transmission lines.

electronic signatures The data equivalent of an actual signature; method must meet certain requirements established by the Uniform Electronics Transactions Act (UETA) and/or the federal E-Sign Act of 2000.

Electronic Signatures in Global and National Commerce Act Allows for the sale or lease of property to be conducted electronically, treating electronic signatures the same as those signed by pen.

emblements Growing crops, such as grapes and corn, that are produced annually through labor and industry; also called fructus industriales.

eminent domain The right of a government or municipal quasi-public body to acquire property for public use through a court action called condemnation, in which the court decides that the use is a public use and determines the compensation to be paid to the owner.

employee Someone who works as a direct employee of an employer and has employee status. The employer is obligated to withhold income taxes and Social Security taxes from the compensation of employees. *See* also independent contractor.

employment contract A document evidencing formal employment between employer and employee or between principal and agent. In the real estate business, this generally takes the form of a listing agreement or management agreement.

enabling acts State legislation that confers zoning powers on municipal governments.

encapsulation A method of controlling environmental contamination by sealing off a dangerous substance.

encroachment A building or some portion of it (for example, a wall or fence) that extends beyond the land of the owner and illegally intrudes on some land of an adjoining owner or a street or alley.

encumbrance Anything—such as a mortgage, tax, or judgment lien; an easement; a restriction on the use of the land, or an outstanding dower right—that may diminish the value of a property.

environmental impact statement Detailed description of a proposed development project with emphasis on the environmental effect of building.

environmental site assessment A report ordered by a potential buyer to determine if the property has any contamination; often called due diligence.

Equal Credit Opportunity Act (ECOA) The federal law that prohibits discrimination in the extension of credit because of race, color, religion, national origin, sex, age, or marital status.

equalization The raising or lowering of assessed values for tax purposes in a particular county or taxing district to make them equal to assessments in other counties or districts.

equalization factor A factor (number) by which the assessed value of a property is multiplied to arrive at a value for the property that is in line with statewide tax assessments. The ad valorem tax is based on this adjusted value.

equitable lien *See* statutory lien.

equitable right of redemption The right of a defaulted property owner to recover the property prior to its sale by paying the appropriate fees and charges.

equitable title The interest held by a vendee under a contract for deed or an installment contract; the equitable right to obtain absolute ownership to property when legal title is held in another's name.

equity The difference between fair market value and indebtedness; equity builds with mortgage payments and appreciation of value.

erosion The gradual wearing away of land by water, wind, and general weather conditions; the diminishing of property by the elements.

errors and omissions (E&O) insurance Errors and omissions insurance carried by real estate brokers.

escheat The reversion of property to the state or county, as provided by state law, in cases where a decedent dies intestate without heirs capable of inheriting or when the property is abandoned.

escrow account *See* impound account.

escrow closing The closing of a transaction through a third party, called an escrow agent or escrowee, who receives certain funds and documents to be delivered upon the performance of certain conditions outlined in the escrow instructions.

escrow instructions A document that sets forth the duties of the escrow agent, as well as the requirements and obligations of the parties, when a transaction is closed through an escrow.

E-Sign Act of 2000 A federal law passed to facilitate the use of electronic records and signatures in interstate and foreign commerce; businesses are required to make certain disclosures to consumers, including signing alternatives.

estate at sufferance The tenancy of a lessee who lawfully comes into possession of a landlord's real estate but who continues to occupy the premises improperly after lease rights have expired.

estate at will An estate that gives the lessee the right to possession until the estate is terminated by either party; the term of this estate is indefinite.

estate for years An interest for a certain, exact period of time in property leased for a specified consideration.

estate from period to period An interest in leased property that continues from period to period— week to week, month to month, or year to year.

estate in land The degree, quantity, nature, and extent of interest a person has in real property.

estate taxes Federal taxes on a decedent's real and personal property.

estoppel Method of creating an agency relationship in which someone states incorrectly that another person is the agent and a third person relies on that representation.

estoppel certificate A document in which a borrower certifies the amount owed on a mortgage loan and the rate of interest.

eviction A legal process to oust a person from possession of real estate.

evidence of title Proof of ownership of property; commonly a certificate of title, an abstract of title with lawyer's opinion, or a Torrens registration certificate.

exchange A transaction in which all or part of the consideration is the transfer of like-kind property (such as real estate for real estate).

exclusive-agency listing A listing contract under which the owner appoints a real estate broker as an exclusive agent for a designated period of time to sell the property, on the owner's stated terms, for a commission. The owner reserves the right to sell without paying anyone a commission if the owner sells to a prospect who has not been introduced or claimed by the broker.

exclusive-right-to-sell listing A listing contract under which the owner appoints a real estate broker as an exclusive agent for a designated period of time to sell the property, on the owner's stated terms, and agrees to pay the broker a commission when the property is sold, whether by the broker, the owner, or another broker.

exculpatory clause A clause that exculpates or excuses a landlord from liability to a tenant for negligence in maintaining leased property.

executed contract A contract in which all parties have fulfilled their promises and thus performed the contract.

execution The signing and delivery of an instrument. Also, a legal order directing an official to enforce a judgment against the property of a debtor.

executor An individual named in a will to oversee the administration and distribution of the estate of a person dying testate.

executory contract A contract under which something remains to be done by one or more of the parties.

express agreement An oral or written contract in which the parties state the contract's terms and express their intentions in words.

expressed contract *See* express agreement.

external obsolescence Reduction in a property's value caused by outside factors (those that are off the property). Also called economic obsolescence.

Fair Credit Reporting Act A law passed to regulate the action of credit bureaus and consumer credit information. It protects consumers from the reporting and use of inaccurate or obsolete credit information. A lender who rejects a loan request because of adverse credit bureau information must inform the borrower of the source of the information.

Fair Housing Act of 1968 Provides that it is unlawful to discriminate on the basis of race, color, religion, sex, or national origin when selling or leasing residential property.

Fair Housing Amendments Act of 1988 Added mental or physical disability and familial status to the federal Fair Housing Act of 1968's list of protected classes.

familial status Fair housing protected class prohibiting discrimination towards children.

Fannie Mae Originally chartered as the Federal National Mortgage Association to purchase FHA and VA loans; as a government-sponsored enterprise (GSE), it purchases both conventional and government loans.

Federal Deposit Insurance Corporation (FDIC) Insures deposits in banks and savings associations.

Federal Emergency Management Association (FEMA) Designates flood zones requiring flood insurance.

Federal Home Loan Bank (FHLB) Supervises savings associations.

Federal Housing Finance Agency (FHFA) Supervises and regulates Fannie Mae, Freddie Mac, and Federal Home Loan Banks.

Federal Reserve System (the Fed) The central banking system of the United States that is responsible for the nation's monetary policy and regulates interest rates and the supply of money.

fee simple absolute The maximum possible estate or right of ownership of real property, continuing forever.

fee simple defeasible An estate that is subject to some condition to determine when it will begin or end.

fee simple determinable An estate that is subject to a special limitation; if the limitation is violated, the original grantor automatically reacquires full ownership.

fee simple subject to a condition subsequent An estate that is in effect as long as a specified condition is satisfied.

fee tail An estate in land in which the right of inheritance is limited to the fee tail tenant's blood descendants, called heirs or issue "of the body."

FHA-insured loan A loan insured by the Federal Housing Administration and made by an approved lender in accordance with the FHA's regulations.

fiduciary One in whom trust and confidence is placed; usually a reference to a broker employed under the terms of a listing contract.

fiduciary relationship A relationship of trust and confidence, as between trustee and beneficiary, attorney and client, or principal and agent.

Financial Institutions Reform, Recovery and Enforcement Act (FIRREA) Provides guidelines for regulation of savings associations (thrifts) and established the Office of Thrift Supervision.

financing statement *See* Uniform Commercial Code.

fixture An item of personal property that has been converted to real property by being permanently affixed to the realty.

flood insurance Required for any property located in a designated FEMA flood zone.

foreclosure A legal procedure whereby property used as security for a debt is sold to satisfy the debt in the event of default in payment of the mortgage note or default of other terms in the mortgage document. The foreclosure procedure brings the rights of all parties to a conclusion and passes the title in the mortgaged property to either the holder of the mortgage or a third party who may purchase the realty at the foreclosure sale, free of all encumbrances affecting the property subsequent to the mortgage.

forfeiture Giving up of a right or financial amount.

four unities of ownership The four unities that are traditionally needed to create a joint tenancy: unity of title, time, interest, and possession.

fraction Part of a whole expressed as a numerator and denominator (e.g., ½).

fractional section A parcel of land less than 160 acres, usually found at the edge of a rectangular survey.

franchise A private contractual agreement to run a business using a designated trade name and operating procedures.

fraud Deception intended to cause a person to give up property or a lawful right.

Freddie Mac Originally the Federal Home Loan Mortgage Corporation established to purchase conventional mortgage loans on the secondary mortgage market. Called a government-sponsored enterprise (GSE); purchases conventional and government loans.

freehold estate An estate in land in which ownership is for an indeterminate length of time, in contrast to a leasehold estate.

front foot Lot line facing the street; measurement often used for special assessments.

functional obsolescence A loss of value to an improvement to real estate arising from functional problems, often caused by age or poor design.

future interest A person's present right to an interest in real property that will not result in possession or enjoyment until sometime in the future, such as a reversion or right of reentry.

gap A defect in the chain of title of a particular parcel of real estate; a missing document or conveyance that raises doubt as to the present ownership of the land.

general agent One who is authorized by a principal to represent the principal in a specific range of matters.

general lien The right of a creditor to have all of a debtor's property—both real and personal—sold to satisfy a debt.

general partnership *See* partnership.

general warranty deed A deed in which the grantor fully warrants good clear title to the premises. Used in most real estate deed transfers, a general warranty deed offers the greatest protection of any deed.

Ginnie Mae The Government National Mortgage Association; administers special housing finance programs; insures Fannie Mae securities backed by FHA and VA loans.

Good Faith Estimate (GFE) Estimate of all costs of closing on both title and loan; Real Estate Settlement Procedures Act (RESPA) requires delivery to borrower within three days of application.

government check The 24-mile-square parcels composed of 16 townships in the rectangular (government) survey system of legal description.

government lot Fractional sections in the rectangular (government) survey system that are less than one quarter-section in area.

government-sponsored enterprise (GSE) Government retains supervisory role; allows tax benefits.

government survey system *See* rectangular (government) survey system.

graduated lease A lease that allows for increases or decreases in the amount of rent being paid during the lease term, or any renewal of that term. Graduated leases are normally either step-up leases, allowing for previously agreed-upon increases in the amount of rent being paid (for example, increases of 10% annually), or index leases, which allow rent increases or decreases periodically based on changes in some designated index, (for example, the cost-of-living or consumer price index). Both provide the landlord with a hedge against inflation, but the index lease with its floating provision is considered to provide the best hedge against increasing costs for the landlord.

graduated-payment mortgage (GPM) A loan in which the monthly principal and interest payments increase by a certain percentage each year for a certain number of years and then level off for the remaining loan term.

grandfather clause Permission for a building that was built prior to prohibitive zoning ordinances.

grant deed Deed of conveyance used primarily in western states. They contain no expressed warranties, but the grantors are obligated by implied warranties established by state law.

grantee A person who receives a conveyance of real property from a grantor.

granting clause Words in a deed of conveyance that state the grantor's intention to convey the property at the present time. This clause is generally worded as *convey and warrant*; *grant*; *grant, bargain, and sell*; or the like.

grantor The person transferring title to or an interest in real property to a grantee.

gross income multiplier (GIM) A figure used as a multiplier of the gross annual income of a property to produce an estimate of the property's value.

gross lease A lease of property according to which a landlord pays all property charges regularly incurred through ownership, such as repairs, taxes, insurance, and operating expenses. Most residential leases are gross leases.

gross rent multiplier (GRM) The figure used as a multiplier of the gross monthly income of a property to produce an estimate of the property's value.

ground lease A lease of land only, on which the tenant usually owns a building or is required to build as specified in the lease. Such leases are usually long-term net leases; the tenant's rights and obligations continue until the lease expires or is terminated through default.

growing-equity mortgage (GEM) A loan in which the monthly payments increase annually, with the increased amount being used to directly reduce the outstanding principal balance and thus shorten the overall term of the loan.

habendum clause That part of a deed beginning with the words *to have and to hold*, following the granting clause and defining the extent of ownership the grantor is conveying.

heir One who might inherit or succeed to an interest in land under the state law of descent when the owner dies without leaving a valid will.

highest and best use The possible use of a property that would produce the greatest net income and thereby develop the highest value.

holdover tenancy A tenancy whereby a lessee retains possession of leased property after the lease has expired and the landlord, by continuing to accept rent, agrees to the tenant's continued occupancy as defined by state law.

holographic will A will that is written, dated, and signed in the testator's handwriting with no witnesses.

Home Affordable Modification Program (HAMP) A government program to help homeowners avoid foreclosure by making monthly payments more affordable.

home equity loan A loan (sometimes called a line of credit) under which property owners use their residence as collateral and can then draw funds up to a prearranged amount against the property.

homeowners insurance policy A standardized package insurance policy that covers a residential real estate owner against financial loss from fire, theft, public liability, and other common risks.

homestead Land that is owned and occupied as the family home. In many states, a portion of the area or value of this land is protected or exempt from judgments for debts.

Housing and Community Development Act of 1974 Added sex (gender) as a protected class to the federal Fair Housing Act of 1968.

Housing for Older Persons Act (HOPA) A federal law that made several changes to the requirements for 55 and older for those properties that are exempt from the provisions barring discrimination on the basis of familial status.

hypothecate To pledge property as security for a loan.

implied agreement A contract under which the agreement of the parties is demonstrated by their acts and conduct.

implied contract *See* implied agreement.

impound account Also called escrow account; a lender collects funds from the borrower to pay taxes and insurance when due.

improvement (1) Any structure, usually privately owned, erected on a site to enhance the value of the property—for example, building a fence or a driveway; (2) a publicly owned structure added to or benefiting land, such as a curb, sidewalk, street, or sewer.

income approach The process of estimating the value of an income-producing property by capitalization of the annual net income expected to be produced by the property during its remaining useful life.

income-property insurance Protects the owner of income-producing property against loss.

independent contractor Someone retained to perform a certain act but who is subject to the control and direction of another only as to the end result and not as to the way in which the act is performed. Unlike an employee, an independent contractor pays for all expenses, Social Security, income taxes, and receives no employee benefits. Most real estate salespeople are independent contractors.

index lease A lease that provides for adjustments for rent according to changes in a price index, such as the consumer price index. The index used in establishing the escalation must be reliable and bear a closer relationship to the nature of a tenant's business. The most frequently used indexes are the consumer price index (cost-of-living index) and the wholesale price index.

index method The appraisal method of estimating building costs by multiplying the original cost of the property by a percentage factor to adjust for current construction costs.

industrial A category of real estate that includes warehouses, factories, land in industrial districts, and power plants.

inflation The gradual reduction of the purchasing power of the dollar, usually related directly to the increases in the money supply by the federal government.

inheritance taxes State-imposed taxes on a decedent's real and personal property.

injunction Court order either forbidding or compelling some action.

installment contract A contract for the sale of real estate whereby the purchase price is paid in periodic installments by the purchaser, who is in possession of the property even though title is retained by the seller until a future date, which may not be until final payment. Also called a *land contract*, a *contract for deed*, or *articles of agreement*.

installment sale A transaction in which the sales price is paid in two or more installments over two or more years. If the sale meets certain requirements, a taxpayer can postpone reporting such income until future years by paying tax each year only on the proceeds received that year.

instrument A formal, written legal document, such as a contract, deed, or lease.

interest A charge made by a lender for the use of money.

interim financing A short-term loan usually made during the construction phase of a building project (in this case often called a construction loan).

Interstate Land Sales Full Disclosure Act A consumer protection act that requires those engaged in the interstate sale or leasing of 25 or more unimproved lots to register the details of the land with the U.S. Department of Housing and Urban Development (HUD). The seller is also required to furnish prospective buyers a property report containing all essential information about the property.

intestate The condition of a property owner who dies without leaving a valid will. Title to the property will pass to the decedent's heirs as provided in the state law of descent.

intrinsic value An appraisal term referring to the value created by a person's personal preferences for a particular type of property.

inverse condemnation A legal process by which a property owner seeks to recover damages due to the fact that a government action has reduced the value to the point that the property owner cannot use the property.

investment Money directed toward the purchase, improvement, and development of an asset in expectation of income or profits.

involuntary alienation *See* alienation.

involuntary lien A lien placed on property without the consent of the property owner.

joint tenancy Ownership of real estate between two or more parties who have been named in one conveyance as joint tenants. Upon the death of a joint tenant, the decedent's interest passes to the surviving joint tenant or tenants by the right of survivorship.

joint venture The joining of two or more people to conduct a specific business enterprise. A joint venture is similar to a partnership in that it must be created by agreement between the parties to share in the losses and profits of the venture. It is unlike a partnership in that the venture is for one specific project only rather than for a continuing business relationship.

Jones v. Alfred H. Mayer Company The decision in this 1968 case, based on the 13th Amendment to the U.S. Constitution, has served as a basis for all subsequent civil rights legislation.

judgment The formal decision of a court upon the respective rights and claims of the parties to an action or suit. After a judgment has been entered and recorded with the county recorder, it usually becomes a general lien on the property of the defendant.

judicial foreclosure Foreclosing on property by a court-ordered sale.

junior lien An obligation, such as a second mortgage, that is subordinate in right or lien priority to an existing lien on the same realty.

kickback Payment made when no service is rendered; prohibited by RESPA.

land   The earth's surface, extending downward to the center of the earth and upward infinitely into space, including things permanently attached by nature, such as trees and water.

land trust   A trust in which real estate is the only asset.

landfill   A waste disposal site.

land contract   *See* installment contract.

last will and testament   Instrument used to direct how an estate is to be distributed after the owner's death.

latent defect   Structural defect not readily discovered by inspection.

law of agency   *See* agency.

lead-based paint   Paint containing lead that could present a hazard; restricted from residential use in 1978.

lease   A written or oral contract between a landlord (the lessor) and a tenant (the lessee) that transfers the right to exclusive possession and use of the landlord's real property to the lessee for a specified period of time and for a stated consideration (rent). By state law, leases for longer than a certain period of time (generally one year) must be in writing to be enforceable.

leasehold estate   A tenant's right to occupy real estate during the term of a lease, generally considered to be a personal property interest.

lease option   A lease under which the tenant has the right to purchase the property, either during the lease term or at its end.

lease purchase   A real property purchase that is preceded by a lease, usually long-term, for a period prior to settlement. Typically done for tax or financing purposes.

legacy   A disposition of money or personal property by will.

legal description   A description of a specific parcel of real estate complete enough for an independent surveyor to locate and identify it.

legally competent parties   People who are recognized by law as being able to contract with others; those of legal age and sound mind.

lender's title insurance policy   Required by the lender to protect a lender's interest in the property.

lessee   One to whom property is rented (or leased); usually called the *tenant*.

lessor   One who rents, or leases, property to another; usually called the *landlord*.

leverage   The use of borrowed money to finance the bulk of an investment.

levy   To assess; to seize or collect. To levy a tax is to assess a property and set the rate of taxation. To levy an execution is to officially seize the property of a person in order to satisfy an obligation.

license   (1) A privilege or right granted to a person by a state to operate as a real estate broker or salesperson; (2) the revocable permission for a temporary use of land—a personal right that cannot be sold.

lien   A right given by law to certain creditors to have their debts paid out of the property of a defaulting debtor, usually by means of a court sale.

lien theory   Some states interpret a mortgage as being purely a lien on real property. The mortgagee thus has no right of possession but must foreclose the lien and sell the property if the mortgagor defaults.

life cycle costing   In property management, comparing one type of equipment to another based on both purchase cost and operating cost over its expected useful lifetime.

life estate   An interest in real or personal property that is limited in duration to the lifetime of its owner or some other designated person or persons.

life tenant   A person in possession of a life estate.

like kind   Properties that may be included in a Section 1031 Exchange.

limited liability company (LLC)   A relatively new business entity that combines the liability benefits of corporations with the tax benefits of partnerships while retaining flexible management. LLCs are governed by state law.

limited partnership   *See* partnership.

liquidated damages   An amount predetermined by the parties to a contract as the total compensation to an injured party should the other party breach the contract.

liquidity   The ability to sell an asset and convert it into cash, at a price close to its true value, in a short period of time.

lis pendens   A recorded legal document giving constructive notice that an action affecting a particular property has been filed in either a state or a federal court.

listing agreement   A contract between an owner (as principal) and a real estate broker (as agent), under which the broker is employed as agent to find a buyer for the owner's real estate on the owner's terms, for which service the owner agrees to pay a commission.

listing broker   The broker in a multiple-listing situation from whose office a listing agreement is initiated, as opposed to the cooperating broker, from whose office negotiations leading up to a sale are initiated. The listing broker and the cooperating broker may be the same person.

littoral rights (1) A landowner's claim to use water in large navigable lakes and oceans adjacent to the landowner's property; (2) the ownership rights to land bordering these bodies of water up to the high-water mark.

loan origination fee A fee charged by lenders to cover the expense in generating a loan. Loan origination fees vary in amount and are usually figured in points (with 1 point equal to 1% of the loan amount).

loan servicing The act of collecting loan payments and making appropriate payments, such as paying real estate taxes and hazard insurance, on behalf of the holder of the mortgage note.

loan-to-value ratio (LTV) The ratio of debt to value; lenders consider a LTV greater than 80% as higher risk and often require mortgage insurance.

lot-and-block (recorded plat) system A method of describing real property that identifies a parcel of land by reference to lot and block numbers within a subdivision, as specified on a recorded subdivision plat.

management agreement A contract between the owner of income property and a management firm or individual property manager that outlines the scope of the manager's authority.

manufactured housing Factory-built housing that conforms to federally approved construction; considered personal property at the time of construction but may be converted to real property.

margin Amount added to an index to derive note rate on adjustable-rate mortgage.

mark Used in place of signature for someone who cannot write.

market A place where goods can be bought and sold and a price established.

market data approach An estimate of value that is based on comparing similar properties that have already sold to the subject property; used most often to appraise residential properties.

marketable title Good or clear title, reasonably free from the risk of litigation over possible defects.

market rent The amount of rent the property would command in a fully informed competitive marketplace; the going market rate for rental space.

market value The most probable price property would bring in an arm's-length transaction under normal conditions on the open market.

master plan A comprehensive plan to guide the long-term physical development of a particular area.

mechanic's lien A statutory lien created in favor of contractors, laborers, and material suppliers who have performed work or furnished materials in the erection or repair of a building.

Megan's Law A federal law that requires that individuals convicted of certain sex offenses, particularly those involving children, to register their home addresses so that community members may protect themselves and their children from child molesters; generally, real estate licensees are not required to discover or to disclose this information.

meridian One of a set of imaginary lines running north and south and crossing a base line at a definite point, used in the rectangular (government) survey system of property description.

metes-and-bounds description A legal description of a parcel of land that begins at a well-marked point and follows boundaries, using directions and distances around the tract, back to the place of beginning.

mill One-tenth of one cent. Some states use a mill rate to compute real estate taxes; for example, a rate of 52 mills is $0.052 tax for each dollar of assessed valuation of a property.

minor Someone who has not reached the age of majority and therefore does not have legal capacity to transfer title to real property.

misrepresentation False statement or concealment of fact.

mistake An unintentional error or misunderstanding; contract voidable with mutual consent.

modified lien theory Allows the lender to take possession of the property if borrower defaults.

mold Fungi that thrive on moisture and that in some forms can cause allergic reactions in humans, ranging from mild to severe, when inhaled or touched.

month-to-month tenancy A periodic tenancy under which the tenant rents for one month at a time. In the absence of a rental agreement (oral or written), a tenancy is generally considered to be month to month.

monument A fixed natural or artificial object used to establish real estate boundaries for a metes-and-bounds description.

mortgage A conditional transfer or pledge of real estate as security for the payment of a debt. Also, the document creating a mortgage lien.

mortgage-backed securities Packages of loans sold on the open market.

mortgage banking companies These institutions operate primarily as loan correspondents. They originate mortgage loans with money belonging to other institutions, such as insurance companies and pension funds, or to individuals, and they act as the liaison between borrower and lender. Mortgage banking companies are involved in all types of real estate loan activities.

mortgage broker An agent of a lender who brings the lender and borrower together. The broker receives a fee for this service.

mortgagee A lender in a mortgage loan transaction.

mortgage insurance premium (MIP) Insurance required of FHA borrowers that protects a lender against a loss in the event of a foreclosure and deficiency.

mortgage lien A lien or charge on the property of a mortgagor that secures the underlying debt obligations.

mortgage reduction certificate *See* reduction certificate.

mortgage tax A tax imposed for recording mortgages.

mortgagor A borrower in a mortgage loan transaction.

multiperil policies Insurance policies that offer protection from a range of potential perils, such as those of a fire, hazard, public liability, and casualty.

multiple listing An exclusive listing (generally, an exclusive-right-to-sell listing) with the additional authority and obligation on the part of the listing broker to distribute the listing to other brokers in the multiple-listing organization.

multiple-listing clause A provision in an exclusive listing for the additional authority and obligation on the part of the listing broker to distribute the listing to other brokers in the multiple-listing organization.

multiple listing service (MLS) A marketing organization composed of member brokers who agree to share their listing agreements with one another in the hope of procuring ready, willing, and able buyers for their properties more quickly than they could on their own. Most multiple listing services accept only exclusive-right-to-sell listings from their member brokers, although any broker can sell a property listed in an MLS.

mutual savings banks Institutions primarily in the northeastern section of the country that operate similarly to savings and loan associations. They are primarily savings institutions and are highly active in the mortgage market, investing in loans secured by income property as well as residential real estate.

National Do Not Call Registry A federal registration process by which consumers have a choice limiting telemarketing calls; applies to some real estate prospecting activities.

National Flood Insurance Program (NFIP) Provides flood insurance for properties in FEMA-designated flood zones.

negotiable instrument A written promise or order to pay a specific sum of money that may be transferred by endorsement or delivery. The transferee then has the original payee's right to payment.

net lease A lease requiring the tenant to pay not only rent but also costs incurred in maintaining the property, including taxes, insurance, utilities, and repairs.

net listing A listing based on the net price the seller will receive if the property is sold. Under a net listing, the broker can offer the property for sale at the highest price obtainable to increase the commission. This type of listing is illegal in many states.

net operating income (NOI) Effective gross income minus all operating expenses.

nonconforming loan Any loan that does not conform to the Fannie Mae/Freddie Mac guidelines.

nonconforming use A use of property that is permitted to continue after a zoning ordinance prohibiting it has been established for the area.

nonhomogeneity A lack of uniformity; dissimilarity. Because no two parcels of land are exactly alike, real estate is said to be nonhomogeneous.

nonjudicial foreclosure Does not require court action as with a deed of trust giving power of sale to trustee.

note *See* promissory note.

novation Substituting a new obligation for an old one or substituting new parties to an existing obligation.

nuncupative will An oral will declared by the testator in final illness, made before witnesses, and afterward reduced to writing.

offer and acceptance Two essential components of a valid contract; a meeting of the minds.

Office of Thrift Supervision (OTS) Regulator of savings associations created by FIRREA.

oil and gas lease Exclusive right to extract oil or gas from beneath the surface of the land.

open-end loan A mortgage loan that is expandable by increments up to a maximum dollar amount, the full loan being secured by the same original mortgage.

open listing A listing contract under which the broker's commission is contingent on the broker's producing a ready, willing, and able buyer before the property is sold by the seller or another broker.

option An agreement to keep open for a set period an offer to sell or purchase property.

option listing Listing with a provision that gives the listing broker the right to purchase the listed property.

origination fee Usually 1% of the loan amount; charged by lender to cover administrative expenses.

ostensible agency A form of implied agency relationship created by the actions of the parties involved rather than by written agreement or document.

owner's title insurance policy Protects owner from anyone making a claim of interest in property.

package loan A real estate loan used to finance the purchase of both real property and personal property, such as in the purchase of a new home that includes carpeting, window coverings, and major appliances.

parol evidence rule A rule of evidence providing that a written agreement is the final expression of the agreement of the parties, not to be varied or contradicted by prior or contemporaneous oral or written negotiations.

partition suit The division of co-tenants' interests in real property when the parties do not all voluntarily agree to terminate the co-ownership; takes place through court procedures.

participation financing Lender provides favorable loan terms in exchange for a percentage interest in the property.

partnership An association of two or more individuals who carry on a continuing business for profit as co-owners. Under the law, a partnership is regarded as a group of individuals rather than as a single entity. A general partnership is a typical form of joint venture in which each general partner shares in the administration, profits, and losses of the operation. A limited partnership is a business arrangement whereby the operation is administered by one or more general partners and funded, by and large, by limited or silent partners, who are by law responsible for losses only to the extent of their investments.

party wall A wall that is located on or at a boundary line between two adjoining parcels of land and is used or is intended to be used by the owners of both properties.

pass-through certificates Certificates issued by Ginnie Mae; passes through income derived from packages of mortgage loans.

patent A grant or franchise of land from the U.S. government.

patent defect Defect easily seen and understood.

payoff statement *See* reduction certificate.

percentage Less than 100% is a part or fraction of a whole unit; more than 100% is more than a whole unit. The general formula for solving percentage problems is percent × total = part.

percentage lease A lease, commonly used for commercial property, whereby rental is based on the tenant's gross sales at the premises; it usually stipulates a base monthly rental plus a percentage of any gross sales above a certain amount.

periodic estate *See* estate from period to period.

personal property Items, called chattels, that do not fit into the definition of real property; movable objects also called personalty.

physical deterioration A reduction in a property's value resulting from a decline in physical condition; can be caused by action of the elements or by ordinary wear and tear.

planned unit development (PUD) A planned combination of diverse land uses, such as housing, recreation, and shopping, in one contained development or subdivision.

plat map A map of a town, section, or subdivision indicating the location and boundaries of individual properties.

plottage The increase in value or utility resulting from the consolidation (assemblage) of two or more adjacent lots into one larger lot.

point of beginning (POB) In a metes-and-bounds legal description, the starting point of the survey, situated in one corner of the parcel; all metes-and-bounds descriptions must follow the boundaries of the parcel back to the point of beginning.

police power The government's right to impose laws, statutes, and ordinances, including zoning ordinances and building codes, to protect the public health, safety, and welfare.

potential gross income The maximum amount of rent plus any other possible income.

potentially responsible party (PRP) Parties that are potentially responsible for hazardous waste site clean-up costs.

power of attorney A written instrument authorizing a person, the attorney-in-fact, to act as agent for another person to the extent indicated in the instrument.

power-of-sale clause A clause in a mortgage authorizing the holder of the borrower's default. The proceeds from the public sale are used to pay off the mortgage debt first, and any surplus is paid to the mortgagor.

predatory lender Lender that takes advantage of a borrower charging exorbitant interest rates or fees.

prepaid items   On a closing statement, items that have been paid in advance by the seller, such as insurance premiums and some real estate taxes, for which the seller must be reimbursed by the buyer.

prepayment penalty   A charge imposed on a borrower who pays off the loan principal early. This penalty compensates the lender for interest and other charges that would otherwise be lost.

price-fixing   *See* antitrust laws.

primary market   *See* secondary mortgage market.

principal   (1) A sum loaned or employed as a fund or an investment, as distinguished from its income or profits; (2) the original amount (as in a loan) of the total due and payable at a certain date; (3) a main party to a transaction—the person for whom the agent works.

principal meridian   The main imaginary line running north and south and crossing a base line at a definite point, used by surveyors for reference in locating and describing land under the rectangular (government) survey system of legal description.

prior appropriation   A concept of water ownership in which the landowner's right to use available water is based on a government-administered permit system.

priority   The order of position or time. The priority of liens is generally determined by the chronological order in which the lien documents are recorded; tax liens, however, have priority over even previously recorded liens.

private mortgage insurance (PMI)   Insurance provided by any private carrier that protects a lender against a loss in the event of a foreclosure and deficiency.

probate   A legal process by which a court determines who will inherit a decedent's property and what the estate's assets are.

procuring cause   The effort that brings about the desired result. Under an open listing, the broker who is the procuring cause of the sale receives the commission.

progression   An appraisal principle that states that, between dissimilar properties, the value of the lesser-quality property is favorably affected by the presence of the better-quality property.

promissory note   A financing instrument that states the terms of the underlying obligation, is signed by its maker, and is negotiable (i.e., transferable to a third party).

property manager   Someone who manages real estate for another person for compensation. Duties include collecting rents, maintaining the property, and keeping up all accounting.

property reports   The mandatory federal and state documents compiled by subdividers and developers to provide potential purchasers with facts about a property prior to their purchasing that property.

proprietary lease   Gives tenant-stockholders in a cooperative the right to occupy a unit.

proration   Expenses, either prepaid or paid in arrears, that are divided or distributed between buyer and seller at the closing.

protected class   A group of people designated as such by the Federal Fair Housing Act—race, color, religion, national origin, sex, familial status, and disability. State and local civil rights legislation may include additional protected classes.

puffing   Exaggerated or superlative comments or opinions made by real estate agent.

pur autre vie   Latin phrase meaning "for the life of another." A life estate pur autre vie is a life estate that is measured by the life of a person other than the grantee.

purchase-money loan   A note secured by a mortgage or deed of trust given by a buyer, as borrower, to a seller, as lender, as part of the purchase price of the real estate.

qualified mortgage   A mortgage that is as beneficial as possible to the consumer (e.g., no prepayment penalty, no balloon payments, points and fees capped at 3%, etc.).

quantity survey method   The appraisal method of estimating building costs by calculating the cost of all of the physical components in the improvements, adding the cost to assemble them, and then including the indirect costs associated with such construction.

quitclaim deed   A conveyance by which the grantor transfers interest in real estate, without warranties or obligations.

radon   A radioactive gas produced by the decay of natural radioactive minerals in the ground; radon is suspected of causing health problems such as lung cancer.

range   A strip of land six miles wide, extending north and south, and numbered east and west according to its distance from the principal meridian in the rectangular (government) survey system of legal description.

ratification   Adoption or confirmation of an act performed without prior authorization; in agency law, when a principal accepts the conduct of someone who acted without prior authorization as the principal's agent; in contract law, the time in which all parties have signed and agreed to the terms of the contract.

ready, willing, and able buyer One who is prepared to buy property on the seller's terms and is ready to take positive steps to consummate the transaction.

real estate Land; a portion of the earth's surface extending downward to the center of the earth and upward infinitely into space, including all things permanently attached to it, whether naturally or artificially.

real estate investment syndicate *See* syndicate.

real estate investment trust (REIT) Trust ownership of real estate by a group of individuals who purchase certificates of ownership in the trust, which in turn invests the money in real property and distributes the profits back to the investors free of corporate income tax.

real estate license law State law enacted to protect the public from fraud, dishonesty, and incompetence in the purchase and sale of real estate.

real estate mortgage investment conduit (REMIC) A tax entity that issues multiple classes of investor interests (securities) backed by a pool of mortgages.

real estate recovery fund A fund established in some states from real estate license revenues to cover claims of aggrieved parties who have suffered monetary damage through the actions of a real estate licensee.

Real Estate Settlement Procedures Act (RESPA) Federal consumer law under the control of the Department of Housing and Urban Development (HUD). The law was created to ensure that the buyer and seller in a residential real estate transaction have knowledge of all settlement (closing) costs. RESPA applies only to transactions involving new first mortgage loans that are federally related.

real property The interests, benefits, and rights inherent in real estate ownership.

REALTOR® A registered trademark term reserved for the sole use of active members of local and state REALTOR® boards or associations affiliated with the National Association of REALTORS®.

realty Referring to real estate.

reconciliation The final step in the appraisal process, in which the appraiser combines the estimates of value received from the sales comparison, cost, and income approaches to arrive at a final estimate of market value for the subject property.

reconveyance deed A deed used by a trustee under a deed of trust to return title to the trustor.

recording The act of entering or recording documents affecting or conveying interests in real estate in the recorder's office established in each county. Until it is recorded, a deed or mortgage ordinarily is not effective against subsequent purchasers or mortgagees.

rectangular (government) survey system A system established in 1785 by the federal government, providing for surveying and describing land by reference to principal meridians and base lines.

redemption The right of a defaulted property owner to recover property by curing the default.

redemption period A period of time established by state law during which a property owner has the right to redeem real estate from a foreclosure or tax sale by paying the sales price, interest, and costs. Many states do not have mortgage redemption laws.

redlining The illegal practice of a lending institution denying loans or restricting their number for certain areas of a community.

reduction certificate (payoff statement) The document signed by a lender indicating the amount required to pay a loan balance in full and satisfy the debt; used in the settlement process to protect both the seller's and the buyer's interests.

regression An appraisal principle that states that, between dissimilar properties, the value of the better-quality property is adversely affected by the presence of the lesser-quality property.

Regulation Z Implements the Truth in Lending Act requiring credit institutions to inform borrowers of the true cost of obtaining credit.

release deed A document, also called a deed of reconveyance, that transfers all rights given a trustee under a deed of trust loan back to the grantor after the loan has been fully repaid.

remainder interest The remnant of an estate that has been conveyed to take effect and be enjoyed after the termination of a prior estate, such as when an owner conveys a life estate to one party and the remainder to another.

remainderman One receiving a remainder interest.

rent A fixed, periodic payment made by a tenant of a property to the owner for possession and use, usually by prior agreement of the parties.

rental market The market for leased real estate.

rent schedule A statement of proposed rental rates, determined by the owner or the property manager or both, based on a building's estimated expenses, market supply and demand, and the owner's long-range goals for the property.

renter's insurance   Covers personal belongings in a rental unit. Also used for personal property in a condominium unit.

replacement cost   The construction cost at current prices of a property that is not necessarily an exact duplicate of the subject property, but serves the same purpose or function as the original.

reproduction cost   The construction cost at current prices of an exact duplicate of the subject property.

reserves   Money set aside for future payments.

residential   All property used for single-family or multifamily housing, whether in urban, suburban, or rural areas.

Residential Lead-Based Paint Hazard Reduction Act   Legislation requiring disclosure of lead-based paint hazard to future owners and renters and the right to a ten-day inspection period for buyers of all residential properties built before 1978.

restrictive covenant   A limitation on use of property.

reverse-annuity mortgage (RAM)   A loan under which the homeowner receives monthly payments based on accumulated equity. The loan must be repaid at a prearranged date or upon the death of the owner or the sale of the property. Disbursement of funds can also be as a lump sum or in an established line-of-credit.

reversionary interest   The interest retained by the grantor after granting a life estate to another person; upon that person's death, the full rights of ownership revert to the original owner.

reversionary right   The return of the rights of possession to the lessor at the expiration of a lease.

right of first refusal   Right that allows the tenant to be offered the property first if the owner decides to sell at a future date.

right of re-entry   Future interest of one transferring rights under certain conditions; requires court action.

right of rescission   Right to cancel a credit transaction within three days; does not apply to first mortgage loans; established as part of Truth in Lending Act.

right of survivorship   Characteristic of joint tenancy by which surviving tenant has all rights to the property without any need for probate procedures.

right-to-use   Right to occupy a time-share unit for a selected time and place.

riparian rights   An owner's rights in land that borders on or includes a stream, river, or lake. These rights include access to and use of the water.

Rural Housing Service (RHS)   Replaced the Farmers Home Administration (FmHA); channels credit to farmers and rural communities.

rules and regulations   Real estate licensing authority orders that govern licensees' activities; they usually have the same force and effect as statutory law.

sale-and-leaseback   A transaction in which an owner sells improved property and, as part of the same transaction, signs a long-term lease to remain in possession of the premises.

sales comparison approach   The process of estimating the value of a property by examining and comparing actual sales of comparable properties.

sales market   The market for purchasing and selling real estate.

salesperson   A person who performs real estate activities while employed by or associated with a licensed real estate broker.

sandwich lease   Created when a sublease is negotiated by a tenant under a lease. Original tenant remains primarily liable for the payment of rent to the landlord and is sandwiched between the owner (landlord) of the property and the end-user (subtenant) of the leased property.

satisfaction   A document acknowledging the payment of a debt.

satisfaction of mortgage   A document acknowledging the payment of a mortgage debt.

savings associations   The most active participants in the home loan mortgage market. They make both short-term and long-term conventional and government loans. By requiring private mortgage insurance (PMI), they will make 95%, 97%, and even 100% loan-to-value ratio (LTV) loans. Also called *thrifts*, they are regulated by the Office of Thrift Supervision (OTS) and supervised by the Federal Home Loan Bank (FHLB).

secondary mortgage market   A market for the purchase and sale of existing mortgages. Mortgages are first originated in the primary mortgage market, then packaged and sold on the secondary market to Fannie Mae, Freddie Mac, and private investors.

section   A portion of a township under the rectangular (government) survey system. A township is divided into 36 sections, numbered 1 through 36. A section is a square with mile-long sides and an area of 1 square mile, or 640 acres.

Section 1031 tax-deferred exchange Allows exchanging of properties of like kind to defer tax liability.

security agreement *See* Uniform Commercial Code.

security deposit A payment by a tenant held by the landlord during the lease term and kept (wholly or partially) on default or destruction of the premises by the tenant.

seller's market An economic condition occurring when the demand for a good exceeds the supply, resulting in an increase in price.

separate property Under community property law, property owned solely by either spouse before the marriage, acquired by gift or inheritance after the marriage or purchased with separate funds after the marriage.

service animal Any animal that assists a disabled person with performing basic life functions.

servient estate Land on which an easement exists in favor of an adjacent property (called a dominant estate); also called a servient tenement.

setback The amount of space local zoning regulations require between a lot line and a building line.

Settlement Statement (HUD-1) The standard HUD form required to be given to the borrower, the lender, and the seller at or prior to settlement by the settlement agent in a transaction covered under the Real Estate Settlement Procedures Act. The lender must retain its copy for at least two years.

severalty Ownership of real property by one person only, also called *sole ownership*.

severance Changing an item of real estate to personal property by detaching it from the land; for example, cutting down a tree.

sharecropping In an agricultural lease, the agreement between the landowner and the tenant farmer to split the crop or the profit from its sale, actually sharing the crop.

shared-appreciation mortgage (SAM) A mortgage loan in which the lender, in exchange for a loan with a favorable interest rate, participates in the profits (if any) the borrower receives when the property is eventually sold.

short sale A sale in which the proceeds do not cover the owed amount; unless the holders of the liens agree to accept less, the mortgagor must bring funds to closing.

single agency A broker who represents only one party, never both, in a transaction.

situs The personal preference of people for one area over another, not necessarily based on objective facts and knowledge.

Small Business Liability Relief and Brownfields Revitalization Act A federal law that provides funds to assess and clean up brownfields, clarifies liability protection, and provides tax incentives to encourage the development of abandoned properties, often in prime urban real estate areas.

special agent One who is authorized by a principal to perform a single act or transaction; a real estate broker is usually a special agent authorized to find a ready, willing, and able buyer for a particular property.

special assessment A tax or levy customarily imposed against only those specific parcels of real estate that will benefit from a proposed public improvement like a street or sewer.

special purpose A category of real estate that includes churches, schools, cemeteries, and government-held lands.

special warranty deed A deed in which the grantor warrants, or guarantees, the title only against defects arising during the period of tenure and ownership of the property and not against defects existing before that time, generally using the language, "by, through, or under the grantor, but not otherwise."

specific lien A lien affecting or attaching only to a certain, specific parcel of land or piece of property.

specific performance A legal action to compel a party to carry out the terms of a contract.

spot survey Shows all buildings, improvements, and easements on a property.

spot zone A single parcel within a zone that has a different use than the zone surrounding it.

square foot method The appraisal method of estimating building costs by multiplying the number of square feet in the improvements being appraised by the cost per square foot for recently constructed similar improvements.

statute of frauds The part of a state law that requires certain instruments, such as deeds, real estate sales contracts, and certain leases, to be in writing to be legally enforceable.

statute of limitations The law pertaining to the period of time within which certain actions must be brought to court.

statutory duties Duties to clients and customers specified in state law of agency.

statutory lien A lien imposed on property by statute (a tax lien, for example) in contrast to an equitable lien, which arises out of common law.

statutory redemption The right of a defaulted property owner to recover the property after its sale by paying the appropriate fees and charges.

steering The illegal practice of channeling homeseekers to particular areas, either to maintain the homogeneity of an area or to change the character of an area to create a speculative situation.

stigmatized property Properties that are said to be psychologically impacted by some event, such as a murder, suicide, rape, ghosts, contamination; most states, but not all, do not require discovery or disclosure by real estate licensees.

straight-line method A method of calculating depreciation for tax purposes, computed by dividing the adjusted basis of a property by the estimated number of years of remaining useful life.

straight loan A loan in which only interest is paid during the term of the loan, with the entire principal amount due with the final interest payment.

subagent One who is employed by a person already acting as an agent. Typically, a reference to a salesperson licensed under a broker (agent) who is employed under the terms of a listing agreement or a cooperating broker who is also representing that principal.

subchapter S corporation Type of corporation treated more like partnership for tax purposes.

subdivider One who buys undeveloped land, divides it into smaller, usable lots, and sells the lots to potential users.

subdivision A tract of land divided by the owner, called the subdivider, into blocks, building lots, and streets according to a recorded subdivision plat that must comply with local ordinances and regulations.

subject property The property that is being appraised.

subletting The leasing of premises by a lessee to a third party for part of the lessee's remaining term. *See also* assignment.

subordination Relegation to a lesser position, usually in respect to a right or security.

subordination agreement A written agreement between holders of liens on a property that changes the priority of mortgage, judgment, and other liens under certain circumstances.

subprime loan Loan made to a borrower with less than perfect credit; usually has a higher interest rate; may require higher down payment and shorter term of the loan.

subrogation The substitution of one creditor for another with the substituted person succeeding to the legal rights and claims of the original claimant. Subrogation is used by title insurers to acquire the right from the injured party to sue in order to recover any claims the insurers have paid.

substitution An appraisal principle that states that the maximum value of a property tends to be set by the cost of purchasing an equally desirable and valuable substitute property, assuming that no costly delay is encountered in making the substitution.

subsurface rights Ownership rights in a parcel of real estate to the water, minerals, gas, oil, and so forth that lie beneath the surface of the property.

suit for possession A lawsuit initiated by a landlord to evict a tenant from leased premises after the tenant has breached one of the terms of the lease or has held possession of the property after the lease's expiration.

suit to quiet title A court action intended to establish or settle the title to a particular property, especially when there is a cloud on the title.

Superfund Popular name of the hazardous waste clean-up fund established by the Comprehensive Environmental Response, Compensation, and Recovery Act (CERCLA).

supply The amount of goods available in the market to be sold at a given price. The term is often coupled with demand.

supply and demand The appraisal principle that follows the interrelationship of the supply of and demand for real estate. As appraising is based on economic concepts, this principle recognizes that real property is subject to the influences of the marketplace, just as is any other commodity.

surety bond Also called a fidelity bond; insurance purchased by an employer to cover employees entrusted with others' money, such as property managers and escrow agents.

surface rights Ownership rights in a parcel of real estate that are limited to the surface of the property and do not include the air above it (air rights) or the minerals below the surface (subsurface rights).

survey The process by which boundaries are measured and land areas are determined; the on-site measurement of lot lines, dimensions, and position of a house on a lot, including the determination of any existing encroachments or easements.

syndicate   A combination of people or firms formed to accomplish a business venture of mutual interest by pooling resources. In a real estate investment syndicate, the parties own and/or develop property, with the main profit generally arising from the sale of the property.

tacking   Adding or combining successive periods of continuous occupation of real property by adverse possessors. This concept enables someone who has not been in possession for the entire statutory period to establish a claim of adverse possession.

taking   Refers to the government taking of private property, either physically through the government's power of eminent domain, or regulatory through excessive restrictions on use. The U.S. Constitution requires the government to pay a private property owner just compensation for the taking of that owner's property.

taxation   The process by which a government or municipal quasi-public body raises monies to fund its operation.

tax basis   *See* basis.

tax credit   An amount by which tax owed is directly reduced.

tax deed   An instrument, similar to a certificate of sale, given to a purchaser at a tax sale. *See also* certificate of sale.

tax levy   The amount charged against a property. *See* levy.

tax lien   A charge against property that is created by operation of law. Tax liens and assessments take priority over all other liens.

tax sale   A court-ordered sale of real property to raise money to cover delinquent taxes.

tenancy by the entirety   The joint ownership, recognized in some states, of property acquired by husband and wife during marriage. Upon the death of one spouse, the survivor becomes the owner of the property with no need of probate.

tenancy in common   A form of co-ownership by which each owner holds an undivided interest in real property as though sole owner. Each individual owner has the right to partition. Unlike joint tenants, tenants in common have the right of inheritance.

tenant   One who holds or possesses lands or tenements by any kind of right or title.

tenant improvements   Alterations to the interior of a building to meet the functional demands of the tenant.

testate   Having made and left a valid will.

testator   A person who has made a valid will.

thrifts   Another name for savings associations.

tier   A strip of land six miles wide, extending east and west and numbered north and south according to its distance from the base line in the rectangular (government) survey system of legal description. Also called township strips.

time is of the essence   A phrase in a contract that requires the performance of a certain act within a stated period of time.

time-sharing   A form of ownership interest that may include an estate interest in property and which allows use of the property for a fixed or variable time period.

title   (1) The right to or ownership of land; (2) the evidence of ownership of land.

title insurance   A policy insuring the owner or mortgagee against loss by reason of defects in the title to a parcel of real estate, other than encumbrances, defects, and matters specifically excluded by the policy.

title theory   Some states interpret a mortgage to mean that the lender is the owner of mortgaged land. Upon full payment of the mortgage debt, the borrower becomes the landowner.

Torrens system   A method of evidencing title by registration with the proper public authority, generally called the *registrar*, named for its founder, Sir Robert Torrens.

tort   An intentional wrongful act from breach of duty created by law.

township   The principal unit of the rectangular (government) survey system. A township is a square with 6-mile sides and an area of 36 square miles.

trade fixture   An article installed by a tenant under the terms of a lease and removable by the tenant before the lease expires.

transaction broker   A broker whose practice is limited to neutrally facilitating a real estate transaction between a buyer and a seller, but represents neither party's interest.

transfer tax   Tax stamps required to be affixed to a deed by state and/or local law.

trigger terms   Credit or financing terms that require that all details of the financing be disclosed in advertising.

tri-merged credit report   A combination report of the three major credit reporting agencies: Experian, Equifax, and TransUnion.

trust   A fiduciary arrangement whereby property is conveyed to a person or institution, called a *trustee*, to be held and administered on behalf of another person, called a *beneficiary*. The one who conveys the trust is called the *trustor*.

trust (escrow) account   A separate account for funds entrusted to a broker in a transaction and regulated by state licensing laws.

trust deed   An instrument used to create a mortgage lien by which the borrower conveys title to a trustee, who holds it as security for the benefit of the note holder (the lender); also called a deed of trust.

trust deed lien   A lien on the property of a trustor that secures a deed of trust loan.

trustee   The holder of bare legal title in a deed of trust loan transaction.

trustee's deed   A deed executed by a trustee conveying land held in a trust.

trustor   A borrower in a deed of trust loan transaction.

Truth in Lending Act (TILA)   Requires full disclosure of all costs of obtaining credit.

underwater loan   A loan amount that is greater than the current market value. *See also* short sale.

underground storage tank (UST)   A tank used to store fuel (primarily petroleum products) underground.

undivided interest   *See* tenancy in common.

unenforceable contract   A contract that has all the elements of a valid contract, yet neither party can sue the other to force performance of it. For example, an unsigned contract is generally unenforceable.

Uniform Commercial Code   A codification of commercial law, adopted in most states, that attempts to make uniform all laws relating to commercial transactions, including chattel mortgages and bulk transfers. Security interests in chattels are created by an instrument called a *security agreement*. To give notice of the security interest, a financing statement must be recorded. Article 6 of the code regulates bulk transfers—the sale of a business as a whole, including all fixtures, chattels, and merchandise.

Uniform Electronics Transactions Act (UETA)   A model law promulgated by the National Conference Commissioners on Uniform State Laws; the basis of most state laws (except Washington, Illinois, and New York); consumer protections added in the federal E-Sign Act of 2000.

Uniform Residential Appraisal Report (URAR)   A form approved for residential appraisals required by many government agencies.

Uniform Residential Landlord and Tenant Act (URLTA)   Model law establishing standards for landlord-tenant relations; adopted in some form by most states.

Uniform Standards of Professional Appraisal Practice (USPAP)   A set of minimum quality control standards that represent the generally accepted and recognized standards of appraisal practice; updated every two years.

unilateral contract   A one-sided contract wherein one party makes a promise so as to induce a second party to do something. The second party is not legally bound to perform; however, if the second party does comply, the first party is obligated to keep the promise.

unit-in-place method   The appraisal method of estimating building costs by calculating the costs of all of the physical components in the structure, with the cost of each item including its proper installation, connection, et cetera; also called the segregated cost method.

urea-formaldehyde   A chemical used in building materials, particularly urea-formaldehyde foam insulation (UFFI).

usury   Charging interest at a higher rate than the maximum rate established by state law.

valid contract   A contract that complies with all the essentials of a contract and is binding and enforceable on all parties to it.

VA loan   A mortgage loan on approved property made to a qualified veteran by an authorized lender and guaranteed by the Department of Veterans Affairs in order to limit the lender's possible loss.

value   The power of a good or service to command other goods in exchange for the present worth of future rights to its income or amenities.

variance   Permission obtained from zoning authorities to build a structure or conduct a use that is expressly prohibited by the current zoning laws; an exception from the zoning ordinances.

vendee   A buyer, usually under the terms of a land contract.

vendor   A seller, usually under the terms of a land contract.

voidable contract   A contract that seems to be valid on the surface but may be rejected or disaffirmed by one or both of the parties.

void contract   A contract that has no legal force or effect because it does not meet the essential elements of a contract.

volume   The space that a space contains, calculated as length × width × height = volume.

voluntary alienation   *See* alienation.

voluntary lien   A lien placed on property with the knowledge and consent of the property owner.

walk-through   Final inspection made by buyer prior to settlement.

warranty deed   A deed in which the grantor fully warrants good clear title to the premises. Used in most real estate deed transfers, a warranty deed offers the greatest protection of any deed.

waste   An improper use or an abuse of a property by a possessor who holds less than fee ownership, such as a tenant, life tenant, mortgagor, or vendee. Such waste ordinarily impairs the value of the land or the interest of the person holding the title or the reversionary rights.

water table   Natural level of water.

will   A written document, properly witnessed, providing for the transfer of title to property owned by the deceased, called the *testator*.

workers' compensation acts   Laws that require an employer to obtain insurance coverage to protect employees who are injured in the course of their employment.

wraparound loan   A method of refinancing in which the new mortgage is placed in a secondary, or subordinate, position; the new mortgage includes both the unpaid principal balance of the first mortgage and whatever additional sums are advanced by the lender. In essence, it is an additional mortgage in which another lender refinances a borrower by lending an amount over the existing first mortgage amount without disturbing the existence of the first mortgage.

writ of attachment   Court order authorizing seizure of real or personal property.

writ of execution   Court order authorizing sale of property.

zoning ordinance   An exercise of police power by a municipality to regulate and control the character and use of property.

Answer Key

Chapter 1: An Introduction to the Real Estate Business

1.   b.   A condominium unit can be either commercial or residential. Page 5.

2.   b.   An increase in the number of homes for sale will lead to a reduction in prices. Page 6.

3.   c.   An increased demand for real estate is most affected by increased employment and wages. Page 7.

4.   b.   The supply of real estate is directly affected by changes in construction costs. Page 6.

5.   b.   Anticipating an increase in population, house prices will likely increase. Page 6.

6.   d.   There are many different specializations in the real estate industry. Page 2.

7.   d.   All states require licensure, but a REALTOR® has chosen to become a member of the National Association of REALTORS®. Page 5.

8.   a.   A real estate counselor provides expertise and advice, rather than showing or listing property. Page 4.

9.   c.   Subdivision is the splitting of property; development is adding improvements. Page 4.

10.   c.   An oversupply of office spaces will lead to a decrease in office rents. Page 6.

11.   c.   Flood insurance is required when the property is located in a special flood hazard area (SFHA) and financed with a federally related loan. Flood insurance is effective 30 days after purchase, unless it is required as a condition of the mortgage loan and is effective immediately. Page 3–4.

12.   a.   An insurance agent must see a copy of an elevation certificate that has been prepared by a licensed surveyor certifying building elevations and is required to show compliance with community floodplain regulations and to determine appropriate insurance rates before the insurance agent can quote a price. Page 4.

13.   b.   Although the businessman is engaged in commercial business, the warehouses would fall under the category of industrial. Page 5.

14.   a.   The price is determined by the specific supply and specific demand for similar properties in the area. Page 6.

15.   c.   Demographics refers to the characteristics of the population in an area. Page 6.

16.   d.   Since the HO-3 homeowner's policy is for owner-occupied properties, owners who vacate their homes should consult their insurance agents to determine when their homeowner's insurance policy converts to a basic fire policy. Page 3.

17.   b.   The cost of flood insurance may significantly change the PITI ratios, so the buyers may not be able to afford a higher value. While it is true that a cash buyer is not required to purchase flood insurance, the buyer is making an unwise decision. Page 4.

18.   a.   When required by the lender, flood insurance is effective as soon as title passes. A homeowners insurance policy is effective as soon as title passes. Page 4.

19.   c.   When buyers pay cash at closing, their flood insurance policy does not become effective for 30 days after closing. Therefore, cash buyers should consider getting a mortgage loan because when the lender requires flood insurance, the policy is effective immediately. Once the insurance is in place, the buyer can pay off the mortgage loan. Hazard insurance is always effective upon transfer of title. Page 4.

20.   a.   Individuals may only insure that which they own; in a rental property, the landlord buys insurance to cover the physical structure, and the renters (tenant) purchase insurance to cover their personal property. Page 3.

Chapter 2: Nature and Description of Real Estate

1. d. Real property includes the land and improvements plus the bundle of rights. Trade fixtures are personal property. Page 11.
2. c. A metes-and-bounds description must begin and end with the point of beginning, thus completely enclosing the described property. Page 17.
3. b. Personal property, also called *chattels*, is characterized by the fact that it can be easily removed from the property. Page 11.
4. b. A subdivision plat shows property divided into block and lot numbers. Page 20.
5. c. All items permanently attached to the land are considered part of the real estate. Page 12.
6. c. Situs refers to the fact that individuals will prefer one location over another. Page 15.
7. d. Prior appropriation rights protect the farmer or rancher that is downstream from others who may tend to divert all available water to their own use. Page 12.
8. a. Emblements are growing crops that the seller of property has the right to harvest. Page 21.
9. a. The fact that land cannot be moved makes it a preferred foundation for a tax basis. Page 15.
10. b. The bundle of rights of ownership are still subject to police power, eminent domain, taxation, and escheat. Page 11.
11. b. The cost of the item has no bearing on determining whether or not it is a fixture. Page 21.
12. c. Land includes air rights and subsurface rights. Page 12.
13. b. A metes and bounds refers to monuments and benchmarks but must return to the point of beginning. Page 17.
14. b. Under the government survey system, a section is 640 acres. Page 19.
15. b. When the trees were growing on land, they were real estate; once cut into lumber, they became personal property; once the deck is complete, the lumber will have returned to real estate as a permanent improvement. Page 22.
16. c. Severance is the process by which real property becomes personal property; the opposite is accession, whereby personal property is so affixed that it becomes real property. Page 22.
17. a. When the commercial lease expires and the tenant has not removed trade fixtures, they become the landlord's property by accession. The tenant has no right to re-enter the property after the lease expires. Page 22.
18. d. The heat pump, although it could be removed, is an essential part of the property, making it a fixture. Page 21.
19. b. Air lots consist of airspace within specific boundaries located over a parcel of land and are typically used to describe each condominium unit in reference to the elevation of the floors and ceilings on a vertical plane above the city datum. Page 21.
20. c. A licensed surveyor is sometimes the only one who can locate the monuments and boundary lines, especially when the metes-and-bounds land description is long and confusing. Page 18.

Chapter 3: Rights and Interests in Real Estate

1. c. Under the right of eminent domain, the government may take property to be used for the common good. Page 28.
2. a. A freehold estate may be sold, leased, or willed to another person. Page 30.
3. d. A life estate allows the mother to remain in the property until her death, at which time the interest goes to the party holding the remainder interest. Page 31.
4. c. A contractor who has not been paid can file a mechanic's lien against the property where the work was done. Page 35.
5. b. An easement in gross is obtained by a commercial company in order to cross over multiple properties. Page 38.
6. d. A lien is an encumbrance that involves money. Page 34.
7. a. The party that is receiving benefit from the easement is called the *dominant tenement*. Page 37.
8. b. A homestead exemption protects the homeowner from debt on a credit card issued by a local bank, but not from mortgage debt, mechanics' liens, or unpaid property taxes. Page 32.
9. b. Under a fee simple determinable estate, the property is conveyed subject to certain restrictions that must be followed or risk reversion to the grantor. Page 30.
10. c. Improvements that will benefit a certain group of homeowners are taxed as special assessments to those homeowners. Page 35.
11. b. The person who will receive the interest in an estate after the termination of a life estate has a remainder interest (reversionary goes back to original grantor). Page 31.
12. d. A mortgage lien is made voluntarily and is specific to one property. Page 34.

13.   b.   Although often replaced today with an elective share, traditionally the husband had curtesy rights to his wife's property. Page 32.

14.   c.   Because of the time involved to file a mechanic's lien, a lis pendens is filed to serve notice that a lien is pending. Page 36.

15.   d.   Easements run with the land and convey when the property is sold. Only the dominant tenement may terminate the easement. Page 39.

16.   c.   Liens are monetary claims against the property, so most buyers require that the liens be paid prior to closing. Page 35.

17.   d.   Any other subdivision lot owner can apply to the court for an injunction to stop a neighboring lot owner from violating the recorded restrictions. Page 40.

18.   a.   Government limitations on ownership of real property are for the general welfare of the community and include police power, eminent domain, taxation, and escheat. Page 28.

19.   b.   Because the woman left a will, her property is not ownerless and will pass to whomever is named in her will. Page 30.

20.   b.   The tenant's right to occupy the land for the duration of a lease is called a leasehold estate, and the ownership interest in the property remains with the landlord, as an estate in reversion. Page 33.

Chapter 4: Acquisition and Transfer of Title

1.   d.   A holographic will is handwritten, prepared, dated, and has no witnesses. A nuncupative will is an oral declaration, usually made upon fear of dying. Page 54.

2.   a.   When a state or federal government conveys title to public land to an individual, it is called a *patent*. Page 45.

3.   a.   The general warranty deed provides the grantee with the covenants of seisin, against encumbrances, of quiet enjoyment, of further assurance, and of warranty forever. A special warranty deed covers only the time the grantor held title. A bargain and sale or quitclaim deed has no warranties. Page 49.

4.   b.   The grantor's signature is required, not the grantee's. The only time the sales price (or consideration) is given is with a court-ordered deed. Page 47.

5.   d.   The person designated to act on behalf of another through a power of attorney is called and must sign all documents as, attorney-in-fact. Page 47.

6.   c.   Accession generally refers to land being added to real property through natural causes. Alluvion is the actual accumulation of soil or other matter. Page 53.

7.   a.   Ownerless property, a result of a person who dies intestate with no heirs, escheats to the state, which is an example of involuntary alienation. Escheat, along with police power, taxation, and eminent domain, are legal rights held by the government. Page 53.

8.   b.   The covenant of quiet enjoyment protects the grantee from any third party making a claim on the property and holds the grantor liable for any damages incurred if there should be a superior claim. Page 49.

9.   b.   If joint tenants are not in agreement as to the disposition of their property, they may file a partition suit to terminate their joint tenancy. Page 53.

10.   d.   A quitclaim deed conveys only whatever interest the grantor may have, which may be nothing; it is often used to clear up minor title issues. Page 51.

11.   c.   To obtain title by adverse possession, the possession must be proved to have been open, exclusive, notorious, and hostile for a specific number of years. Page 53.

12.   c.   Title passes when the deed is delivered and accepted—either at the settlement table or through an escrow agent. Page 48.

13.   b.   Fiduciaries, such as trustees and executors, generally convey property with a special warranty deed because they cannot warrant against the actions of earlier holders of the title. Page 49.

14.   b.   Each state has specific laws regarding the length of time that a claimant must have made open, exclusive, notorious, and hostile use of land for it to be claimed under adverse possession. Page 53.

15.   c.   The granting clause of a general warranty deed is often all-encompassing, including the words *grant, bargain, sell,* and *convey*. Page 49.

16.   b.   A valid deed must be in writing and signed by the grantor, but not the grantee. It must also include a granting clause, a legal description, and a recital of consideration. Page 46.

17.   a.   Dedication is an example of voluntary alienation in which the owner turns over private property to the government for public use. Page 45.

18.   d.   The notary public only verifies that the signature is genuine, not a forgery, and is voluntarily given. This acknowledgement does not examine or verify the truthfulness of the document. Page 48.

19.   d.   A court order for specific performance transfers property involuntarily when the sellers have decided to not transfer the property. Although dying is not voluntary, writing a will is. Dedication is a voluntary process of turning over private property for public use. Page 53.

20.   a.   Erosion is the slow loss of land, but avulsion is the sudden tearing away as when the river changes course or a hurricane changes the beach in a matter of a few hours. Accession is the process of gaining land, often by accretion, through the accumulation of soil, rock, and other matter. Page 53.

Chapter 5: How Ownership Is Held

1.   b.   A cooperative is a unique form of ownership in which the owner actually owns shares in the corporation that owns the property and has a proprietary lease that gives the right to occupy a specific unit. Page 68.

2.   a.   In a condominium, each owner has a fee simple interest in an individual unit plus an undivided interest in all of the common areas. Page 69.

3.   d.   The four unities required to establish joint tenancy are time, title, interest, and possession. Rights of survivorship may or may not be included. Page 62.

4.   c.   The trustor is the one who establishes the trust; the trustee is the one who administers the trust; and the beneficiary is the one who ultimately benefits from the trust. Page 65.

5.   c.   With a joint tenancy with rights of survivorship, a deceased party's interest automatically conveys to the surviving owner. Page 63.

6.   b.   Two unmarried individuals often prefer that any interest they have in a property will convey to their heirs upon their death, rather than to the surviving party. Page 61.

7.   c.   The states in the western part of the United States are primarily influenced by Spanish law. Married couples are recognized as equal partners and hold title to all property accumulated during the marriage as community property. Page 64.

8.   c.   A corporation must pay taxes, and its stockholders must also pay taxes on the profits received. A subchapter S corporation is taxed only at the shareholder's level. Page 67.

9.   b.   With a limited partnership, the investor does not take an active part in the management of the business and only risks the loss of the money originally invested. Page 68.

10.   b.   A real estate investment trust (REIT) is formed of at least 100 members who hold shares in the trust that will purchase several different properties. Page 66.

11.   c.   Any time tenants in common cannot agree voluntarily to terminate their co-ownership, they can file for a court-ordered partition suit. Page 63.

12.   a   The form of time-share that conveys a fee simple interest in a specific property for a certain time each year is a fee simple ownership, which is treated like any other real property; a right-to-use form of time-share is limited to a specific time period. Page 70.

13.   b.   When no specific type of co-ownership is stated in the deed, a tenancy in common is presumed. Page 61.

14.   c.   When a joint tenancy is broken by one party conveying that party's interest, the remaining parties remain as joint tenants, along with the new owner as a tenant in common. Page 61.

15.   b.   Although the four brothers are acquiring their interest at the same time, they received title through one instrument; they have equal ownership interest, and they each have undivided possession of the property. This does not necessarily indicate joint tenancy. Tenants in common could receive title through one instrument; they have equal ownership interest and they each have undivided possession of the property. Page 62.

16.   a.   A corporation can take title in severalty or as a tenant in common. Because a corporation never dies, it may not take title as a joint tenant with rights of survivorship. Page 67.

17.   c.   A married couple may not take title in severalty, but, depending on the state, may take title as tenants in common, joint tenancy, or tenancy by the entirety. Page 61.

18.   d.   When a joint tenant dies, the remaining joint tenants receive the interest of the deceased tenant by right of survivorship. Page 61.

19. a. Real estate owned by a husband and wife as tenants by the entireties is considered to be held by one indivisible legal unit; the couple generally has no right to partition. Page 64.

20. b. The licensee is proposing a limited partnership with himself as the general partner doing the work and the investors as limited, or silent, partners who are not involved in running the business and can be held liable for any losses only to the extent of their investment. Page 67.

Chapter 6: Title Records

1.   b. Under the right of subrogation, a second party acquires all rights that were formerly held by an original party. Page 78.

2.   b. The Torrens system is a form of land registration used in some states. The registrar of titles issues a certificate title and provides a duplicate to the property owner. Page 79.

3.   c. Actual notice occurs when an individual personally examines public records or inspects a property. Constructive notice is the presumption of law that makes the purchaser responsible for acquiring this information. Page 76.

4.   d. The abstract of title is a summarized list of all instruments relative to taxes, judgments, special assessments, and conveyances of property from the original owner of the property up to the present time. In older states, the search may be limited to the past 60 years. Page 77.

5.   a. Constructive notice is a presumption of law that makes the buyer responsible for searching the public records, as well as inspecting the property. Failure to do so is no excuse for not knowing of another right or interest. Page 75.

6.   c. Title evidence is necessary in order to insure that the grantor is conveying marketable title that has no significant defects that might need to be defended in the future. Page 77.

7.   c. The chain of title provides a record of ownership dating from the present time back to the original patent issued by the U.S. government. Any gaps in this chain might require a suit to quiet title. Page 77.

8.   a. Because the deed was not recorded, there is no constructive notice, but a buyer is responsible for inspecting both the property and public records. An inspection of the property would have made it obvious that it was occupied. Page 75.

9.   d. Although local recording statues may vary slightly from one area to another, all written instruments affecting any estate, right, title, or interest must be recorded in the county where the property is located. Page 75.

10. a. The Uniform Commercial Code is a codification of commercial law adopted in most states. It does not generally apply to the conveyance of real estate. Page 80.

11. c. The standard title insurance policy does not protect against unrecorded rights of parties in possession. An extended coverage policy will cover risks that could only be uncovered through actual inspection of the property. Page 78.

12. c. A mortgagee's title insurance policy only protects the lender. An owner-mortgagor must purchase an owner's title insurance policy to receive title protection. Page 78.

13. a. Constructive notice makes it the responsibility of the purchaser's to inspect both property and public records. The fact that a deed is recorded provides constructive notice to any potential purchaser. Page 75.

14. c. The absence of a recorded mortgage only provides a potential purchaser with the knowledge that the current owner has not placed a mortgage; it does not assure the purchaser of issues relating to taxes, title, or occupancy of the property. Page 76.

15. a. The concept of caveat emptor, or buyer beware, is based on old English common law that charges the buyer with the responsibility of learning about the interests of other parties. Page 75.

16. b. Constructive notice is information that should have been known because information that is recorded is readily available. A person has actual notice upon reviewing the information or visiting the property. Page 76.

17. a. A lender's policy can be transferred to the holder of the note if the loan is sold, and the face amount decreases over the life of the loan. An owners' policy amount remains the same but terminates when title is transferred to another party. Page 79.

18. c. Title insurance premiums are due only once, at closing, and the policy remains in effect until title is transferred again. Page 78.

19. d. Title insurance never covers defects known to the buyer or any defects or liens listed in the policy or changes in land use brought about by zoning ordinances. Page 78.

20. b. The extended coverage usually protects against unrecorded liens not known by the policyholder, but no insurance policy will protect against changes in land use by zoning changes, defects known to the buyer, or any defects known at the time of issuance. Page 78.

Chapter 7: Real Estate Agency and Brokerage

1. b. A special agent is authorized only to represent the principal in one specific piece of business (e.g., finding a ready, willing, and able buyer for a property). Page 88.

2. b. Appraisers must be licensed or certified by their state, but they do not have to have a real estate license. Page 93.

3. b. A broker must be licensed at the time of employment to act as an agent on behalf of a client in order to be entitled to a commission. Page 95.

4. a. A salesperson can only receive payment from the principal's broker. The seller pays the listing broker who has agreed to provide payment to a selling broker who then pays the salesperson based on their brokerage agreement. Page 97.

5. c. A case may be made that the broker is actually representing both parties. Because neither knows about the other's representation, the broker could be charged with undisclosed dual agency. In some states, dual agency is legal with full disclosure to both parties and with their informed consent. In other states, dual agency is illegal, even if disclosed. Page 92.

6. a. The exaggeration used by some listing agents in describing a property is not illegal and is called *puffing*. Page 91.

7. b. Most states limit the actions of an unlicensed assistant to administrative or clerical tasks that do not involve acting in any way on behalf of either a seller or buyer. Page 85.

8. c. Regardless of circumstances, a broker must never deposit monies that belong to either a seller or buyer in either a personal or operating account. This is a violation of law called *commingling*. Page 85.

9. c. The person with whom there is a contractual agreement for representation is the client; the other party is a customer. Persons seeking general information about property are customers until such time that they sign a brokerage agreement. Page 89.

10. b. An independent contractor in real estate is primarily a category in the Internal Revenue Code in which the independent contractor is responsible for paying all income and Social Security taxes. Three requirements must be met: the individual must be licensed, must have a written contract with the broker, and must get 90% of income from production. The individual must in no way be treated as an employee. Page 95.

11. d. Although courtesy is certainly an important professional standard, it is not one of the fiduciary responsibilities of a broker toward a principal. Page 86.

12. c. The commission is generally accepted as earned upon acceptance of the offer to purchase, but in reality it is not actually paid until the transaction is settled. Page 95.

13. b. A salesperson may assume any responsibilities assigned by the employing broker but must be under the supervision of the broker. Page 93.

14. d. There is no average or usual commission to be paid to a broker. All commissions are negotiable between the broker and the seller. Any reference to anything other than freely negotiated commissions is a violation of the Sherman Antitrust Act. Page 97.

15. c. The seller who has signed a listing agreement with a broker may be called the seller, the principal, or the client. The customer is the other party to the transaction. Pages 90.

16. a. Disclosing the lowest price that the seller would accept is a direct violation of either the fiduciary or the statutory duties owned to the seller client. Page 87.

17. b. A broker is still entitled to a full commission if the transaction is not consummated due to a seller changing the seller's mind, refusing to sign the deed, being unwilling to correct title defects, committing fraud during the transaction, insisting on terms not in the contract, or making an agreement with the buyer to cancel the contract. Page 96.

18. c. In some states, the broker may act as a transaction broker who does not have any fiduciary or statutory responsibilities to either party, but merely facilitates the transaction. This is a nonagency relationship, but all parties should still be treated honestly and competently. Page 92.

19. a. Agreeing to divide a geographic area into market shares is a violation of antitrust laws if it occurred between different brokers. Within one brokerage firm, this is allowable. Page 98.

20. b. A salesperson may only receive compensation from the broker. Any type of bonus would have to be given to the broker for distribution to the agent. Page 93.

Chapter 8: Contracts

1. a. The parol evidence rule states that any oral agreements made prior to the writing of a contract may not be used to dispute or contradict the written word. Page 106.

2. b. Between the time a contract is ratified and settlement, the contract is executory; it will become executed at settlement when all parties have performed the conditions of the contract. Page 103.

3. c. A novation occurs when new parties are substituted for the original parties, but the existing terms of the contract are retained (novation can also mean a new contract between the same parties). Page 106.

4. b. The statute of frauds in all states requires that real estate contracts be in writing in order to be enforceable. Page 105.

5. b. With a unilateral contract, one party agrees to take action upon the performance of another. The second party is not obligated to act. Page 103.

6. c. Deliberate misrepresentation by the seller would give the buyer the option of canceling the contract, making it a voidable contract. It would only be void if the buyer chose to make it so. Page 103.

7. c. A counteroffer rejects the original offer from the buyer and becomes a new offer from the seller. The contract is not valid until it is accepted by the buyer. Page 104.

8. a. With a bilateral contract, each of the parties agrees to take some action; in the case of real estate, the seller offers to sell and the buyer offers to purchase. Page 102.

9. b. An exclusive-agency listing gives only one broker the right to sell the property, but the owner retains the right to sell it without any commission due to the broker. The open listing would allow any broker to sell, and the exclusive-right-to-sell provides that the broker be paid regardless of who sells the property. Page 114.

10. d. The right to make an assignment may or may not be a condition of a contract, but it is not one of the essential elements required to make a valid contract. Page 106.

11. c. A contract made with a minor is voidable, but not automatically void, at the time the minor reaches legal age. Page 104.

12. b. A contract is assignable unless specifically prohibited in the contract. The retiree acquired equitable title at the time the contract was created. Page 106.

13. c. An open right to represent the buyer is the same as an open listing with a seller; the buyer agrees to pay any broker who finds a property that the buyer decides to purchase. Page 114.

14. a. An option can only be enforced by the optionee (buyer). If the buyer chooses to exercise the option, the seller (optionor) must agree to go through with the sale at the agreed upon terms. Page 128.

15. d. Earnest money is not required to a create a valid contract; the agreement of the parties is sufficient. However, the earnest money deposit gives evidence of the buyer's intent to go through with the contract because in most cases, it is forfeit if the buyer backed out of the transaction. Page 105.

16. b. A net listing is based on the amount of money the seller will receive if the property is sold. The broker keeps any amount over that. A net listing is not allowed in many states and discouraged in others because the broker might act in a fraudulent manner by not informing the owner of the true worth of the property. Page 114.

17. c. A suit for specific performance would force the seller to perform the contract (i.e., sell the property under the original terms of the contract). Page 108.

18. c. Liquidated damages are the amount of money that one party will pay the injured party in case of a breach of contract; in real estate contracts, it is often the earnest money deposit. Page 108.

19. b. An agency contract with either a seller or a buyer may be terminated by the client on the grounds of abandonment if the broker has spent no time on it. Page 109.

20. b. Any counteroffer cancels the original offer and becomes a new offer coming from the seller. The buyers now have the option to accept, reject, or modify that offer. Page 126.

Chapter 9: Landlord and Tenant

1. a. A lease is a bilateral agreement and can be terminated when the period of time has expired or by mutual agreement between landlord and tenant. Page 145.

2. a. The 11th District Cost of Funds is an economic index that could be used as the basis for an index lease. Page 148.

3. b. When a lease extends for a very long period of time and the tenant takes on many obligations of a landowner, some states give the tenant some of the privileges of a freehold estate. Page 134.

4. b. An estate for years is for any definite period of time (even one month); no termination notice is required. A period-to-period estate is for an indefinite number of periods and does require termination notice as required by state law. Page 134.

5. d. Constructive eviction allows the tenant to abandon the premises and terminate the lease if it can be proven that the property is no longer habitable due to the conscious neglect of the landlord. Page 144.

6. a. With a gross lease, the tenant pays a fixed amount and the landlord pays all other expenses related to the property. This is most common in residential leases but may also be used in commercial leases. Page 147.

7. b. When a tenant remains in the property without the consent of the landlord, it is called an estate at sufferance. Page 135.

8. c. Reduction of mortgage debt is not considered an operating expense. Page 147.

9. c. A percentage lease is often used with retail tenants who pay a fixed amount each month, plus a percentage of profit over a certain amount. Page 148.

10. c. A lease purchase is often used when buyers need more time to obtain financing. With a lease purchase, the purchase agreement is the primary consideration and the lease is secondary. With a lease option, the lease is primary and the option is secondary. Page 149.

11. c. A graduated lease begins with a set amount for a predetermined period and then is increased at agreed-upon intervals to a higher amount; this lease is especially advantageous for long-term commercial tenants. Page 148.

12. d. An estate from period to period may be month to month, year to year, or for another designated period of time that is automatically renewed until one of the parties gives notice to terminate. The notice requirement is determined by state law. Page 134.

13. b. A leasehold interest is considered personal property and may be an estate for years, estate from period to period, estate at will, or an estate at sufferance. Page 134.

14. c. An important safeguard for tenants is that their lease contract extends to any new owner of a property. Page 134.

15. a. With an assignment, the person now occupying the property is primarily responsible for the rent, but the original tenant may still be held responsible if the assignee defaults. Page 144.

16. a. A lease may be assigned without either party's prior written consent, unless the terms in the lease prohibit assignment. Page 144.

17. d. The parties to a lease are the landlord (lessor) and the tenant (lessee). The manager is not a party to the lease. Page 133.

18. d. A residential lease should not contain a provision to use the premises for a business. It should include building rules, possession date, specific address, et cetera. Page 142.

19. b. Ground leases are generally net leases that require the lessee to pay rent plus real estate taxes, insurance, upkeep, and repairs. Page 142.

20. b. The landlord may regain possession through a suit for possession, a process called actual eviction; when the court issues a judgment for possession, the tenant must peaceably vacate the premises or a court officer will forcibly remove the tenant. Page 146.

Chapter 10: Real Estate Taxation

1. b. An equalization factor might be used when the tax assessments for one county are found to be a percentage less than in the rest of the state. The assessed value of properties in that county is multiplied by the equalization factor, and the tax rate is applied to the equalized assessment. Page 153.

2. c. Market value of $80,000 assessed at 25% of value = $20,000 times the tax rate of 30 mills ($20,000 × 0.030) = $600. A mill is $\frac{1}{1000}$ of a dollar. Page 154.

3. a. Ad valorem taxes are based on the value of the land and are levied as general real estate taxes because they may vary according to the value of the property. Page 153.

4. c. Basis usually refers to the initial cost an investor pays for a parcel of real estate. The adjusted basis represents the basis, plus the cost of any physical improvements to the property, minus depreciation. Page 158.

5. c. One of the major benefits of an installment sale is that taxes are due only on the monies actually received during the tax year, rather than on the entire sales price. Page 159.

6. b. The property was valued at $135,000 but only assessed as $47,250. The assessed value was multiplied by the equalization factor of 125% ($47,250 × 1.25), for a new assessed value of $59,062.50 times the tax rate of 25 mills ($59,062.50 × 0.025) for a total real estate tax of $1,476.56, or $1,477. Page 154.

7. c. Most state laws allow a period of redemption after the tax sale in which the owner can redeem the property by paying the amount paid at the tax sale plus all interest and charges. The period of redemption varies by state. Page 155.

8. c. When property is sold, the seller generally pays a transfer tax, sometimes called a *grantor tax,* that is based on the sales price. In the case of an assumption, the tax is based on the difference between the sales price and the amount of the assumed mortgage. Page 153.

9. d. Married taxpayers who file a joint federal income tax return have a $500,000 exemption from capital gains tax on the sale of their property, as long as they have lived in the property for two out of the past five years. If the profit is less than $500,000, no capital gains tax is due. A single person has a $250,000 exemption. Page 158.

10. a. Under most state laws, properties owned by municipalities (schools, parks, playgrounds), federal and state governments, religious organizations, hospitals, and educational institutions are exempt from real estate taxation. Usually the property must be used for tax-exempt purposes. Page 153.

11. a. The married couple has a full exemption of $500,000 because they have owned and lived in their home for three years. The single man has a full exemption ($250,000) because he has lived in his home for 17 years. Use of the proceeds from either sale has no effect on the exemption. The single woman might be eligible for a partial exemption because she is having to sell her home due to a new job in another city. The IRS would determine what amount she is eligible for as an extenuating circumstance. Page 158.

12. a. Because land never wears out or becomes obsolete, it cannot be depreciated. Only an improvement can be depreciated based on the period of its useful life that may have little relationship to the actual physical condition of the property. Page 159.

13. b. The adjusted basis includes the original cost of the property, plus any physical improvements, less depreciation, and it is used to determine taxable gain. Page 159.

14. d. A special assessment is levied by a municipality in order to pay for improvements such as curbs and gutters or street lights that will benefit a particular group of homeowners. These homeowners will be assessed an amount based on certain criteria established by state law. Page 156.

15. c. New homeowners are able to deduct all mortgage interest paid during the year, any discount points paid at settlement (by either the seller or the buyer), and all real estate taxes paid during the year on their federal income tax return. Homeowners' insurance cannot be deducted. Page 158.

16. b. Hospitals, schools, property owned by the city or county, and others are exempt from paying real estate taxes. Many state laws allow certain owners a reduction, not an exemption, in real estate taxes, such as homeowners, seniors, military personnel, and those owning agricultural land. Page 153.

17. c. The tax process begins with the adoption of a budget by each taxing body. Taxes cannot be imposed until the taxing body can demonstrate how the taxes will be used, hence the need for a budget. Page 154.

18. d. Because the delinquent taxpayer is still the owner of the property, under the equitable right of redemption, the delinquent taxpayer can avoid a tax sale by paying the delinquent taxes plus interest and charges. In some states, the owner may redeem the property after the sale under a statutory right of redemption. Page 155.

19. a. The county will pay for the improvement along one road through a special assessment on the properties that will benefit from the improvement. Page 156.

20. a. The capital gain is calculated by subtracting the purchase price from the sold price, $545,000 minus $35,000 or $510,000. A married couple is exempt from the first $500,000 of capital gain, so must pay taxes on $10,000. Page 158.

Chapter 11: Real Estate Appraisal

1. b. The gross rent multiplier is used to estimate value of rental property. The value is determined by multiplying the monthly rental income by the gross rent multiplier ($15,000 annual ÷ 12 = $1,250 monthly rental × 125 = $156,250). Page 174.

2. d. The final and most important step in the appraisal process is the reconciliation of all of the findings from the three approaches to value: sales comparison (market data), cost, and income. Depending on the type of property, one approach may be given more weight than others, but all three should be taken into consideration. Page 175.

3. c. Functional obsolescence exists within the property, and it is generally curable, although in some cases it may not be cost effective. The owner must weigh the cost of the improvement against the anticipated increase in value of the property. Page 172.

4.   b.   The cost approach to appraisal is generally used for properties for which there are no real comparables. It takes into account the value of the land, the current cost of construction, and the accrued amount of depreciation. Page 170.

5.   c.   Management fees are part of operating expenses and will be taken into consideration later to calculate the net operating income. The effective gross income is derived by taking the potential gross income and subtracting an allowance for vacancies and collection fees. Page 173.

6.   a.   The merging of several smaller pieces of property into one larger property will generally result in a higher value. This is the principle of plottage, and the process of merging the parcels is called *assemblage*. Page 167.

7.   c.   In most cases, cost does not represent market value because location is an important determining factor. Only when a property is new and represents the highest and best use would cost and market value be approximately the same. Page 175.

8.   a.   The capitalization rate is determine by comparing the relationship of net operating income with the sales price of comparable properties. An investor divides the net income by the capitalization rate to estimate value. Increasing the amount of expected capitalization rate (rate of return on investment) will decrease the value of the property. $270,000 value × 0.09 capitalization rate = $24,300 income. $24,300 income ÷ 0.10 capitalization rate = $243,000 value. Page 173.

9.   c.   The principle of substitution assumes that the value of one property cannot be higher than that of another property that a buyer would find equally desirable. Page 166.

10.   a.   A reproduction duplicates both form and function at current construction prices. A replacement eliminates obsolete features and takes advantage of modern materials and techniques. For historic properties, reproduction is often desired regardless of cost. Page 170.

11.   d.   Unfortunately, external obsolescence is outside the control of the property owner and is therefore incurable. Page 172.

12.   d.   Based on the principle of contribution, the value of an improvement must be considered as to what it will add to the total value of the property to determine if it will be cost effective. Page 167.

13.   c.   To determine replacement cost of an improvement, the appraiser can use the quantity survey of raw materials needed, the finished unit-in-place of individual components, or the average cost per square foot of comparable properties. Due to the time involved in either of the first two options, the most common practice is the square-foot method. Pages 170.

14.   b.   The principle of regression applies when a higher-quality property is located in a neighborhood of lesser-quality properties. The opposite is true of a lesser-quality property located in a higher-quality neighborhood. This is called *progression*. Page 167.

15.   b.   The income approach to value starts with the effective gross annual income, subtracts all allowed operating expenses, and divides by a capitalization rate ($250,000 − $175,000 = $75,000 ÷ 0.10 = $750,000). Page 173.

16.   a.   To have value in the real estate market, a property must have demand, the need or desire for the property or ownership, backed up by the financial means to satisfy that need. Page 164.

17.   b.   Cost and market value are most likely to occur with the sale of a newly constructed property. For older properties, the original cost is unlikely to influence today's buyer; the market value is based on the buyer's desire to buy this particular property. Page 165.

18.   c.   Progression states that the worth of a lesser property tends to increase if it is located among better properties. People will pay more to live in the subdivision, even if it is a smaller home. Page 167.

19.   d.   To have market value, the buyer and seller must be unrelated (father to son) and acting without undue pressure (tax sale and foreclosure). Therefore, the buyer who purchased after viewing a number of other properties is an acceptable comparable. Page 165.

20.   a.   The anticipation that jobs are leaving the community is depressing the demand and the prices. On the other hand, if the rumor were that a plant was opening, anticipation of new jobs coming to the community would help increase the prices. Page 167.

Chapter 12: Real Estate Financing Instruments

1.   c.   Security for a promissory note may be in the form of either a mortgage or a deed of trust. This varies by state. Page 190.

2.   d.   Subordination always refers to one party taking precedence over another. A mortgage loan for the purchase of land often contains a clause agreeing to subordinate to a construction loan. Page 196.

3.   a.   A straight or term loan requires interest-only payments for a certain term, at the end of which the entire principal amount is due. Page 205.

4.   b.   Discount points are considered prepaid interest, increase the yield to the lender, and have no effect on the term of the loan. Page 208.

5.   b.   Lenders like using a deed of trust to establish security for a loan because the nonjudicial foreclosure does not require any court action due to the power of sale clause granting the right to foreclose to the trustee acting on behalf of the lender. Page 199.

6.   a.   In a title theory state, the actual title to the property conveys to a trustee on behalf of the lender. In a lien theory state, the borrower retains the title and the lender has a lien on the property. Many states use a modified lien theory. Page 189.

7.   b.   An equitable right of redemption allows the borrower to pay all outstanding charges and reinstate the loan right up to the time of the foreclosure auction. Some states also allow a statutory right of redemption granting additional time after the foreclosure sale for the borrower to reinstate the loan. Page 199.

8.   c.   All adjustable-rate mortgages start with an index to which a margin is added to determine the rate of interest to be charged. The index may be any one of several economic indicators that are published daily in newspapers. Page 193.

9.   b.   A seller is still responsible for the repayment of the loan if the purchaser defaults under a purchase "subject to" the existing mortgage. Under an assumption, both the buyer and the seller remain liable for the repayment. Only under a novation where the lender releases the original borrower is the seller released from responsibility to repay the loan. Page 197.

10.   a.   On a VA loan, the VA issues a certificate of reasonable value based on an appraisal made by a VA-designated appraiser. If the purchase price is greater than the certificate of value, the purchaser can pay the difference in cash with VA approval. Page 203.

11.   d.   Allowed in some states, the statutory redemption period (the length of time varies) gives the borrower a chance to repay all outstanding charges and reinstate the loan. Page 200.

12.   b.   With an installment contract, the seller does not actually convey title to the property until the buyer has paid the full amount of the sales price. This type of contract is also called *a land contract, contract for deed*, or *agreement of sale*. There is no mortgage or deed of trust. Page 206.

13.   c.   An elderly couple who need cash, but do not wish to sell their paid-for home, can obtain a reverse equity mortgage where the bank will provide either a lump sum or regular monthly payments to the owners based on their equity in the home. The loan is eventually repaid from the sale of the property or from the estate upon the borrower's death. Page 205.

14.   d.   A sale and leaseback has advantages for both the seller and the buyer. The seller now has operating capital and continues to conduct business in the property, paying rent to the new owner who receives certain tax breaks on the investment property. Page 206.

15.   a.   A balloon payment is the final payment of a partially amortized loan. This final payment is much larger since it represents the remaining balance of the loan. Page 206.

16.   b.   A package loan consists of both real and personal property and is often used in resort properties when the security consists of the real estate plus all of the furnishings. Page 204.

17.   d.   Interim financing implies a short-term period. It is often used for construction financing that must then be taken out with a permanent loan when the construction is completed. Page 205.

18.   c.   An open-end loan starts with a note that includes an initial advancement of funds plus any future advances (the interest rate on the advances may change). The equity line of credit is a type of open-end loan that is often used to make improvements to a property. Page 204.

19.   a.   A shared appreciation mortgage allows the lender to originate a mortgage or deed of trust at a favorable interest rate in return for a guaranteed share of the gain (if any) realized by the borrower when the property is eventually sold. Page 205.

20.   a.   The graduated payment mortgage allows for smaller payments in the early years of the loan with increased payments over the remainder of the term. Unfortunately, the lower payments made in the early years are not usually adequate to cover the interest due, resulting in negative amortization; in effect, owing more than the amount originally borrowed. Page 206.

Chapter 13: The Real Estate Financing Market

1.   b.   The Truth in Lending Act requires credit institutions to disclose the true cost of obtaining credit so that it can be compared with making a purchase in cash. Page 219.

2.   c.   A mutual savings bank issues no stock and is mutually owned by its investors. It operates much like a savings association. Page 214.

3.   b.   The Real Estate Settlement Procedures Act (RESPA) does not require that the borrower be given a copy of the loan package submitted for underwriting. Page 219.

4.   b.   Although originally chartered by the government, both Fannie Mae and Freddie Mac are now called *government sponsored enterprises (GSEs)* and fall under government supervision through the Department of Housing and Urban Development (HUD). Page 216.

5.   b.   Originally chartered to provide a secondary market for conventional loans, Freddie Mac today also purchases FHA and VA loans. Page 217.

6.   c.   Age, marital status, and source of income are all included under the Equal Credit Opportunity Act (ECOA), but are not listed as protected classes in the Fair Housing Act. Page 220.

7.   b.   Regulation Z applies to personal loans under $25,000 and all loans secured by a residence such as a mortgage or home equity loan. Page 219.

8.   b.   The secondary mortgage market comprises Fannie Mae, Freddie Mac, and individual investors who purchase blocks of conventional or government loans. Page 216.

9.   d.   Regulation Z defines trigger terms that require that all credit terms be disclosed as amount of down payment, number of payments, amount of payment, period of payment, and amount of any financing charges. If any of the trigger terms are mentioned, full disclosure must be made of cash price or amount of loan; required down payment; number, amount, and frequency of payments; total of all payments; and the annual percentage rate (APR). Page 220.

10.   b.   The annual percentage rate (APR) comprises the interest rate, any discount points, and all loan fees or financing charges. The broker's commission is not included. Page 220.

11.   c.   The Community Reinvestment Act was passed to help prevent redlining and discrimination by lenders. It requires a bank to make a reasonable percentage of loans in their local business area. Page 226.

12.   c.   When the Federal Reserve wants to slow down the economy, it can raise the discount rate, raise reserve requirements, and sell government securities. Any of these actions makes less money available for lending that may slow down the economy. Page 218.

13.   d.   RESPA was created to insure that buyers and sellers have knowledge of all costs of settlement. The RESPA regulations are very specific about preventing any form of kickback between lenders and real estate brokers. Page 221.

14.   b.   RESPA regulations apply to all federally related loans, such as loans made by banks and savings associations that are covered by FDIC, FHA-insured loans, VA-guaranteed loans, and any loan intended to be sold to Fannie Mae or Freddie Mac. Page 221.

15.   d.   FICO is the method of scoring most commonly used by the major credit reporting agencies. The scores are a numerical number ranging from 400– 900 and indicate the level of credit risk to the lender. Page 215.

16.   b   The lender is permitted to require no more than $1/12$ of each year's charge. In this situation, $1,800 +$600 ÷ 12 = $200 per month. Page 226.

17.   b.   The lender may accumulate no more than $1/6$ of the total disbursements for the year, as a cushion, which in this situation amounts to $400. $600 + $1,800 = $2,400 ÷ 6 = $400. Page 226.

18.   c.   The broker's request is illegal even though the licensee doesn't actually acquire something of value immediately. Any referral must be made based on the quality of service, not in the hopes of winning a vacation to Hawaii. Page 225.

19.   b.   The interest for the mortgage loan may not be increased just before closing. If it is increased, the lender must provide a new good-faith estimate and closing will be delayed by three business days. Page 225.

20.   c.   The lender may charge for only a credit report until the lender has delivered a good-faith estimate of all loan charges. If the lender decides to deny the applicant due to the report, the lender is not required to provide the good-faith estimate. Page 221.

Chapter 14: The Control and Development of Land

1. a. A variance is a permanent exception to zoning regulations and is intended to relieve a hardship suffered by a homeowner. The homeowner will have to present evidence that the restriction against a porch is detrimental to health, limits access to the home, or causes some other definite hardship. Page 236.

2. b. A developer (or a subdivider) is the one that divides a large parcel of land into smaller building lots. The builder is the one who actually builds the improvements. The term *developer* is often used today to include both the initial development of the project and the building of homes or office. Page 231.

3. b. Police power provides the government with authority to adopt regulations to protect the health, safety, and general welfare of the public, such as zoning regulations. Private restrictions are created by covenants, conditions, and restrictions (CC&Rs) and deed restrictions. Page 234.

4. b. Building codes deal with the specific details of the construction of a building, including electrical and plumbing services and all materials used. Page 237.

5. d. Zoning ordinances are established by local government based on the authority given to them by state enabling acts. Page 235.

6. a. The Interstate Land Sales Full Disclosure Act was created to protect the public from project developers who were not always honest about the properties they were selling (e.g., parcels of land that were in fact swamps in Florida or near-desert land in California). Page 231.

7. c. Zoning for a PUD permits a higher density of dwellings, mixed uses, and greater use of open space. The combination of residential and commercial uses provides a more convenient community for the occupants plus more green space. Page 235.

8. a. One way that the Interstate Land Sale Full Disclosure Act protects the public is by requiring that prospective buyers receive a property report containing information about distance of paved roads to other communities, number of homes currently occupied, soil conditions, type of title to be received, and any existing liens on the property. The report must be received at least three days before signing a sales contract. Page 231.

9. c. Most municipalities have a zoning board of appeals where members of the public may present their complaints about the adverse effect of a particular zoning ordinance on their property. The petitions may be made for either changes or exceptions to existing zoning laws. Page 236.

10. c. Buildings that were constructed prior to a zoning law that would now make them in violation are acceptable as a nonconforming use permit. If the building is ever destroyed or torn down, the nonconforming use would most likely no longer be permitted. Page 236.

11. b. A new property or business will be expected to conform to current zoning ordinances. If special approvals or exceptions will be necessary, these facts need to be known prior to entering into a sales contract. Page 235.

12. d. Private deed restrictions are a way for an owner to control future use of property; however, such restrictions may not be violations of fair housing laws that prohibit discrimination based on race, color, religion, national origin, sex, familial status, or disability. Page 233.

13. a. Sometimes a local zoning authority will bend its own rules and grant a conditional use permit if it appears that such permission would serve the best interests of the community (e.g., a school, park, recreation center, hospital, or country club). Page 236.

14. a. The Interstate Land Sales Full Disclosure act affects interstate sales or leasing of 25 or more lots. Some states have enacted additional laws for intrastate sale or leasing of property. Page 231.

15. d. The plat map must contain all necessary approvals and be recorded in the county where the land is located. It includes detailed information about easements, land dedication, and set asides for roads and right-of-ways, but no information about present or future sales prices of the lots. Page 232.

16. b. Many states require that municipalities produce master plans to provide the public with notice on planning, controlling subdivision development, and zoning ordinances. Page 234.

17. d. A planned unit development (PUD) consists of a combination of diverse uses; homeowners contribute to an association that is charged with maintenance of community areas. Page 235.

18. a. A transit-oriented development (TOD) is a variation of a planned unit development in that it mixes retail, residential, and other uses around access to public transportation. A TOD is not similar to traditional suburbs in which residents depend on their cars for nearly everything. Page 236.

19. c. Local municipalities can enforce zoning ordinances and building codes, but they may not enforce private restrictions, such as deed restrictions, restrictive covenants, and CC&Rs. Page 233.

20. a. The issuance of building permits is a method by which building codes are enforced. Through the permit requirement, city officials become aware of construction or alterations and compliance with both building codes and zoning ordinances. Page 237.

Chapter 15: Fair Housing Laws and Ethical Practices

1. c. The Fair Housing Act was created to give those seeking a new home the right to buy or rent any property they can financially afford in an unbiased market place. Page 240.

2. b. Blockbusting, also called *panic selling*, is the illegal practice of encouraging property owners to sell and move by preying on their bias or prejudices about a particular race, ethnic, or religious group moving into the neighborhood. Page 244.

3. d. The Civil Rights Act of 1866 was the first antidiscrimination law and dealt solely with the right of any person, regardless of race, to inherit, purchase, lease, sell, hold, and convey real and personal property. Unlike other antidiscrimination laws, there are no exceptions. Page 241.

4. a. Any indication on the part of the real estate agent that they may be encouraging, or denying, access to any given neighborhood is considered to be steering and is directly prohibited by fair housing law. Page 241.

5. a. Although many discrimination complaints may be taken to HUD or to state fair housing authorities, any complaint regarding discrimination under the Civil Rights Act of 1866 must be brought to a federal court. Page 247.

6. b. Redlining is the illegal practice of denying loans to property owners based on the neighborhood's racial or other ethnic composition instead of making a business decision based on income, debts, and so on. Page 244.

7. b. The two new protected classes added in 1968 were disability and familial status. Disability may be either a mental or physical impairment that substantially limits one or more major life activities. Familial status refers to anyone with children under the age of 18, pregnant women, and those in the process of securing legal custody. Page 241.

8. c. The only way that a person should be denied housing is on a financial basis: poor credit, insufficient income, or lack of funds for a down payment or security deposit. Page 242.

9. a. Undercover volunteers called testers may visit real estate offices, lenders, and insurance companies to test for discriminatory practices. Testing is legal and is allowed by the courts as the only means available to check for compliance with fair housing laws. Page 249.

10. b. In the real estate business, it is important that all customers and clients be treated in the same way. There must be no special conditions, either positive or negative, or any particular group. Page 248.

11. d. It is important to know that prior to the Housing and Community Development Act of 1974, women could not have credit or purchase property in their own name if they were married. The protected class of sex is sometimes called gender to clarify that it refers to either male or female, not to sexual preference. Page 241.

12. d. A real estate broker is expected to always act in the best interests of the client, but this does not extend to accepting a client's directions if doing so is considered to be discrimination or a violation of fair housing law. Page 249.

13. b. A private club or religious institution may limit housing to members of that particular group as long as anyone may become a member of the group, but no one is allowed to limit housing to singles or to prohibit children. Page 244.

14. d. An administrative law judge may impose penalties ranging from $10,000–$50,000; however, there is no dollar limit to cases heard in federal court. Page 247.

15. c. Because occupation is not a protected class, the landlord would not be in direct violation of fair housing to deny lawyers. This would still be risky, however, because it is very possible that a lawyer could claim the denial of housing was due to race, religion, national origin, or another protected class. Page 243.

16. c. Although the landlord wants to protect small children, she is practicing a form of steering and taking on a responsibility that is not hers to take. She must show all available apartments and let the parents decide which to choose. Page 244.

17. a. *Jones v. Mayer* reaffirmed the Civil Rights Act of 1866 that prohibits all racial discrimination, public as well as private. Under no circumstances may an owner or seller discriminate on the basis of race or color. Page 241.

18. c. Under fair housing, families consist of at least one person under the age of 18; this familial unit includes foster children and pregnant women. Page 241.

19. b. Owner occupants of two-, three-, or four-unit properties may not use discriminatory advertising, but they may discriminate by not renting to families with children or someone with a disability. Under no circumstances may they discriminate by race or color. Page 241.

20. d. The Equal Credit Opportunity Act prohibits discrimination in the granting of credit; creditors, such as landlords and property managers, may not discriminate on the basis of race, color, religion, national origin, sex, receipt of public assistance, age, or marital status. Page 242.

Chapter 16: Environmental Issues and the Real Estate Transaction

1.   b.   The act requires that the disclosure statement be attached to all sales contracts and leases, that all buyers and sellers receive the lead hazard pamphlet, that the known presence of lead-based paint must be disclosed, and that purchasers of property built before 1978 be given a 10-day period to conduct an inspection. Page 254.

2.   c.   Encapsulation is preferable over removal because the removal itself could release hazardous airborne asbestos. Page 254.

3.   c.   Urea-foam insulation was first used in the 1970s, but lead-based paint was used for decades until 1978 when it was banned. A licensed salesperson should never attempt to personally inspect and/or remove any type of environmental hazard. Pages 254–255.

4.   a.   Asbestos is a good form of insulation and was used extensively prior to 1978 when it was banned. It is only harmful when it is disturbed or exposed, and attempting to remove it from one part of a building might contaminate other areas. Pages 254.

5.   a.   Lead was used in paint and plumbing pipes and does appear in soil or even in the air, but was not typically used in roofing tiles. Pages 256.

6.   d.   Intact asbestos is nonfriable and does not constitute a danger, unless it is disturbed and becomes airborne. Page 254.

7.   b.   A landfill is one type of waste disposal site primarily used for garbage and refuse. The process involves lining a large hole with an impermeable membrane, filling it with garbage and/or refuse, and then covering it with soil and plantings. Hazardous and toxic materials go to hazardous waste disposal sites that are much more complex. Page 254.

8.   b.   The Comprehensive Environmental Response, Compensation, and Liability Act (CERCLA) established the Superfund to clean up hazardous waste sites. A landowner is held liable for cleanup along with previous owners, property managers, and any other persons who caused the contamination. Page 260.

9.   c.   Radon is a radioactive gas produced by the decay of minerals in the ground and is believed to be a direct cause of lung cancer. The presence of radon can be found by testing and can be removed by installing an adequate ventilation system. Page 256.

10.   b.   Asbestos contamination is most prevalent in public or commercial buildings, especially schools built prior to 1978. It was also used as insulation material in residential property build before 1978. Pages 254.

11.   d.   Mold has become a very controversial environmental problem, although only a few types of mold are actually toxic. The only way to effectively control mold is to remove the source of the moisture that is providing the environment conducive to the growth of mold. Page 257.

12.   b.   Although all forms of hazardous substances are dangerous for both adults and children, lead-based paint is particularly damaging to children under six years old. Page 254.

13.   c.   The biggest problem with carbon monoxide (CO) is that it is both odorless and colorless and, therefore, impossible to detect. Because CO emissions come from all types of heating systems, proper ventilation and maintenance is essential. Page 257.

14.   d.   Based on experience, a licensed agent may be very aware of potential environmental hazards in a property but should always direct any parties involved to seek professional inspections and make no attempt to correct the situation. Pages 260–261.

15.   c.   Mold usually has a very distinct odor and is easily detected. The toxic form of mold that has been under much discussion is Stachybotrys, which has caused serious health problems. The EPA has not established any allowable level of mold spore count. Page 257.

16.   d.   Some 300 deaths a year are caused by carbon monoxide, a deadly by-product of an improperly burning stove. Page 257.

17.   a.   Since 2010, the EPA requires the use of lead-safe practices; all contractors disturbing more than six square feet of painted area in a home, day care, or school built before 1978 must be certified. Page 256.

18.   b.   Mold requires oxygen, food source, warmth, and moisture to thrive. The easiest to control is moisture. Page 257.

19.   c.   Before any government funded project can take place, an environmental impact statement (EIS) must consider what will happen if the project takes place. The EIS considers population expansion that may require additional funding for public services, among other things. Page 259.

20.   b.   Brownfields legislation has changed attitudes about these formerly stigmatized properties; now, their values have increased as developers see their potential and less liability. Page 258.

Chapter 17: Closing the Real Estate Transaction

1.   d.   An item that is owed by the seller and that has not been paid for is prorated as a debit to the seller and credit to the buyer. For example, the seller has not yet paid the current taxes that will ultimately be paid by the buyer; debit the seller, credit the buyer. Page 270.

2.   d.   Accrued interest on the seller's mortgage that is assumed by the buyer is always prorated to the day of closing. The seller is responsible for paying the interest for the days of the month when the property was owned by the seller; debit the seller, credit the buyer. Page 272.

3.   c.   RESPA regulations require that the Settlement Statement (HUD-1) be used for all mortgage loans that are financed by all lending institutions covered by FDIC insurance or that are intended to be sold to Fannie Mae and Freddie Mac. Page 270.

4.   b.   The deed may be delivered to the buyer at the settlement table (as in a face-to-face closing) or may be deposited with the escrow holder when settled in escrow. Page 267.

5.   a.   The earnest money is submitted along with the sales contract and counts as part of the total sales price. Page 268, 274.

6.   a.   The annual percentage rate (APR) is disclosed on the truth-in-lending statement that is provided to the borrower. The settlement statement contains all costs of closing on both the property and the loan, but it does not include all financing details. Page 270.

7.   d.   The lender provides a check for the amount that the buyer is borrowing in order to purchase the property that shows as a credit to the buyer on the statement. Page 270, 274.

8.   d.   The biggest difference between closing in escrow and a face-to-face closing is that neither party needs to be present. The escrow agent collects all necessary documents and funds, disperses monies due to the seller, and records the deed and any mortgage or deed of trust. Page 268.

9.   b.   A buyer must be assured that there are no encumbrances or liens on the property other than those mentioned and agreed upon in the sales contract. For example, a tax lien would have to be paid off before settlement in order to provide a clear title. Page 269.

10. a.   A lender is concerned about having a clear title to the property in case the borrower should default on the loan and the lender should need to foreclose. The lender requires the buyer to purchase a lender's title insurance policy to protect that interest. It is up to the buyer to decide whether to also purchase an owner's policy. Page 266, 268.

11. d.   The deed, property disclosure form (if required), and lead-based paint booklet (if required) are deposited with the escrow agent by the seller. The buyer deposits the cash to complete the transaction, the loan documents, and all required insurance policies. Page 268.

12. b.   Because a lease continues in effect after the sale of a rental property, the security deposit will eventually be returned by the new owner and will be credited to the buyer and debited to the seller. Page 273.

13. b.   The seller collected the September rent of $550 but only actually owned the property for 15 days. One-half of the rent ($275) will be credited to the buyer and debited to the seller. Page 274.

14. b.   The buyer is borrowing 70% of the $80,000 sales price ($56,000) and has made a $5,000 earnest money deposit. The buyer will need $19,000 to complete the transaction. $80,000 × 70% = $56,000 + $5,000 EMD = $61,000; $80,000 − $61,000 = $19,000. The buyer will need additional funds for closing costs. Page 274–275.

15. d.   The buyer is borrowing 90% of the $200,000 sales price ($180,000) with a 10% down payment ($20,000). A point is 1% of the loan amount ($1,800); three points is $5,400. The buyer will need $25,400 to complete the transaction. $200,000 − $180,000 = $20,000 + $5,400 = $25,400. The buyer will need additional funds for closing costs. Page 277.

16. d.   The buyer deposits the cash necessary to complete the transaction, the loan documents, and all required insurance policies. The seller must deposit the deed, property disclosure form (if required), and a lead-based paint statement, if required. Page 270.

17. c.   The payoff statement includes not only the final amount owed, but also the interest required to the day of closing. Most residential loans do not include prepayment penalties. Page 271.

18. d.   Nothing must be filed with the IRS, unless the gain is more than exempted by law; $500,000 is exempt for couples who are married and filing jointly. Page 269.

19. a.   Prepaid items are those that have been prepaid by the seller but which the buyer is now receiving the benefit of. Therefore, the buyer is debited the same amount that is credited to the seller. Page 270.

20. c.   Generally, the day of closing is the responsibility of the seller who must pay any expense incurred that day. However, the seller also benefits because the rent for that day belongs to the seller. Page 272.

Chapter 18: Real Estate Mathematics

1. b. $11,150. The buyer is borrowing 95% of the $223,000 sales price with a 5% down payment. The buyer will need $11,150 in cash for the down payment ($223,000 × 95% = $211,850; $223,000 − $211,850 = $11,150). Page 287.

2. a. $1,557. The 6% commission on a $173,000 home is $10,380, ($173,000 × 6% = $10,380), which the brokers split evenly ($10,380 ÷ 2 = $5,190). The listing agent receives 30% of the broker's share ($5,190 × 30% = $1,557). Page 288.

3. a. $312. Sales price of $195,000. State conveyance tax of 0.11% plus town conveyance tax of 0.05% = 0.16% tax ($195,000 × 0.0016 = $312). Page 290.

4. c. $345,000. The conveyance tax of $448.50 represents 0.13% of the sales price ($448.50 ÷ 0.0013 = $345,000). Page 290.

5. d. 80% ($356,040 ÷ $445,000 = 80%). Page 290.

6. c. $3,485. Sales price of $205,000 with LTV of 85% ($205,000 × 85% = $174,250). Each point equals 1% of $174,250 loan amount ($1,742.50); two points are $3,485 ($1742.50 × 2 = $3,485). Page 291.

7. b. $170,720. Last year's sale price represents 103% of this year's sale price. Therefore, $176,000 ÷ 1.03 = $170,873. Page 291.

8. d. $26,250. Five years ago value of $15,000 appreciated by 75% ($15,000 × 175% = $26,250). Page 291.

9. b. 25%. Today's price of $50,000 − original value of $40,000 = $10,000 ($10,000 ÷ $40,000 = 25%). Page 291.

10. b. 10,626.63. Front footage of 75 ft. 6 in. (width) equals 75.5 ft, and depth of 140 ft 9 in. = 140.75 ft (75.5 × 140.75 = 10,626.63 sq ft). Page 292.

11. c. 940. Two sides of 125 feet = 250 ft; two sides of 350 ft = 700 ft. 250 + 700 = 950 running feet − 10 ft gate = 940 running feet of fence. Page 292.

12. b. $1.81. 125 ft width × 150 ft depth = 18,750 sq ft. Sales price of $34,000 ÷ 18,750 sq ft = $1.81 per sq ft. Page 292.

13. d. 4,000,000. 400 ft length × 250 ft width × 40 ft height = 4,000,000 cu ft. Page 292.

14. b. $396.86. Total tax for the year is $1,282, or a daily rate of 3.512 ($1,282 ÷ 365 = 3.5123). Settlement is April 23 with taxes to be prorated through the day of settlement. Calculated on the calendar year, the seller owes for January (31), February (28), March (31), and April (23), for a total of 113 days at 3.512 per day, or $396.86. This amount will be credited to buyer and debited to seller. Page 294.

15. a. $26.66 credit to the buyer. Settlement is March 20. The annual water bill is $120. Because the buyer will pay the bill, the seller will owe for 80 days: January (30), February (30), March (20) calculated on banker's year and prorated through day of closing at the daily rate of $0.3333, or $26.66 credit to buyer. Page 294.

16. b. $190,909. $10,500 ÷ 0.055% = $190,909. Page 295.

17. c. 6%. 15,000 ÷ $250,000 = 6%. Page 288–289.

18. b. $1,993.75. $435,000 × 0.055 ÷ 12 = $1,993.75. Page 291.

19. a. Debit seller $616.64, credit buyer $616.64. $3,000 ÷ 360 = $8.333 × 74 days = $616.64. Page 290.

20. b. Debit seller $5,350, credit buyer $5,350. Generally, the day of closing is the responsibility of the seller who must pay any expense incurred that day. However, the seller also benefits because the rent for that day belongs to the seller. In this situation, the seller has to pay for the repair, but that has no impact on the number of days of rent that the seller must turn over to the buyer. $535 × 20 = $10,700 ÷ 30 days × 15 = $5,350. Page 295.

Practice Examination

1. d. $175,532. The amount the seller wishes to net represents 94% of the sales price (100% − 6% = 94%). $165,000 ÷ 94% = $175,532. If you just add 6% of $165,000 ($9,900) to the net amount ($165,000), the price will be $174,900; deducting a 6% commission from that amount will not allow enough for the desired net [$165,000 + $9,900 = $174,900; $174,900 − 6% ($10,494) = $164,406]. Page 289.

2. d. Joint tenancy usually includes rights of survivorship where if one party dies, the surviving parties automatically receive the deceased party's interest. With tenancy in common, the deceased party's interest goes to the deceased's heirs. Page 62.

3. b. The statute of frauds requires that all real estate contracts and all leases for more than one year be in writing in order to be enforceable. Pages 126.

4. a. When the certificate of reasonable value is less than the agreed-upon sales price, the veteran can pay the difference in cash (with VA approval). The veteran can also walk away from the sale without penalty. Page 203.

5. c. A cloud on the title may mean that there is a problem in the history of the conveyances of the property (chain of title). A quitclaim deed releases any potential interest someone may have in the property and clears the title. Page 51.

6. d. Real property includes the land and everything above or below, all improvements, and the bundle of rights that go with the real estate. It does not include personal property (chattels). Page 13.

7. b. Real estate taxes will be prorated between buyer and seller according to the number of days the property is owned. Both seller and buyer have separate recording charges and earnest money, and the amount of the new mortgage loan are credits to the buyer. Page 272–273.

8. a. Only the grantor is required to sign the deed with the acknowledgment of two witnesses. It may be signed by an attorney-in-fact acting under the authority of a power of attorney. The grantee must be named in the deed, but no signature is required. Page 47.

9. c. An open listing is a unilateral agreement where the seller agrees to pay a commission to any broker producing a ready, willing, and able buyer. Brokers prefer to have an exclusive-right-to-sell where a commission is paid regardless of who produces the buyer. With an exclusive-agency listing, the seller retains the right to sell the property without paying a commission to the listing broker. Page 114.

10. b. The Fair Housing Act prohibits the denial of housing and any change in the terms being offered for sale or lease on the basis of race, color, religion, national origin, sex, familial status, and disability. Pages 243.

11. a. Resort or vacation properties are often sold as a package deal with all furniture and appliances included along with the property. This spreads the cost of furnishing the unit across the term of the loan and reduces the amount of initial investment by the new owner. Page 204.

12. b. The easement in gross may be personal but is most often used for a commercial purpose where multiple properties are affected (e.g., railroad tracks, sewer lines, and power lines). It is not appurtenant to any ownership interest and may be inherited, assigned, or conveyed. Page 38.

13. c. An encroachment occurs whenever a portion of a building, a fence, or a driveway extends over into an adjoining property. Page 40.

14. c. Tenancy by the entirety applies only to a married couple and is not available in all states. The real estate is considered to be held by one indivisible legal unit with full rights of survivorship. Any future conveyance of the property must be signed by both parties, and there is no right to partition. Page 64.

15. d. The Taxpayer Relief Act of 1997 granted an exemption from capital gains tax on the sale of a personal residence of $250,000 for a single person who has lived in the property for at least two of the past five years. That person will owe no federal tax ($306,100 − $177,800 = $128,300). Page 158.

16. b. A lien is a money encumbrance such as a mortgage loan that affects the title. An encumbrance is anything that diminishes the value or use of a property. Nonmoney encumbrances include easements, encroachments, and restrictions. Page 35.

17. a. Functional obsolescence is one of the three classes of depreciation. It refers to outdated function or poor design. It is within the control of the owner and in many cases is curable, although cost or other factors may make it incurable. Page 172.

18. b. Many municipalities assess property for tax purposes as some percentage of actual value. If one section of a larger area is assessed much lower (or higher) than the rest of the area, an equalization factor may be used. The percentage is then applied to the new figure and the tax rate calculated on the new assessment ($40,000 × 1.5 = $60,000 × 40% = $24,000 ÷ 100 = $240 × $4 = $960). Page 153–154.

19. d. To be valid, a contract must have been signed as a free and voluntary act. A contract signed under duress, menace, or undue influence is voidable at the option of the distressed party. Page 103.

20. a. A building that was erected prior to a zoning ordinance that would now prohibit its construction is considered a nonconforming use. This is often called *grandfathered*. At any time the building is either torn down or destroyed, any new structure would have to conform to the current zoning ordinance. Conditional use refers to the use of the property rather than the structure, and a variance is a permanent exception. Page 236.

21. b. The chain of title shows the record of ownership from the original owner to the present time. The abstract of title is a history of all documents pertaining to that property and is one form of title evidence along with title insurance policy, Torrens certificate, and certificate of title. Page 77.

22. a. The fiduciary relationship that calls for the duties of care, obedience, accounting, loyalty, and disclosure is a relationship based on trust and confidence and is an important aspect of the common law of agency. In many states today, these duties have been replaced with a statutory law of agency that specifies certain duties owned to both clients and customers. Some states have abrogated the common law of agency; others have incorporated the fiduciary duties into the statutory. Page 86–87.

23. d. Insurance companies, pension funds, and other large fiduciaries are interested in long-term investments to protect the funds entrusted to them. Providing a lower rate of interest in a commercial property can prove to be a better investment over time due to the share of anticipated appreciation. Page 214.

24. a. Property taxes may be collected at the beginning of, end of, or at intervals during the year. Depending on which party must pay the taxes and when, the other will owe for each day that the property was in their possession. The seller paid a total tax of $1,116 for the calendar year. With settlement on November 15, the buyer will need to credit the seller for 45 days; November (15), December (31). Total tax of $1,116 ÷ 365 days = daily rate of $3.058 × 46 = $140.67. Page 274–275.

25. c. The Federal Housing Administration (FHA) made it possible for more people to buy a home by providing for an amortized loan with equal payments over a set term and a low down payment. To encourage lenders to make these loans, FHA agreed to insure the full value of the loan. Page 201.

26. b. 8 width × 9 depth × 12 height = 864 cu ft ÷ 2 = 432 cu ft × $1.82 = $786.24, rounded to $786. Page 293.

27. d. A counteroffer is a rejection of the original offer and becomes a new offer that may be accepted, rejected, or countered. A counteroffer can be withdrawn prior to being accepted, but it is not possible to return to an acceptance of the earlier offer. Page 126.

28. b. The Real Estate Settlement Procedures Act (RESPA) requires disclosure of all fees and charges involved in the settlement of both conveyance of a property and closing of a loan. The Truth in Lending Act refers only to the cost of credit. The Equal Credit Opportunity Act prohibits discrimination by lenders, and the Real Estate Reinvestment Trust refers to a real estate investment trust (REIT) investment group. Page 220–221.

29. c. A balloon loan is also called a partially amortized loan because the payments for a set number of years are based on a fully amortized payment schedule. At the end of the specified number of years, the remaining balance of principal becomes due in one final payment. Page 192.

30. d. A licensed salesperson must always act under the supervision of a principal broker. All actions must be taken in the name of the broker, and any compensation must be paid by that broker. Page 93.

31. a. With a unilateral contract, one party offers to take some action if another party performs (for example, an open listing). There is no initial agreement between the parties. Page 102.

32. d. With a land contract, there is no mortgage or deed of trust and title does not pass to the buyer until the terms of the contract have been completed. Between the time of signing the contract and the passing of the title, the buyer has an equitable interest. Page 206.

33. b. The Equal Credit Opportunity Act prohibits discrimination on race, color, religion, national origin, and sex (also protected classes under fair housing law), plus marital status, age, and source of income. The only legal way to refuse credit is if the party cannot make the payments. Page 220.

34. d. Demographics is the study of the population, and although it may have an effect on the supply and demand for real estate, it is not categorized as one of the principles of value. Page 6.

35. b. The estate from period to period is for an indefinite number of definite periods, such as week to week, month to month, or year to year, and is automatically renewed. The time required for notice to terminate is set by state law. An estate for years ends at the time specified in the lease. An estate at will and an estate at sufferance require notice to quit. Page 134.

36. d. A tenant may remain in the property after the expiration of the lease either with the landlord's permission (tenancy at will) or without permission (tenancy at sufferance). A tenancy at will is indefinite as to term. Page 135.

37. d. In some states after a foreclosure sale, a statutory right of redemption permits a defaulting party to pay all debts and expenses to redeem the property. A borrower who is in default on a mortgage loan almost always has the right to pay all past due charges and reinstate the loan prior to the foreclosure auction sale. This is equitable right of redemption. Page 155.

38. d. Fair housing law allows a person to specify the gender of a person with whom living space will be shared. Page 243.

39. b. State law may vary slightly, but basically all states have a statute of descent that specifies to whom property will be conveyed when a person dies without a will but does have heirs. The property of a person who dies without either will or heirs reverts to the state by the law of escheat. Page 53.

40. a. A life estate is created to allow someone to live in a property, even though it has been conveyed to another party, as long as that person lives. Upon the death of the person with the life estate, the property may either revert to the owner (reversionary interest) or go to the third party previously designated (remainder interest). Pages 31–32.

41. c. Appraisers use all three approaches to value (sales comparison, cost, and income), but the one most commonly used for residential properties is the sales comparison (or market data) approach. The subject property is compared to other similar properties located in the same area and sold within a reasonable time period. Page 168.

42. b. Each month the lender may collect one-twelfth of the amount due for taxes and insurance as part of the mortgage payment (PITI). At settlement, the buyer pays the lender an amount roughly equivalent to two months' worth of taxes and insurance payments to start the escrow account from which these payments will be made. Page 196.

43. b. Although all hazardous substances obviously present a risk for both adults and young children, studies have shown that lead-based paint has a neurological effect on children under the age of six. Page 254.

44. a. In an effort to obtain working capital, a business owner might sell a building to an investor and then lease back the property and continue to operate the business. The original owner is now the lessee, and the new owner (buyer) is the lessor. The buyer holds title and receives any mortgage interest deduction. Page 206.

45. c. In a state that allows designated agency, the broker may designate one agent to work with a seller client and another to work with a buyer client in the same transaction (both seller and buyer have signed brokerage agreements). Both seller and buyer have full representation by their designated agent. In a dual agency situation, both agents would have equal responsibility to both parties. All dual or designated agency relationships must be disclosed to all parties. Page 92.

46. a. The income approach to value is based on the present worth of the future rights to income. The appraiser must first look at the potential income, then deduct all operating expenses to derive the net income. This figure is then divided by a cap rate (derived by comparison with comparable businesses sold in the area) to estimate the value of the property ($72,000 income – $60,000 expenses = $12,000 net income ÷ 8% capitalization rate = $150,000 value). Page 172–174.

47. d. Unless a broker limits a business to single agency, the broker will have both seller and buyer clients who will have signed brokerage agreements. The broker owes either fiduciary or statutory duties to all clients. The other party to a transaction involving one of the broker clients is a customer. Page 92.

48. d. Although it would sound exactly contrary, a gross lease is one in which the lessee pays only a specified rent. The lessor pays all other expenses of the property, including taxes, insurance, and maintenance. A net lease is when the lessee pays some, or all, of the other expenses in addition to the rent. Page 147.

49. b. An easement grants one party the right to use some portion of another's property. The party who is benefiting from the easement holds the dominant tenement, the party who has lost something in value holds the servient tenement. Pages 37–38.

50. d. Sometimes the auction sale does not produce enough money to pay off the total amount due to the lender. The lender can then file for a deficiency judgment against the defaulting borrower. Page 200.

51. d. General liens apply to any properties held by a person. A specific lien only applies to one specific property. Mortgage liens, mechanics' liens, and tax liens are all specific liens. Page 34–35.

52. c. An option gives all of the control to the optionee. The optionor must agree to convey the property on the specified terms if and when the optionee decides to exercise the option. The optionee may choose to exercise that option or not. Pages 128.

53. a. First, the debits must be determined before subtracting the credits to arrive at the amount due at closing. Debits include the purchase price of $184,500, plus taxes of $1,488.33 ($1,880 ÷ 12 × 9.5 = $1,488.33), and other closing costs of $4,250. Total debits = $190,238.33. Credits include new mortgage of $166,050, plus earnest money $4,000 = $170,050. Debits minus credits ($190,338.33 – $170,050) = $20,288.33. The actual down payment is never entered on the closing statement. The sellers' closing costs are immaterial to what the buyers owe. Page 273–274.

54. b. A contract with a person who is known to have been judged incompetent by the court is void. Page 104.

55. a. If a broker deposits money belonging to an individual in the broker's own account, it is a violation of the law and is called *commingling*. That is why brokers maintain a trust, or escrow account, for all monies belonging to others. Misappropriating funds from a trust or escrow account is called conversion. Page 85.

56. a. Steering is a violation of fair housing law and occurs whenever an agent takes any action that appears to either lead to, or away from, a particular area because of racial or religious overtones. Even if agents believe they are acting in the client's best interest, any suggestion of steering must be avoided. Page 244.

57. b. Estate for years would seem to imply a period of years, but in fact it is any specific period of time with a definite termination date. It could be for weeks, months, quarters, or any other specified interval. It does not require notification to terminate. Page 134.

58. c. Each discount point counts for 1% of the loan amount ($138,500 × 0.01 = $1,385 × 4 = $5,540). Page 202.

59. b. The Civil Rights Act of 1866 was the first of the civil rights acts and prohibits any discrimination regarding sale or rental of housing on the basis of race. There are no exceptions. Page 241.

60. a. The loan origination fee is 1% of the loan amount ($260,000 × 90% LTV = $234,000 × 0.01 = $2,340). Page 202.

61. c. A variance provides an exception to a zoning ordinance based on hardship. Nonconforming use refers to a structure that predates the zoning. Building permits are issued to control construction. Page 236.

62. b. An alienation clause, often called due-on-sale, provides that upon the sale of the property by the borrower, the lender has the choice of declaring the entire debt immediately due or permitting a qualified buyer to assume the loan at current market rates. Page 197.

63. a. Asbestos was used for insulation in many schools and office buildings. The problem is that attempting to remove the asbestos is liable to further contaminate the building through the release of airborne asbestos spores. Page 254.

64. b. A special warranty deed warrants only that the property was not encumbered during the time of that person's ownership. A general warranty deed provides numerous warranties, or covenants. The bargain and sale and quitclaim deeds have no warranties. Page 49.

65. d. Accrued depreciation results from physical deterioration, functional obsolescence, and external obsolescence. It is difficult to determine the depreciation in these areas on a building over 70 years old. Page 172.

66. a. RESPA permits a real estate licensee to refer buyers to appropriate lenders. However, RESPA prohibits kickbacks from a lender, settlement agent, or title insurance company to a broker. A kickback is any payment made when no service is actually performed. Pages 221, 225.

67. b. The church received 12% of the estate (54% + 18% + 16% = 88% and 100% − 88% = 12%). The church's part is $79,000 ÷ 12% = $658,333 for the total estate. The daughter's share is $118,500 ($658,333 × 18% = $118,499.90 or $118, 500). Page 288.

68. d. The presence of vacant or abandoned buildings in the area is an example of external obsolescence because the deterioration is beyond the control of the owner of the property being appraised. Physical deterioration (e.g., a roof leak) is curable, functional obsolescence (e.g., pillars and cornices) may or may not be curable depending on cost, but external obsolescence is always incurable. Page 172.

69. c. An adjustable-rate mortgage (ARM) is calculated by starting with a selected economic indicator as an index, then adding on the margin of profit desired by the lender to determine the note rate. As the index fluctuates, the note rate will change (the margin never changes during the life of the loan). Changes are made in an adjustment period that may be monthly, quarterly, annually, or multi-year. Page 192–193.

70. d. During the time between the ratification of a contract and settlement, the buyer has what is called an *equitable interest*. Page 127.

71. c. Listing broker received one-half of the 6.5% commission ($2,593.50 ÷ 3.25% = $79,800). Page 289.

72. a. In a cooperative, each homeowner owns shares of stock in the corporation that owns the building and receives a proprietary lease for the unit they occupy. It differs from a condominium where each owner has fee simple title to a unit plus an undivided interest in the common elements. Page 68–69.

73. c. A cubic yard is calculated by dividing the cubic feet by 27 (36 × 200 × 12 = 86,400 cu ft ÷ 27 = 3,200 cu yd at $1 per month × 12 = $38,400 annual rent). Page 292.

74. d. With an exclusive-right-to-sell listing, the listing broker is entitled to a commission regardless of who procures the ready, willing, and able buyer. In open or exclusive-agency listings, brokers must prove they are the procuring brokers. The net listing is not recommended. Pages 114.

75. a. The cabinets were made a part of the permanent structure and are, therefore, fixtures that become a part of the real estate. Trade fixtures used in a business may be removed at the end of the lease term regardless of the means of attachment, adaptation, or intended use. Pages 21–22.

76. d. Quoting an interest rate is a trigger term under Regulation Z that requires the disclosure of all other information regarding the credit involved, including the annual percentage rate (APR). Page 220.

77. d. The lender requires that the borrower (the buyer) protect the lender's interest in the property by purchasing a lender's title insurance policy. It could, however, be made a condition of the contract that the seller would pay for this policy. Page 78–79.

78. b. If property has increased 27% over a three-year period, calculate the increase in value by multiplying the original cost by 127% ($142,500 × 127% = $180,975 present value). Page 291.

79. a. Broker commissions are always negotiable, and there is nothing illegal about charging a different rate of commission to different parties. There may, however, be a question of ethics in this situation depending on how this was presented to the seller. There is also the question of good will in the community. Page 95.

80. a. Under the government survey system, a section has 640 acres. The NW quarter of a section is 160 acres, the NW quarter of that is 40 acres, and half of that is 20 acres. It is easiest to start with the full section and work backwards to determine the number of acres in a parcel. Page 19.

81. c. Under the Comprehensive Environmental Response, Compensation, and Liability Act (CERCLA), present landowners may be designated as personally responsible persons (PRPs) and held responsible for cleanup and damages, even if they were not responsible for installing the underground storage tank. Page 259–260.

82. d. A property manager functions under the direction of the individual employment contract, called the *management agreement*. The agreement spells out the expected property manager duties that include all day-to-day operations, but most likely would not include calculating depreciation for tax purposes. Page 2.

83. d. The veteran can proceed with the refinance loan and pay the discount points. On a new purchase, either the veteran or the seller can pay the discount points as well as other closing costs. Page 203.

84. a. The Real Estate Settlement Procedures Act (RESPA) regulations apply to all residential transactions that involve a mortgage loan through any bank or savings association that is covered by FDIC insurance or will be sold to the government-sponsored enterprises Fannie Mae and Freddie Mac on the secondary market. A state may have additional regulations. Price has no bearing. Page 221.

85. d. Even the most thorough search of the public records would fail to find any unrecorded documents, but a recorded mortgage would definitely become part of the abstract of title. Page 77.

86. b. The capitalization or cap rate is calculated by comparing the relationship of net operating income (NOI) with sales prices of comparable properties sold in the area. The net operating income of the subject property can then be divided by the capitalization rate to determine value. If a property is listed for a higher price than this estimated value, this is probably not a good investment. Page 173.

87. d. Market value is determined by several factors: there must be motivated, well-informed parties; a reasonable time on the market must be allowed; and payment must be made in U.S. dollars with no special or creative financing or concessions a part of the transaction. Page 165.

88. a. A counteroffer is a rejection of the original offer. The counteroffer becomes a new offer that can be accepted, rejected, or further countered. Any offer or counteroffer can be withdrawn prior to its acceptance by the other party. Page 104.

89. a. The lender must execute a satisfaction of mortgage that is recorded to show that the debt has been paid and the mortgage released. When the collateral for the loan is a deed of trust, the trustee executes a deed of reconveyance that restores the rights of the trustee back to the owner-borrower. Page 195.

90. d. Points are prepaid interest on the loan charged by the lender to increase the anticipated yield on the loan. A borrower can pay or request the seller to pay discount points in order to lower the interest rate. Page 208.

91. a. A metes-and-bounds legal description must start at a point of beginning and the boundary must return to that point. The description will describe various degrees, distance in linear feet, and both natural and artificial monuments. The point of beginning is often related to a specific benchmark. Page 17–18.

92. a. If a broker is involved, fair housing law applies whether or not the broker does any advertising. The sale of an individual residence is exempt from fair housing law as long as no broker is involved and the owner does not use discriminatory advertising. Private clubs and religious institutions have special exemptions as long as no discrimination is made for membership. Pages 243–244.

93. b. Adverse possession is an involuntary transfer of title. The claimant is required to prove open, exclusive, notorious, hostile, and uninterrupted possession for the number of years required by state law. No compensation is made to the original owner. Page 53.

94. b. Area is calculated by multiplying width by length for square footage. The number of square feet is divided by 9 for square yards (15 ft × 20 ft = 300 sq ft ÷ 9 = 33.3 sq yd at $6.95 = $231.66 plus installation of $250 = $481.66 or $482). Page 292.

95. c. In a case where the property has become uninhabitable due to neglect by the landlord, a tenant may abandon the premises as a constructive eviction and no longer be held responsible for payment. Page 144.

96.   c.   The Truth in Lending Act applies when credit is extended to individuals for personal, family, or household uses and the amount of credit is $25,000 or less. It does not apply to business or commercial loans of any amount or to agricultural loans over $25,000. With most consumer credit transactions, the borrower has three days to rescind the transaction. This does not apply to first mortgage loans. Pages 219–220.

97.   a.   The total commission for the $84,500 sale is $5,915 ($84,500 × 0.07 = $5,915). The listing broker receives 40% of the commission ($5,915 × 0.40 = $2,366). The salesperson receives 50% of the broker's share ($2,366 × 0.50 = $1,183). Page 289.

98.   a.   A personal right to use is considered a license and may not be sold, inherited, or otherwise transferred to another party. On the other hand, an easement is said to run with the land; in other words, it conveys whenever a property is sold. The nephew has no interest in the property. Page 40.

99.   b.   Fannie Mae and Freddie Mac are government-sponsored enterprises (GSEs) that purchase blocks of conventional and government loans on the secondary market. They then sell securities based on the packages of loans, providing the GSE with additional funds to purchase more loans from primary market lenders. Page 216–217.

100.   b.   Not every potential homeowner has stable income, cash reserves, and a clean credit history. If the borrower presents a high risk to the lender (as evidenced by a low credit score), the lender may still be willing to provide the loan if the borrower pays a higher rate of interest, makes a larger down payment, or agrees to a short term of the loan. This is not a predatory loan unless the lender has coerced the borrower into the loan when circumstances did not warrant it. Page 215.

Index

Notes

Notes

Notes

Notes

Notes

Notes

Notes

Notes

Notes

Notes

Notes

Notes